The Pragmatist

The Pragmatist

Bill de Blasio's Quest to Save the Soul of New York

JOSEPH P. VITERITTI

OXFORD
UNIVERSITY PRESS

OXFORD
UNIVERSITY PRESS

Oxford University Press is a department of the University of Oxford. It furthers
the University's objective of excellence in research, scholarship, and education
by publishing worldwide. Oxford is a registered trade mark of Oxford University
Press in the UK and certain other countries.

Published in the United States of America by Oxford University Press
198 Madison Avenue, New York, NY 10016, United States of America.

CIP data is on file at the Library of Congress
ISBN 978–0–19–067950–7

1 3 5 7 9 8 6 4 2

Printed by Sheridan Books, Inc., United States of America

Joseph P. Viteritti is the Thomas Hunter Professor of Public Policy at Hunter College, CUNY, where he is Chair of the Urban Policy and Planning Department. Prior to Hunter, he taught at Princeton, New York University, Harvard, and the State University of New York at Albany.

This is his twelfth book. He has published widely in social science journals, law reviews, and popular venues such as the *New York Times, Washington Post,* and *Huffington Post,* covering topics that include city politics, education policy, criminal justice, and law. His work has been translated into four languages other than English. Over the years, he has advised governmental leaders on a variety of public policy issues.

A brown-haired boy with hazel eyes, John was only six when his mother died. He barely got to know her. The Spanish influenza swept through New York like a tidal wave in 1918, taking 30,000 lives with it. Angelo had been doing well enough before his wife Annunziata, still in her twenties, was snatched away. The building of the subway provided plenty of work for immigrants like him, and he was promoted to foreman. He had been able to move his wife and six children from a Brooklyn tenement on Front Street to a small house in Ridgewood, Queens. Unable to care for them now, Angelo sent John and his three brothers off to St. Malachy's Orphanage in Rockaway. His two girls, just a few years older than John, stayed home to assume domestic responsibilities.

Angelo and the girls traveled out to the peninsula on weekends to visit the boys. On one Sunday afternoon, he met an Italian widow and mother of six who was visiting her own children. Angelo and Mildred decided that if they got married, they could bring their children home and unite their families. The couple moved back to Brooklyn, and Mildred gave birth to five more. Now there were seventeen. They were good Catholics and didn't know it. Angelo still labored in the subway, and took whatever extra work he could to make ends meet. As the children got older, they were expected to help out. John dropped out of PS 9 when he was in the sixth grade to shine shoes and sell newspapers.

At one point, Angelo rented some space to open a candy store in Bedford-Stuyvesant, not far from where he lived. The kids pitched in to keep the place going. His landlord, Annibale, lived upstairs with his wife Mary. They had six children. The two men got along. They had emigrated from the same province in Southern Italy, with not much more than the clothes they wore. Neither had the gift of literacy, and their English was very broken.

Annibale had a shoe repair shop, and through wise investing managed to buy a few pieces of property that he rented out, as many as seven after he got through the Great Depression. A man of few words, he liked to spend evenings in his rocker, smoking his pipe, and listening to the opera on Italian radio. The shoemaker understood that in hard times tenants occasionally would miss their rent. Even after a few lapsed months, he never considered putting anybody out. "It would be wrong to throw a struggling family onto the street," he would say, especially for a man like him who had been so fortunate to own property.

One day, when John was behind the counter, Mary walked into the store with her youngest daughter Catherine. She was a slight woman with olive skin, chestnut hair, and the biggest blue eyes he had ever seen. He didn't think he had a chance with her.

She was accustomed to a more comfortable life than he, and was better educated. She had attended Prospect Heights Girls Commercial High School for three years, and quit before graduating to take an office job. John didn't know anybody with an office job. Catherine did marry him. They had a nice wedding in the backyard -- just the immediate family and close friends. They drank homemade wine produced in their fathers' cellars.

After losing his job filling pie pans at a local bakery, John started to attend school in the evenings, and learned how to read blueprints. That got him hired as a ship fitter in the Brooklyn Navy Yard, where he worked overtime shifts during the war, and was kept on until the yard closed in 1966. He then took a position working in a hospital tool room and joined the union. It carried him to retirement, when social security and a federal pension gave him and Catherine a decent life.

John and Catherine had two sons. I am the younger.

This book is dedicated to all those mentioned above, who pursued the American Dream in a different city (in a different country) called New York.

CONTENTS

PREFACE

Why This Book?

It was purely random that, just months after Bill de Blasio became mayor, I published a book about John Lindsay, who had served as mayor of New York from 1966 to 1973.[1] The manuscript was already off to the printer before I paid much attention to de Blasio's candidacy. After the election, people kept asking me to compare the two progressive chief executives. I would explain how difficult that is because they lived in different times and faced different challenges.[2] Each mayor, in fact, inherits the legacies of all those who went before him—both the good and the bad. For progressives, looking back can be daunting. They all face the irresistible comparison with La Guardia—the idol of all modern mayors—who remains perched on such a mythical pedestal that no other local leader can ever measure up.

There is a voluminous body of literature on New York mayors. It makes interesting reading because New York is so interesting. This city is like no other place in the country, yet you ought to keep an eye on it if you want to know where the rest might be heading. Gotham's mayors are a collection of colossal characters, for sure: the timid need not apply. Bill de Blasio is no exception: his personal story is compelling. He arrived on the scene at a critical time in the history of the city and country. His election itself was monumental after three consecutive terms of Michael Bloomberg. His aim is nothing less than an attempt to recapture a time long ago when New York was a place of opportunity for people from all over the world. We cannot understand him or the challenges he faces unless we review that history and explain how far the city has come since then, putting those aspirations out of reach for many New Yorkers.

Bill de Blasio is the first progressive to serve as mayor of New York in twenty years. Except for David Dinkins's single term from 1990 to 1994, de Blasio is the first unabashed progressive to govern the city in four decades. He follows in a tradition that dates back to Franklin D. Roosevelt's New Deal. The policies that kept the tradition alive began to fade in 1975, when the city stood on the brink of bankruptcy. The political climate grew more conservative, and fiscal constraints eroded a spirit of generosity that once defined politics and policies in New York. Mayors became preoccupied with the bottom line. They needed to attract and retain wealthy people and businesses that could produce revenue. The city that once served as an engine for democracy became an engine for prosperity.

This historically informed study assesses Bill de Blasio's rise to power and the priorities he sets as mayor: his building of an electoral coalition, the distinct challenges he faces, the strategies he adopts, the success with which he has governed, and the significance of his tenure in the history of progressive government. It is a series of snapshots—contemporary portraits presented in full color, and a series of black and white photos from the past.

De Blasio's mayoralty came along at time when American politics was deep in the grip of moneyed corporate interests, and Bernie Sanders was about to launch a "revolution" against the establishment that ruled the Democratic Party. Even though Sanders did not gain the nomination of his party, the defeat of Hillary Clinton by Donald Trump in the general election has given new momentum to the progressive wing of the Democratic Party. The party remains divided between those on the left who want to distribute the rewards of American life more fairly, and those at the center who cooperated with Republicans to usher in an era of political and social inequality that continues to prevail, and could grow worse with time.

Bill de Blasio has inhabited both camps. As an elected official and advisor to mainstream politicians, including Hillary Clinton, his feet are firmly planted in the world of real politics, but he also has a long association with progressive causes that animated his run for mayor. Although he won his party's nomination by a slim margin, he also managed to assemble the broadest progressive coalition in city history for the general election. Whether de Blasio's rise will recast New York politics toward a more progressive bent the way Ed Koch's three terms in office moved it to the center remains to be seen. It's not easy being Bill de Blasio. He leans too far to the left to fit comfortably within the mainstream of his own party, yet many of those who elected him are unhappy with the accommodations he has made to achieve his objectives.

In trying to blend his philosophical commitment to progressive government with the practical realities of city politics and finance, de Blasio defies conventional labels. He is both insider and outsider, a gadfly and a seasoned operative; but he clearly has his sights set on changing policies that have contributed to the growing disparities he regularly decries. At times it seems as though he needs his own nomenclature: he's something of a *pragmatist*.

Like every mayor that preceded him, Bill de Blasio has had to make compromises in order to function. His challenges are particularly acute because the progressive agenda that he espouses does not easily align with the structure of political power he inherited from Mayor Michael Bloomberg. Like those before him, de Blasio will be judged on the basis of those compromises, and the extent to which they either advanced or undermined his promise to make New York a better place for less advantaged people. He needs to do that without losing the support of everyone else, whose interests the mayor also needs to represent while confronting the challenges of growth.

There are some who wonder whether pragmatism and progressivism are compatible. That is a crucial consideration today because what is at stake here is bigger than either Bill de Blasio or New York. With Bernie Sanders defeated in the national primaries and Donald Trump occupying the White House, Bill de Blasio's mayoralty is a test case for progressivism itself. This is, after all, New York, New York, the city that La Guardia built. If progressivism can't make it here, it can't make it anywhere.

Chapter 1 is an introduction to our main character, Bill de Blasio. Rather than try to describe him, I chose to present him through five vignettes that exhibit his response to a variety of situations and provide insight into his personality and instincts. Although these stories may seem disconnected at first, common themes of leadership, philosophical commitment, and compromise emerge that lace through subsequent chapters, and ultimately help frame the book. Read it as an overture to the work, if you will.

The remainder of the book is divided into three parts, each with two or more chapters. Part I contains two chapters that dig deeper into de Blasio's personality and the factors that contributed to his formation. Chapter 2 ties together pieces of his family history. It reaches back to his childhood in Massachusetts, through his days as a college and graduate student in New York, to the raising of his own family with Chirlane McCray. McCray is not just de Blasio's wife and the mother of his two children: she is his closest political advisor and partner.

Chapter 3 traces de Blasio's early career, beginning with his work as an aide in the office of Mayor David Dinkins, and his roots in third party politics tied to labor movements. It takes us through his experience as a campaign advisor for Harlem congressman Charles Rangel and East Harlem assemblyman Francisco Diaz Jr., then on to the presidential campaign of Bill Clinton, in which he functioned as a state coordinator. After serving for a brief time as an assistant to City Council Speaker Peter Vallone, he was called upon to run the U.S. Senate campaign of Hilary Clinton. By the time de Blasio took his first major government job as a deputy to U.S. Secretary of Housing and Urban Development Andrew Cuomo, he had an established reputation as a skillful political operative for Democratic Party candidates. To the surprise of many, he eventually applied those skills to launch his own electoral career, first serving as a member of the City Council, and later as Public Advocate before running for mayor.

This is a book about mayoral leadership. If Bill de Blasio is the main character in the story, those who preceded him in the office of mayor are the supporting cast. They help us to understand him—as he sheds light on them. In order
to assess de Blasio's role in history, we need to appreciate how his predecessors
and the city they left behind shaped his aspirations and challenges. The three
chapters in Part II elaborate on that history. Chapter 4 describes the evolution
of progressivism in New York, beginning with Fiorello La Guardia through the
mayoralties of Robert Wagner and John Lindsay, and its eventual demise during
the fiscal crisis of 1975 when Mayor Abraham Beame served. Focusing on these
first three chief executives allows us to identify the basic precepts of progressive
government, the coalition each mayor formed to bring it about, the compromises
they made to keep it afloat, the limits of their leadership, and the overall political
climate—locally and nationally—that emerged during Franklin D. Roosevelt's
New Deal and Lyndon B. Johnson's Great Society to enable their leadership.

Chapter 5 deals with post-fiscal crisis New York and the administrations of
Edward Koch, David Dinkins, and Rudolph Giuliani. At that point, American
liberalism had lost its shine, the federal government was divesting from social
programs, financial constraints narrowed the range of government activity,
and each mayor became increasingly reliant on private investment to sustain
the city's fiscal health. As the city grew more vulnerable, mayors had to reward
wealthy corporations with tax breaks and other benefits to prevent them from
leaving. The terms of the deals became more generous. The bargains they made
kindled suspicion and accusations, but they continue as a usual part of doing
business in New York.

Michael Bloomberg's election as mayor, the subject of Chapter 6, was the culmination of the process in which New York City became increasingly dominated
by corporate interests. By the end of Bloomberg's third term, many leaders in
the business, real estate, and financial sectors that had become part of the unoffi-
cial permanent government convinced themselves that what was good for them,
was good for the rest of the city. Bloomberg shared that view to a large extent.
He used his power as mayor to rezone nearly half the city, and convert valuable
waterfront property from industrial to high-end residential and commercial use.

Bloomberg inscribed his mark on New York's physical landscape like no other
mayor in history. Some of the reforms he implemented with regard to transportation, health, and the environment are praised by progressive planners, but
other policies he championed reinforced his image as a mayor of the privileged
class. Bloomberg's tenure also coincided with a final transformation of the federal role in policymaking. As the New Deal and Great Society became distant
memories, Washington continued to use its powers to redistribute wealth, but in
the opposite direction it once had, contributing to a polarization of income that
defines the city and the country.

Bill de Blasio's ascension to City Hall, the subject of Part III, occurred at a time when America had entered a new Gilded Age. Chapter 7 describes his sudden rise to power: his campaign strategy, the competition he faced, the contours of the contest, the significance of the electoral coalition he built, the administration he assembled, and the agenda that he set.

Chapters 8 and 9 explore that agenda more carefully with a close examination of policies he enacted, their impact on the city, and their alignment with the goals he originally set out to accomplish. They do not purport to be a comprehensive analysis of de Blasio's tenure; nor do they pretend to fully assess his success or effectiveness at such an early point in his tenure. These chapters focus on his administration's policy initiatives, its measurable priorities. Such changes are visible early in the life of an administration.

Chapter 8 begins by looking at the budget, which tells us where the administration is committing its discretionary resources. Then we will look at programmatic and legislative initiatives. Particular attention will be paid to his administration's economic, criminal justice, and education initiatives. We will also consider questions that have been raised about de Blasio's campaign practices and a number of investigations that have haunted him and those around him. Chapter 9 will focus on homeless and housing policies, the latter of which is shaping up to be the cornerstone of de Blasio's first term in office.

Chapter 10 will serve as a conclusion. We will look back at New York's distinct role in the history of progressive politics, the developments that derailed it, and Bill de Blasio's role in restoring it. This brings us to the larger question of the project. It concerns the prospects for progressive governance at the local urban level at a time when the national climate appears so prohibitive, and not likely to get better with Donald Trump in the White House and Republicans controlling both houses of Congress. As if those challenges were not enough, Bill de Blasio's tenure at City Hall shows how the progressive agenda itself is full of tensions that, depending on the issues, sow seeds of dissent within its own camp.

ACKNOWLEDGMENTS

Every book project relies on the contributions of many people, and this one is no exception. I first want to thank New York City Mayor Bill de Blasio and First Lady Chirlane McCray for their openness and candor, and for being so generous with their time as I went about my research to learn more about them. I also want to thank Steven Wilhelm and Jean Wilhelm, who were very kind in letting me poke into their lives.

First Deputy Mayor Anthony Shorris was extraordinarily helpful in opening the doors of the government and helping me gain access to information and people who offered their cooperation, including, among others, Steven Banks, Carl Weisbrod, Alicia Glen, Shola Olatoye, Phil Walzak, Eric Phillips, Wiley Norvell, and Vicki Been. Ronnie Lowenstein, Doug Turetsky, Ray Domanico, and their colleagues at the New York City Independent Budget Office, as always, served as a reliable source of objective information and analysis.

I am indebted to many friends, colleagues and professional acquaintances, who shared with me their insights and expertise on New York City government, history, politics, and policy, including Marc Shaw, Lilliam Barrios Paoli, Dennis Rivera, Dan Cantor, Betsy Gotbaum, David Chen, Alexandra Hanson, James Parrott, Thomas Main, Allan Dobrin, Kevin McCabe, Steve Aiello, Sid Davidoff, Lisa Gulick, Jane Quinn, Emily Goldstein, and Brad Lander. Allan Frei and Peter Dicpinigaitis shared personal stories and memories I could not have acquired anywhere else.

At Hunter College, I benefited from assistance provided by Matthew Lasner, Owen Gutfreund, Sigmund Shipp, Roger Karapin, Donna Haverty-Stacke, Melanie Breault, and Stephanie Margolis. Marisol Otero-Morales and Miriam Galindez always deserve recognition for making my life on 16 West better. My students in the Urban Policy and Planning Department continue to challenge me, and remain a constant source of intellectual stimulation.

One could not hope for a better team of collaborators than the one I had at Oxford University Press. My editor, Dave McBride, was supportive from the moment I brought the project to his attention, and his detailed comments on an early draft were invaluable in shaping the final product.

I am especially grateful to Hunter College President Jennifer Raab for her continued support over the years, going back to the day she told me in no uncertain terms that I "need to" come to Hunter to teach. She, by the way, was right.

There is nothing more rewarding for a teacher than to learn from his students. In this project, I have been especially fortunate in having two research assistants—partners I should say, from beginning to end. Nicole Krishtul and Erika Wang, proud daughters of immigrants, not only assisted me in gathering important data, reports, news clips, and other relevant documents; our weekly meetings grew into a mini seminar on how to develop raw material into a historical narrative. By the end of the project, they were critiquing draft chapters I had written and providing me with their own constructive insights. I am not at all exaggerating when I say that I could not have completed this book without them.

My wife Rosemary Salomone and our son Andrew make all things worthwhile, and usually better, no matter what it is I am up to.

I accept full responsibility for the final product.

1

Who Is Bill de Blasio?

He seemed to appear from nowhere. He had served for one term as Public Advocate for New York, the least consequential of three citywide elective offices. The position is a remnant of an office once called President of the City Council, which itself made no sense outside the arcane customs of city government in old New York. Like most legislative bodies, the council had always elected its own leadership, and the council president's role was mostly ceremonial, but it had another purpose. In the day, New York City needed three citywide electoral offices to help balance a ticket along ethnic lines that more often than not included an Irishman, an Italian, and a Jew. No serious candidate for mayor would ever throw his hat into the ring without trying to assemble such a triumvirate of ethnic diversity around him. The third citywide position belonged to the City Comptroller, who had a real job as chief fiscal officer of the municipal corporation.

A commission empaneled by Mayor Edward Koch to rewrite the City Charter in 1989 had seriously considered eliminating the council president position. There were more important things to think about after the United States Supreme Court decided that the City Board of Estimate—an executive body composed of the Mayor, Comptroller, Council President, and five borough presidents—violated the constitutional standard of one person-one vote because all the boroughs had equal representation regardless of their population size.[1] Attuned to the changing demographics of the city, the Charter Commission of 1989 was intent on creating a larger City Council, expanded from 35 to 51 seats, that would better represent growing African American, Caribbean, Hispanic, and Asian communities. Even gay residents who were beginning to congregate in Chelsea, just north of Greenwich Village, had their own district carved out.[2]

When the Charter Commission was deliberating in 1989, the position of City Council President was held by a man named Andrew Stein, the son of a wealthy and influential businessman who published the *New York Law Journal* and could boast of powerful friends such as John F. Kennedy, Lyndon B. Johnson, and Nelson Rockefeller. Notwithstanding his father's connections, Andy was unable to advance beyond the council president position, so he was determined to hold on to it for as long as he could. He petitioned members of the panel to save the office in some form or another. The position and its incumbent survived under the revised charter. In 1992, Mayor David Dinkins and City Council Speaker Peter Vallone, intent on removing any pretense of a serious legislative role, renamed the office *Public Advocate*, which emphasized a responsibility assigned to it in the charter revision of 1975. That's the job Bill de Blasio held when he ran for mayor in 2013.

Mayor Michael Bloomberg had thought the office of Public Advocate was "a total waste of everybody's money," and had an equally unflattering view of those who held the title.[3] He kept cutting its budget and tried to have the post eliminated entirely when he appointed his own charter revision commissions. Mayor Bloomberg, of course, had a way of thinking that anybody in a position to question what he did had no logical purpose. His self-assured behavior supported an argument, made by many during the Bloomberg years, that you can't have too many checks on the power of the mayor, particularly when the position seems to be a magnet for strong personalities such as Bloomberg and his predecessor Rudolph Giuliani. Betsy Gotbaum, who held the position for eight years immediately prior to de Blasio, explains:

> In a city where the mayor has such administrative and budgetary discretion, there can never be too many checks on his power. In performing its ombudsman role, the Public Advocate gives the people of the city a place to be heard when they can't get satisfaction from the mayor's office or the agencies. If there is anything wrong with the present institutional arrangement, it is that the mayor has control over the budget of the person who is supposed to serve as his watchdog.[4]

In all actuality, being the Public Advocate was a fitting assignment for Bill de Blasio because he had a contrarian disposition about politics, and a keen sense of how dysfunctional government could be. Moreover, it would be difficult to find another politician whose priorities were as adverse to those pursued by Michael Bloomberg. They were a perfect match for underscoring the merits of a checks and balances governmental arrangement. Mark Green, the first occupant of the position, had tried to use it as a steppingstone to the city's big electoral prize, but de Blasio was the first to make it happen.

At the outset, De Blasio's principal opponents in the Democratic Party primary for mayor in 2013 were Christine Quinn and William (Billy) Thompson. Quinn had been Speaker of the City Council, a true leadership position that held the power to make or break an incumbent mayor's aspirations regarding the budget, local legislation, and real estate development. Quinn rarely used her power that way. Her support for Bloomberg in the council made it possible for him to have a third term after the electorate of the city twice approved referenda—by overwhelming margins—that limited the mayor to two terms.[5] (The council and mayor have the power to amend the charter.) She was generally perceived to be Bloomberg's choice to succeed him—so long as Bloomberg's Police Commissioner Raymond Kelly did not enter the race, and she hoped to turn that support into a historic opportunity to become the city's first woman and openly gay chief executive. Thompson was the former City Comptroller. As a mayoral candidate in 2009, he came very close to denying Michael Bloomberg that third term and becoming the second black man to rise to the city's highest office.

De Blasio was not perceived as a serious challenge in the Democratic primary to either of these two seasoned candidates, who benefited from wider name recognition. Early polls predicted that de Blasio would get no more than 11 percent of the vote.[6] For reasons that will be discussed in a later chapter, de Blasio managed to take slightly more than 40 percent (40.3) of the vote in the September balloting against Thompson (26.2 percent) and Quinn (15.5 percent). Squeezing past the 40 percent mark allowed de Blasio to avoid a runoff against Thompson, which could have ended differently. Winning the nomination put de Blasio in a head-to-head race with Republican candidate Joseph Lhota, a former Chair of the Metropolitan Transportation Authority, who had gained a reputation as a tough-minded manager serving as Deputy Mayor to Rudy Giuliani.

Reaching back into de Blasio's history as a student radical who was a supporter of the Marxist Sandinista government in Nicaragua, Lhota portrayed his opponent as a wild-eyed lefty ideologue whose attempts to promote "class warfare" were "right out of the Marxist playbook."[7] Wearing the mantle of an anti-crime candidate who stood beside Rudy Giuliani when the former mayor famously crusaded against unsafe streets and quality-of-life infractions, Lhota warned that making de Blasio mayor of New York would bring the city back to the bad old days when murder rates were high and street vagrants harassed law-abiding citizens. One Lhota campaign ad used news footage from a recent biker gang's assault on a motorist, and other violent street scenes from the 1970s and 1980s to urge voters not to let Bill de Blasio "take New York backwards."[8]

Lhota proved to be a lackluster campaigner and his strategy failed. Bill de Blasio, as it turned out, was very much in touch with the sentiments of New Yorkers. It was a rout. The man from nowhere took 73 percent of the vote, compared to Lhota's 24 percent.[9] As a campaigner, Bill de Blasio embraced his roots as an advocate for social justice and ran on a platform of economic equality, a theme that resonated with everyday New Yorkers who had just sloughed through twelve years of a billionaire mayor who enjoyed feasting with Gotham's lords of finance and real estate in his East Side townhouse. And for anybody who was watching, de Blasio demonstrated that the demand for social and economic justice was more than slogan tossed out by a few angry protesters who "occupied" Wall Street in the fall of 2011. It had a solid political reach.

For sure, there was more to the de Blasio victory than his appeal to class interests. Yet, there was something new in the air, at least in New York City, and maybe in the country. That's what makes Bill de Blasio such an interesting character in the drama of American politics. He is a test case for the rise of a new left movement that would reach across the boundaries of class, race, and gender (including sexual identity). The city and the country watched in wonder. How would this tall lanky fellow, whose cronies once referred to in his younger radical days as "Big Bird with a Beard," govern the greatest city in the world? Was his rise to power the beginning of the end of law and order? Would the fat cats whom Michael Bloomberg coddled for twelve years take flight from the city, and carry off their riches with them? Could de Blasio really make a difference? If so, for better or for worse?

Let the following five vignettes from his early tenure serve as an introduction to his complex and not entirely predictable character.

With nearly a month to go before officially taking office, Mayor-elect Bill de Blasio announced one of his first major appointments—his choice to replace Raymond Kelly as Police Commissioner. It was not just any Police Commissioner that he chose; it was Rudy Giuliani's Police Commissioner, William Bratton. De Blasio had passed over the names of two department insiders who were on the short list for the job: Philip Banks III, the chief of the department and highest ranking uniformed officer, who is African-American; and Deputy Commissioner Rafael Pineiro, who is Hispanic. The bonding of Bill de Blasio and Bill Bratton was a shotgun marriage of sorts that was brought together at a tender moment when two ambitious careers happened to meet in a place called New York City politics. The most celebrated law enforcement officer in the country, at the twilight of his professional life, wanted to cap his career with a second run at the most sought after job in the business; the new mayor, at the pinnacle of his own career, wanted to dispel any thoughts that he intended to be soft on crime.

Bratton had been the top cop in Boston before his first tour of duty in New York, and then went on to serve for seven years as commissioner in Los Angeles, where the name Rodney King was synonymous with a history of police brutality. Asked about Bratton's record, Los Angeles mayor Antonio Villaraigosa attested that Bratton, whom he had appointed to two successive terms, "helped transform the L.A.P.D.'s relationship with the community while bringing crime down to historic lows."[10] Bratton, however, was still a controversial choice among de Blasio supporters who longed for a softer approach to policing. Bratton was widely associated with the "broken windows" theory. It held that aggressive enforcement against quality-of-life annoyances such as intrusive panhandling, or minor offenses such as marijuana use, served as a deterrent to more serious crimes.[11]

By the end of Bloomberg's third term, civil rights advocates and leaders in black and Latino communities were already reeling from a "stop-and-frisk" policy implemented by Commissioner Raymond Kelly that disproportionately targeted people of color and subjected them to police suspicion and harassment. The Bloomberg administration had appealed a federal court decision declaring aspects of the practice an unconstitutional violation of individual rights. As a candidate for mayor, de Blasio promised to curtail the controversial policy and develop new legal guidelines for police searches. Commissioner Bratton supported de Blasio's campaign pledge, even though he himself had utilized a "stop-and-frisk" strategy in Los Angeles.[12]

The relationship between these two men from different worlds—a supporter of Latin American revolutionaries and an Irish cop from Boston—was fascinating, and it was real. As former deputy mayor Lilliam Barrios-Paoli observed, "De Blasio really admires Bratton. No other member of the administration enjoys such independence within the hierarchy of city officials."[13] In return, Bratton pledged to serve the mayor loyally through his first four years in City Hall. It would not be easy; nor would it last through the mayor's first full term in office.

Cities across America were simmering with anger as more and more black men fell to police bullets. In February of 2012, Trayvon Martin, an unarmed seventeen-year-old high school student in Florida, was shot to death by George Zimmerman, a neighborhood watch captain. Martin was visiting his father's fiancée in the racially integrated gated community near Orlando. There is no evidence of any wrongdoing on his part. The shooting occurred in the course of an altercation between the two after Zimmerman, without identifying himself, started following Martin and notified police that he had spotted a suspicious-looking black man in the complex that had experienced a rash of burglaries. Zimmerman himself is of mixed race, having a great-grandfather who was Latino and black.

The Trayvon Martin shooting drew national attention, and things came to a head in the summer of 2013 when Zimmerman was acquitted of charges of second-degree murder after claiming self-defense. The political temperature kept rising during the summer of 2014 when police officer Darren Wilson killed eighteen-year-old Michael Brown, a robbery suspect in Ferguson, Missouri, after the young man struggled with the officer in an attempt to take his service revolver. Wilson shot Brown twelve times in the course of the scuffle. Then later that fall Tamir Rice, a twelve-year-old boy in Cleveland, was shot to death by a police officer who responded to a call about a young man brandishing a gun in a city park. The gun turned out to be a toy. These events and others like them in urban locales gave birth to a national "Black Lives Matter" movement demanding an end to racial profiling, police violence, and the general state of racial inequality.

During Mayor de Blasio's first summer in office, New York City experienced its own eruption of angry protest when a black man on Staten Island died of a chokehold administered by a white cop. Eric Garner had been selling untaxed single cigarettes known as "loosies" when he was confronted by police officers. Garner, who had been arrested many times before on charges that included assault, resisting arrest, and grand larceny, denied the allegation when approached. He resisted when the officers tried to handcuff him, prompting Officer Daniel Pantaleo to put Garner into a headlock with his forearm around Garner's neck.

"Chokeholds" are prohibited by Police Department policy, except in extreme circumstances of self-defense. Several other officers assisted in holding Garner to the ground while compressing his chest, at which time Garner, an asthmatic, repeatedly cried out, "I can't breathe." Garner went unconscious at the scene, and had a fatal heart attack in an ambulance on the way to Richmond University Medical Center. The Medical Examiner ruled the death a homicide, but in December a Grand Jury empaneled by the local District Attorney failed to indict Officer Pantaleo, who was reported to have other complaints pending against him.

Immediately after the Grand Jury's dismissal of the case, "I can't breathe" became the rallying cry for anti-police demonstrations in more than fifty locations around the country. New York was now at the center of a national controversy about police-community relations. A video of the incident was flashed across the screens of every major news outlet from coast to coast. Political allies of the mayor had already begun to raise doubts about the direction he and the city were heading on police matters. Donna Lieberman, executive director of the New York Civil Liberties Union, issued a reminder to de Blasio that he was "elected on a promise to end the tale of two cities that plagued New York through the Bloomberg years" and noted "the death of Eric Garner at the hands of the NYPD is tragic, poignant, powerful evidence that we have a long way to go."[14]

The Reverend Al Sharpton, who had been instrumental in gaining black support for de Blasio's mayoral bid, held an anti-police protest on Staten Island two days after Garner died. After aides to the mayor talked Sharpton out of holding a more disruptive demonstration across the busy Verrazano Bridge, he later organized a peaceful march on the island that attracted more than a thousand sympathizers and received national media attention. Sharpton has established himself as a prominent spokesperson for the African-American community. Presidents Barack Obama and Bill Clinton have both praised him for his leadership on civil rights issues; political candidates travel near and far to pay homage at his National Action Network on West 145 Street in the heart of Harlem to curry favor with black voters.

The flamboyant dramatist of racial politics can also be a lightning rod for opponents. Sharpton's inflammatory use of language has offended whites, Jews, gays, and lesbians on various occasions.[15] His record of unpaid taxes is well established. And many remember Sharpton's role in the Tawana Brawley case dating back to 1987. The fifteen-year-old girl from Wappinger Falls, New York had been found wrapped in a plastic garbage bag covered in feces with racial epithets written across her body in charcoal. She claimed that she had been raped by six white men, some of whom were police officers. Sharpton became her spokesman, and in the course of the trial he accused Dutchess County prosecutor Steven Pagones of being one of the girl's assailants. The girl's claims turned out to be a hoax. Pagones was awarded a handsome judgment in a defamation suit against Sharpton and other Brawley advisors. This is the episode that put Al Sharpton's name on the media map. His friendship has been a mixed bag of tricks for Bill de Blasio.

The Garner incident was the first major test in the short political marriage of Mayor Bill de Blasio and his police commissioner Bill Bratton, and it was surrounded by other controversies that made the early days of the relationship even more challenging. With the "stop-and-frisk" issue put safely behind them, at least for a while, the Garner case still raised questions about Bratton's signature "broken windows" philosophy that targeted minor offenses to control more serious crime. If the police had just ignored Garner's street peddling, his tragic death would not have occurred. Whatever harm may have been caused by the illegal cigarette sales certainly does not measure up to the abrupt loss of a human life.

A few days after the incident, Mayor de Blasio held a press conference joined by Commissioner Bratton and other criminal justice officials. Bratton defended the police intervention, stating that the immediate area was a constant source of complaints by residents and merchants over the past six months—646 emergency calls resulting in 98 arrests and 100 summonses, mostly for quality-of-life infractions.[16] He further explained that the officers involved were acting in the performance of their "lawful duties." Referring to the videotape of the incident, Bratton noted that when the officers informed Mr. Garner of their intention to arrest him, he made it known to them that he was going to resist. "I do not expect my officers to walk away from that type of situation," Bratton declared.

Mayor de Blasio stated that he was "very troubled by the video," but noted that the men and women of the NYPD assume enormous responsibility in keeping the city safe, and have to make "difficult split second decisions in trying circumstances."[17] He went on to say that the police must be "compassionate, constitutional and respectful;" then emphasized, "The NYPD is the most effective police force in the nation and is at its best and most effective when it has the respect and support of those it protects."

The mayor and the commissioner promised a full investigation by both the department and the district attorney. The Justice Department also made an inquiry. At no point did de Blasio raise any doubts about the wisdom of Bratton's "broken windows" approach. Was there at least a tacit understanding between the mayor and his top cop about the merits of aggressive law enforcement? Had they discussed these matters deliberately? In any case, it was clearly apparent that as the commissioner had gone along with curtailing the controversial "stop-and-frisk" policy identified with his predecessor and sometimes critic Raymond Kelly, the mayor had no intention to second-guess the implementation of a program upon which Bratton built his professional reputation.

A couple of weeks later, Mayor de Blasio hosted a City Hall forum on police-community relations that was attended by his key cabinet officials, police brass, City Council members, local ministers, and community leaders. Seated on either side of the mayor were Police Commissioner Bratton and the Reverend Al Sharpton. Sharpton ripped into the commissioner and his "broken windows" policy, claiming that it is applied disproportionately in black and Latino communities. He then looked straight at the mayor and said, "If Dante wasn't your (biracial) son, he'd be a candidate for a chokehold."[18] Bratton took exception to the comment, retorting that race was not a factor in Mr. Garner's death. Police union members were outraged that the mayor had given Sharpton an equal place at the table with the Police Commissioner, and had set their boss up to be demeaned so publicly.

The relationship between the mayor and police unions had already begun to sour at the very beginning of his tenure when he clumsily tried to intervene in the arrest of an influential black pastor. Bishop Orlando Findlayter, a member of the mayor's inaugural committee, had two outstanding warrants when he was apprehended at a traffic stop. Then, in the fall, it was disclosed that the mayor's wife, Chirlane McCray, was employing a chief of staff who was living in New Jersey with a convicted killer and drug trafficker. Rachael Noerdlinger had previously served as a close advisor to Al Sharpton. She had attended sensitive meetings with police department officials concerning the Eric Garner case, and she was in the audience the night that Sharpton confronted Bratton at the City Hall forum. Noerdlinger's live-in boyfriend, Hassaun McFarlan, had almost run over a policeman at a traffic detour in New Jersey while driving her car, and he had used social media to post hateful statements against the police.

When the news about McFarlan was disclosed, the head of the Policemen's Benevolent Association (PBA), the city's largest police union, demanded that Noerdlinger be fired. At first, de Blasio's office defended Noerdlinger, arguing that she could not be held responsible for the behavior of another individual. Noerdlinger eventually took a leave of absence in November when her own son was arrested on West 164th Street on charges of criminal trespassing. She resigned permanently at the end of the year when it was revealed that she had failed to disclose crucial information on a routine background check by the Department of Investigation when she was hired. By then it was also public knowledge that the former chief of staff for the First Lady had multiple federal tax liens against her.

His relationship with the police deteriorated further when Mayor de Blasio appeared on television in December, saying that he feared for his own son's safety at the hands of the police. He remarked, "I think every night about my son, making sure he comes home safe."[19] While acknowledging, "Our police keep us safe," he also referred to "decades of problems, a history of centuries of racism that undergird this reality." He went on to explain how parents who have children of color have for decades taught young men to be careful when encountering a police officer. De Blasio had just returned from a meeting on police relations with President Barack Obama, who himself once commented that if he had a son, he might look like Trayvon Martin, the unarmed seventeen-year-old who was killed in Florida by a neighborhood watch volunteer. De Blasio's words could also be read as validating the assertions made by Reverend Sharpton at the City Hall forum.

Ed Mullins, president of the Sergeants Benevolent Association, called de Blasio's statement "moronic."[20] He reminded the mayor that a police security detail protects his family every day and suggested that if de Blasio does not have faith in the police who work in his own city, he should move out. PBA president Patrick Lynch accused the mayor of throwing cops "under a bus."[21] Former Mayor Rudolph Giuliani described de Blasio's remarks as "racist."[22] Commissioner Bratton stuck by his boss, in a manner of speaking, telling reporters "This mayor, my mayor, Bill de Blasio, is *probably one of the best* I've ever worked with."[23]

The union leaders were not swayed by the police commissioner's guarded support for the mayor. Under the title, "Don't insult my sacrifice," the PBA posted a form on its website offering cops an opportunity to register their opinion on whether Mayor de Blasio and City Council Speaker Melissa Mark-Viverito—an ally of the mayor's and the highest-ranking Hispanic woman in city government—should be barred from police funerals when officers die in the line of duty.[24] The question became more than a hypothetical a few days before Christmas when a deranged man approached two officers sitting in their radio car in front of a public housing project in Brooklyn and opened fire at point blank range, hitting both in the head, killing them instantly. Police in Baltimore confirmed that the shooter had traveled from Maryland to New York intent on avenging the deaths of Eric Garner and Michael Brown.

The cold-blooded murder of Officers Rafael Ramos and Wenjian Liu—one Hispanic, the other of Asian descent—was greeted by an outpouring of sympathy in the mostly black community of Bedford-Stuyvesant where it took place.

The Reverend Al Sharpton denounced the use of Eric Garner's and Michael Brown's names in connection to violence against police as "reprehensible." PBA president Patrick Lynch was less conciliatory, using the occasion to goad both the mayor and Sharpton, charging: "There is blood on many hands, from those who incited the violence under the guise of protest to try to tear down what police officers do every day." He continued, "That blood on the hands starts on the steps of City Hall in front of the mayor."[25]

When Mayor de Blasio attended the funeral mass for Officer Ramos in Glendale, Queens, he embraced Commissioner Bratton, and their wives did the same, as would old family friends sharing a solemn moment. When the mayor got up to deliver his remorseful remarks, more than two hundred police personnel assembled in their dress blues turned their backs on him. The act of defiance organized by union leaders drew mixed reactions in police circles. Some wondered if it was an ill-conceived attempt by the unions to gain an upper hand in ongoing contract negotiations with City Hall.

Police Commissioner Bratton called the demonstration inappropriate, and urged his troops to refrain from doing it again. Roy Richter, president of the Captain's Endowment Association, sent a memo to his members indicating that such a visual display at the slain officer's funeral "caused pain for his loved ones," and he beseeched his colleagues not to repeat the actions at the funeral of Officer Liu, which was scheduled to take place the following week.[26] The protest was repeated at the Liu service, this time by many fewer officers who were in attendance.

Bratton remained police commissioner through September 2016. When it came time to replace him, de Blasio chose James O'Neill, a Bratton protégé, who had known the commissioner since 1990, when the two served with the city transit police: Bratton as its chief, O'Neill as a young officer on the rise. In naming O'Neill to the top job in the department, de Blasio passed over Benjamin Tucker, an African-American career veteran whom Bratton had appointed to the number two spot.

Times Square is called the "crossroads of the world." Annually the busy intersection at Broadway and Seventh Avenue between West 42nd and 47th Streets becomes the world's focal point as a giant ball of lights slides down a 140-foot pole at midnight to celebrate the start of a new year. For the 2007 centennial anniversary of the "drop," one million revelers looked on in awe at the descending six-ton ball containing 2600 Waterford Crystal triangles lit by 32,256 Philips Luxeon bulbs. Once called Long Acre Square before the newspaper publisher moved its headquarters there in 1904, Times Square remains one of the most popular tourist attractions on earth. Through most of the twentieth century, however, Times Square was more famously recognized as the city's intersection of pathology and pleasure. The brothels, hotels, and theaters had long ago migrated north from the Tenderloin district, making the area a fertile environment for multiple forms of entertainment.

The transition was gradual but steady. By the turn of the century, the city itself was undergoing a great transformation. Immigration had peaked in 1880, and the constant influx of newcomers from Europe made New York the world's leading destination for people seeking a better life. At the stroke of a pen, the population doubled to 3.4 million in December 1897, when the original municipal corporation occupying Manhattan and parts of the Bronx was consolidated with the larger city of Brooklyn and towns located in Queens, Staten Island, and parts of Westchester.[27] By the turn of the century, 69 corporate headquarters and 185 of the financial trusts being organized by J.P. Morgan were located in New York.[28]

The opening of Grand Central Station in 1913 brought travelers to the district from all parts of the country, and a new subway system, still being built, made Times Square a popular stop for commuters from downtown and the outer boroughs.[29] One of the first major American boulevards to be illuminated by electricity, Broadway became the Great White Way. As if following a law of natural evolution, the lights kept getting bigger and brighter, but the Great Depression also brought seedier attractions to the area. By the 1960s the neighborhood was downright dangerous.

Lusty billboards and brightly lit marquees enticed adventurous visitors to succumb to temptations offered by pornographic movie houses, strip joints, sex shops, massage parlors, and drug dealers—all at their own risk of course. You could buy just about anything there, and return home with a souvenir, the kind your doctor attempted to remove with shot of penicillin. In his entertaining history of this raunchy outpost, James Traub refers to Times Square as "The Devil's Playground." If you want to see what it was like, you can spend two enticing hours with the street hustlers portrayed by John Voight and Dustin Hoffman in John Schlessinger's *Midnight Cowboy*. Until the last decade of the past century, city leaders tended to look the other way from what was there for everyone else to see, except for an occasional police raid to keep up appearances, before letting business get back to "normal." In earlier days crooked cops and Tammany "pols" were rewarded for their oversights with an opportunity to skim off profits from the proceeds of illicit enterprises.

As Y2K approached, Times Square became a symbol of new aspirations and an opportunity for reigning politicians to determine how they wanted to be remembered. Edward Koch hoped it would serve as an emblem of the city's remarkable rebound from a ruinous fiscal crisis that nearly ended in bankruptcy. Rudy Giuliani wanted to clean it up so that law-abiding people could feel safe walking the streets at any hour of the day.[30] Michael Bloomberg wanted to make it sparkle so that millions of tourists would be drawn there to spend money on legitimate forms of entertainment. For Bill de Blasio, it became a precocious battleground for civil rights—not altogether how he wanted to be remembered, but close.

By the time Mayor Giuliani shut down the sex establishments and drove out the drug merchants with an increased police presence, city officials were working with local businesses to create the Times Square Alliance. The business improvement district (or BID) launched a successful effort to attract corporate headquarters, pricey restaurants, fancy drinking establishments, big box stores, and huge multiplex theaters, creating an urban Disneyworld unrecognizable to former visitors. At midnight on January 1, 2002, Mayor Giuliani swore in Mayor Bloomberg at an unprecedented inauguration ceremony held right in Times Square. It took some time, but before Bloomberg left office he came up with a plan to make his own mark on the busy thoroughfare: The crossroads of the world were closed to traffic.

In 2009 the city Department of Transportation (DOT) announced the Green Light for Manhattan initiative. Beginning on Memorial Day weekend, Broadway between 42nd and 47th Streets was converted into a pedestrian mall with café tables, planters, and bike paths. The experimental initiative, which also included Herald Square on West 34th Street, was part of a larger push by Bloomberg's imperious DOT Commissioner Janette Sadik-Khan to rid the city of automobile congestion and pollution. Her campaign to make the city more pedestrian and bike friendly was praised by progressive city planners. The experiment was made permanent after DOT studies documented improved traffic flows and a decline in injuries to motorists and pedestrians.[31]

With a week to go before leaving office, Mayor Bloomberg announced that the 30,000-square-foot pedestrian plaza along Broadway between 42nd and 43rd Streets would be paved in granite.[32] Seating and a sound system would be installed for public events. Seventh Avenue between 43rd and 47th Streets would be redesigned for strolling. Sewer and water mains that had been rusting underground for a century would be replaced. The $55 million project was handed over to *Snohetta*, the prize-winning architectural firm based in Oslo, Norway. The project was scheduled to be completed in 2016 as Mayor Bill de Blasio was wrapping up his third year in office, and it was.

Build them a Pedestrian Plaza and they will come: So they did, 300,000 a day; 480,000 in peak tourist periods.[33] And so did Spider-Man, Wonder Woman, Mickey and Minnie, Snow White and her Dwarfs, Elvis, Ninja Turtles, Catwoman, Cookie Monster, Naked Cowboy, Naked Black Cowboy, Toy Story Cowboy, Lady Liberty, Darth Vader, Queen Elsa, Queen Elizabeth, and more— all working the crowd for tips. I once saw Abraham Lincoln and Richard Nixon having a heated discussion with Donald Trump—about the changing fortunes of the Republican Party, I would suppose. Elmo is a favorite with the youngsters, but he can have an attitude if you don't tip well after he poses for a picture. He cursed out a mom from Utah one day, right there in front of everybody. Another time, he grabbed somebody's butt and got hauled off by the cops. Then came the painted ladies, who figured that the less they wore, the more they earned. They became known as *desnudas* after a few started removing their tops. Some were suspected of offering special services for the dads as night fell. It all belonged to de Blasio now. Bloomberg's Great Plan for Times Square became Bill's Great Pain.

Maybe Joe Lhota was right all along. At least in the old days the strippers kept the show indoors. During the mayoral campaign, Bill de Blasio said that he had "profoundly mixed feelings" about Bloomberg's yet to be completed alteration of Times Square.[34] Identifying himself as "a motorist" who was "often frustrated," he also acknowledged the traffic and safety benefits and a positive impact on tourism. As mayor, his reaction to the sight of half-naked ladies prancing on New York's busiest thoroughfare was less circumspect, declaring, "It's wrong." He promised to do everything he could as chief executive to regulate it.[35]

What that action might be was less obvious. Panhandling is not illegal in New York, nor is it illegal for women to appear topless in public. As creative performers, the *desnudas* were also protected by a First Amendment right to artistic expression. Although not denying the civil liberties issues involved, the mayor insisted that the city had the authority to regulate the painted ladies as a business, insofar as they earn money for their performance. Tim Tompkins, President of the Times Square Alliance, supported that approach, citing a survey by his organization finding that during a single week 120 costumed characters and 11 painted ladies were sighted in the area, and that 45 percent of the people working there had either experienced or witnessed an unpleasant incident with one or the other.[36]

Police Commissioner Bratton took a stronger stance, proposing, "I'd prefer to just dig the whole damn thing up and put it back the way it was," which, in his mind, would eliminate opportunities for loitering and put vehicular traffic back on the streets.[37] At first the mayor agreed that eliminating the plaza was a possible solution, but the idea drew an immediate negative reaction from progressives around town. Planners expressed disappointment that de Blasio would consider turning the clock back to a time when cars took precedence over people. Leaders in the artistic community called him insensitive and intolerant. Tim Tompkins of the Times Square Alliance accused the administration of surrendering to the problem rather than solving it, recalling the days when overcrowded sidewalks were forcing pedestrians into the streets and oncoming traffic.[38]

In the end, the administration arrived at a compromise. A Task Force appointed by the mayor that was cochaired by Commissioner Bratton and City Planning Chair Carl Weisbrod released a set of recommendations in the fall of

2015 that the mayor immediately agreed to adopt.[39] Construction on the plaza continued as planned. Street performers were restricted to a designated time and place in which they can solicit the public. More police officers were added to the area to protect people from aggressive panhandling, which is illegal. And the painted ladies were permitted to display their wares under the watchful eyes of city regulators.[40]

Metzitzah b'peh (MBP) is part of a circumcision ritual practiced by ultra-Orthodox Jews on the eighth day of a child's life. It is carried out by a mohel, who in the Orthodox tradition must be an adult Jewish male with specialized training. Sometimes the mohel is a rabbi, sometimes not; sometimes he has formal medical training as a physician, usually he does not. Circumcision, or a bris, involves the use of a sharp knife or scalpel to cut away the foreskin of a boy's penis. When a medical circumcision is performed in a hospital, the surgeon applies an anesthetic to prevent pain; but among some Haredim no medication is applied, and pain, punctuated by the child's screams, is an ordinary part of the ceremony. After the foreskin is cut away, the mohel places his mouth on the boy's penis and sucks on it to drain blood from the wound, supposedly to prevent clotting. This sucking ritual (MBP) only occurs among a small fraction of Orthodox Jews. In most circumcision procedures, religious or medical, a sponge, cloth, or suction device is used to remove blood.

MBP has been associated with herpes infection in babies, which can be fatal to an infant with an undeveloped immune system. The risk of infection is one in 4,000 among babies on whom the procedure is performed, and approximately 3,600 babies undergo it in the city each year.[41] In 2012 the New York City Health Department issued a strongly worded warning against the practice, citing data indicating that since 2000, eleven cases of herpes tied to the ritual had been discovered.[42] Of ten children who were hospitalized, two were diagnosed with brain damage and two other babies died. Based on the city Health Department findings, the Centers for Disease Control and Prevention in Washington posted an advisory declaring the procedure "not safe."[43]

These reports prompted the Bloomberg administration to adopt a health regulation requiring informed parental consent prior to the bris. The purpose of the signed form was to alert parents to the medical risks they were assuming, and to specifically advise against it.[44] A mohel would be expected to retain the signed form for a year. There was no plan for enforcement put into place. Investigations would be conducted on a case-by-case basis in response to a specific complaint, without regular monitoring. A mohel violating the policy could be subject to a fine or a letter. Some members of the medical community believed that the new regulation was too weak, arguing that in light of evidence of serious risk, the procedure should be outlawed. Leaders in the Orthodox Jewish community claimed that the regulation—or any regulation for that matter—is an unconstitutional infringement of religious freedom. Some Orthodox rabbis instructed their communities to ignore the mandate, and most parents did.

With support from the Rabbinical Council of America, the largest organization of Orthodox rabbis in the world, local Jewish leaders pleaded with Mayor Michael Bloomberg to work with them to develop safe protocols. Bloomberg stood by the regulations enacted by his Health Commissioner, Thomas Farley. The rabbis then took the matter into federal court. After a trial court sided with the city on the First Amendment matter, an appellate court remanded the case back to the trial judge to develop more precise standards. This left the regulation in place, but with an uncertain future.

As a mayoral candidate in 2013, Bill de Blasio vowed to discontinue the regulation and find a new solution, criticizing his predecessor's disrespect for religious tradition and his failure to have a constructive dialogue with the community.[45] De Blasio delivered on his promise in February 2015, when nine of eleven members of the Board of Health, including his new Health Commissioner Mary Bassett, voted to revoke the consent requirement. The mayor had reached a tentative agreement with the influential rabbis earlier, but he waited until he was able to replace Bloomberg appointees on the health board before bringing the issue to a vote. The Orthodox community had largely ignored the Bloomberg administration's regulation, and the city never attempted to collect any consent forms. Between 2012 and 2014, six new cases of herpes had been detected, and only two sets of parents agreed to identify the mohel responsible.[46]

Under the new policy, the rabbis agreed to help identify any mohel associated with a herpes infection and prohibit him from practicing for life. A brochure describing the dangers of the procedure was distributed in hospitals located in Orthodox communities. Once again, there were no enforcement mechanisms put into place. City Hall issued a statement acknowledging that "MBP carries with it health risks," but in consideration of the "sacred nature of this ritual in the community," the administration stood by its policy "centered around education of health risks by the healthcare community and respect for traditional practices by the religious community."[47]

The change was not well received in the larger liberal Jewish community and among groups that found it to be an unreasonable accommodation of religion. Coming forward on the basis of their "responsibility to speak out," a group of Jewish doctors from prestigious medical institutions in the city published an op-ed in *The Jewish Week* calling the new policy "shameful and simply wrong" because it "ignores the teachings of modern medicine."[48] They further pointed out that because numerous DNA tests are required to determine whether a particular mohel is responsible for a herpes infection, the enforcement of protections for innocent children would not be effective. Six new cases of herpes were detected between 2015 and 2017, during which time the mayor stepped up the city's information campaign and banned the infected mohels from practicing; but the voluntary practice of reporting remained in place with no effective enforcement mechanisms established.

There were other accommodations of religion promulgated by the de Blasio administration during the first two years of his tenure at City Hall, some of which specifically benefited the Jewish Orthodox community, some of which had larger implications. Community organizations, including religious institutions and schools, were allowed to host classes in the mayor's sweeping universal pre-kindergarten program. Rather than totally ban any instruction with religious connotations as other jurisdictions had, the city set ambiguous guidelines for the estimated 180 sectarian (of 1,200 private) institutions participating, which allowed religious texts to be included in lessons so long as they were "presented objectively as part of a secular program of instruction" so that students can learn about their cultures.[49]

Civil libertarians protested that the arrangement was "ripe for overstepping" the legal boundaries between church and state. In order to accommodate the sectarian institutions further, half-day rather than full day instruction was permitted as an exception to program designs in the rest of the school system so that children at private institutions could receive religious instruction during the other hours. The mayor again drew fire from liberal rights groups at the end of 2015 when he signed a City Council bill that paid for private security guards at independent and religious schools. The program had been supported by a cross-section of Jewish, Catholic, and Islamic organizations. One City Council member called the measure "a regressive bill" that is a "step in the direction of subsidizing private education."

De Blasio seemed unmoved by criticism from liberal allies who prefer to maintain a strict wall of separation between church and state. Despite differences on social issues such as gay marriage, he has managed to develop a cooperative relationship with Cardinal Timothy Dolan, the spiritual leader of the Catholic Archdiocese. When the mayor was running into political headwinds over the death of Eric Garner on Staten Island, he asked the cardinal to assemble an interfaith coalition of religious leaders to help with the process of healing and reconciliation. Just days before the historic visit of Pope Francis to New York, the mayor and the cardinal announced that the two would leverage properties in the archdiocese's portfolio to provide 150 beds for homeless people. Taking a note from the pontiff's message on combating inequality, de Blasio remarked, "Pope Francis is calling us to action."[50]

Bill de Blasio owes a lot to the Clintons. During his presidency, Bill Clinton gave de Blasio his first big executive job in government as regional director of the Department of Housing and Urban Development, serving under Secretary Andrew Cuomo. When Hillary Clinton decided to make a run for a U.S. Senate seat in New York State, she asked de Blasio to manage her campaign, which later gave him a huge boost when he launched his own career in electoral politics. The day Bill de Blasio took the oath of office as mayor of New York, it was former president Bill Clinton who swore him in at the ceremony in front of City Hall. But when Hillary Clinton declared her candidacy for the presidency in 2015, Bill de Blasio was the last major Democrat in the state to give her an endorsement. How can one explain such behavior?

Bill de Blasio signaled that he was on a different path from that of the Clintons early on in a September 2014 interview published in *Politico* under the title "The New Icon of the Left."[51] Although the newly chosen mayor praised the former president as being "ahead of his time" for trumpeting the decline of the middle class, he also admitted, "I was never comfortable with the DLC (the now-defunct centrist Democratic Leadership Council allied with the Clintons). I think the DLC's time came and went." When asked about the 2016 presidential race, he predicted, "Clearly, throughout the 2016 election cycle, there will be a call for what we often call populism." He continued, "there will be sort of sharp truth-telling about the reality of the economy and the need for more profound answers." He elaborated, "The campaign is about the issue of inequality." When asked whether he would endorse Hillary Clinton, he said he would not support a candidate who had not yet formally declared.

De Blasio was even more precise in his appraisal of the Democratic Party and its need to change direction in December, 2015 when he argued,

> I think the Democratic Party needs to get back to its roots. We are a party that is supposed to be about progressive economic policies and economic populism. And we're supposed to speak for the needs of working people of every background, of every region. And I don't think as a whole the party has done a good enough job.[52]

When Hillary Clinton finally did declare in June, de Blasio did not attend the elaborate ceremony on Roosevelt Island, and again withheld his support, stating that he wanted to wait for her to articulate a vision and clarify her position on the issues.[53] He was very certain about the issues he had in mind. Emphasizing that the country is experiencing the "worst income inequality since the Great Depression," he mentioned progressive taxation, increases in wages and benefits for workers, and taxation of the wealthy.[54]

As a matter of fact, Hillary Clinton did not endorse Bill de Blasio for mayor until he had won the Democratic Party primary. But the circumstances were different then. It is not unusual for politicians at the top of the party food chain to withhold an endorsement while there is an intramural primary battle going on for a local office, especially when there are several contenders with strong claims for party support, as was the case in the 2013 mayoral contest. When a leader at the head of the state party hierarchy becomes a serious candidate for president, it is more common for other politicians to line up in support of a "favorite son." In this case, the presidential candidate was a prominent woman.

Instead of falling in with the rest, Bill de Blasio turned his energy toward working with like-minded people within the party to develop a "Progressive Agenda," which was put forward as a left-of-center alternative to the conservative "Contract for America" once propagated by Republican leader Newt Gingrich. It was really an alternative to the moderate politics as usual that has come to define the centrist mainstream of the Democratic Party.

The Progressive Agenda Committee had planned to host a forum in Iowa that December in anticipation of the early primary there. Candidates from both parties were invited to share their views on the issues. The committee especially wanted to call out candidates on the question of income inequality. The announcement of the planned forum further incensed people in the Clinton camp, who felt that it could upstage their candidate at the moment of her announcement. Hilary Rosen, a leader of a pro-Clinton super PAC called Ready for Hillary warned that the mayor's "self-aggrandizing" actions "won't go unnoticed," asserting, "Hillary Clinton fought for the middle class and poor families long before Bill de Blasio could even articulate any vision at all."[55]

At no point did Bill de Blasio make any disparaging remarks about Hillary Clinton or her campaign. To the contrary, he consistently complimented her on her progressive record and expressed confidence that she would articulate a plan to address his policy concerns. Other than a well-publicized meeting that took place in Brooklyn at Bernie Sanders's request, de Blasio never gave any indication that he was seriously leaning toward the Vermont senator, whose priorities seemed almost perfectly aligned with his own. Although he did praise Sanders on occasion, hacked emails released in 2016 indicated that de Blasio never intended to support him. He, instead, offered to help bring Sanders into the Clinton fold.[56] When Vice President Joe Biden threatened to interrupt Hillary's momentum with public speculation that he might challenge her, de Blasio remarked, "I don't think we need additional candidates."[57]

Mayor de Blasio finally delivered his belated endorsement of Hillary Clinton on October 30th. It was an un-ceremonial statement made in response to a question during a television interview covering a number of topics. Hillary Clinton was not herself present, as is usually the case on such occasions, to hear the mayor say, "The candidate who I believe can fundamentally address income inequality effectively, the candidate who has the right vision, the right experience and the ability to get the job done is Hillary Clinton."[58] The Clinton campaign hardly recognized the statement except for an email sent to reporters suggesting that the mayor's support was "a sign of the campaign's continued momentum."[59] The same email noted that the campaign was about to announce a joint endorsement from more than eighty-five mayors across the country. Just a few days earlier, Clinton had formed a New York "leadership council" composed of the one hundred most prominent Democrats in the state who stood behind her candidacy. Bill de Blasio's name was not on the list.

By this time, the former U.S. Senator and Secretary of State had celebrated a spectacular performance at the first Democratic Party presidential debate, moving her ahead in national polls. The storm over a possible Biden candidacy had passed. The presidential forum that the mayor's progressive coalition had planned to stage in Iowa never materialized. Bernie Sanders and former Maryland governor Martin O'Mally had said they would attend; the Clinton campaign never made a commitment.

In the end, the de Blasio endorsement drew more media attention for its poor timing than its impact. One local reporter from New York poignantly observed, "Mayor Bill de Blasio's long national politics nightmare is over."[60] However, Hillary Clinton's worst nightmare was just about to begin.

* * *

This is a story about a man who acts as though the American political process is a diseased system that preys on the weak, and understands that in order to help bring it back to health, he himself needs to occupy the malignant body. If he were a physician, we might wonder whether the healer would be consumed while administering the cure. We can easily ask the same about Bill de Blasio. He could lose his head—or worse, lose his soul.

In the American system, radical thinkers usually inhabit the fringe of politics, and haul their criticisms from the outside. For that reason they often remain marginalized. De Blasio jumped right in, and drilled his long legs into the mud. I had considered subtitling the book, "Bill de Blasio's Quest to Save the Soul of New York (and his own a_ _ in the bargain)," but a polite editor advised me that such a colloquialism on the cover of a serious book might give readers the wrong impression. In truth, that is a main query of the project. This is a book about survival, not just Bill de Blasio's, but the progressive cause he has adopted, not to mention the compromised system of democracy we now have. The Democrats were too absorbed in their own internecine battles to appreciate the enormity of the threat that Donald Trump posed as he worked his way through the Republican primaries and on to a final victory on Election Day. As a result, Trump was given four years to remind them of what they had missed.

Even as a mature political actor, this man who once dabbled in Marxist causes remains an odd player on the American scene. What could de Blasio have been thinking when he snubbed the most powerful woman in American politics after she had treated him like a friend? One explanation I have heard from several people who know him well is overconfidence—seasoned with an ounce of arrogance, and a drop of innocence. As the newly elected mayor of New York City, he may have truly believed that he could lead a progressive movement in the mainstream of the Democratic Party and coax the presumptive standard-bearer to take a serious stand on income inequality. Against formidable odds, the same message worked well for him in his own election.

The Hillary episode must have been the most grueling experience of his short tenure: measuring loyalty to a friend and former ally against loyalty to an ideal. Maybe he overestimated her, hoping that the old Hillary Rodham would show up at the end of the day and act less Clintonesque, taking a firm position on income equality because she really believed in it, rather than because her pollsters were cautioning her to tilt left or lose ground to Bernie Sanders. Bill de Blasio kept waiting. He never lost hope in her; never latched on to her opponent, a more natural ally philosophically; and snapped into action to help put down a serious threat by a popular vice president of the United States who was also pivoting leftward.

Most insiders saw de Blasio's handling of the endorsement as a political disaster bordering on suicide. How foolish a move it was for a career politician. Doesn't Bill know how the system works? Then again, maybe Bill does know. Maybe he understands that if political leaders don't finally draw a line in the sand, business as usual will just maintain an unacceptable status quo in which powerful lobbyists ply decision-makers with money to protect privileges for the few at everybody else's expense. Drawing that line is what he tried to do. He took it as far as he could, then fell in with the party regulars who convinced themselves that Hillary Clinton would be the next president. In the end, he was pragmatic and loyal to the candidate who had helped him build his own career.

Throughout it all, de Blasio never abandoned his demand that Democrats address the growing economic inequality that their own party had helped to grow. As he explained in an interview with *The Atlantic* in December 2015, "What I am trying to do with the progressive agenda goes far beyond the boundaries of the Democratic Party. It is about changing our national debate and ultimately changing national policies."[61] This is the man whom Joe Lhota accused of promoting class warfare during the 2013 mayoral campaign. That war was well underway before de Blasio spoke up. It's not clear who started it: the poor homeless guy living in a cardboard box on Lexington Avenue, or the guy in the office high above. Undeniably it is ongoing. Bernie Sanders got that; too many other Democrats did not. When Bill de Blasio embraced it in 2013, he was portrayed as an ideologue.

"Ideologue" can be a vexing appellation for an active politician, and we must use it advisedly. There is a difference between an ideologue and a principled actor. Ideologues can ignore facts that don't support their worldview. Ideologues tend to be inflexible and single-minded. Bill de Blasio doesn't quite measure up that way. As black leaders who supported his candidacy lamented aggressive police tactics, he hired one of the toughest lawmen around to head up the NYPD, and the two managed to get along splendidly, despite the mayor's lasting relationship with the ever-defiant Reverend Al Sharpton. De Blasio's reaction to the carnivalesque happenings in Times Square was also revealing. He identified with the motorists before the cyclists. He swooped in with moral outrage at the sight of public nudity, declaring it to be just plain "wrong." As civil libertarians cringed from the sidelines, he worked closely with his police commissioner to maximize regulation without breaking the law—all the while threatening to dig up the showcase experiment in progressive planning.

This left-leaning politician who does not go to church (except to campaign) is no enemy of organized religion either. He has befriended the cardinal of the Catholic Archdiocese; Pope Francis is one of his heroes. His forays into Latin American Marxism were nurtured in the liberation theology of the Jesuits. He is close to Orthodox Jewish rabbis. He finally crossed the line when he lifted regulations that would have better protected infants put at risk by an ancient religious ritual. Health professionals believed the Bloomberg regulations regarding *metzitzah b'peh* were too weak from the start. De Blasio's compromise stank of political opportunism.

Bill de Blasio is a *pragmatist*. That can cause concern in some circles. If using the term *ideologue* to describe him provokes alarm among those on the political right, the label *pragmatist* evokes a similar reaction with those on the left. So we need to be clear here about how the term is intended in this volume, and more important, how it is not—especially as the term appears on the jacket cover to describe our main character. Pragmatism is not an antonym of conviction, although we have grown accustomed to believing that today, when all things seem negotiable in the face of power and money.

The slick inside operatives will tell you that compromise is what keeps government moving. More principled folks will remind us that government does not always move in a desirable direction. There are no simple rules to apply in judging the merits of any political action. Some pragmatists effectively safeguard their cherished convictions; others have shallow guiding principles from the start. A reasonable assessment of public actions requires that we analyze decisions of key actors in the context of the actual choices they faced at the time. That is the cruel reality of public life that will become more apparent when we review the history of New York mayors. It is the standard by which people will judge Bill de Blasio.

Politics, in the more enlightened sense, is about the pursuit of basic human values. *Equality,* the core value that animates Bill de Blasio, is one that Americans have been struggling with since the founding. Reasonable people can debate the details regarding its meaning and requirements. In politics, pragmatism is a calculation that considers the compromises actors must make in the pursuit of such core values. Promoting *economic equality,* which we will hear about more in these pages, is arguably a pragmatic step to addressing a host of inequities ranging from healthcare to homelessness, from education to affordable housing, not to mention public safety, childcare, and an assortment of other policy dilemmas. To state it another way, income inequality is arguably at the root of many issues that plague our cities and our country. The rest may be symptomatic.

These are the kinds of policy assertions that progressives such as Bill de Blasio and Bernie Sanders have made. They are arguable, perhaps also refutable. Such claims are contested by advocates and analysts who believe that government is not equipped to effectively redistribute wealth, or that poverty and inequality are natural outcomes of a competitive economy. Many of the same philosophical antagonists believe such an intrusive governmental role is an assault on basic freedoms. We will discuss these debates at greater length in future chapters.

For now, let's accept these progressive assertions as a hypothesis for understanding the mind of Bill de Blasio, whose commitment to a redistributive governmental role has personal and historical roots that we will explore further. We do not need to agree with them. We may also acknowledge a cynical assumption, common even among many who share his priorities, that what he is trying to achieve politically is impossible: that his progressive march could be a fool's journey. As stated earlier, he is a ripe case for testing the progressive proposition. So far the record is not encouraging. The outcome of the 2016 election makes the prospects for real progress more discouraging.

That said, Bill de Blasio's aspirations for the city and the country extend a long progressive tradition in New York that goes back to Fiorello La Guardia. If New York has a soul, it is because the city produced leaders who believed it should create a better life for all people, and that government had a role in ensuring it. For those who are true believers, it is not just good policy. It can also be considered smart policy, which we may describe as policy that, though refutable, is a reasonable approach to addressing societal problems. The progressive legacy has been carried forward by other mayors since La Guardia, including Robert Wagner, John Lindsay, and David Dinkins—with varying degrees of success and compromise.

La Guardia, Wagner, and Lindsay were able to advance the cause because they had the backing of strong presidents in Washington who propped them up with sympathetic laws and programs. And even they suffered from serious limitations. Franklin D. Roosevelt, who served as La Guardia's patron of aid toward the needy, was reluctant to antagonize Southern Democrats in Congress with a serious agenda for racial equality, so the liberal coalition he built was not all inclusive. It took a pass on civil rights.

Lyndon Johnson took the bull of racial injustice by the horns, and New York benefited from his outstanding legislative leadership, but Johnson became distracted by an ill-advised war in Vietnam that eventually brought him down. New York mayors at the time faced serious obstacles to the progressive agenda in their own backyards. Although the white working class unions Robert Wagner empowered advanced economic equality, they were not always receptive to a vigorous racial agenda. Lindsay took a stronger stand on racial equality than his predecessor, but his antagonism with the white working class also built long-standing resentments between the races. By the time David Dinkins became mayor, the city was in such a fiscal tailspin that the opportunities to act progressively were limited.

Bill de Blasio has turned a new page in New York City history. The electoral coalition he built on the basis of class interests cut across racial boundaries. Being able to transform that electoral coalition into a governing coalition and then to repeat the performance in 2017 is his continuing challenge; this, we have seen, is no walk through Central Park on a sunny afternoon. His burden as mayor weighs heavier because policies that have contributed to a growing inequality are made in Washington, with the cooperation of both major political parties. A mayor has little control over these policies. It is his job to deal with their consequences, in the form of homelessness, social disruption, inadequate housing, and a city less hospitable to people of modest means. It is no wonder that de Blasio, like his predecessors, has such an interest in national politics. His stake is not just philosophical.

Bill de Blasio's career, although awesome in its velocity, has proceeded down a rocky road full of twists and turns. Given his stated aspirations, he needs support along the way from players who really don't agree with his goals, at least not enough to take a chance against the odds, whose friendships and alliances may be temporary at best and less than heartfelt. How can somebody like him govern such a complex city like New York and remain an effective player on the national scene? We'll see. Don't expect the usual game. Bill is an original, and his jagged stripes run deep.

PART I

EARLY YEARS

2

All in the Family

It was right after the Second World War when Warren and Maria married. They had met at *Time* magazine, where he was a business reporter, and she a research assistant. They were both thirty-two years of age when they wed—late for a first marriage in those days. Originally from lower Manhattan, Maria was one of three daughters born to Italian immigrants from Southern Italy near Naples. Her parents, Giovanni and Anna, ran a dress shop. She was raised Catholic and had an Uncle Alberto who was a priest in Sant' Agata de' Goti; but she moved away from religion as an adult, and it was never an important factor when she and Warren raised their own family. Warren—of mixed German, English, French, and Scotch-Irish heritage—was born on Staten Island. His father, Donald Wilhelm, was originally from Ohio. He had come east to attend Hobart College in upstate New York on a football scholarship, and after a year of study he transferred to Harvard, where he took on various part-time jobs to support himself. On one visit back home, he met a girl at a dance named Nina May Warren, a recent graduate of Ohio Wesleyan who taught high school English in Defiance, Ohio. They later married.

The elder Wilhelm (Donald) was a prolific writer. He had been a staff reporter for the *Washington Post*, and was the author of nine books, including one on the college years of Theodore Roosevelt, which he wrote as an undergraduate student.[1] He contributed to popular magazines such as *Saturday Evening Post*, *Scribner's*, *Collier's*, *Harper's*, and *Ladies Home Journal*. Donald also served as a personal assistant to Herbert Hoover when Hoover was secretary of commerce, and was dispatched to Russia for a time to report on the starvation crisis there. Smart and ambitious, he apparently got to know Roosevelt and Hoover through the Harvard alumni network, with which he was actively involved.

Warren's older brother, Donald Jr., served as an advisor on Far Eastern affairs for the United States government, and wrote a series of Cold War books celebrating how the West was going to prevail over communism. In the mid-1950s, Donald was appointed a visiting professor of political science at the University of Tehran in Iran. While there, he became a close associate of the

Shah, Mohammed Reza Pahlavi, who had assumed the throne with the help of a CIA (Central Intelligence Agency)-supported coup. The two men became so close that Donald helped the Shah write his personal memoir. Donald is thanked in the preface, where the Shah refers to him as a "personal friend" and friend of his country.[2] Despite Donald's fondness for the Shah and conservative political causes, his own son John was destined to have a career as a progressive labor leader in the New Haven area where he grew up. John later crossed paths with his cousin Bill who shared his political leanings.

Like his father and older brother, Warren Wilhelm was interested in world affairs. After attending the Loomis School (now Loomis Chafee), an elite boarding academy in Connecticut, he acquired a degree in economics from Yale. Warren was more liberal than his brother Donald, and quite skeptical about his relationship with the Shah.[3] As a student at Yale, Warren became involved in a campaign to get higher wages for the chambermaids who tended to the daily needs of boys who attended the Ivy-clad institution. Years later, nephew John, another Yale alumnus, also took on the university when he unionized its clerical and service workers and organized a series of strikes to raise their salaries and benefits.

Warren was also proudly patriotic. Four months after the bombing of Pearl Harbor, he enlisted in the army. He had tried to join the Navy earlier, but was rejected for being too tall (6'5"). Initially, he was engaged in three combat missions in the Pacific Islands, for which he earned a Bronze Star. He was then deployed to participate in the Battle of Okinawa, one of the bloodiest engagements of the entire war. A few weeks before the battle ended, Wilhelm advanced ahead of his company to establish an observation post, where a Japanese soldier emerged from a foxhole with a grenade. Warren was able to take down the advancing enemy soldier, saving many American lives, but the grenade exploded and took off part of his left leg just below the knee. While the young hero was recuperating in a hospital in Atlantic City, he asked for a temporary leave so that he could return home to marry Maria. He was later discharged with a Purple Heart.

After the war, Warren acquired a master's degree in economics at Harvard, where he worked at the Russian Research Center and began to study the economy of the Soviet Union. Upon graduating, he took a job in Washington working as an analyst for the Bureau of the Budget. He was later hired to become the chief economic analyst at Texaco Oil, commuting from his home in affluent Rowayton, Connecticut, to its offices in the Chrysler Building in Midtown Manhattan. The giant petroleum company held major interests in the Middle East and South America.

Texaco profited greatly when the Shah denationalized Iran's oil industry and went into business with American firms. The company also lost a huge amount of money in 1959 after Fidel Castro took power in Cuba and seized its oil refineries there. Philosophically, Warren remained a New Dealer. Occasionally he used his knowledge of world economies to assist Senator Jacob Javits, the liberal Republican from New York, developing programs to increase American investments in Latin America.

In 1966, Warren and Maria moved to Cambridge, Massachusetts, when Warren accepted an offer from the Arthur D. Little consulting firm, hoping to reconnect to the Harvard stratosphere. By then, the couple had three boys— Steven, Donald, and Warren Jr.—the youngest always referred to as Billy. The family lived in a beautiful Victorian home on Brewster Street, a tree-lined block just a short walk to the Charles River. The house, built in 1886, had belonged to the celebrated lesbian poet and essayist Adrienne Rich. Literary icon Robert Frost once lived just a few doors down in a four-unit townhouse that is now on the National Register of Historic Places.

The couple seemed to fit well in the rarefied intellectual community near the Harvard campus. They enjoyed reading, listening to classical music, and talking politics. Warren was able to keep trim by rowing a small one-person shell with a sliding seat he built for himself that was specially fit to accommodate his missing leg. He relished the time he spent teaching his older sons how to navigate the family's 26-foot Wianno Senior sloop that they named the *Solange* (French for *Dream*), the same kind of vessel that the Kennedy family could be spotted sailing along Cape Cod in those days. According to his younger sister Jean, Warren had learned to sail as a boy after taking a job at boatyard where they lived near the Mianus River in Connecticut. After that, being on the water became a lifetime passion that the two shared.[4]

Maria de Blasio Wilhelm was not the typical daughter of Southern European immigrants. She had acquired two degrees in English from Smith College, and was always proud that she was one of only two Italian-Americans in her graduating class. She not only married late: she pursued her own career, both before and after marrying. She was employed by the Office of War Information during the great conflict, and later worked in public relations, first for the Italian consulate, then for Polaroid.

Maria was just about to turn forty-four years of age when her youngest son, Billy (later called Bill), was born in 1961. Because late age births were especially risky then, she and her husband, Warren, traveled from their Connecticut home to have the baby at Doctor's Hospital on the Upper East Side of Manhattan, across the street from Gracie Mansion, where they could get better care for mother and child. Tending to the needs of three children did not dissuade Maria from pursuing her own literary ambitions.

The mother of three kept her hand in publishing, and wrote for several magazines, including *Working Women*, a periodical that was way ahead of its time.

Maria was also the author of several books, including a well-received study of the Italian Resistance published in 1988 that merited a favorable review by Herbert Mitgang in the *New York Times*.[5] Writing under her married name, Maria Wilhelm, she highlighted the important role women played in the Resistance— crossing battle lines under German fire, carrying ammunition in shopping bags and baby carriages, distributing clandestine newspapers to keep spirits high during the perilous struggle against the Nazis. She recounts the episode as one of the first times in Italian history that men and women worked side by side as equals for a common cause.

Maria and her husband seemed to have put together an idyllic life in Cambridge. But, in fact, their life was riven with turmoil. During the McCarthy era, they were both accused of being Communist sympathizers. Warren had brought suspicion upon himself for having studied the Soviet economy while affiliated with Harvard's Russian Research Center. Maria was an active member of a labor union, and drew further attention from government authorities when she attended a concert featuring Soviet musicians. None other than Whittaker Chambers, the former Soviet agent whose testimony brought down Alger Hiss, laid claims against the couple, who were employed by *Time* magazine when he was editor there.[6] The accusations could not be substantiated by an FBI investigation.[7]

In 1950, the regional Loyalty Board brought the couple in for questioning. Warren, a recipient of both a Bronze Medal and a Purple Heart for the sacrifices he made during the war, swore complete allegiance to the United States. On the basis of a three-hour hearing that took place in mid-July, the board found that there was no compelling evidence to conclude the Wilhelms were disloyal, and the charges were dismissed. The board also determined that "Mr. Wilhelm and his wife had had a sympathetic interest in Communism," and consequently denied him access to classified documents.[8] The latter determination seriously limited his career in the federal government, so he decided to leave public service.

Having suffered through the Great Depression, the war, McCarthyism, unemployment, and devastating humiliation by the government he served, Warren Wilhelm developed deep psychological problems. He experienced long bouts of depression and became an excessive drinker. Despite pleas from Maria and others, he refused to get professional help, reasonably concerned that any admission of psychological trauma would further damage his already compromised career. These ailments also took a toll on the family. In 1969, three days before her twenty-fourth wedding anniversary, Maria did something else that Italian women of her generation would never contemplate. She filed for divorce, claiming abusive treatment by her troubled husband. It was a difficult decision for a woman from her background, especially with three boys to raise on her own, and it further weakened Warren's mental condition. As a single mother with limited earning power, Maria was forced to move to a modest apartment in a working class part of town. By then, her oldest son, Steven, was grown and pretty much off on his own.

Despondent, unemployed, and guilt-ridden for having failed his family, Warren moved back to Connecticut, not far from where the Wilhelms lived when he commuted to New York City as a young executive at Texaco. He continued to visit the family on occasion, but the visits were usually painful for Maria and not very pleasant for the children. He was now also suffering from lung cancer and emphysema brought on by heavy smoking. On June 28, 1979, after two unsuccessful attempts to take his own life, Warren drove to the Rocky River Inn that sat along the Housatonic River in New Milford, Connecticut, and shot himself to death. Steven, at age twenty-one, got the call when police identified his father. Knowing that he was losing his fight with cancer, Warren left a note saying that he did not want to die in a hospital with tubes running through his body. He apologized to the family for the grief he had caused them, and to the police and motel-keeper for the bloody mess he had left behind.

Steven, who was very close to his dad, looks back on the sad yet admirable life of a father who was caring, highly intellectual, physically adventurous, and heroic, but ultimately defeated by a chain of unbearable circumstances that life dealt him, commenting,

> I have come to understand my father as a warrior, overcome by wounds from the Second World War and its aftermath.
>
> I remember a creative and energetic man who kept on despite the limits of his wooden leg. He taught me to sail, to use wood-working tools.
>
> As I came of age I slowly realized how wounded he was on the inside, from the war and from being falsely accused of treason.
>
> I think the era failed him. He might have recovered but the societal and institutional support wasn't there. So he turned to drink and isolation.
>
> My dad shot himself partly because he was dying from cancer, but also from trauma unresolved. This remains a great and unnecessary tragedy.[9]

It is difficult to measure the lasting damage this kind of hardship has on a family, especially the children. Bill was only seven when his father left home, and just eighteen when his father died. He has fond memories of Little League baseball and sunny afternoons cheering on the Red Sox with his dad at Fenway Park, still his favorite baseball team, but he never really got to know his father well. Bill spent some time in psychotherapy during his twenties trying to figure out the man who was his father, never quite succeeding. He is quick to say that it was strong women—his mother and two aunts—who got him through it. In a 2013 interview with the *New York Times*, Bill is quoted as saying, "My father was a picture of courage in terms of his war service and strength, and yet in his decline, I learned primarily negative lessons."[10] In a more recent interview with the author, de Blasio identified his maternal grandfather Giovanni and his older brother Steven as his two principal male role models during childhood.[11]

Bolstered by her two sisters Dorothy and Yole, Maria remained dedicated to giving her three sons any advantages that her fragile middle class status could offer. After living for a while on a commune in Connecticut, Steven has had a career as a journalist for local newspapers and magazines in the State of Washington. He also became involved with the Tibetan Nuns Project, which supports refugee nuns in India, and the Northwest Dharma Association, a North American organization that promotes collaboration among 137 Buddhist groups and publishes a quarterly that he edits. Donald, the middle son, now retired, has had a career as a journalist and union activist in the Boston area.

Bill inherited his parents' passion for politics, and carried it over into a lifelong career. He remains ever grateful to his mother and the strong pragmatic idealism that she embodied throughout her lifetime. He holds her up as "the greatest influence in my life." In a 2013 *New York Magazine* interview published a week before his election as mayor of New York City, he admiringly and sympathetically described Maria as follows:

> She was often very, very sad about things that had happened to her, but she had a fierce resilience—a very sharp, purposeful resilience. She was very practical. She always talked to me about a kind of Italian understanding of the world—she would juxtapose somewhat my father's upbringing and what she saw as sort of an American affectation for a certain romanticism, a certain idealism, with her own Southern Italian sense of practicality. She was nobody's fool, and when the whole McCarthy thing happened, it bothered her intellectually and it troubled her personally, but she was not surprised one bit. She came out of that experience further armored. My father came out of that experience further troubled.[12]

Maria did manage to place her youngest son at the Pilot School, an experimental public high school founded on the Harvard campus in 1969 as a collaboration between faculty from the Graduate School of Education and public school teachers who believed that the regular public schools were too regimented. Similar to today's public charter schools, students were chosen by lottery, and the campus functioned outside the usual bureaucratic constraints imposed by the local school district. In this case though, applicants were selected to represent different neighborhoods throughout Cambridge, so the 180-member student body was diverse. Children whose ancestors came over on the Mayflower would sit next to students whose forefathers arrived in slave ships; academic standards were kept high by boys and girls whose fathers taught at Harvard and MIT. The curriculum was progressive, and students were encouraged to address teachers by their first names.

Bill thrived at the Pilot School. He reveled in the diversity and immediately took to the school's egalitarian practice of shared decision-making. According to his 1979 high school yearbook, Bill was a member of the Student School Committee, the Fairness Committee, and the National Honor Society. While at Pilot, he started using his mother's name, calling himself Warren de Blasio Wilhelm, and at his request it appeared on his diploma when he graduated.[13] His strong Italian self-identification began to manifest itself in 1975 after he visited the hometown of his grandparents, Sant' Agata De Goti, in southern Italy. As de Blasio explains, "For the first time in my life, I felt my ancestry beyond the United States, a sense of having roots that I could connect to."[14]

Young Bill was popular among his classmates and elected to student government—affectionately referred to among his peers as "Senator Provolone" in recognition of his Italian identity and love of politics. They jokingly hummed the tune to "Hail to the Chief" when his gawky, oversized figure entered the room. It was there at the Pilot School that Bill first became involved in contentious issues of the day, joining protests against the use of nuclear power, and reading for the first time *The Autobiography of Malcolm X*, destined to become one of his favorite books. Reading it gave him the confidence to choose a name that better reflected his identity.[15]

Because his parents were older than those of his peers, de Blasio grew up hearing stories about the Great Depression and the New Deal that made a distinct impression on him, and helps us to understand his strong political inclinations. As he explains,

> We would have these family gatherings, and everyone would be around the table and it felt like there were two empty chairs for Franklin Roosevelt and Fiorello La Guardia. There was a reverence for them in our family. I was steeped in the notion that you take heart from a government that is trying with all its might to find a solution for you.[16]

A Presidential Scholarship with free tuition at New York University brought Bill to New York City in 1979, just a few months after his father was laid to rest. He had always been fascinated with New York, and Aunt Yole was living nearby in Greenwich Village. On his first day there he met Peter Dicpinigaitis, another presidential scholar who is now a critical care physician practicing in the Bronx and teaching at the Albert Einstein College of Medicine. The two became fast friends, sharing a dorm room in Weinstein Hall at 5 University Place. They have remained friends ever since, even though Peter was a science major and conservative Republican, while Bill majored in Metropolitan Studies and leaned so far to the Left that his long body would practically topple over. He took courses such as "The Politics of Minority Groups" and "The Working Class Experience."

As Peter recalls, "We would talk politics late into the night. Although we passionately disagreed, our politics never got in the way of our friendship."[17] Their NYU fellowships permitted the two roommates to travel every year, and they used these opportunities to visit Israel, Senegal, Spain, Morocco, and the Soviet Union. Between stays in Moscow and Leningrad, Bill accompanied Peter on an emotional trip to Lithuania, the homeland his parents had fled after World War II following several years at a displaced persons camp in Germany. The two young men got to know each other's families and attended each other's weddings. Thirty-eight years later, Peter remembers that this "Red Sox fan from Massachusetts" (another point of contention) "was determined to live in New York City and become involved in local politics."

According to Allan Frei, another classmate, post-college roommate, and longtime friend, who is now a geography professor at Hunter College in New York, "Bill impressed those around him as being highly intellectual, very funny, and passionately committed to political causes."[18] As in high school, Bill continued to be a student activist. In 1989 he launched a hotly contested campaign (his first ever) to become dorm president at Weinstein, working day and night to defeat an unscrupulous opponent who tore down his campaign posters when nobody was looking. He cofounded the Coalition for Student Rights, led demonstrations against tuition hikes (even though his fellowship covered those costs), and demanded student representation on the university Board of Trustees. He got into steep trouble with university authorities at one point when he organized a sit-in at Bobst Library, which was off limits to protesters.

Although the NYU campus in Greenwich Village had an ample supply of drugs and alcohol, Bill, who enjoyed a good social life, had no particular interest in either. He admits to smoking marijuana only a few times while there, and never again since. Right after graduating, Bill formally filed papers to change his legal name to Warren de Blasio Wilhelm, explaining in the application that after his parents' divorce, it was his mother and her Italian family who really gave him his identity.[19]

In 1983 Bill won a prestigious Truman fellowship, and went on to study Latin American politics as a graduate student at Columbia University. While there, he worked on the 1984 presidential campaign of Walter Mondale, and had his first taste of city government as an Urban Fellow in the Department of Juvenile Justice. Taking classes at the School of International and Public Affairs, he met Dan Cantor, another campus activist. They would have a lasting friendship and become Brooklyn neighbors in later years. In 1998 they collaborated with labor organizers and other like-minded activists to form the Working Families Party (WFP). Cantor would become the party's national director. The party advanced a progressive political agenda in New York and a handful of states that were receptive to its message of political and economic justice. It would also become a key asset to Bill as his political career matured.

At Columbia, Bill's attention soon extended beyond American borders. He became fascinated with the revolutionary Sandinista government that over-threw the American-backed dictatorship in Nicaragua that had ruled for forty-six years. The Marxist regime that came into power in 1979 enjoyed a close alliance with Fidel Castro and the Soviet Union. Bill was impressed with the Sandinista efforts to implement mass literacy, healthcare, housing, and other services to depressed populations in urban and rural areas.

After earning his master's degree in 1987, Bill was hired by the Quixote Center in Maryland. Housed in a converted apartment decorated with peace posters, the group raised money to send food, clothing, and other supplies to Nicaragua. Founded by Jesuit Catholic leaders who espoused a theology of liberation, the organization did not officially take sides in the civil war. De Blasio, himself, was becoming an effective provocateur, and was twice arrested in Washington for participating in disruptive rallies against American policies in the region.

Missing New York, he left the Maryland-based center after a year, but before returning, he got to spend ten days at a health clinic in Masaya, Nicaragua. While there, he and his Quixote colleagues worked shoulder to shoulder with doctors, nurses, nuns, and other volunteers serving poor communities dev-astated by war and poverty. As he explained to the *New York Times* in 2013, observing the Sandinista government in action affirmed his conviction that government must protect and enhance the lives of the poor. It showed him what a robust government attuned to human needs could achieve, and it taught him "how hands-on government needs to be, how proactive, how connected to the people it must be."[20]

When Ronald Reagan became president in 1981, he condemned the Sandinistas for joining Fidel Castro in supporting Marxist revolutionary move-ments throughout Latin America and suppressing human rights in their own country. Both claims were valid. Vowing to depose the government, Reagan authorized the CIA to finance, arm, and train a militia force known as the Contras to conduct a civil war. Already controversial at home, the Contras and American foreign policy drew criticism from other corners of the world.

In 1983, the Republic of Nicaragua filed a complaint with the International Court of Justice (ICJ) alleging that the United States was using force against its country in violation of international law. In 1986, by a vote of 12-3, the ICJ ruled that the United States had breached international law by intervening in the affairs of another state. The court also found that President Reagan, in an attempt to disrupt navigation, had authorized a government agency to mine the harbors of El Bluff, Corinto, and Puerto Sandino, which were in either international waters, territorial seas, or both, causing personal and material harm to civilians.[21]

Congress suspended funding to the Contras, and the civil war ended in 1989, after it was discovered that the Reagan administration was still secretly channeling resources to the Contras. The Sandinista government went down in defeat the next year in a peaceful democratic election, but the party managed to maintain a plurality of seats in the legislature, and continued to get support from political sympathizers in the United States, including Bill de Blasio.

When de Blasio returned to New York in 1989, he volunteered with the Nicaragua Solidarity Network, which was located on the top floor of a three-story building at the corner of Bleecker and Lafayette Streets in Greenwich Village. This band of thirty volunteers was a ragtag collection of peace activists, left-leaning Democrats, and Marxists. They organized dances and other fundraisers to send money to the Sandinistas after the revolutionary government lost its power in 1990.

That year a twenty-nine-year-old leader of the solidarity network named William Wilhelm was quoted in the New York Times praising the Sandinistas for giving the world "a new definition of democracy" that "was striving to be economic and political, that pervaded all levels of society."[22] Although his name has changed, that young man's convictions about political and economic equality have stuck with him throughout. As mayor of New York, he makes no excuses for his past political activity with the revolutionary government. Although he has been critical of the Sandinistas' crackdown on dissenters, de Blasio insists that his support was "the right thing to do."[23] Nor did he waver as a candidate for office—despite jibes from his Republican opponent, Joseph Lhota.

Bill de Blasio met the love of his life in 1991 while working as an aide in the office of Mayor David Dinkins, New York's first and only black mayor. Like Bill's own mother, Chirlane McCray is smart, well-educated, and ambitious; a powerful blend of practicality and idealism; a writer and a poet. She too is an alumna of a fancy women's college, Wellesley—one of about thirty African-American women in the predominantly white upper-class institution at the time. She too has roots in New England. Chirlane's great-grandmother had emigrated from Barbados to Claremont, New Hampshire, to take a job as a domestic.

Chirlane's parents, Robert and Katherine McCray, had both attended high school. He, who never knew his father and emigrated from the South, had worked as a civilian employee at a U.S. Air Force base. She, unable to break through the employment barriers black women faced at the time, worked in a factory. According to Chirlane, "My parents were not ordinary people. They were extremely hard working and politically active, and had a vision for the future."[24] Although they were working class folks with modest incomes, Robert and Katherine managed to eke out a relatively comfortable life for their three girls and a much older boy that Katherine had before she met Robert. They owned a four-family house in Springfield, Massachusetts, which produced rental incomes from three apartments. The Village area where they lived was predominantly white. The McCrays were attracted to it because of its better schools; however, being the oldest of the three girls with her brother off to college, Chirlane was at first the only black girl in attendance.

In 1964 Robert and Katherine hired an African-American contractor to build them a new ranch house in Longmeadow, Massachusetts, another predominantly white suburb with good schools. They were only the third black family to reside there, and once again Chirlane, now ten years of age, was left to break the color line in her school. She recalls that local residents petitioned the family to leave the area.[25] Chirlane and her siblings were subjected to racial taunts and isolation. When she complained to her mother about the mean treatment she got, she was told, "You're not here to be popular, you're here to get a good education." As Chirlane's sister Cynthia Davis recalls, "You were just expected to deal with life as it came."[26] Chirlane persevered. She was determined to distinguish herself in a positive way, to become a leader. She went out for the swim team; she became a lifeguard, a camp counselor, and president of the YWCA Leaders Corps; she took piano lessons and learned to dance.

Chirlane's hard work earned her admission to Wellesley College. The elite institution had a more diverse student body than Longmeadow, but Chirlane was still in a minority. She could not even relate to the strong feminist ethos that wafted through the Gothic halls of the all-girls campus. Her issues were different from those of the privileged white girls who dominated the school culture. She then joined some thirty other black feminists to form the Combahee River Collective. With its focus on the connections among race, gender, sexuality, and class, the support group helped her relate issues of economic and psychological oppression to her own life experiences. After graduating from Wellesley in 1977, Chirlane enrolled in the Radcliffe Publishing Course, then landed an editing job in New York City at *Redbook*. The popular magazine had published the work of prominent women authors such as Betty Friedan, Mary Gordon, and Jane Smiley. Even as a low-level editor, the job was quite a prize for somebody just out of college, and living in New York gave Chirlane wings to fly.

Chirlane came into her own at a time of growing self-awareness for black women artists. Alice Walker had recently published *The Color Purple,* a Pulitzer Prize winning novel about the effects of sexism, racism, and brutality committed against black women in the South during the 1930s. Ntozake Shange had just staged *For Colored Girls Who Have Considered Suicide When the Rainbow Is Enuf,* an Obie Award winning contemporary play about the travails of nine women of color.

In New York, Chirlane immersed herself in a community of black, mostly gay and bisexual women who met in private homes, coffee shops, and bars to conceive and incubate artistic expression through literature, theater, and dance. She took occasional freelance editing gigs, and dabbled in public relations. For a while she worked as an editor at the *Salsa Soul Gazette.* She eventually landed positions at *Essence, New York Magazine,* and *Conde Nast.* She spent ten years in publishing, and dreamed of founding her own magazine for women of color that would be more substantive than those already available. Then, her interest in social issues drew her into government service and speech-writing assignments for the Commission on Human Rights and local politicians. She eventually wound up in the administration of David Dinkins, in which she composed speeches for the mayor.

Chirlane McCray is petite, thoughtful, articulate, and reserved—a straight-backed New Englander with a clear sense of her own values and a direct manner. As the story goes, she met Bill in 1991 when she needed information for a press release she was writing, and found out that Bill was the guy in the office who had it. As Bill tells it, "I was totally struck."[27] He reminisces about meeting a woman with long black braids, wearing a batik dress, sporting a provocative nose ring—who rocked his world.[28] He told Barbara Walters, "I heard the angels sing. I heard the violins. The thunderbolt hit."[29] Bill had dated a lot, but Chirlane seemed different. Despite her evident lack of interest in him, he continued his pursuit. He finally got up the courage to ask her to lunch at a vegetarian restaurant near City Hall. After they had seen each other a few times, Chirlane handed him an essay she had written for *Essence* magazine in 1979 entitled "I Am a Lesbian."[30]

The 5,000-word *Essence* piece is an intimate revelation of a young woman's decision to come to terms with her own sexual identity. Ten years had passed since the momentous Stonewall incident, when the patrons of a gay bar on Christopher Street in Greenwich Village offered resistance to an early morning police raid, marking the inception of the gay rights movement; nevertheless, sympathetic discussions about homosexuality were not yet part of mainstream journalism, especially in black venues. McCray's editor at *Essence,* Marcia Ann Gillespie, described the article as "brave" and "fierce." In a *New York Magazine* interview published in 2014, Gillespie also acknowledged a protective motherly reluctance at the time of its publication regarding Chirlane's absolute certainty about her sexuality, exclaiming, "I thought, 'She's so young. She's going to have a long life.' "[31]

In the essay, McCray describes how she first began to explore her attraction to other women when she was a freshman in college. She shares the thrills and the anxieties of her first lesbian relationship, at once exuberant about finding a lover, yet frightened that they would be discovered. She tells of conversations between the two young women, wondering who they should tell about their feelings, whether their parents would still love them, whether their closeted sisters would shun them for coming out, whether their straight friends would ostracize them, whether they would be able to get jobs, whether they would need to sacrifice having children. It is a thoughtful and insightful exploration about the dilemmas of same-sex relationships in a straight world, as instructive today as it was nearly four decades ago.

Prior to this experience, McCray had dated men and had told herself that she was heterosexual, but she expresses gratitude in the essay that she had found herself when she was still relatively young, before getting involved with a man or having a family with one. She writes about nightmares and scratching fits, of being covered with hives at the thought of other people's reactions. She conveys a sense of relief about her coming out. She writes about relationships she later had with other women, and dreamy dances in lesbian bars. She relates a painful story about introducing her parents to a woman, twelve years her senior, with whom she thought she would spend the rest of her life. Katherine liked Candace and got along with her well. Robert never quite understood how two women could be attracted to each other, and refused to accept any kind of living arrangement for either Chirlane or her heterosexual brother outside of marriage. The relationship between father and daughter was never the same after that.

Chirlane and Bill were married in 1994. The ceremony, performed by two gay ministers, took place in Brooklyn's Prospect Park. Maria distributed party favors of glazed almonds wrapped in little white nets, a Neapolitan tradition. Imported Peroni beer was served. Former Mayor David Dinkins offered kind words about the bride and groom, who, in a manner of speaking, he had brought together. Guests were entertained by an Italian folk band and a group of African drummers. There was a special table with kosher food to accommodate several guests who were strict religious observers. After the celebration, the bride and groom took off for a honeymoon in Cuba—by way of Canada of course, as the American State Department prohibited travel to the Communist-run island. Their daughter Chiara was born seven months later.

Chirlane and Bill had known each other for three years before they married, but had been living together for more than two. They were by most definitions the ultimate odd couple. Apart from all the other differences, Chirlane initially was taken aback when she learned that Bill was seven years younger than she, but got over it. She wondered how his family would receive her. Bill introduced her to Maria and her two sisters early on in the relationship. Maria objected to the relationship at first, but eventually came around. Chirlane was struck with how much Bill adored the three women who raised him. He refers to them as the "Three Graces."

When Chirlane and Bill first met, she was living in Flatbush, Brooklyn, and he in Astoria, Queens. They found an apartment to share on Twelfth Street in Park Slope (Brooklyn), and never left the neighborhood. Both of their children were born nearby in the Maimonides Hospital on Sixth Street, where Chirlane worked as an administrator for a while. Dante came along three years after his sister. In time Bill and Chirlane's differences seemed to wash away in a tide of common values and aspirations. As one reporter has put it, they were each other's opposites "in all the ways that don't really matter."[32]

In fact, prior to his election as mayor, Bill and Chirlane had a fairly traditional marriage. Like many career women who marry and have children late in life, she acknowledges real anxieties about the loss of independence and assuming the responsibilities of motherhood with her first child, even though she always wanted children and cherishes them. As she explains:

> I was forty years old. I had a life. Especially with Chiara—will we feel guilt forever more? Of course, yes. But the truth is, I could not spend every day with her. I didn't want to do that. I looked for all kinds of reasons not to do it. I love her. . ... But I've been working since I was 14, and that part of me is me. It took a long time for me to get into, "I'm taking care of the kids" and what that means.[33]

Chirlane continued to accept writing and consulting assignments with government officials. Things changed when Dante was born in 1997. She was almost forty-three now, the same age Maria was when Bill was born. In order to allow her husband to build his career, Chirlane became the parent-in-charge. It was she who would pick the kids up after school, she who would put meals on the table, she who would handle most of the chores. She could only work part-time. In 2005, the couple decided to move their aging widowed mothers into a house down the street from their own, so that it would be easier to care for them and manage their doctor appointments. Katherine, who suffered from multiple myeloma, lived on the top floor; Maria, who had a heart condition, lived downstairs. Chirlane assumed most of the responsibility for the two grandmas too.

By the time their mothers were in place, Chirlane and Bill had already moved into 442 11th Street near Seventh Avenue in Brooklyn. It was not far from the apartment they originally rented together on Twelfth Street, and within the boundaries of the City Council district where Bill would launch his political career. The 100-year-old attached frame clapboard house has three bedrooms, oak floors, and a brick fireplace with hand-painted tiles. The first floor contains a combined living room and kitchen. It has only one bathroom, and that is on the third floor. The backyard is large enough to accommodate a patio with a picnic table, a crab apple tree, and a landscaped garden with perennials, evergreens, and fresh herbs. It was comfortable place to raise a family, but modest compared to the elegant brownstones that give tony Park Slope its turn-of-the-century character.

The family lived on 11th Street for thirteen years before Bill became mayor and they moved into the official residence at Gracie Mansion. Bill never seemed to leave the neighborhood though. He continues to raise eyebrows among reporters when he returns for regular workouts at the Ninth Street Y while living in the elegant mansion on the Upper East Side and assuming a busy schedule as the city's chief executive. He still holds important meetings at Bar Toto, an unadorned dining establishment down the block from his house that serves omelets, panini, pizzas, burgers, and full dinners. The most expensive pasta on the dinner menu, *Pappardelle alla Bolognese*—a chopped beef, veal and pork ragu sauce with *parmigiano* cheese and extra wide noodles—will set you back $18.00. When I took my research assistants there for lunch one Wednesday afternoon, the waiter told us that Bill had already been there twice that week.

Chirlane returned to full-time government service in 2002 when Dante started elementary school. She lent her hand at writing speeches for City Comptroller Bill Thompson, the man whom Bill would later defeat in the contest for mayor. Chiara and Dante lived a rather charmed life growing up. Their parents' political connections gave them opportunities most kids don't have. By the time Chiara was five and Dante was two, they were treated to a sleepover at the White House with their parents and the Clintons.

Chirlane also has fond memories of family gatherings at a farmhouse her parents had built in Westminster West, Vermont, and a house that Maria occupied in Hastings-on-Hudson. She recalls, "And so Westminster West and Hastings-on-Hudson were destinations for us and our kids for roughly ten years—until our Moms relocated to Brooklyn." She further reminisces, "My Mom made the best apple pie and ginger snap cookies, and could provide a sledding hill, sleigh rides, hay rides, blueberry picking, and bedrooms for all. Very New England! Bill's mother baked terrific blueberry pie and eggplant parmesan."[34]

The brother and sister attended local public schools—which in Park Slope were integrated demographically and above city averages academically—until Dante got accepted into Brooklyn Technical High School. Located in downtown Brooklyn, *Tech*, as it is familiarly known, is one of New York City's very selective high schools in which admission is granted by a special exam. Less than 15 percent of the student body is black or Hispanic. Dante stood out there as an extraordinary student and champion debater. Accepted into every college where he applied (ten in all), Dante, already the son of the mayor, decided to attend his grandfather's alma mater, choosing Yale over Harvard.

Chiara has distinguished herself differently. When her father was elected, she was already enrolled at Santa Clara University, a small Jesuit school in the San Francisco Bay area with a declared commitment to "faith inspired values of ethics and social justice." On the Christmas Eve after de Blasio's election, a week before his swearing in, his team released a YouTube video in which Chiara discussed her history of clinical depression and addiction to drugs and alcohol.

It was a startling revelation for the daughter of a newly elected public official. Pundits commented that it was wise for the family to get the bad news out of the way, allowing the new mayor to have a fresh start and move on. In other circles the message was received with praise for a different reason. *Ebony* magazine lauded Chiara for jump-starting a conversation that is "long past due" in the African-American community. The article cited data indicating that although 63 percent of the black population admitted to depression, 38 percent had failed to get treatment because of embarrassment and shame.[35]

Chiara was not done yet. Five months into her father's tenure at City Hall, she published an article in *xojane.com*, an online magazine that features new and established women authors and encourages readers and writers alike to be their "unabashed selves." Chiara did just that. This particular piece read, "I'm Chiara de Blasio and I'm a Young Woman in Recovery."[36] As she describes it, the essay is a journey "through death and rebirth, defeat and victory." She notes again her addiction to alcohol, which she partially attributes to a genetic predisposition she was born with. She also describes her road to recovery and the help she got learning to lead a healthy life by meditating, exercising, and simply getting out of bed when she didn't want to.

In a separate video that accompanies the essay, Chiara declares that getting better is the most difficult thing she has ever done, and accepts it as a lifelong battle. She acknowledges being privileged, surrounded by an unconditionally loving unbroken family, going to good schools, and living in a beautiful neighborhood. But she declares, "Mental illness does not discriminate." It was clear now: De Blasio's revelation about his daughter's struggle was not just an inconvenient truth to get out of the way. The family wanted to convey a message. Once again Chiara's revelation drew praise for its bold honesty.[37]

In Washington, Secretary of Health and Human Services Kathleen Sebelius got the point, and conveyed an award to Chiara for coming forward and using her own crisis as an opportunity to advocate for millions of Americans suffering from mental health issues. When asked by reporters about her daughter's latest revelation, Chirlane McCray again emphasized the need for individuals and society in general to deal with such problems openly, and noted how difficult it was for their own family to find the right mental health professionals to get help. She added, "The first step to recovery is reaching out to others. It's the first step to healing."[38] Right then and there, the de Blasio administration vowed to invest millions of dollars to improve personalized mental health services in the city.

Mayor Bill de Blasio delivered on his mental health promise in November, 2015 as he was about to reach the halfway mark of his first term of office. Appearing at Hunter College's Silberman School of Social Work in East Harlem surrounded by his wife and two children, who returned from college to attend the event, de Blasio unveiled *Thrive NYC,* a comprehensive mental health plan for New Yorkers. The new effort was the culmination of a year-long inquiry led by First Lady Chirlane McCray in which she consulted with mental health professionals, service providers, agency heads, clients, parents, senior citizens, homeless people, and advocates in order to assess needs and develop a "roadmap" of services. It would become her project, her personal cause to put into action. The plan offered fifty-four initiatives and $305 million in new funding to supplement $548 million that had already been committed to similar services. The roadmap covered six strategic areas of action designed to change the culture, act early, close treatment gaps, partner with communities, use data better, and strengthen government's ability to lead.[39]

Beyond the programmatic details of the initiative, the first family of the city was there to deliver an experience-based lesson about mental healthcare and the city's need to come to terms with it openly and honestly. As never before, an emotional, teary-eyed Bill de Blasio spoke publicly about his own father, who most likely suffered with post-traumatic stress disorder (PTSD) from his experience in the war, although it was never diagnosed and he was too ashamed to admit his pain. Nor was society prepared to deal with it at the time, out of both ignorance and denial. It seemed as though Bill de Blasio was publicly coming to terms with the father he never really knew, whose very name he literally had erased from his life.

Admiring a Warren Wilhelm who was brave and heroic, highly intelligent and accomplished—a man who like himself had married a bright, unconventional, ambitious, no-nonsense, family-oriented woman—de Blasio regretfully admitted, "I never really got to know everything about my father I would've liked to, because by the time I knew him, he was already really starting to decline." De Blasio continued, "I saw what happens when a problem is not addressed. I saw what happens when someone's suffering and doesn't know where to turn for help or can't be reached."

In the course of the event, Chirlane disclosed to the audience and reporters who were present that her own parents suffered from depression, and that she had extended family members who were victims of substance abuse and bipolar disorder, none of whom sought or received help. She mentioned a close friend who had taken her own life at an early age. She then turned to her daughter, Chiara, and complimented her for having the courage to come forward to share her own struggle and recovery publicly, setting an example so that others would feel comfortable doing the same.

* * *

The mental health press conference in East Harlem beamed like a window into the heart of New York's first family, luminous and large, like Saks Fifth Avenue the week before Christmas. For them the personal and the political are the same. One acts as one feels. No need to take a poll or confer with a focus group to determine a position on an issue. Bill and Chirlane are a package deal and their children are part of the package. They play by their own rules, but are governed by a larger set of values acquired by harsh experience. They had seen bigotry and pain, privilege and power. They had crossed conventional boundaries, yet could serve as a role model for a traditional loving intact family—an extended family at that—wanting what's best for their children, including a safe pleasant living environment, a good education, and support in times of hardship.

They had seen what government could do to help those most in need; they had seen government turn its back when it chose to, only to speak the words of justice and compassion without delivering on the promise. There is an authenticity about them that is all too rare in American politics. You might not like everything about them, but they are who they are—no secrets, no riddles to solve. Perhaps that was Bill's appeal in the contest against favorites to determine who would succeed Michael Bloomberg as mayor of New York. Perhaps he struck a chord in the conscience of New York that was kind and fair and caring to the struggling people who made the city what it once was. Perhaps it was his calling to recapture the soul of the city that La Guardia built and seemed to be lost forever.

A "Radical" in the Mainstream

Radicalism has had a distinct place in American politics—usually tucked away out of sight in the remote regions of the political process. This is largely a result of our two-party system in which Democrats and Republicans historically have built electoral constituencies based on broad, politically moderate alliances that are unable and unwilling to accommodate activists who do not accept the underlying assumptions that keep the broader mainstream alliances functioning. Party discipline was stronger in the days when regulars from state delegations chose presidential candidates at conventions rather than through the popular primaries that we now have.

The 2016 presidential election suggests that such discipline is in further decline, and we may be entering a new era of politics. Donald Trump's emergence as the Republican candidate through a hard-fought set of primary contests and his subsequent election surprised party regulars and maybe even Trump himself. Although the Democratic Party nominated another Clinton, Bernie Sanders's demands for economic justice have challenged the centrist conventions that have allowed Democrats since Bill Clinton to "triangulate"—that is, chart a course midway between progressive Democrats and conservative Republicans on policy issues. For mainstream Democrats, the lure of moderation often finds politicians leaning toward the Left on civil liberties issues and to the Right on economic issues—a philosophy referred to by some, not admiringly, as *neoliberalism*.[1] That inclination may prove to be more difficult to carry off in the future as the party tries to reconnect with its old white working class base.

Other democracies with multiparty systems more easily integrate smaller parties with strong philosophical identities into the ordinary political process. These smaller parties collaborate with competitors to build governing coalitions within legislative bodies. Since the end of World War II, for example, the German government has been dominated by two major parties, the center-right Christian Democratic Union (CDU) and the center-left Social Democratic Party (SPD). Because neither has been able to assemble a majority on its own, legislative politics in the Bundestag that chooses the chancellor is characterized by coalition government. The CDU always forms a coalition with the Christian Social Union of Bavaria (CSU), and they are commonly referred to collectively as the Christian Democrats. Other parties with representation in the Bundestag include the the free market Free Democratic Party (FDP), the former communist Left Party, and the Alliance 90/Green Party.

France, another multiparty system, has had a left-wing Socialist Party, center-right Republican Party, centrist party En March, the far-right National Front, Democratic Movement Party, Federation for a Social and Ecological Alternative, French Communist Party, Left Party, Europe Ecology Party, New Center Party, Radical Party, Left, Radical Party of the Left, Centrist Alliance, and the Movement for France (social conservatives), all with a distinct representative role. As we saw, the Sandinistas, who originally came to power in Nicaragua by means of a violent revolution in 1979, remained a mainstream party in the democratically chosen national legislature after losing the presidential election of 1990.

Young Bill de Blasio did not see a need to make a choice between radical causes and conventional politics, but he knows the difference. As a twenty-eight-year-old man, two years out of graduate school, still working on behalf of the Latin American Marxists, he enlisted as a volunteer in the 1989 campaign to elect David Dinkins mayor. That decision changed his life forever.

If there is a single edifice that embodies the guts of New York City government, it is the Municipal Building at 1 Centre Street, across from City Hall. The McKim, Mead & White structure that shoots forty stories into the air was completed in 1914 to accommodate the ever-growing government of the newly consolidated city. Six years in the making, its cavernous interior is a million square feet and spacious enough to accommodate thousands of city workers. It remains one of the largest government office buildings in America. Its beautifully tiled central arch enhanced by Corinthian columns once served as a passageway for automobile traffic. It was the first building in New York to have its own subway station inside, with underground tracks carrying commuters to and from every borough, including Staten Island, which runs a ferry to the Battery Park Station further downtown. Huge Roman-like sculptures once lined the corners of the plaza. A 20-foot high figure of *Civic Fame* still gracefully balances her bare feet on a globe atop the building's wedding cake tower.

In 2015, toward the end of his second year in office, Mayor Bill de Blasio announced that he was naming the building after his former boss, David Dinkins. The dapper former chief executive had spent fourteen years toiling in the Municipal Building, first as the City Clerk, then as Manhattan Borough President, before becoming mayor. Bill de Blasio presided over the dedication ceremony on an unusually mild October morning with his wife, Chirlane McCray, and the honoree at his side, effusively proclaiming, "He left an indelible impact on this city and on Chirlane and my lives."[2] Dinkins beamed.

It was at once a fitting and anomalous tribute to the eighty-eight-year-old veteran of public service. There can be no doubt that the mayor and the First Lady have a special place in their hearts for their former patron, who was indirectly responsible for their meeting. De Blasio has often praised Dinkins for his dedication to social justice, his historic role as the city's first African-American mayor, and his success in channeling additional resources to fight the city's long-standing crime problem during his tenure at City Hall. De Blasio's love for the man who gave him a start, however, was not always mixed with admiration. On the eve of his own mayoral election less than two years earlier, de Blasio recalled that working in the Dinkins administration had taught him what not to do in running a government: a remark about negative lessons similar to one he once made about his own father. De Blasio had described the City Hall operation under Dinkins as disorganized and divided, without a clear singular purpose.[3]

Dinkins has critics who would agree with that unflattering assessment.[4] The frank remarks, nevertheless, said as much about de Blasio as they did about the former mayor. Could this man who had an alternative vision about the ends of government ever be fully comfortable as an actor in the system that had undermined his democratic ideals? If de Blasio has any characteristic that distinguishes him from most other public officials, it is his overarching focus on one issue: economic equality. And this ideal is the lens through which he evaluates everything and everybody—including those he loves.

Ironically, the landmark Municipal Building, with its classic contours heralding grand civic aspirations, also can be depicted by government critics as a grand monument to the colossal bureaucracy that perpetuates dysfunction within the sprawling municipality. De Blasio, who is torn by the tensions derived from his own insider/outsider perspective, does not quite fit within the government he is running. He can seem ambivalent about the entire enterprise and what it means. He is constantly re-establishing himself in his beloved Brooklyn, even while his own home is rented out, practically setting up a government in exile in neighborhood cafes where important meetings can be held with close aides. He also understands that without playing the game as a key insider, his dream of realizing what government could achieve will remain pure fancy. Working for David Dinkins gave him the needed entree.

Young de Blasio made friends in the Dinkins administration who shaped the course of his career. Among them were two of his political mentors: Deputy Mayor Bill Lynch, to whom de Blasio reported as a low-level aide, was the rumpled strategist who orchestrated Dinkins's winning election and remained the mayor's most trusted confidante; and Harold M. Ickes, who had been an advisor to the 1989 Dinkins campaign before he went on to serve as chair of Bill

Clinton's 1992 presidential race in New York State, and later as an assistant to the president and Deputy Chief of Staff. It was Ickes who introduced de Blasio to the Clintons, paving the way for de Blasio to develop a reputation as a political operative working on Bill Clinton's 1996 presidential campaign, and Hillary Clinton's 2000 senate campaign.

Patrick Gaspard was another young staffer who worked under the tutelage of Deputy Mayor Lynch. According to Ken Sunshine, the public relations guru who was Lynch's chief of staff at the time, "Bill and Patrick were by far the stars of all the young aides back then."[5] Bill and Patrick were also a study in contrasts. Bill was the disheveled unshaven student radical; Patrick was the elegant French-speaking Haitian who looked like he had just stepped out of a fashion magazine. The two junior staffers bonded over the Italian sandwiches that Bill brought into work from his mother's kitchen, and became inseparable. In later years, Bill coached the Brooklyn Little League team both their sons played on, and Chiara was a flower girl at Patrick's wedding. When Bill was hired as an assistant to HUD Secretary Andrew Cuomo in 1997, Patrick took him out to buy a suit.

After leaving the mayor's office, Patrick served as chief of staff for City Council member Margarita Lopez, then he became the political director of Local 1199, the healthcare workers union whose leadership was close to the Dinkins administration. Like many people in the more left-leaning union, he also worked on Jesse Jackson's 1988 presidential campaign. Ten years later, he sided with Barack Obama rather than Hillary Clinton in the 2008 presidential primary. He went on to be political director for Obama's presidential campaign, served in the White House, and headed up the Democratic National Committee. He was later appointed U.S. Ambassador to South Africa, where he remained through the end of the Obama administration.

Patrick was usually there to lend assistance when Bill ran for office, and helped field questions from the press when Chiara revealed her struggle with addiction the week before Bill's inauguration. Although Bill and Patrick took different paths ascending the Democratic Party hierarchy, they simultaneously made common cause with organizations determined to provide party members and voters with alternatives when that same hierarchy forsook their progressive ideals. Both also remained close to organized labor, especially left-of-center unions that aggressively fought to protect the interests of working and disadvantaged people.

Rather than use his connections to advance his policy agenda within government, Bill de Blasio decided to hone his skills as a political operative, organizing campaigns for politicians who were more or less like-minded. The boundary between politics and policy is thin for sure, but to the extent that it exists, Bill de Blasio turned his energies to the former—more pragmatic, less ideological, without losing sight of his clearly defined egalitarian mission. At City Hall, he helped Bill Lynch with constituency work, learning how to build alliances with key support-ers in city neighborhoods. He had a front row seat during the Crown Heights riots that pitted blacks against Jews in Brooklyn, and saw the price that an elected official can pay by neglecting the concerns of the well-organized Orthodox com-munity. He later conceded that Crown Heights "wasn't handled right."[6]

De Blasio was also present when Lynch ran Mayor Dinkins's unsuccessful re-election campaign in 1993. While working on the campaign, de Blasio became involved with the formation of something called the *New Coalition Party*. The latter was a descendant of two other organizing efforts—one local, the other national. Locally, there was the *Majority Coalition for a New New York*, an alliance sponsored by Local 1199 that worked on city elections in 1991. Nationally, there was the *New Party*, which was founded in 1992. These organizations, directly and indirectly, were crucial parts of the network that nourished Bill de Blasio's evolving political career and the changing politics of New York as it approached the twenty-first century.

The principal architect of the Majority Coalition was Dennis Rivera, the presi-dent of Local 1199. The healthcare workers union has a storied history. It was founded in 1932 by Leon Davis, a legendary figure in the American labor move-ment who endowed the organization with its militant pedigree. During his career, Davis had twice been jailed for organizing illegal strikes, and was questioned by Congress in the late 1940s regarding his possible connections to the Communist Party, which he refused to validate or deny. What started off as an association of drug store clerks grew into the largest health employees union in the country. Under Davis's leadership, 1199 was one of the first labor organizations to provide education, health, and housing benefits for its members. The Reverend Martin Luther King Jr. called 1199 the "authentic conscience of the labor movement" and referred to it as his "favorite labor union."[7] Davis was at King's side in the Montgomery bus boycott of 1955 and the March on Washington of 1963. In 1998, the membership of Local 1199 voted to affiliate with the Service Employees International Union (SEIU), which represents employees in social services and a variety of titles at the state and local levels of government.

More recently SEIU and the American Federation of State, County and Municipal Employees (AFSCME) announced plans for closer cooperation in organizing workers, launching political campaigns, and coordinating collective bargaining efforts, feeding rumors of a possible merger.[8] The two unions have somewhat different cultures. AFSCME represents public sector workers exclu-sively; SEIU's membership is divided almost evenly between public and private sector employees. They have common interests in bucking anti-labor legislation and taking on income inequality. Their combined membership of 3.6 million members would make them the largest labor union in the nation.

Dennis Rivera became Local 1199's fourth president in 1989, and carried on its activist tradition. The union commands a well-oiled get-out-the-vote political machine in New York City that can have a decisive impact on any election, but especially in low-turnout Democratic Party primaries that often determine the next mayor. It has spawned an impressive lineup of local leaders that included Patrick Gaspard, Bill de Blasio, and Melissa Mark-Viverito, the present Speaker of the City Council—all of whom have been involved in the union's political causes at various points in their careers.

In 1991 Rivera put together the Majority Coalition to advance a diverse slate of City Council candidates representing blacks, Hispanics, women, gays, and environmentalists. Their unambiguous objective was to challenge the leadership of City Council Speaker Peter Vallone, a more moderate politician with a firm hand on the chamber's leadership. The coalition operated out of the union's midtown Manhattan headquarters. The revised City Charter adopted in 1989 that expanded the size of the City Council from thirty-five to fifty-one members promised to create a more diverse and representative legislative body for the changing city. The Majority Coalition was determined to seize on that promise.

Many of the Majority Coalition's organizers, including Deputy Mayor Bill Lynch, hoped the group would function to bolster the 1993 re-election campaign of David Dinkins. Others wanted to separate the group from the mayor, because they were either doubtful of his electability, or felt that he was too close to mainstream politicians supported by Vallone's own political action committee. Their council campaign was unsuccessful. Only four of their thirty-two candidates won nominations in the September primary.[9] Referring to Vallone by name, a *Newsday* article summed up the election results by concluding, "The person who gained the most by yesterday's council primary election was not even on the ballot."[10]

As chair of the commission that redrew council districts for the enlarged legislature, Vallone subsequently worked with progressive leaders to carve out new minority districts. The Majority Coalition soon ran into financial trouble and disbanded. But it was the beginning of something larger that would take time to mature. As Rivera remembers, "We were ambitious, but short on experience. We had plenty of ideas, but few specific plans. We learned how to take it to the next step, which we would."[11]

The national New Party was cofounded by a University of Wisconsin activist professor named Joel Rogers, and Daniel Cantor.[12] This is the same Dan Cantor who met Bill de Blasio in a graduate school class on Latin American politics at Columbia in 1985. Dan was a former organizer with ACORN (Association of Community Organizations for Reform Now), in which he had been employed for six years. ACORN was the largest community-based alliance ever assembled to promote affordable housing and social justice on behalf of low- and moderate-income families. Before its demise in 2010, it claimed 175,000 member families, living in 850 neighborhoods across 75 cities in the United States, Canada, the Dominican Republic, and Peru.[13] Cantor left ACORN to work for the National Labor Committee on Central America, where he fought against the AFL-CIO's support for President Reagan's attempt to bring down the Sandinista government in Nicaragua. Cantor also played a role in lining up labor support for Jesse Jackson's 1988 presidential campaign. ACORN remained an important factor in the accelerating political career of Bill de Blasio.

The New Party was an attempt to coordinate disparate efforts around the country to elect progressive candidates. Its strategy was to provide voters with a third party fusion option, allowing people to cross party lines while voting for their favorite Democratic (and sometimes other) candidates—a gentle protest against the regular organizations that had gravitated more toward the center. As Cantor and Rogers explained, "We propose a cross between the 'party within the party' strategy favored by some Democratic Party activists and the 'plague on both your houses' stance adopted by some critics of both major parties."[14]

New York was one of the six states that permitted fusion, and in 1993 progressives behind the local Majority Coalition were receptive to a broader labor-based alliance with the New Party. Jan Pierce of the Communications Workers of America (CWA) and Jay Mazur of the International Ladies Garment Workers Union cooperated with Dennis Rivera in the organizing effort, and eventually the creation of the New Coalition Party. Grass roots activists and an assortment of left-leaning politicians came on board. Public service unions with strong ties to the Democratic Party were less enthusiastic, as were some leaders in black and Hispanic communities who were closest to mainstream Democrats. Many of those involved with the formation of the Majority Coalition had been part of a political action committee formed to promote the candidacy of Mayor David Dinkins in 1989, and they had strong loyalties to the Democratic Party; but they also shared a deep concern that party regulars were not always in tune with the needs of average working people. As Rivera explains, "The real targets of a third party are those that you are close to. You want them to move closer and you believe that they will."[15]

Pierce of the CWA saw it somewhat differently, saying, "I am a Democrat and will be until the New Party becomes a [reality], but I have never found the Democratic Party to be progressive. It ceases to exist the day after Election Day."[16] Pierce was even critical of Franklin Roosevelt, who, he claimed, ran on a balanced budget platform at a time when one in three Americans was unemployed. But what better place to galvanize a true progressive alliance than, in his words, "the political capital of the world." He was hopeful that more sympathetic leaders such as Bill Clinton, Mario Cuomo, or Dinkins could form the backbone of a national movement to demand reforms in Congress that would be beneficial to working people.

Bill de Blasio was more equivocal. Working with the New Coalition Party in 1993, he emphasized, "While we know that there are many progressive Democrats, we know that millions are alienated from the process."[17] Now Democrats had an alternative. They could vote for Democratic candidates on another party line, recording their progressive preferences without entirely breaking ranks, all the while pushing the party leftward. And if that failed, as Pierce suggested, the New Coalition Party conceivably could replace the old Democratic Party. Progressive hopes for the Democratic Party did not quite pan out, though. Bill Clinton very deliberately moved the party to the center. David Dinkins was about to lose his re-election bid to Rudolph Giuliani. In the next year, Mario Cuomo suffered a stunning defeat to George Pataki, handing the Empire State's governorship over to the Republican Party.

By 1993 the New Party was operating ten chapters across the country.[18] Its fusion strategy proved to be fundamentally flawed, however, because only six states allow fusion candidates to appear on the ballot. An office seeker could appear only on one line in the remaining forty-four states. In 1997, the Supreme Court rebuffed the party's attempt to remove such prohibitions, affirming the right of states to regulate their own elections, and sealing the party's end.[19]

With the demise of the Majority Coalition and the New Party, progressives in New York yearned for a rallying point and a line on the ballot that allowed left-leaning voters to voice their preferences without entirely abandoning Democrats still deemed worthy of their allegiance. So in 1998, ACORN's top leaders in New York, Bertha Lewis and Jon Kest, as well as regional leaders from the CWA and United Auto Workers, joined up with remnants of the New Party to take one more try at forming a new political party in New York. It was called the Working Families Party (WFP). Dan Cantor, Bill de Blasio's classmate from Columbia University who was cofounder of the New Party, became the WFP's national director. As its name suggests, the WFP has a strong pro-labor thrust, dedicated to "tackling the political, economic and educational inequality that deprives maintenance staff, doormen, building engineers, school and food service workers, railroad workers and factory workers."[20] Once again, some of the larger public employee unions, such as the United Federation of Teachers, remained reluctant to abandon old alliances with regular Democrats in favor of a third-party option.

After David Dinkins was turned out of office in 1993, Bill de Blasio began to cultivate his skills organizing political campaigns for local Democratic politicians, keeping one foot firmly planted in the camp of party regulars. In 1994 he managed the re-election campaign of Harlem congressman Charles Rangel. Rangel is a close friend of David Dinkins. He was first elected to Congress in 1970, when, in a hard fought primary, he put an end to the reign of Representative Adam Clayton Powell Jr., who had dominated Harlem politics for twenty-six years. Powell's name adorns the State Office Building on 125th Street and the street signs on one of the neighborhood's major boulevards.

Rangel's chief opponent in 1994 was City Council member Adam Clayton Powell IV, a son of the former congressman. If the younger Powell had history on his side, Rangel had the New York political establishment. By then, Rangel was the senior member of the state congressional delegation, and in line to become chair of the powerful House Ways and Means Committee, the first black man to do so. He ran on a slogan, "Keep the Power," and defeated his opponent in the Democratic Party primary by a margin of 61 percent to 33 percent, assuring him the November election.[21] It was also another victory for Bill de Blasio; but when de Blasio ran for mayor in 2013, Rangel threw his support behind his old friend and Harlem neighbor William Thompson. De Blasio, as mayor, returned the favor in 2014, withholding his endorsement when the congressman was steeped in a closely fought primary challenge that he won against Adriano Espaillat, his main rival, and two other candidates. After that, Rangel joined with other African-American leaders to criticize the new mayor's handling of police issues.

In 1995, Bill de Blasio agreed to manage the campaign of Francisco Diaz Jr. in a special election to fill the vacant state assembly seat left by Angelo Del Toro, who had died in office. Del Toro was the boss of an entrenched Democratic Party organization located in the El Barrio district of East Harlem, West Harlem, and parts of the Upper East Side. His brother William Del Toro, a local minister, was among three other candidates competing for his job. Del Toro was the official candidate of the Democratic Party. Diaz had served as district manager of Community Board 11, an appointed position designed to help coordinate city services at the neighborhood level. He was also secretary of local Community School Board No. 4. Known widely in the district, but new to electoral politics, he had previously lost a bid for a seat in the City Council when William Del Toro was one of the other losing candidates.

Although Diaz ran on the Liberal Party and Independent lines, he was able to capture the support of local Democratic Party luminaries such as former Mayor Dinkins, Congressman Rangel, Congresswoman Nydia Velazquez, State Senator (and future Governor) David Paterson, and an array of labor unions that had been involved with the formation of the New Coalition Party. He also won an endorsement from the *New York Times*. In an amazing upset against an entrenched machine, Diaz came out ahead with 59 percent of the vote.[22] Del Toro came in second with 35 percent.[23] It was an impressive grass-roots victory for Diaz, de Blasio, and an emerging progressive coalition.

In 1996, with his reputation and political contacts on the rise, Bill de Blasio was selected to coordinate the Clinton-Gore re-election campaign for the state, serving as a liaison between the Clinton organization and the state committees. This contest would give de Blasio high-powered exposure, lifting his career to another level. A *Daily News* article described the rising star as "politically savvy, well-connected and highly skilled in managing people."[24] Another news source referred to him as a "longtime Democratic operative in local elections."[25] Clinton and Gore were heavy favorites in New York, and nothing happened to change that. All the while, the campaign provided de Blasio with an extraordinary opportunity to enter the Clinton sphere of influence, and extend his political connections.

After the presidential campaign, de Blasio took a job with City Council Speaker Peter Vallone, the very man whose power the Majority Coalition had come together to challenge back in 1991. De Blasio held the title special assistant to the speaker and director of operations. He focused on policy issues and helped with outreach. Vallone's former chief of staff, Kevin McCabe, remarks, "Bill was decent and well liked. He had strong relationships with people in neighborhoods throughout the city and he helped Peter incorporate the concerns of these diverse constituencies in the work of the council that had recently been expanded from 35 to 51 members."[26]

Vallone was a respected old school member of the New York political establishment. He had been elected Majority Leader of the Council in 1986, and was the first person to hold the office of speaker (similar to majority leader) after the City Charter had been revamped with designs for the local legislature to become an effective check on the power of the mayor. The City Council has not been able to fill the vacuum left from the demise of the powerful Board of Estimate, but it has played a more meaningful role in the government than it had prior to the revised charter. Vallone's shaping of the Speaker's office, where he served for sixteen years as party leader, was foundational. He not only cooperated in carving out minority districts in the legislative body—including a gay district in Chelsea—he was an early supporter of a living wage bill.

In 1998, Vallone launched a campaign to unseat the Republican governor George Pataki. He was the front runner in the Democratic primary, starting out with a $1 million war chest.[27] He had the support of party stalwarts such as David Dinkins and Charles Rangel, but incumbency has its advantages, even for a GOP governor. Many labor leaders who had managed to cultivate productive relationships with Pataki were reluctant to cross him. Dennis Rivera, who was able to extract generous raises and a jobs package for his healthcare workers from the governor, endorsed him, as did the leaders of the United Federation of Teachers and the Public Employees Federation. Stanley Hill of District Council 37 and Brian McLaughlin of the Central Labor Council remained neutral.

One group that did support Vallone was the Working Families Party. It was an ironic turn of events for these insurgents, insofar as many of its members were part of the Majority Coalition that Dennis Rivera had put together to unseat Vallone years earlier. The gubernatorial election of 1998 was the budding organization's first opportunity to place a candidate on the ballot. It proved to be a historic milestone. Because Vallone was able to get the minimum required number of votes (50,000) on their ballot line, the Working Families Party could now legally claim a place on the ballot in the next election without going through an arduous petition process. Vallone had helped legitimize it. An affable campaigner, Vallone won the primary with 55.9 percent of the vote.[28] He was unable, however, to depose the incumbent governor George Pataki, who took 54 percent of the vote in the November election.[29]

As it turned out, Bill de Blasio left Vallone's office before the gubernatorial race took off to work with HUD Secretary Andrew Cuomo. The two had become acquainted in 1996 working for the Clinton-Gore campaign. Upon assuming the federal post, de Blasio was portrayed in the press as a "political ally" of Cuomo's and "czar" of his New York Office.[30] He oversaw federal housing and economic development programs for the New York and New Jersey region, and managed a staff of twenty. The metropolitan region was a top priority for the young secretary—directly aligned with his own future in electoral politics.

Apparently there was a deep reservoir of trust between de Blasio and Cuomo at the time. Subsequently, de Blasio was one of the few Democrats to support Cuomo in 2002 when he ran against State Comptroller Carl McCall for governor. Black leaders were incensed when Cuomo declared his candidacy against the man who could become New York's first black chief executive. According to Cuomo biographer Michael Shnayerson, when Cuomo finally decided that he would drop out of the race, de Blasio was one of the emissaries he sent to negotiate the terms with McCall.[31]

Andrew Cuomo was an ambitious young man. He was the son of former governor Mario Cuomo, a Democratic Party icon whose oratory skills mesmerized the nation when he delivered a keynote address at the Democratic National Convention in 1984. He himself had married into American royalty when he wed Kerry Kennedy, the daughter of Robert. He envisioned a big future for himself in national politics, the place he thought his father always deserved. Perhaps he believed Bill de Blasio could apply his considerable political skills to help the cause. Bill de Blasio, instead, was on his way to something bigger.

The 2000 senate campaign was Bill de Blasio's greatest opportunity yet. Hillary Clinton is the only first lady in American history to run for a major elected office. This was her first try, and her future was in his hands. She was a carpetbagger who had never lived in New York, but not the first outsider to come to New York to build a political career. Robert Kennedy had relocated from Massachusetts to win a Senate seat in New York in 1964 after serving as Attorney General under his brother John. Hillary was different. Although Hillary was a political celebrity, she had never held public office, and she had started out in Arkansas. Once again, de Blasio's arrival on the campaign scene was greeted with high anticipation. Hillary praised the thirty-eight-year-old campaign veteran for his "broad knowledge of the state, extensive experience in New York politics, and strong leadership skills."[32]

Bill's New York connections paid off. He was chummy with key labor leaders, and the full complement of constituent organizations that backed the Clinton-Gore ticket, an established base with proven capabilities to get voters to the polls. He was able to deliver an endorsement from the Working Families Party, whose members were ambivalent about the former first lady—a proponent of welfare reform who was once quoted as saying, "There is no left in the Clinton White House."[33] Once again expedience won out, as the train of inevitability barrelled down the track. There was no other Democrat.

De Blasio also helped the first lady reach out to the Orthodox Jewish community. Congressman Rick Lazio, the socially conservative Republican from Suffolk County, Long Island, would ordinarily be more to their liking. Hillary had already offended rabbinical leaders when she was photographed kissing Suha Arafat, the wife of Palestinian leader Yasser Arafat. Bill drew on his relationship with Assemblyman Dov Hikind, who represented the Orthodox stronghold of Borough Park, Brooklyn. Together they were able to soothe hurt feelings within the influential voting bloc. And why wouldn't they? This was not just any woman: this woman happened to be married to the president of the United States. The rabbis had a history of crossing party and ideological lines when it suited their needs.

The Orthodox community from the village of New Square in Rockland County had a particular point of interest when it came to the Clintons. In 1999, four men from the Hasidic enclave north of the city were convicted of swindling $40 million dollars from the federal government. A federal appellate court upheld their convictions. In desperation, political leaders from the 7,000-member religious community approached several New York politicians for help in getting a presidential pardon for the felons, or at least a commuted sentence, arguing that a large share of the stolen money was put to good use for education and social services in the relatively poor community. They got nowhere with Senator Charles Schumer, and were turned away by Mayor Giuliani, a celebrated former federal prosecutor.

In the midst of Hillary's senate campaign, Paul Adler, the Democratic Party Chair from Rockland County, arranged for the first lady to meet with New Square's Grand Rebbe David Twersky. The meeting in Twersky's home was attended by State Assembly Speaker Sheldon Silver, who had close ties to the Orthodox community. They were also joined by Israel Spitzer, the Grand Rebbe's top political advisor and New Square's deputy mayor. In the course of conversation, Twersky revealed that the town was planning to name a street after President Clinton, and suggested to the first lady that a visit by the chief executive to commemorate the event would be welcome. All accounts indicate that the pardon issue was not mentioned.[34] On Election Day, all but a few of New Square's some 1,400 votes were deposited in Hillary's column, while Lazio prevailed by large margins in neighboring communities.

President Clinton did not visit the naming ceremony in New Square. Instead, Rabbi Twersky and his associates were invited to the White House in December for a meeting with the president. Hillary Clinton, now senator-elect, was in attendance. This time the pardon issue was broached by the town's delegation. This time the religious leaders had their prayers answered. On his last day in office, President Clinton granted clemency to the four convicted felons from New Square, reducing their sentences from a maximum of seventy-eight months to a maximum of thirty—some of which had already been served.

The U.S Attorney from Manhattan Mary Jo White, and Deborah Landis, the lead prosecutor in the case, publicly objected to the president's decision to offer clemency. White initiated an investigation to determine whether there was any impropriety involved in the action.[35] The inquiry was closed by her successor James Comey because "we determined it wasn't appropriate to bring charges against anybody in the case."[36] Paul Adler and Sheldon Silver have since been convicted on federal corruption charges that have nothing to do with the Clintons or the clemency issue. One day President Obama would choose Comey to head the FBI, and he would direct the investigation of Hillary Clinton's use of her private email account while she was Obama's secretary of state, again putting Comey smack in the middle of Hillary's political ambitions. And Comey would eventually get tangled in the intrigues of the Trump administration's relationships with the Russians.

Hillary's senate race got a lucky break when Mayor Rudy Giuliani for health reasons cancelled his intended run. Rick Lazio, less well known than the hard-charging mayor, turned out to be more formidable than expected, but the woman from Arkansas prevailed, beating the Long Islander by twelve points.[37]

In the meantime, press reports indicated that tensions had developed within the Clinton campaign operation. There were stories of friction between de Blasio and some people in Hillary's high-powered Washington-based organization, who evidently held more sway.[38] What could have happened? The answer to this question sheds light not only on the 2000 senate campaign, but also on de Blasio's behavior toward Hillary Clinton in the more recent 2016 presidential campaign. And, I would argue that, taken together, the two pivotal episodes reveal the character of Bill de Blasio better than anything we have seen.

Let us take the two Hillary episodes in order.

According to de Blasio, he was somewhat ambivalent about the 2000 race at the start. One reason he offered was personal. As he explained, "I had two small children at the time and had just worked on a string of campaigns. I knew that taking on the senate campaign would require more sacrifice by my family."[39] The second reason he offered was professional: "I was not sure that I was prepared in this early part of my career to take on the enormous responsibility of running the first lady's U.S. Senate race. It was a huge leap."

Given his reservations, I asked why he agreed to do it at all, to which he responded in more detail:

> I had no doubt she would be a very good Senator. But it was also neces-
> sary to beat Giuliani, and I believed she was the only person who could
> do it. I had been the New York State director for Clinton-Gore in 1996,
> which was the first time I worked in the Clinton world. And because
> I was working in the Clinton administration at HUD as a political
> appointee, I felt a loyalty to the Clintons. So when it was finally made
> clear to me in the fall of 1999 that Hillary wanted me to take the cam-
> paign manager role, I thought the right thing to do was say yes—despite
> the family challenges.

So what was the source of the friction that had been reported? According to de Blasio, "There were several reasons and they developed over months as the year 2000 progressed." He explained, "Some issues were strategic, some had to do with key personnel decisions to be made, and some were philosophical." On the latter, he elaborated when pressed, "There was a split within the campaign between the progressives and the moderates, and the latter won out." With the benefit of hindsight, after what has happened over the past two years, the emergence of such a division is not difficult to comprehend.

Let's now move to 2016. There it was apparent all along that de Blasio had certain philosophical misgivings about Hillary. But he never suggested that he would support anybody else, including Bernie Sanders, whose unswerving stance on economic inequality was more in line with de Blasio's own predilections. He admits, "Although I opposed the DLC (Democratic Leadership Council) and its centrist politics, I had real hope for Hillary. I thought she would eventually take a stronger position on income inequality. She could have generated more support if she had taken a stronger stance, and done it sooner." He continued, "I like Bernie Sanders, but I had a certain loyalty to Hillary going back to 2000 that I could not dismiss. And I also thought that she would do a better job at putting those ideas into action as president."

The two Hillary episodes expose a fissure in the de Blasio psyche that helps us understand his place as an insider/outsider in the political process—as a man who has strong philosophical commitments, yet appreciates the need to function within the system to have his goals realized; who understands the need to compromise, but is not entirely comfortable with its bargains. Bill de Blasio, after all, is the progeny of two prodigious personalities: an idealistic father who embraced Franklin Roosevelt's New Deal aspirations, but was bitten by Joseph McCarthy's Cold War hysteria; and a pragmatic mother who did not allow her high-minded ideals to overwhelm her Southern Italian predisposition against entirely trusting government to do the right thing. Bill de Blasio harbors similar doubts, but he soldiers on in a way that is confusing to those who are accustomed to the ordinary machinations of American politics. He can stun the regulars and dismay the dreamers.

De Blasio ended the 2000 campaign on good terms with the Clintons. Both Bill and Hillary Clinton continued to support his political ambitions and endorsed him for mayor once the party primary was resolved. Hillary was in attendance when the former president swore in the new mayor—an extraordinary gesture of friendship for a former first couple. There apparently were no hard feelings on their part about the Senate race.

Bill de Blasio did something else that was unusual in 2001. He decided to run for a seat in the New York City Council. It was an odd move for somebody who was functioning at the apex of American politics. By this time Bill had become such a prominent figure inside the Washington beltway that in one episode of the popular television series *West Wing*, the character played by Rob Lowe is seen discussing strategy in front of a board with an inscription reading, "CALL B. DE BLASIO."

Covering de Blasio's entry into the race, a *New York Observer* article referred to his decision as a "Midlife Crisis Council Race," speculating as to why somebody who could cash in as a high-priced political consultant or influential policy advocate in the office of a celebrity senator was returning to the neighborhood to ring doorbells.[40] There were clear signs, though, that de Blasio had been planning the run all along. Chirlane and Bill had already moved one block over to the house on 11th Street, just inside the boundary of the 39th council district, so that he would be eligible. And their change of residence wasn't the only sign that Bill was harboring political aspirations that were more local.

In 1999, after working in the Department of Housing and Urban Development for Andrew Cuomo, he had decided, at the urging of his friend Patrick Gaspard, to run for his local school board. By then school boards in New York City were virtually meaningless when it came to governance. A law passed by the state legislature in 1969 had originally divided authority between the central school administration at 110 Livingston Street in downtown Brooklyn and thirty-one, eventually thirty-two, locally elected school boards. The central board, appointed by the mayor and five borough presidents, retained most of the power, presiding over the school budget, personnel policy, and the city high schools. The local boards hired a district superintendent who oversaw elementary and middle schools, and selected their principals and other administrators.

Rarely did 5 percent of the eligible voters turn out for school board elections, and many of the districts were ridden with petty corruption. In 1996, the state legislature took away the hiring power of the local boards. The act was a prelude to their complete annihilation in 2001, when Mayor Michael Bloomberg convinced decision-makers in Albany to put him in charge of the schools. By 1999, there was little attraction to serving on local school boards. When de Blasio declared his interest, individuals in the district who had previously served were dropping off. For him, it was an opportunity to engage voters and lay the foundation for something else. Being on the school board gave him a chance to learn something about education—and a reason to cultivate his relationship with the politically potent United Federation of Teachers, which would later endorse his council bid.

The question still remains: Why at this point in a high-powered career would he run for the local city council? De Blasio himself has reported on the disparate life he was leading—in the course of a single day consulting with the White House on the first lady's election strategy, then running home for a school board meeting. Besides that, there was no guarantee that the guy who helped the leader of the free world retain power in 1996 could win himself a seat in the local legislature. It was a crowded field. His principal opponent, Steven Banks, was a prominent legal aid attorney with the wherewithal to raise campaign money from wealthy liberal donors. Banks had won endorsements from former mayor Edward Koch and former Manhattan Borough President Ruth Messinger. The left-leaning Messinger had also been involved with the formation of the New Coalition Party. Koch later expressed regrets about endorsing Banks before de Blasio entered the contest, suggesting he might have stayed neutral.

In response to the "why" question, Bill's wife Chirlane McCray attested, "he always had a dream of being an elected official."[41] Bill's answer may have been more to the point when he said, "I'm supposed to go for the highest-paying or biggest-sounding job. But *I prize my ideological independence*, and think I have something to contribute. I have the experience to *move the Council in a progressive direction*."[42] In another interview during his race for the council seat, he proclaimed, "Now I get to talk to real people with real concerns. They ask questions, and I can actually answer however I want. I'm not worried about straying from the party line."[43]

Bill wasn't exactly starting off with an empty hand. Pursuing the office he should have had no interest in was something he had been preparing for all along. In true strategic fashion, it was a matter of ends and means. He perceived those factors differently from most other politicians. Long anticipated, the seat became open when its incumbent, Steve DiBrienza, was term limited. Bill had time to think about this.

City Council District 39 in Brooklyn comprises Park Slope, Cobble Hill, Carroll Gardens, Windsor Terrace, Kensington, Red Hook, Gowanus, and Borough Park—an amalgamation of Brownstone Brooklyn, Limestone Brooklyn, and Clapboard Brooklyn, infiltrated by a toxic canal, and offset by an eighteenth-century theocracy with laws against birth control that generate large families, rapid population growth, and tightly wrapped packages of votes. Bill de Blasio was already the darling of the Working Families Party. His well-publicized associations with the Clintons, the Cuomos, Peter Vallone, David Dinkins, and Charles Rangel granted him stature that was hard to match, and helped him snatch a blue chip endorsement from the *New York Times*. His connections also fed a surge of fundraising. More than 90 percent of his $150,000 in donations came from outside of Brooklyn, giving him a lower in-district funding rate than any of his opponents.[44] Bill was a composite insider/outsider. He was angling for a position on a minor league team with name brand sponsors behind him.

Among de Blasio's earliest and most generous supporters was Israel Spitzer, the Deputy Mayor of New Square, and political advisor to the Grand Rebbe. The donation was made two weeks before Spitzer and Rabbi Twersky met with the president and senator-elect Clinton. De Blasio claims he had no knowledge of the religious leaders' intention to bring up the pardon issue at the White House. Spitzer remained a loyal contributor to de Blasio for some time, as has the Rockland County power broker and convicted felon Paul Adler.[45] Spitzer's father, Avrohom Chaim Spitzer, was a rabbi at a Borough Park synagogue; Adler has no direct link to Brooklyn or the city. De Blasio has known the two politicos from Rockland County since the Clinton-Gore campaign of 1996. They have been a source of embarrassment for him on occasion, but not especially damaging. De Blasio swept 71 percent of the vote in 2001.[46]

As a freshman in the City Council, Bill de Blasio joined a seventeen-member progressive coalition of members calling itself the "Fresh Democracy Council." They sought to make the governance of the body more democratic by weakening the power of the Speaker's office and disbursing it among the members. We had heard this plea from the Left before. Under Peter Vallone, the Speaker determined the legislative calendar, committee assignments, stipends, and staffs associated with those assignments, and "member items" were awarded to loyalists so they can dispense goodies in their home districts. This is not an uncommon practice in legislative bodies. Despite its nondemocratic features, which can be modulated through the personal style of an individual leader, such discipline can also strengthen the hand of a legislature vis-à-vis the executive. There is something to be said for it in a municipality with such a strong mayoralty.

De Blasio was not shy about criticizing the ways of the man under whom he once served. Despite all the back and forth about power sharing, however, not much changed in the way the council was run, although Vallone's successor as Speaker, Gifford Miller, was more inclusive and less sure of his command over the chamber. Spurred on by the Working Families Party and ACORN that were now more influential among the members, a loose alliance of progressives remained intact to challenge Mayor Michael Bloomberg on issues that were important to organized labor and underprivileged New Yorkers. Among them were a living wage bill to raise the compensation of employees in private companies doing business with the city, and the maintenance of funding for basic neighborhood services.

Because council districts were redrawn as a result of the U.S. Census, there was a special election in 2003 in which winners would retain their seats for two years instead of the usual four. After winning re-election in 2003 with 72 percent of the vote, de Blasio challenged Council Member Lew Fidler for the chairmanship of the seventeen-member Brooklyn delegation.[47] It was a first step in an attempt by de Blasio to ascend to the Speaker position. De Blasio ended up making a deal with Al Vann, an influential former state assemblyman from Bedford-Stuyvesant, to cochair the Brooklyn delegation. They both aligned themselves behind Gifford Miller, who took the top legislative post, even though they had each eyed the position for themselves from the moment they entered the council as freshmen in 2001.

De Blasio simultaneously signed on to become state chair of the John Edwards campaign for president. He took some flack in opinion circles when it was disclosed that he was accepting consulting fees as an advisor to the North Carolina senator, which is not usually the practice for a campaign chair. De Blasio had also been earning money on the side consulting with SEIU 1199. It was all legal, and in keeping with his class-based politics. Bill was one of the few elected Democrats in the state to support Edwards.[48] He expressed admiration for the "clarity and sharpness" of the senator's "populist" message on inequality.[49] Most of his Council colleagues, including Speaker Miller, backed Vermont governor Howard Dean, who was seen as a prohibitive favorite until Senator John Kerry of Massachusetts swooped in to take the nomination. This was typical Bill de Blasio: aggressive, in-your-face, out of the box, carrying the banner of a less traditional, somewhat unsafe candidate who was unambiguous about his policy goals and willing to discuss inequality.

Reelected in 2005 with 83 percent of the vote, de Blasio made another unsuccessful bid to become Speaker.[50] One of seven Council members in contention, he was edged out by Christine Quinn, whom he would later battle for the mayoralty. While in the council, de Blasio served as Chair of the General Welfare Committee, giving him a forum for advancing causes close to his heart, such as better services for the homeless, job training for the unemployed, expanded eligibility for food stamps, programs for the elderly, subsidized day care, and affordable housing. On the economic front he fought to pass a living wage bill, impose a commuter tax, raise income taxes for the wealthy, and lower regressive property taxes.

As a member of the Council Education Committee, de Blasio joined with its chair Eva Moskowitz to criticize Mayor Bloomberg for excluding parents from decisions about their schools. He also adamantly opposed a Bloomberg plan to close eight firehouses, including one in his Park Slope district. That battle forever won him the allegiance of the firefighters union, paying political rewards later on. At the urging of several union leaders, de Blasio also sponsored legislation that significantly loosened the cap on donations that unions could make to political campaigns, drawing criticism from the Campaign Finance Board and Mayor Bloomberg, who preferred to spend his own money on campaigns. When the City Council took up Bloomberg's request to extend his term limit for four more years, de Blasio unsuccessfully led a fight to put the question to a popular referendum, where it had been twice defeated before.

After losing his bid for Council Speaker to Christine Quinn, Bill de Blasio explored other opportunities to advance his political career. In 2006, he announced that he would challenge Vito Fossella, the only Republican in New York City to hold a seat in Congress. The idea went nowhere. De Blasio did not live in the 13th Congressional District that took in Staten Island and parts of Brooklyn, and the local Democratic Party committee had already pledged its support to somebody else.

In 2009, de Blasio considered a run for Brooklyn Borough President. The position carried little weight after the Board of Estimate was eliminated in 1989, and became even more irrelevant when the central Board of Education was abolished with the passage of mayoral control of the schools in 2001. Although de Blasio managed to pick up endorsements from influential minority leaders such as Congresswoman Nydia Velazquez and Yvette Clarke, the contest promised to be highly charged racially. Brooklyn contained the largest concentration of black voters in the city, and had never elected a black borough president. The stakes got higher when City Councilman Charles Barron, a former Black Panther prone to volcanic rhetoric, entered the race, leading de Blasio to drop out.

A better opportunity emerged when Betsy Gotbaum announced that she was not seeking a third term as Public Advocate. Betsy, who was married to the much admired labor leader Victor Gotbaum of District Council 37, had accumulated an impressive record of public service in New York going back to her days as a young aide to Mayor John Lindsay, including turns as Parks Commissioner and President of the New York Historical Society before being elected to the post.

She had become frustrated with the budget cuts she was forced to absorb by Mayor Bloomberg, and she was uncomfortable seeking a third term made possible by the City Council's decision to overturn two popular referenda imposing term limits on office holders. That was Michael Bloomberg's deal, not hers. For Bill de Blasio, the vacancy opened the door to a citywide arena—a stepping-stone to the mayoralty.

De Blasio launched his public advocate campaign with a well-trained army of organizational support that was wide and deep, including the Working Families Party, ACORN, SEIU 1199, the United Federation of Teachers, and the Uniformed Firefighters Association. His main opponent in the Democratic primary was Mark Green. Having served as Public Advocate between 1994 and 2001, Green benefited from better name recognition with the general public. The consumer advocate and champion of liberal causes had been a reliable critic of Republican mayor Rudy Giuliani, who liked to return fire, and seemed to enjoy the constant banter. Together Green and Giuliani provided City Hall reporters with a feast of controversy, and the two of them basked in the attention.

The other candidates in the 2009 contest for Public Advocate were civil liberties attorney Norman Siegel, and Queens council member Eric Gioia, the most aggressive fundraiser in the pack. The crowded field made it difficult for any candidate to get the required 40 percent vote to avoid a runoff. De Blasio (33 percent) and Green (31 percent) nearly tied for first place in the September primary.[51] The strong organizational support de Blasio mustered from years as a local political operative paid off, making a decisive difference (63 percent to 37 percent) in the low turnout runoff. [52] He prevailed in the November election over his Republican opponent Alex Zablocki by a margin of more than four to one.[53]

As a third-term mayor, Bloomberg lost no time sniping at the office of Public Advocate, questioning its utility and cutting its budget to the bone, a pattern he began when Betsy Gotbaum held the office. Between 2000 and 2009, budget cuts reduced the size of the staff from forty-five to twenty-two.[54] At its peak in 1990, the office counted sixty-five staff members. A loss of resources on that scale does have a substantive impact on the capacity of an office to function. Looking toward his own future, de Blasio used the post to gain visibility for causes he wanted to champion. On one level there was the usual carping at the mayor: constituent items such as school bus delays, repair backlogs in public housing, a lack of transparency in city agencies, and freedom of information requests left unattended.

On another level, there was the posturing in national debates, like how the Supreme Court's *Citizens United* decision of 2010 allows corporations to funnel money into politics. Then there were gestures of gratitude to powerful allies: opposing teacher layoffs and school closings, standing by taxi owners who fought the mayor's plan to expand the taxi fleet, creating a landlord watch list to protect tenants. And of course there were signature issues that de Blasio carried forward into his own mayoralty: complaints about "stop and frisk" tactics in the police department, and allegations of abuse at detention centers for immigrants.

Most curious was de Blasio's cautious positioning on issues that should have been to his liking. He did not participate in the Occupy Wall Street protests staged in Zuccotti Park in 2011, as many of his friends and allies had. Here again he relied on the *focus* and *clarity* arguments, commenting, "My concern is that it's not particularly organized, there's not a particularly clear set of demands."[55] Was this crowd too far out for a man anticipating a run for mayor? Or was their movement just too discombobulated for a serious politician with a clear sense of purpose? They were outsiders to the system, self-described radicals; he was an insider now—in a manner of speaking.

De Blasio also refused to play ball when Speaker Christine Quinn, a rival for mayor, finally caved to union pressure to support a living wage bill, baffling progressive advocates who had demanded such legislation for decades. De Blasio described the bill as "watered down."[56] Was it really? Did Bill have serious policy concerns here? Or was he once again more focused on politics? Quinn was a latecomer who had delayed progress on the issue all along. Why let her rack up the credit now when she was going after the big prize? Bill felt obliged to remind folks about Christine's dalliance, and how she was lost in action on issues important to working people, noting, "repeatedly, we've seen her look the other way on issues like paid sick leave and living wage. That's what the public will ultimately judge, the substance, whether someone is on their side or not."[57] He eventually supported the bill, and it passed.

The landscape of progressive politics in New York shifted quickly after de Blasio became Public Advocate in 2010 with the sudden dissolution of ACORN, a substantial part of his political base. The hastened decline of the housing/social justice coalition was precipitated by a series of scandals. There had been allegations of voter registration fraud and embezzlement dating back to 2008, and damaging accusations that the organization had violated its tax-exempt status by engaging in partisan politics. The most embarrassing episode involved the release of a video from 2009 in which political adversaries posing as a prostitute and a pimp received advice from the organization's counselors on how to acquire a mortgage to open a brothel. Republicans in Congress capitalized on the incident as a justification to cut off ACORN's funding.[58] Many private donors followed suit. After a federal judge rebuked the House of Representatives for punishing the organization without a trial, an appellate court upheld the suspension of funds. This led to bankruptcy and the shuttering of ACORN's New York offices by April 2010, followed by the folding of its operations throughout the rest of the country.

In order to continue its political organizing and legislative advocacy, the New York-based office of ACORN resurrected itself under the name New York Communities for Change (NYCC). Jon Kest, ACORN's former executive director and cofounder of the Working Families Party (WFP), became its executive director and remained on WFP's board. The structures of the NYCC and the WFP continue to be interwoven by common threads of progressive politics, and the two organizations have shared office space in downtown Brooklyn for nearly twenty years.

Together these political companions are a force to behold. They cooperated to win Democratic primaries for the City Council in 2009 and 2013, creating a base of support for progressives to eventually assume leadership within the local legislative body. When de Blasio became mayor, they cooperated with him to elect Melissa Mark-Viverito the Speaker. These relationships are reciprocal. With friends at City Hall, the WFP plays a more prominent role than it (or ACORN) ever could have imagined in Mayor Bloomberg's New York. Progressive politics is more alive in the city now than it has been in fifty years. This was true to form for Bill de Blasio. Looking back, Dan Cantor remarked, "Bill was always involved in progressive causes, but he was also very pragmatic, concerned about achieving tangible results for real people who needed help."[59]

In November 2015, the WFP announced that it was granting its presidential ballot line to Bernie Sanders. In a landslide, 87.4 percent of its membership voted for Sanders over Hillary Clinton (11.5 percent). Speaking for the party, Dan Cantor exclaimed, "we want to live in a nation that allows all people to live a decent life," further elaborating, "the super rich have used their economic muscle to buy political muscle."[60] Unlike Bill de Blasio, who did not seem to lose hope that Hillary Clinton would come around on economic equality, his friends from the WFP had given up on her—at least until she secured the nomination. Then they switched.

* * *

If we are about to start a new chapter in the life of the national Democratic Party, observing Bill de Blasio's transition from a young radical to a respected political operative can be informative. This is not the first time progressive forces in New York have moved the establishment leftward, nor is it the only time third parties have played a role in the process. Mayors Fiorello La Guardia and John Lindsay both relied on third-party lines to get elected in New York. They, however, were Republicans who aligned their fortunes with local Democrats (and Democratic presidents) sympathetic to their goals. Bill de Blasio is a progressive Democrat whose agenda is not entirely aligned to the mainstream of his own party. His political partnerships with Democratic leaders can be short stops on a longer journey. He prizes his own independence. These political arrangements do not always end on a fully amicable note. At times they appear utilitarian: necessary accommodations that allow him to remain relevant; or, to put it another way, that prevent him from becoming irrelevant and marginalized, as activists with "radical" inclinations usually are in American politics.

Bill de Blasio's commitment to political and social equality was conspicuous from his high school and college days. His sentiments were reinforced by a mother who had a profound influence on him, and are ratified by a wife who shares the same values. Even when he took his first steps in politics wearing smiles for David Dinkins and Bill Clinton, he was associated with the more progressive Majority Coalition, the New Party, and their fused New Majority Coalition. This is where he found his true soulmates, with the likes of Patrick Gaspard, Dan Cantor, Bertha Lewis, and Melissa Mark-Viverito. In spirit, these entities comprised the gestation, infancy, and adolescence of a loose band of advocates who matured into the Working Families Party. Their strategy was always the same: Win Locally, Build Nationally.

To ascertain what they are and always have been about, take a look at the website of the New Party from 1996, when Bill Clinton was seeking a second term. A section reading, "Thinking about '96" starts off with a quote by an independent congressman from Vermont, named Bernie Sanders, complimenting the party for taking care of business at the local level, as "We did in Burlington."[61] Pining over "what's missing" from the ongoing political debate surrounding the presidential election, the site mentions, "falling wages, rising inequality, millions of impoverished children, rotting cities, rollbacks in environmental and consumer protections, the ongoing corruption of the political process itself with big money."

Here is what the New Party website had to say about the re-election prospects of President Bill Clinton: conceding it to be "good" that he will probably beat Republican Bob Dole, the site hardly heaps praise on the sitting president. Noting, "how disappointing President Clinton has been," it dares to point out:

> He has fought hard and successfully for bad policies (NAFTA, GATT), claimed great victories on relatively inconsequential policies (Americorps), but on most crucial matters of the day he either started from a bad premise (see health care), caved in without much of a fight at all (eg. the budget, economic stimulus, labor law reform), or just ignored it (minimum wage) until recently.

In perhaps the most biting criticism Democrats can make of a fellow Democrat, the New Party folks held, "the Clinton administration resembles a moderate Republican administration much of the time." And the critics went on to explain why, asserting "there is no serious durable, visible, progressive presence in American political life," which forces him (Clinton) to "concede to the bond market, or the corporations, or the media elite." That's why, unfortunately, "all American politics is a debate between Clinton and Newt Gingrich." Looking toward the future, the progressives demanded, "what we need is a debate between Clinton and, say, Ted Kennedy or Jesse Jackson or Bernie Sanders."

Twenty years later, there was that debate between a Clinton and Bernie Sanders. Bernie did not win, but he pushed the discussion further than anybody ever expected he could. With Hillary's defeat in the general election, he now has another chance to work with some of the original organizers of the New Party to change the direction of the national Democratic Party itself. In the meantime, the wily operative who ran Bill Clinton's '96 re-election campaign in New York State was elected mayor of its largest city on a progressive platform crafted by many of same folks. In order to understand how that was possible, and why it matters, we need to dig further back into history.

PART II

PAST AS PROLOGUE

4

The Soul of New York

New York is exceptional. Its expansive harbor, ringed by the most spectacular skyline on the planet, is more than an entrance to a city. For generations, New York has been a gateway to the American Dream. Going back some four hundred years, it has offered pilgrims from every land the promise that if they worked hard, life would be better for them and their children. In fits and starts, the city delivered on that promise for successive waves of newcomers. The seeds of modern progressivism, where this story begins, can be traced to the mid-nineteenth century with the rule of Democratic Party bosses, who saw the immigrants as an opportunity to accumulate power. A process of assimilation and growth lasted for more than a century.

Then, as we moved into the last quarter of the past century, a fiscal crisis that brought the city to the brink of bankruptcy changed everything, altering the city's view of itself and its potential.[1] The lofty language of possibility was replaced by sobering warnings of constraints and limitations. By the 1970s commentators wondered whether New York would survive. In 1990, *Time* magazine published a cover story on "The Rotting of the Big Apple."[2] Political leaders, with good reason, obsessed over the bottom line. They became more focused on generating prosperity than opportunity, on corralling the wealthy instead of rescuing the needy.

Becoming a New Yorker was never easy. Each generation of new arrivals did its best to close the door behind them once they had passed through; but the golden threshold remained open all the while, if more narrowly for some than for others. By the 1820s virtually the entire population was composed of immigrants.The next wave brought the Irish, who fled famine in the 1820s and continued to arrive by the boatload for twenty years. They were not welcomed by nativists of Protestant ancestry, who resented their rowdiness, condemned their church, and feared they would eventually take the town over. The nativist fears of a political takeover proved to be well founded. By 1870, the Irish constituted 21.4 percent of the city population.[3]

Boss Tweed and his Tammany cronies had seen it coming all along, so rather than fight the Irish and spill more blood on the streets as the nativists did, the machine embraced them.[4] Tweed personally greeted their tall ships as they approached the harbor. A cup of watered-down soup was a delectable treat after a long journey on a damp, stinking, rat-infested vessel: a lovely reception for the tired and poor. The machine also helped the newcomers find jobs and shelter. Employment was sporadic and the tenements were dilapidated, but it was a start in a new land—not any worse than what they had fled, but it held promise for a future. More than anything, the machine gave the immigrants citizenship and the right to vote. Tammany opened its Naturalization Bureau in 1840, converting 11,000 foreigners into Americans within four years. Between 1856 and 1868 the machine naturalized 9,207 immigrants per year; it added an additional 41,112 in 1868.[5]

Historians differ over whether the machine really helped the Irish or exploited them. Steven Erie believes that Tammany consigned Erin's sons and daughters to dead end, low-skilled jobs that ultimately inhibited their advancement. Immigrant votes certainly fueled the growth of the corrupt party organization that made its chieftains wealthy. In time, however, the Irish became the machine, and the machine took care of its own. Tammany controlled 40,000 patronage jobs by 1880. By 1900, 36.6 percent of the public sector jobs in the city were held by Irishmen; by 1930 the figure had risen to 51.7 percent.[6] Patronage could be kind for those on the receiving end, and it was especially appreciated by those in need.

Apart from the corruption, there was something fundamentally democratic about the machine.[7] First of all, it was decentralized, so that real power resided with local aldermen who presided over their small districts. That local politician was more likely to be a saloon keeper or butcher than a lawyer or other professional. He was a familiar and accessible figure to those of humble origins. A citizen could reach out to him personally. If you or your brother needed a job, he was the guy to see about joining the police force or the fire brigade. No test required. If you had relatives arriving from abroad, he could help acquire citizenship papers so they could stay. No questions asked. It was real service, without government bureaucracy. In return for such patronage, you would be expected to vote, and perhaps knock on a few doors to get your neighbors out to the polls on Election Day. The arrangement was empowering. Every time you walked up a flight of creaking tenement stairs to rap on your neighbor's door, you were affecting the outcome of an election—not to mention your standing with the local alderman.

Tammany was less enthusiastic about welcoming the next wave of immigrants arriving toward the end of the century. Most of them came from Italy, Russia, and Poland, and did not speak English. The public schools could be harsh with them.[8] It did not help the Jews that they did not want to be Christians. The machine did not need any more immigrant votes, nor did it want more foreigners begging for a share of the spoils. Reformers were already complaining about excessive governmental costs and high taxes. Progressives were demanding that sound management practices be adopted from the private sector, where business was conducted more efficiently. They wanted the civil service to be professionalized so that public administration would be put in the hands of university-trained experts, and patronage would be ended. Revisionist historians couldn't help but notice that the reform movement was orchestrated by bankers and businessmen. Accordingly, they depicted it as a class war designed to displace ethnic rule and put the elite in charge.[9]

There is no denying that urban government was corrupt, wasteful, and poorly managed. The schemes were the stuff of legend. The grandiose courthouse that carries Tweed's name—now the headquarters for the school department— exceeded its original cost estimates by a multiple of fifty, much of it set aside to pay for kickbacks demanded by the bosses. Back in Tweed's day, it was the responsibility of the City Chamberlain to decide which banks would hold the city's deposits. As a matter of course, the chamberlain got to keep the interest paid on the accounts for himself. That practice was formally ended in 1866 when Peter Sweeney proudly announced that he would no longer take the money. Writing about America in 1888, British political theorist James Bryce called our cities "the most conspicuous failure of the United States."[10]

There was another side to the story. The localism embedded by the machine remained an essential component of New York's political culture. In the name of reform, power was increasingly centralized in the office of the mayor; yet the concerns that shaped the executive agenda continued to percolate from the city's diverse communities. City life was formed within neighborhoods when common people patronized family-run stores, attended houses of worship where their language was spoken, played in city parks, and were helped by local charities. That is the way New Yorkers cope with the anonymity of the giant city and develop a sense of belonging. The neighborhood is the place—with credit from the grocer, a used coat from the pastor, a kind gesture from a playground attendant (once called a *parkee*), or a warm meal from the neighborhood pantry—where residents imbibe the ethos that underlies New York's social contract, which implores all: "Give a poor guy a break." It runs through the city bloodstream and keeps the place alive.

Fiorello La Guardia was born in Greenwich Village and served in Congress between 1923 and 1932 representing East Harlem while he lived in the Bronx.[11] Raised mostly in Arizona, he was half Italian and half Jewish, and spoke six languages. His first wife was a Catholic. After she died, he married a Lutheran. He himself was an Episcopalian and a Mason. He had won the 1922 election as a Republican by less than two hundred votes. He was turned out of office in 1932 when Franklin Roosevelt was swept into the White House at the top of the Democratic Party ticket.

La Guardia attributed the loss to his eroding base of support as Puerto Ricans replaced Jews in the multi-ethnic 20th Congressional District. It did not help being toward the bottom of a Republican ticket headed by Herbert Hoover. His own party was suspicious of the irascible young congressman who was unpredictable and not shy about challenging Hoover on his handling of the economy.[12] La Guardia was also an outspoken critic of prohibition—a GOP cause—which he believed was class-based, hypocritical, and anti-immigrant. Why deny a workingman a drink while the rich sip their martinis at private clubs and bootleggers score profits for illicit produce?

La Guardia demonstrated political independence during his second year in Congress when he abandoned the GOP presidential nominee to support the third party candidacy of Wisconsin senator Robert La Follette on the Progressive Party ticket. That cost him the Republican Party line when he sought another term in 1924, so he was re-elected as the candidate of the Socialist Party. Unable to caucus with one of the major parties, he was denied influential committee assignments, weakening his effectiveness as a legislator. His legislative record was unremarkable, except for the passage of the Norris-LaGuardia Act that occurred during his last year in the House. That landmark labor legislation removed judicial and legal barriers that limited the rights of workers to join unions, strike, picket, or organize boycotts. Enacted in 1932 in the midst of the Great Depression, the law signaled a growing public sentiment behind the needs of workers exploited by bosses in the private sector.

Representing the slum residents of East Harlem put La Guardia in touch with the effects that poverty can have on the human spirit, and cemented his commitment to do something about it. Toward the end of his tenure in Congress, La Guardia joined with other Republicans and representatives from the Midwest to form the Allied Progressives. If nothing else, their legislative agenda would prove prophetic. Their debates instigated the idea that government had a moral obligation to eradicate the misery caused by the Depression. La Guardia proposed a program of direct relief that would employ men in much-needed public works projects. When Hoover created the Reconstruction Finance Corporation in 1932 to make loans to ailing banks and industries, La Guardia branded it the "millionaire's dole." Why rescue the banks whose reckless speculation with other people's money imposed hardship on innocent people? Why reward brokers who peddled worthless stocks to their clients?

When Hoover proposed a regressive sales tax to raise federal revenues, La Guardia and his allies were able to stop it. La Guardia's alternative "soak the rich" scheme to impose a luxury tax and eliminate loopholes in the tax code never saw the light of day, but his progressive message did. *Time* magazine praised the congressman from East Harlem for refusing to be accountable to any authority other than his conscience. The more conservative *Evening Journal* admonished La Guardia for his attempt to "strangle" business, declaring "it is a shame you are classed as a Republican," suggesting "next time you should run as a Red."[13] Fearing that progressives could override his veto, Hoover finally signed an Emergency Relief and Construction Act to aid states and municipalities—a modest prelude to FDR's New Deal.

La Guardia lost his congressional seat in 1932, but he successfully ran for mayor of New York the next year. It was his second attempt to rescue City Hall from the clutches of Tammany. In 1929 incumbent mayor Jimmy Walker was too popular and his machine backing still too powerful. Beau James had been one of the most popular mayors in city history. A smooth-talking charmer, he liked to be seen about town with his best girl, Betty Compton, a Broadway actress half his age whose luscious smile captivated tabloid cameras. Walker's flamboyance irritated former governor Al Smith, who chided his old roommate that such behavior was unacceptable for a married man and against the teachings of their Catholic faith.

Smith refused to endorse his charismatic friend until he mended his ways, which never happened. The two Tammany men, nonetheless, continued to share a commitment to public construction that outpaced all other areas of city spending in the 1920s.[14] As governor, Smith signed a pioneering law that dedicated public funds for the creation of subsidized urban housing. Such expenditures were good for the city that had become a center for world commerce, rewarding for laborers who pulled the lever for machine candidates, and profitable for politicians who had lucrative contracts to play with. As Tammany would have it, this was larceny with a heart. Everybody—nearly everybody—got a piece of the action.

Walker, a man of humble origins, truly identified with the working class tenant dwellers who kept him and the machine in power. He was their hedonistic naughty hero.[15] Tammany's lease on life began to run out in 1931 when Governor Franklin Roosevelt, wanting to clean up the Democratic Party's reputation before his run for the White House, appointed a commission headed by Judge Samuel Seabury to investigate the magistrate courts. Later that year, with Roosevelt's approval, the state legislature appointed a joint committee to investigate the affairs of the municipal government, choosing Seabury as counsel. In the famous "duel at Foley Square" Walker fast-talked his way through testimony when Seabury put him on the stand, and the celebrated corruption fighter was unable to make any of his charges of bribery stick. Roosevelt raised the temperature on Walker, when he personally brought the mayor to Albany for questioning. Al Smith finally persuaded his friend to resign for the good of the party five weeks before Roosevelt was elected president.

Now out of a job, La Guardia decided to make another try for the position he had long coveted. City government was not new to him. He was President of the Board of Aldermen in 1920 and 1921, an office that was a precursor to the Public Advocate position Bill de Blasio held before becoming mayor. In those days, though, that official was also a member of the powerful Board of Estimate, which voted on the budget and key land use issues having to do with real estate. La Guardia used the board position to educate himself on the mechanics of the municipal government, and occasionally to tweak Mayor John Harlan, a Brooklyn Democrat who needed his vote.

La Guardia ran for mayor as a Republican and City Fusion Party candidate, hoping to draw support from a broad and diverse coalition. Republican leaders who had become disenchanted with his performance in Congress warmed to La Guardia because he adopted a good government platform promising to end corruption and institute management reforms. Organized labor considered him a friend. Jews and Italians loved him. Wealthy WASPs were persuaded that he was best equipped to take down Tammany and its budget-breaking shenanigans. The poor who exercised their franchise stayed with the machine. Roosevelt, now in the White House, remained neutral. Helping things along for La Guardia, two Democrats split their party's vote, and he won with barely 40 percent of the total.[16] His Fusion ticket also took the comptrollership, the presidency of the Board of Alderman, and three borough presidencies, giving him control over the powerful Board of Estimate.

Among those who have succeeded him, the "Little Flower" remains the most admired man to hold the office of New York City mayor. Every modern day mayor—whether Democrat or Republican, liberal or conservative—has put him on a pedestal and held him up as a role model. Bill de Blasio is no exception, explaining, "He was the first true progressive mayor and was beloved in a way none of us will ever achieve. . . .. La Guardia brought this real sense of caring, of a personal give-and-take with every New Yorker. After that, people had this new vision of the mayor."[17]

La Guardia spent his first year in City Hall dealing with a gaping budget deficit, and it wasn't pretty. He cut jobs and required payless furloughs; he imposed a regressive sales tax, much like the one he opposed as a congressman. These tough decisions put the city on sounder financial footing for a while, but the three-term mayor also had a larger agenda to fulfill. In the course of his tenure, La Guardia created a civil service system for the municipal government that replaced the notorious patronage system. Although this brought better-educated people into public service who were capable of passing required written exams, it also displaced lower class workers who needed the jobs and may have had the skills to perform them. The Irish, who enjoyed a disproportionate share of Tammany's handouts, were especially hard hit.

La Guardia enacted a new City Charter that strengthened the mayor's powers and created a City Planning Commission to deliberate on the capital budget and land use. The charter also replaced the Board of Aldermen with a smaller, weaker City Council, a further blow to Tammany's base of support—with collateral damage inflicted on the strong localism that the machine had inscribed onto the political culture of the city.

La Guardia's most significant legacy to the city he ruled for twelve years arose from the collaboration he forged with President Franklin Roosevelt and the partnership between the city and the federal government that came of it. The two men's relationship was built on a common understanding that government has a moral obligation to assist those in need. That commitment was in keeping with the spirit of New York that inhabited both men.

In 1931, when Jimmy Walker was still mayor, labor leaders had persuaded the city fathers to finance public works projects to create jobs that maintained parks and streets. The year before, New York's major private charities banded together to create the Emergency Employment Committee to coordinate relief.[18] That same year, New York State—with Roosevelt still residing in the governor's mansion—became the first state to offer direct relief to victims of the Depression. The Temporary Emergency Relief Administration appropriated $20 million to reimburse local relief agencies for 40 percent of their expenditures on such efforts. In its first year of operation, the program helped 48,000 families in the city with jobs and an additional 90,000 with food, rent, and clothing vouchers.[19] The city began to build low-income housing on its own in 1934 with the creation of the New York City Housing Authority (NYCHA).

Before he was sworn in as mayor, La Guardia was traveling to Washington to beseech the new president that there needed to be federal assistance for cities. His pleas fell on sympathetic ears: not at first on the president's, but rather on the ears of the people around him such as Harry Hopkins, who asked La Guardia to help assemble the Civil Works Administration (CWA), and Interior Secretary Harold Ickes, who was in charge of the Public Works Administration (PWA); his son by the same name would one day mentor a young Bill de Blasio. La Guardia had always believed that public resources should be invested in public programs to alleviate public problems, rather than intervening through the private sector. As he insisted in Congress, "The highest function of government is the preservation of life."[20] Hoover had not agreed; Roosevelt eventually did. La Guardia brought a planner to Washington with him by the name of Robert Moses to convince the administration that New York City was an ideal place to realize that public potential.[21] The Big Apple was about to become New Deal City.

A week before taking office, La Guardia had sealed an agreement to employ 200,000 CWA workers in New York City. That was just the beginning. On La Guardia's third day in office, Harold Ickes allocated $25 million to the city—a quarter of the PWA housing budget—to build public housing. In February, La Guardia charged NYCHA with responsibility to carry out the task.[22] Disagreements ensued between Ickes and the mayor over how to administer land clearance, construction, rental, and upkeep. NYCHA, nonetheless, grew into the largest low- and middle-income public housing project in the history of the country—and it still is, providing homes for more than 400,000 residents.[23] Roosevelt eventually got behind a public housing program that its sponsor, Senator Robert F. Wagner of New York, sold as a tool for economic recovery.

The direct employment approach adopted by the federal government not only provided relief for those who were out of work, but also it allowed the city to build its infrastructure in ways that were unfathomable to even the most ambitious planners. New York ultimately received $58 per capita in federal grants to fund 107 projects under the PWA program, which was much above the $33 per capita national average for the program.[24] The funds were used to build schools, roads, bridges, viaducts, tunnels, libraries, parks, playgrounds, beaches, zoos, hospitals, and treatment plants. Some of the most impressive monuments to this ambitious set of programs include the Triborough Bridge, Whitestone Bridge, Henry Hudson Bridge, Lincoln Tunnel, Queens-Midtown Tunnel, FDR Drive, Belt Parkway, Hunter College, Brooklyn College, and LaGuardia Airport. Federal support allowed the city to align its three existing subways into a unified underground network that surpassed urban transit systems around the world. Robert Moses oversaw a newly unified parks system that consumed 35 percent of the entire CWA appropriation.[25] Borough presidents got to use federal money for long overdue street and sewer repairs.

With all its fine attributes, there was a dark stain on the fabric of New Deal liberalism. It had to do with race. As Italians and Jews moved out of Northern Manhattan, Harlem became the "Black Mecca" and East Harlem "El Barrio." In 1941, La Guardia teamed up with A. Philip Randolph and other black leaders to convince Roosevelt to sign Executive Order 8802, which created the Fair Employment Practices Committee and forbade discrimination by federal agencies and contractors on the basis of race, creed, or color. FDR, however, was not about to go to Congress to seek more meaningful civil rights legislation.[26] His New Deal legislation was too reliant on the cooperation of Southern committee chairs to challenge racial segregation and violence in the South, where lynching and church burnings were all too common. Both FDR and La Guardia tried to satisfy black voters by giving them jobs. Their high-level minority appointments broke a historic color line, but minorities were still consigned to a separate existence, even in New York. Those who were politically active in the city belonged to a parallel party organization called the United Colored Democracy. As a matter of policy, NYCHA's public housing was segregated by race.

La Guardia was surprised when a riot broke out in Harlem in 1935. He had befriended black leaders and enjoyed cordial relations with key organizations such as the NAACP and Urban League, but he did not fully understand the simmering resentment bred by isolated slum living. He never went public with the report he had commissioned in response to the riot. The panel's study on "The Negro in Harlem," conducted over the course of a year, had been directed by the prominent black sociologist E. Franklin Frazier, drawing on testimony from 160 witnesses at twenty-five public hearings. It traced the cause of the disturbance to racism and the effects of poverty, and made an impassioned plea for the city to deal with problems such as job discrimination, substandard services, and police abuses. [27] Its recommendations were reasonable, given the level of dissatisfaction voiced by the community, but too costly and ambitious for the times.

La Guardia invested resources to improve housing, education, and health services in Harlem, but discrimination continued. When the city signed a contract with the Metropolitan Life Insurance Company in 1943 to develop low-income housing in Stuyvesant Town, the agreement maintained the company's hiring policy of racial discrimination, and the apartments were kept segregated. That summer another disturbance broke out in Harlem when a white policeman shot at a black soldier and his mother after a brief altercation in a hotel. The melee was finally put down when the Little Flower personally supervised an army of 5,000 police personnel occupying the area.[28] In 1944, the City Council passed the first anti-discrimination housing law in the country, but Stuyvesant Town remained segregated, as did the city at large.

Fiorello was elected to a third term in 1941 by the closest margin of any mayor since 1904. For the second time, the Republican incumbent also wore the American Labor Party label. But, he probably should not have run at all. With all his major challenges and triumphs behind him, he seemed to have lost interest in the job. The city and the country were consumed by the war. As the federal government cut the flow of money to states and localities, the city had to pick up a larger part of the tab for many of the New Deal initiatives that had brought it through the Depression, requiring the embattled mayor to raise taxes. The colorful father figure, who had once read the funny sheets to children over the radio during a newspaper strike, increasingly displayed an angry, intemperate side. His opposition to public employee unionism and collective bargaining in local government did not sit well with organized labor, whose leadership once saw him as a hero for landmark legislation he sponsored in Congress to advance the union cause in the private sector.

La Guardia's departure from City Hall in 1946 opened the door for a much chastened Tammany to return. William O'Dwyer, an immigrant from Ireland, fit the bill nicely as the machine's candidate. He managed to keep much of the New Deal coalition intact, drawing support from organized labor, government workers, Irish and Italian immigrants, and a smattering of government reformers, including Eleanor Roosevelt—now the widow of the late president. With the New York postwar economy booming, the new mayor continued to improve services and build facilities to everyone's delight, leading to his re-election for a second term. His tenure was cut short in 1950, when he was forced to resign in the wake of a police corruption investigation involving organized crime. O'Dwyer was immediately succeeded by City Council President Vincent Impellitteri, who was next in the line of succession. Tammany did not support Impellitteri when he ran in a special election to complete O'Dwyer's term, but he managed to edge out a plurality in a three-way race by running on an independent line called the Experience Party.

Impellitteri ran for re-election in 1953, but Tammany again had its own candidate to put forward. This time it was Robert F. Wagner Jr., the son of the prominent New Deal senator who had written the National Labor Relations Act in 1935. Commonly referred to as the "Magna Carta of Labor," the Wagner Act, for the first time, gave employees the right to join unions and engage in collective bargaining. Wagner senior was a German immigrant of modest beginnings and a graduate of City College who had been a product of the machine. Beginning as a ward heeler, he worked his way up the ranks as a state legislator, state judge, and finally U.S. senator. He was a close ally of Franklin Roosevelt and authored laws to provide work relief, housing, and social security.

The younger Wagner's political pedigree gave him easy access to labor, machine, and reform circles, not to mention other privileged networks. He was a graduate of Yale. A Catholic upbringing furnished by his Irish mother qualified Wagner to balance citywide tickets complemented by Italian and Jewish running mates. He was elected Manhattan Borough President in 1949 with Tammany support, after serving as chair of the City Planning Commission. His decision to run for mayor caused a dispute among the county bosses, bringing opposition from Brooklyn and Queens, but blessings from Manhattan and the Bronx, the latter getting him elected. Through the first half of his three-term tenure at City Hall, Wagner dispensed a bounty of patronage through the notorious Tammany leader Carmine De Sapio, and just enough jobs to keep Bronx boss Edward Flynn content with the choice he had made at election time. Wagner also gave the machine a semblance of New Deal respectability.

Fixed on his father's legacy, Wagner had promised to pass a "Little Wagner Act" for organized labor in New York, and to carry on programmatic commitments for a "Little New Deal." With Dwight Eisenhower in the White House and Republican Thomas Dewey in the governor's mansion, this would have to be a local bootstrap effort on the part of the city administration. Wagner delivered.

In his first year as mayor, he issued an Interim Order declaring that city employees "had full freedom of association . . . to negotiate the terms and conditions of employment," granting to city workers the unionization and collective bargaining rights that his father had given to private sector employees on a national level.[29]

In 1958, at the beginning of his second term, Wagner signed Executive Order 49, which empowered a newly created city Department of Labor, controlled by the mayor, to certify exclusive bargaining rights to particular groups of representatives. In so doing, Wagner granted himself the authority not only to administer collective bargaining, but also to recognize which labor leaders were personally empowered to negotiate on behalf of city workers. The era of municipal labor was officially launched. Wagner, single-handedly, made it happen.

An astute politician, Wagner understood that the power of the bosses to deliver votes was waning. And there was always the possibility that one of the scoundrels would do something to embarrass him. In 1959, reformers had taken seven of thirty-three district leadership positions against Tammany; Carmine De Sapio had won his own district by only 600 votes out of 9,000 cast.[30] In addition to fulfilling deeply felt philosophical commitments that were part of his birthright, aligning with labor was a better investment in Wagner's political future. In 1961, Wagner asked De Sapio to step down as county leader of the Democratic Party. It was a bold move by Wagner against the man who had helped him attain power and with whom he had shared it so grandly.

Tammany put up State Comptroller Arthur Levitt Sr. to oppose the incumbent mayor in the 1961 primary. Wagner defeated him handily. The machine lost fourteen of sixteen contested district leadership positions to boot, including De Sapio's.[31] The stubborn old boss tried to make a comeback in 1963, but this time he was stopped by a young reformer from the Village Independent Democrats by the name of Edward Koch. The infamous man behind the dark sunglasses was later convicted in a bribery scandal involving local judgeships. Wagner, concerned that his falling out with Tammany might hurt him with Irish and Italian voters in 1961, turned to his union friends for help in winning a third term. Harry Van Arsdale, President of the Central Trades and Labor Council, came through, founding the Brotherhood Party, a labor coalition that mobilized blue collar workers and assured Wagner an additional ballot line.

The election of 1961 marked a turning point in New York City politics. Get-out-the-vote campaigns, which for more than a century had been efficiently carried out by county political machines, were eventually assumed by organizations representing municipal workers. Office seekers who once vied for the good graces of the party bosses increasingly sought the favor of union chiefs who spoke for teachers, policemen, firefighters, sanitation men, transit workers, office workers, and hospital employees.[32]

As mayor, Wagner moved forward with the thrust of municipal reforms that had begun under La Guardia a generation earlier. He adopted a "Career and Salary Plan" that rationalized job titles, career paths, salaries, and benefits, fully implementing a merit system for city personnel.[33] He recruited former Roosevelt advisor and civil service reformer Luther Gulick to serve in a newly created position of City Administrator. In 1961, Wagner adopted a revised City Charter that further consolidated power in the office of the mayor. By transferring oversight of public works projects from the borough presidents' offices to his own, Wagner was able to significantly reduce the influence of the county bosses and advance a process of municipal centralization that began with La Guardia and has proceeded largely unabated through the mayoralty of Michael Bloomberg.[34]

Wagner was especially attentive to the redistributive aspects of the New Deal pledge to improve the lives of middle class and less advantaged New Yorkers. During his tenure, Wagner built five new city hospitals and 123,000 units of public or publicly aided housing.[35] He was instrumental in creating the Mitchell-Lama Housing Cooperative with the state, a program in which public loans and subsidies were given to private developers as an incentive to build means-tested affordable housing. Mitchell-Lama was a departure from the New Deal formula, which, as La Guardia insisted, was wholly public, but it was a harbinger of things to come when federal decision-makers decided to further divest from social programs. From 1955 through the 1970s, 105,000 housing units were built under its urban renewal programs.[36] In 1957 the City Council passed a law prohibiting private landlords from discriminating by race, color, national origin, ancestry, and religion. It was the first comprehensive law of its kind in the country.

Under Wagner, New York City also boasted the most generous public assistance program in the country, making it a destination for Puerto Ricans and Southern blacks who could not get aid elsewhere. This commitment preceded the inception of President Lyndon Johnson's Great Society programs, under which Washington assumed most of the costs for social services. Once again, New York City was ahead of the country in extending a helping hand to people in need. In order to finance his ambitious projects, Wagner persuaded Albany to allow him to impose a new sales tax, business taxes, and nuisance taxes on items such as cigarettes, meals, and taxis. It also granted Wagner permission to borrow, borrow, borrow.

Wagner presided over New York at a time when the civil rights movement was coming into its own. Ten years after the landmark *Brown v. Board of Education* desegregation ruling was handed down by the United States Supreme Court, attention was focused on schools. Whereas students in the South were segregated by law, racial isolation in the North was a function of segregated housing. New York was no exception. The Brooklyn chapter of the NAACP sponsored massive demonstrations and crippling school boycotts. In response to demands from a newly empowered teachers union, Wagner funneled money into education to raise salaries, improve services, and construct 300 new buildings. To the delight of advocate groups such as the United Parents Association and the Public Education Association, he also remained firmly committed to a governance arrangement that gave the school system virtual autonomy from City Hall. For the mayor, such a structure was a political convenience that allowed him to remain aloof from controversial battles over racial integration.[37]

When it came to race, Wagner seemed to take a page from the playbook written by La Guardia. He appointed more African Americans and Puerto Ricans to high-level government posts than any of his predecessors. Also like La Guardia, however, he treated minority constituents as a substrata of mainstream politics. It was not so difficult to do that in a segregated city where whites were still a true numerical majority of the city population. He dispensed most of his black patronage through J. Raymond Jones, the crafty Tammany-based political entrepreneur of Harlem, and to a lesser extent through Gardner Taylor in Brooklyn. The arrangement kept minority voters aligned behind Wagner, but it was not enough.

As the civil rights movement gave way to demands for "Black Power," militant leaders in the minority community rejected handouts from the white power structure. They wanted to control their own institutions; their demands for change became angrier. Matters finally came to a head in the summer of 1964, two weeks after President Johnson signed the historic Civil Rights Act, when a white off-duty police lieutenant shot and killed a fifteen-year-old black boy in Harlem. The community erupted into five nights of violence and destruction. Gangs plundered 125th Street, then turned up Lenox Avenue to inflict more chaos. The rioting spread to Bedford-Stuyvesant, Brooklyn. The disorder finally ended with a blunt show of force by the police that further enraged the black community.

In a now familiar manner, the stormy episode made the issue of police brutality a central focus of attention in the city and beyond. Local activists demanded the resignation of Police Commissioner Michael Murphy and the creation of a civilian review board to investigate allegations of brutality and misconduct. Like La Guardia, Wagner's response to discontent in Harlem was sympathetic but inadequate. He defended his police commissioner and an existing review board composed entirely of police personnel. The old Tammany hand-turned-reformer was beginning to appear out of his element. His cautious incremental style of decision-making could not keep pace with the rapidly changing politics of the time.

In January 1965, as Wagner began his last year in office, the *Herald Tribune* ran a four-month series of articles called "New York City in Crisis." It drew a portrait of a city with fleeing businesses, a middle class on the run, a smoldering

Harlem, rising crime, a lethal drug epidemic, a more dependent population, unsafe streets, dirty sidewalks, ailing hospitals, an expensive bureaucracy, crumbling infrastructure, polluted environment, growing debt, and a political system incapacitated by one-party rule. The series was edited by Barry Gottehrer, who compiled its contents into a small book later that year.[38] The book carried jacket endorsements from Kenneth Clark, the black psychologist from Harlem who had given persuasive testimony in the landmark *Brown v. Board of Education* Supreme Court decision; Whitney Young Jr. of the National Urban League; Franklin D. Roosevelt Jr.; Republican Senator Jacob Javits; and Republican Congressman John V. Lindsay.

The series was not just a statement of findings; it was a politically motivated personal indictment designed to discourage Wagner from seeking a fourth term. In one early essay, Congressman Lindsay warned that Mayor Wagner's inept leadership could transform New York into a second-class city. Lindsay believed he could do a better job—as did John Hay Whitney, the owner of the *Herald Tribune,* who became one of Lindsay's major financial backers, when the legislator from the Upper East Side Silk-Stocking District finally declared his candidacy for mayor. And so did the series editor Barry Gottehrer, who would become one of the young mayor's top aides.

Like Fiorello La Guardia, John Lindsay was a Republican running for mayor in a Democratic city, so he entered the race of 1965 as a Fusion candidate. Like La Guardia, Lindsay had developed a progressive congressional profile in his earlier career, joining with other liberal Republicans—at a time when the label was not an oxymoron—to support the passage of the Civil Rights Act of 1964, the Voting Rights Act of 1965, and landmark Great Society legislation designed to address the social needs of many Americans. Like La Guardia, Lindsay had an ally in the White House who supported his programmatic priorities—even though the independent-thinking mayor never hesitated to speak his mind on issues that divided them, such as the Vietnam War.

Unlike any New York mayor before him, John Lindsay fearlessly took on the issue of racial inequality and stood up to the ugly political backlash it would foment throughout the rest of his career. Unlike all but maybe a few leading politicians in his time, John Lindsay took action against gender discrimination, broadly defined to include women, gays, and lesbians. Lindsay's aggressive approach to race often put him at odds with the same labor leaders who embraced the moderately progressive politics of Robert Wagner. As mayor, John Lindsay assumed the role as a spokesperson for the needs of not just his own city, but for all of urban America.[39]

There was little ambiguity about Lindsay's intentions. The young congressman from Manhattan used his first campaign speech in May 1965 as an occasion to denounce police brutality and declared that if elected he would appoint a civilian review board to hear complaints.[40] Intended to assure the city's growing black and Puerto Rican populations that they would finally have a chief executive who heard their concerns, the speech also set the acrimonious terms of the relationship he would have with the Patrolmen's Benevolent Association (the officers union), and much of organized labor for that matter.

So far as the labor chiefs were concerned, following Robert Wagner as mayor would be difficult for any politician. Wagner had not only recognized their unions, he authorized each and every one of them to speak for their workers, making them into political powerhouses. Lindsay's patrician Upper East Side manner did not help matters in the rough-and-tumble world of New York ethnic politics. Lindsay could also lend a deaf ear to their concerns, which was self-defeating. However you sliced it, he was not their kind of guy, especially if he was expecting them to make concessions on racial issues not raised in the past.

To Lindsay's good fortune, Wagner decided not to seek a fourth term. Robert F. Kennedy's 1964 acquisition of a U.S. Senate seat in New York blocked the chance for Wagner to pursue the only other job he could have wanted to cap his career, diminishing his incentive to stay in office. His wife's death that same year finally sapped him of the energy needed to make another run.

Lindsay entered the contest as a Republican, with a cross nomination on the Liberal Party line, an organization with labor roots in the garment industry that dated back to the La Guardia days, and was still philosophically true to its own label. He identified himself as a progressive, which, to wealthy Republicans who supported him, meant another chance to install efficient, professional, non-partisan government.[41] His major financial backer in the race was the liberal Republican governor Nelson Rockefeller, who was looking for a junior partner in the city as he planned his own bid to take the party's nomination for president. Lindsay had aspirations of his own, though, and was not interested in being anybody's sidekick, so it did not take long for the relationship between the two Republicans to deteriorate into a public rivalry once Lindsay took office.[42] Lindsay eventually ran his own disastrous campaign for president at the end of his second term.

Lindsay's major opponent in the 1965 mayoral election was Democrat Abraham Beame, an accountant and career civil servant from the Brooklyn clubhouse who had been Wagner's budget director before being elected City Comptroller in 1961. Lindsay was also opposed on the Conservative Party line by the right-leaning celebrity intellectual William F. Buckley, who crusaded to save the state GOP from the election of another liberal leader, and capitalized on Lindsay's hostility with the police union as the public became increasingly alarmed about rising crime.

Lindsay conducted an unorthodox campaign. Lacking a clubhouse operation that could usually be relied on to get Democratic voters to the polls, he set up his own volunteer organization of 122 storefronts, manned mostly by reform-minded Democrats. They were joined by Republicans who either sympathized with Lindsay's progressive posture, or were desperate finally to elect one of their own. Lindsay also recruited media genius David Garth, who took advantage of Lindsay's movie star good looks to run the first successful television campaign in city history, changing the nature of local elections forever. Lindsay won with a slim 43.3 percent share of the total to defeat Beame (39.5 percent) and Buckley (12.9 percent). According to Harris poll data, he drew support from a diverse constituency usually identified with the Democratic base—garnering 40 percent of the Jewish vote, 40 percent of the African-American, 40 percent of the Catholic, and 25 percent of the Puerto Rican, but with no commanding majorities. He took 61 percent of the vote among WASPs.[43]

There was no labor leader closer to Robert Wagner than Michael Quill, a cantankerous Irish immigrant with a thick brogue who was president of the Transport Workers Union. Even before Wagner granted collective bargaining rights to municipal unions, the city was negotiating with representatives of the subway and bus workers who had originally been employees of the privately owned transit lines. As John Lindsay was taking the oath of office on New Year's Eve with La Guardia's widow by his side, Quill called a strike that closed the transit system down for twelve days. No labor leader would have pulled a move like that on Robert Wagner, but Lindsay was a target. He had already set himself up on the wrong side of labor when he took on the PBA during the campaign. Quill personally despised the well-born mayor and his Ivy League (Yale) pedigree. When Quill finally ended the walkout with a generous settlement in hand, he proved to other union negotiators that militancy pays off.[44]

During Lindsay's first term, the city was hit with a nine-day sanitation strike that filled the streets with mountains of rotting garbage. During his second term, police officers and firefighters staged work slowdowns that threatened public safety. Labor militancy spread beyond the municipal workforce. Because of contract disputes at the state level, bridge operators left drawbridges open for two days causing traffic mayhem, while workers at treatment plants let raw sewage pour into city waterways. In the private sector, workers went out on strike in the airline, construction, newspaper, and electrical utilities industries, as did cab drivers, deliverymen, oil truck drivers, and gravediggers.

Whatever the merits of the union pleas (and they were debatable), organized labor, a significant link in the progressive coalition, was on its way to developing a reputation as being a public menace in a town that was instinctively pro-worker. More damaging to the possible advent of a broad progressive coalition, the most spectacular controversies that emerged between Mayor Lindsay and the unions revolved around race. A year after his election, the PBA organized and won a popular referendum that prohibited the use of civilian personnel to hear complaints about police misconduct, further antagonizing the relationship between officers and minority communities.[45]

In 1968, the United Federation of Teachers (UFT) called three teacher strikes—the longest lasting for five weeks—after twelve white teachers and six administrators were transferred from their jobs by black administrators in Brooklyn's Ocean Hill-Brownsville experimental school district without being afforded the due process protections to which they were entitled. Ocean Hill-Brownsville was one of three demonstration districts that had been set up as an experiment in community control. It was taken over by a group of militants who believed that the white teaching staff was out of touch with the educational needs of the black students who attended the schools. The dismissals drew an angry reaction from UFT President Albert Shanker. Shanker had been one of the few union leaders in the city who supported Lindsay's attempt to create a police review board, and his predominantly Jewish membership was more sympathetic to the mayor's liberal agenda than were most other city workers. Amid countercharges of racism and anti-Semitism between teachers and school administrators, the Ocean Hill-Brownsville episode was one of the most divisive in city history, creating a schism between blacks and Jews—and within a nascent progressive coalition—that would take years to heal.[46]

Lindsay did not step away from the battle over race. Whereas Robert Wagner defended the civil service merit system as a tool to curb patronage and recruit qualified employees, Lindsay challenged the written exams as an unfair barrier to hiring more blacks and Puerto Ricans. In fact, Lindsay used his executive power to circumvent civil service rules and hire more minorities, provoking accusations of favoritism.[47] He made conspicuous appointments to register his disapproval of the white ethnic enclaves that controlled the administrative hierarchies of agencies. For his first cabinet appointment, he selected Robert Lowery, a black firefighter, as commissioner in the Fire Department, the most segregated agency in the government, sowing deep resentment among the rank and file. Lindsay's internal battles over race inside the government were ever spilling out into the larger community. When white residents in Queens opposed the construction of integrated public housing, Lindsay brought in a young lawyer by the name of Mario Cuomo to settle the dispute. The project moved forward.[48]

Previous progressive mayors might have avoided such conflicts. The pitched battles certainly disrupted the civic peace. But how else would change occur if political leaders were not willing to take unpopular stands on issues that could no longer be put aside? Lindsay did the same on issues concerning gender. When McSorley's, the storied drinking establishment located in the East Village,

refused to amend its "male only" policy in 1970, Lindsay signed a local law prohibiting discrimination against women in public accommodations. He subsequently issued an executive order requiring city contractors to take affirmative
action to eliminate sex discrimination in hiring. In 1971, after the City Council
refused to pass a bill outlawing employment discrimination against homosexuals, Lindsay stepped in with an executive order to do the same—the first such
government provision of its kind anywhere in the country.

Lindsay was reelected in 1969 with 42 percent of the vote in a three-way race
against Democrat Mario Procaccino (33.8 percent), who ran a weak campaign,
and Republican senator John Marchi (22.1 percent), who had beat the incumbent mayor in a primary. This time running as a Liberal-Independent, Lindsay
won by wide margins among blacks (85 percent) and Puerto Ricans (65 percent), while his Jewish support remained at about 45 percent.[49]

Yes, New York has a habit of leading the nation in progressive causes. As we have
seen, such causes are more likely to gain traction when local leaders have a partner in Washington. Federal intervention is more probable in troubled times, and
the sixties were troubled times. The country was torn by protests against racial
inequality, and cities were powder kegs of the frustration being vented. The riot
that occurred in Harlem in 1964 seemed like a minor disruption the following
year when the community of Watts in Los Angeles exploded in rage and was
nearly burnt to the ground following an incident between a white policeman
and a black motorist.

Violent outbursts against people and property became a rite of summer in
urban America. National Guard troops with bayonets mounted on the tips of
their rifles were routinely summoned to restore order. Riots broke out in thirty-
eight cities in 1966. The most devastating occurred in 1967 when parts of
Detroit and Newark literally went up in flames. Riots also occurred in Chicago,
Cleveland, Philadelphia, Milwaukee, Atlanta, and Minneapolis. A Commission
on Civil Disorders appointed by President Johnson in 1967 recorded 187 disturbances that year.[50] Johnson's selection of John Lindsay as vice chair of the
panel anointed the New York mayor as a national spokesperson for America's
troubled cities. Lindsay was able to keep New York relatively calm with his
famous walking tours in minority neighborhoods where he was often greeted
as a hero. Thanks to LBJ, he backed up his personal gestures with concrete
programs.

Lyndon Johnson had idolized Franklin Roosevelt. As a master of the legislative process, he was at least Roosevelt's equal. Roosevelt had mobilized Congress
to respond to a national depression that affected every American. It made him
popular and enhanced his power. Johnson's great achievement, against steeper
odds, was to get Congress to lift the burdens of discrimination and neglect from

the shoulders of a small conspicuous minority of Americans, most of whom had been legally disenfranchised from the voting booth. The Texas politician knew that his Civil Rights and Voting Rights laws would make him and the Democratic Party unpopular in the South, and some parts of the North and West, but he proceeded, with great effect.

Johnson declared war on poverty in 1964. What happened after that was arguably the most impressive demonstration of presidential leadership in history. He proposed 200 pieces of legislation to the 89th Congress and got 181 (90.5 percent) enacted.[51] The array of programs touched all aspects of American life, most of which we now take for granted, some of which disappeared under subsequent presidents: food stamps, Medicare, Medicaid, elementary and secondary education, bilingual education, higher education, preschool, housing, immigration reform, law enforcement, high speed transit, clean air, clean water, manpower training, child safety, urban mass transit, auto safety, farms, Appalachia, the wilderness, community health, vocational rehabilitation, rent supplements, a minimum wage, the arts and humanities, drug rehabilitation, bail reform, drug control, and affirmative action.[52]

Later on, Johnson's avalanche of domestic legislation addressed age discrimination, increased Social Security benefits, public broadcasting, college work-study, summer youth programs, product safety, fair housing, school breakfasts, aid to handicapped children, consumer protection, and vocational education. Recognizing cities as a national priority, Johnson created the Department of Housing and Urban Development. He appointed Robert Weaver as secretary, the first black man to ever hold a Cabinet position in the federal government.

Lyndon Johnson understood better than most that if black Americans were going to be full participants in the American promise, they would need more than rights and programs. They needed—as militant activists insisted—power to control their own destinies. The Community Action Program (CAP) administered by Johnson's Office of Equal Opportunity (OEO) required the "maximum feasible participation of the poor" in antipoverty programs. Federal funds were directly appropriated to more than a thousand local corporations in cities whose boards were locally elected.[53]

To the dismay of local officials, Johnson's method of appropriation put federal funds in the hands of some of the most combative and inexperienced neighborhood activists who were assuming control in their own communities. These same black activists had been forced to sit on the sidelines of urban power structures controlled by white ethnic coalitions. The old guard was not ready to let go. Robert Wagner was one of the mostly Democrat signatories of the resolution adopted by the United States Conference of Mayors in 1965, accusing the OEO of fostering "class struggle" and demanding that antipoverty monies be put under their control. Johnson could not ignore his fellow Democrats. Congress eventually acceded to the conference's wishes and amended the law with no opposition from the White House.

As mayor, John Lindsay gravitated to the idea of community empowerment as a means to overcome the political alienation of people who lived in poor segregated communities. He sought to establish neighborhood institutions that connected local residents with decision-makers in city agencies. When he proposed setting up neighborhood city halls, the Democratically controlled City Council rejected the idea as an attempt to rival their local clubhouse organizations. He subsequently established task forces and eventually an Office of Neighborhood Government that placed high-ranking officials from his administration in communities to reach out to residents and give them better access to service providers.

Although Lindsay initially embraced the community corporations created by the federal OEO under the CAP program as a way to reach neighborhood leaders, he also got burnt by their belligerent style and mishandling of federal monies. He, like other urban chief executives, was relieved when President Johnson's Model Cities Program replaced the "maximum feasible participation" language of CAP with a less ambitious expectation of "widespread citizen participation," and put funding under the control of City Hall.[54] The program did encourage community-based planning for the coordination of housing, education, health, recreation, and employment services.

In 1969, as he was up for re-election, Lindsay reluctantly signed a local law that established sixty-two community boards with advisory power on matters pertaining to planning, budgeting, and service delivery. The plan was adapted from one that Robert Wagner had instituted when he was Manhattan Borough President in 1953. Like Wagner's Manhattan arrangement, it gave the respective borough presidents the power to appoint all local board members. The following year, Lindsay proposed a new law that would have merged the community boards with the neighborhood task forces he had created, and would have shared the power of appointment among the mayor, the borough presidents, and City Council members. He further suggested that eventually the boards might be directly elected by community residents, but neither proposal was ever taken up.

In 1972, Governor Nelson Rockefeller appointed a State Charter Commission for New York City. An outgrowth of the community revolution that had been unfolding for nearly a decade, the charge of the panel was "to encourage genuine citizen participation in local city government."[55] He selected state senator Roy Goodman as chair, a liberal Republican from Lindsay's former congressional district who had served as finance commissioner in Lindsay's administration. Goodman was determined to incorporate into the charter features of community government that already had been adopted by local law under Lindsay's tutelage. By the time the work of the commission was completed in 1975, other concerns emerged that had to be addressed. The city had fallen victim to a fiscal crisis that put it on the brink of bankruptcy, leading to demands for more managerial scrutiny.

The Goodman charter of 1975 represents the only significant break in a pattern of governance that had begun to centralize power in the office of the mayor since the Thatcher Commission appointed by La Guardia in 1935.[56] Adding community- and borough-level boards with advisory powers over land use, budgeting, and service delivery, it institutionalized a feature of decentralization that had not formally existed in the charter. As John Lindsay had originally suggested, community boards were also staffed with district managers who chair service cabinets composed of local administrators from city agencies who work together to coordinate services on a neighborhood level.

The 1975 charter also curbed the discretion of the mayor. He was now required to present a balanced preliminary budget to both the Board of Estimate and the City Council. He was no longer permitted to vote on the budget as a member of the Board of Estimate, nor could he veto reductions made by the board or the Council. He could veto increases the board and the Council made, but his veto could be overridden by either a simple majority vote in both bodies or a two-thirds supermajority in either body. The mayor also was required to submit an annual management report to the two other branches of the government. In order to improve the council's analytic capability to monitor city services, a Legislative Office of Budget Review, modeled after the Congressional Budget Office, was created. The president of the City Council, still a citywide elected office, was assigned new responsibility to serve an ombudsman function.

The song of community government was still in the air, but, with the fiscal crisis looming, its sounds were soon drowned out by calls for greater accountability.

John Lindsay took seriously the promise he had made to progressive Republicans to run the government more efficiently and effectively. He recruited the most talented team of managers the city had ever seen.[57] So called "whiz kids" were leaving the federal government—an interesting place itself back then—to take on the municipal bureaucracy in New York. They set up project management teams, created "superagencies" to better coordinate services, developed the latest program planning and budgeting systems (PPBS), and implemented a productivity program that became the foundation for the present city management plan and reporting system for city agencies. New York was the first place in the country to have an Environmental Protection Administration—before the word "environment" became an ordinary part of the vocabulary in government circles. When Lindsay's managers could not come up with answers to operational problems on their own, they brought in consultants from The Rand Corporation and McKinsey to lend their expertise.

Sound management was not enough, however, for a city whose social conscience was misaligned with the changing economy. Between 1960 and 1965, 800,000 middle class whites departed New York City, mostly for the suburbs, and they were replaced by a near equal number of blacks and Puerto Ricans, who were more dependent on government services and less capable of contributing to the tax rolls. The erosion of a middle class tax base was exacerbated by the loss of 100,000 manufacturing jobs between 1959 and 1964. By the end of Lindsay's second term, these job losses would triple in volume.[58] The hopeful mayor made a gallant bid to restore small industries and revitalize the city's once vibrant port, which for generations had provided decent jobs for the unskilled laborers who were still arriving in droves; but, with technology, automation, and globalization taking hold, economists deemed these well-intentioned efforts to be countercyclical and therefore futile.

City planners had hoped that the bleeding within the blue-collar sector would be offset by a growth in office jobs, but declines occurred there also. Between 1967 and 1974, forty *Fortune 500* companies abandoned New York, taking with them four of the seven corporate headquarters that had just relocated to the city between 1968 and 1971.[59] Departures by name brand companies such as American Can, PepsiCo, and Shell Oil contributed to a general perception that New York was in decline and no longer a good place to do business. Lindsay attempted to balance the budget by imposing new personal income and commuter taxes and increasing sales and business taxes, but these burdens only gave revenue-producing corporations and families more incentives to flee.

Lindsay was the first mayor to blur the boundaries between public and private construction through the process of incentive zoning, which granted developers the opportunity to build higher and bulkier buildings in return for amenities such as public space at no direct cost to the public.[60] The practice was certainly innovative. It, however, also paved the way for bigger deals between the city and the private sector, which in the hands of greedier developers and complicit politicians created opportunities for abusive practices with only meager rewards for the city.

Lindsay himself could not help but to remain hopeful and idealistic. At a time when American cities were being abandoned as wasteful, unlivable artifacts of another time, John Lindsay continued to believe that cities—with their abundance of human energy, their spectacular array of creative and performing arts, and their enriched cultural institutions—were the centers of civilization. He celebrated these features of urbanism as resources that make cities more attractive places to live and to work.[61] He understood, as no mayor before, their developmental potential in an era defined by despair.

Such bright rays of sunshine could not penetrate the dark fiscal clouds that hung overhead, however.[62] When Robert Wagner left office, the city was already a quarter billion dollars in debt.[63] During Lindsay's first four years in office, the operating budget of the city rose 49 percent, social service spending doubled, expenditures at the city university leapt by 121 percent, and health costs grew by 58 percent. Some of the increase was driven by labor costs, although New York's contract settlements were no more generous during this period of union militancy than those in other cities. Much of the growing deficit had to do with a spike in the welfare rolls that more than doubled to 200,000, increasing spending from $400 million to $1 billion. Although the federal government picked up a large portion of the social service budget, New York's benefits remained among the most charitable, and state laws required the city to pick up a disproportionate share of costs.

New York was unique among American localities for the range of public services it offered. It was the only city to run its own hospital and university systems. With the introduction of Medicare and Medicaid, the municipal hospital budget more than doubled to $1 billion between 1970 and 1975. Lindsay had expanded higher education programs in his first term and instituted a policy of open admissions in his second, so the university budget ballooned from $84 million in 1965, to $320 million in 1970, to $613 million in 1975.

Since the time Robert Wagner was mayor, New York had made it a practice of covering its excess costs by borrowing. The city took loans to cover its operating expenses, which, according to municipal law, are only supposed to be used to finance capital investments that will benefit future generations of taxpayers who eventually pay the loan. But borrowing was politically expedient. As Wagner was known to say, "A bad loan is better than a good tax." To make matters worse, city administrators habitually balanced their budgets by using accounting gimmicks to overstate anticipated revenues. It was the dirty little secret that everybody knew: the mayor, City Comptroller Abraham Beame, members of the City Council and Board of Estimate, Governor Rockefeller, state legislators, and many of the bankers who covered the loans. Lindsay had managed to restore budget shortfalls with new taxes during his first term, but he fell back on the old ways when the financial strains of the second term sank in.

Lindsay had been out of office nearly a year when it was discovered that New York was about to default on its debt and bankers were no longer willing to underwrite its notes and bonds. He was succeeded by Abraham Beame, the clubhouse politician who had served as Mayor Wagner's budget director before being elected City Comptroller. In order to avoid bankruptcy, Governor Hugh Carey snapped into action, and placed the municipal government in virtual receivership. Carey forced Beame to fire his close friend and deputy James Cavanaugh, and install

City Planning Commissioner John Zuccotti—a Lindsay holdover with credibility among all parties involved—as First Deputy Mayor.[64]

Carey had served in Congress for seven terms before becoming governor. A Brooklyn Democrat, he had been a key player in crafting President Johnson's legislative agenda, and was a tough-minded pragmatist. Gerald Ford was already completing Richard Nixon's term as president, and Carey was well aware that Washington Republicans were not about to become fast friends with New York in its moment of crisis. None of the major stakeholders in New York wanted to see the city declare bankruptcy. It would have been embarrassing to politicians in the city and state, with serious financial repercussions for both governments. Union leaders such as Victor Gotbaum and bankers such as David Rockefeller, who usually sat on opposite sides of the table, had a common interest in avoiding bankruptcy, because everybody knew that a federal bankruptcy judge had the power to reduce outstanding debt and abolish existing labor agreements. David's brother Nelson was now vice president, which softened the posture of the White House. He could gently remind his colleagues that if the credit markets in New York failed, the damage would spread nationally and internationally.

In order to secure federal aid from a reluctant President Ford, and calm Republicans in the Albany legislature, Governor Carey established several oversight institutions assigned the task of putting the city's fiscal house in order.[65] The basic premise behind their existence held that the city was no longer capable of governing itself. The two most significant institutions rolled out were the Municipal Assistance Corporation (MAC), and the Emergency Financial Control Board (EFCB).

The MAC board included five appointees of the governor and three of the mayor. The chair and most influential member of the board was Felix Rohatyn, an investment banker admired by Carey. A majority of members were recruited from the finance or business communities. MAC's charge was to restructure the city debt, monitor the city's fiscal health, and protect creditors. For all practical purposes, this meant that the city could not enter the credit market without MAC's approval. And MAC—Big MAC, as it became known—was empowered to collect city sales and stock transfer taxes and to issue its own bonds as a state agency.

The EFCB board was composed of the governor, the mayor, the city and state comptrollers, and three private citizens appointed by the governor, giving Carey control of the body. The EFCB had substantial authority to oversee the creation and implementation of the city financial plan. This meant it was officially empowered to approve revenue estimates, the operating and capital budgets, labor agreements, and all borrowing. What the late political scientist Robert Bailey called "The Crisis Regime," meaning MAC, the EFCB, and a host of other ad hoc agencies, constituted a profound transfer of authority from elected city officials to authorities controlled by state officials and private citizens. Bailey described the new governance arrangement as an era of "post interest group politics" with the emergence of private economic elites whose public power was now legitimized.[66] Functionally, The Crisis Regime lifted decision-making out of the reach of unions, policy advocates, racial and ethnic group activists, community organizers, and all those local political actors blamed for pushing New York City to spend beyond its means.

The policy outputs of the new institutions were of great consequence. On the positive side, they forced the city to discontinue accounting gimmicks, institute modern financial management systems, operate according to sound business principles, and balance its budget. In order to alleviate the financial stress, creditors reduced interest rates. The state assumed financial responsibility for senior colleges at the City University and a larger share of costs associated with hospitals, some social services, and the courts. Fiscal discipline also required significant cutbacks that would fall hard on poor and working people, such as increases in transit fares, tuition charges at the once-free City University, a 20 percent reduction in the workforce, and the closing of five city hospitals. Municipal unions put $3 billion in pension funds on the line to secure credit and back the badly needed loans that kept the city afloat.

The fiscal crisis of 1975 was a time of reckoning for sins of the past. What were these sins? It depends on whom you ask. There were no excuses for the lies, gimmicks, and poor management that made the Big Apple go bust. For conservative scholars such as Vincent Cannato, the graver sins exposed by the calamitous fiscal breakdown were philosophical and political. The crisis heralded the decline of the city and a crisis of liberalism. The political coalition brought together by Franklin Roosevelt in the 1930s had begun to disintegrate. As Cannato wrote, "Union members, urban Catholics, blacks, middle-class liberals, and white Southerners could no longer be held together under one tent."[67] Washington was no longer there to feed the grandiose expectations of ambitious politicians from New York. The infusion of federal funds had caused an artificial high that was bound to collapse once the flow was cut off. New York was the prime example of what went wrong in urban America; John Lindsay, its attractive mayor, was the personification of an era that had ended. The conversation about cities and their historic purpose had changed forever.

* * *

There was a sweet wisdom to the familiar localism that was bred in Tammany's mischievous ward-based structure. Its domains were small and within reach. They could be comforting to those from faraway places trying to make a go of it in an unfamiliar land. That same localism was conducive to a parochialism that could nurture prejudices against those who broke the common rules of conformity established by petty hierarchies of culture, race, religion, and gender. Those biases were first manifest when the machine turned its back on the Italians and Jews. When the door finally opened, the bundle of rewards behind it was already shrinking in the name of reform.

Just a crack of light could be seen—a few jobs here and there—by the small numbers of blacks and Puerto Ricans who were kept in their place in segregated communities during the La Guardia years. By the time people of color arrived in greater numbers, the white ethnics who had formed the foundation of the New Deal coalition were, thanks to the Wagners, exercising their power through the ranks of organized labor. The agencies they inhabited functioned like ethnic villages, and they harbored the same parochial biases as the comfortable neighborhoods from which the workers commuted to their jobs. Occasionally, union members could be counted on to throw up a line of defense and delay the march of progress when blacks and Puerto Ricans came knocking. John Lindsay discovered that the hard way, but persevered. Women, gays, and lesbians got a wink of attention for the first time; Asians were hardly noticed; transgendered never heard of. Somebody always gets caught behind a pause.

Only when government, Big Government, intervened did the march advance at a quickened pace. The starting gun would usually go off in New York, but if the shot wasn't heard in Washington, the energy would subside. Some would argue that this constant federal jolt was unhealthy and doomed to fail. The exuberance it generated was momentary, and the dependence it created could be destructive. They sought alternatives. We could ignore the vulnerable amongst us and let each man fend for himself to keep the costs of government down and out of people's business, or pretend that their condition is self-imposed, the result of flawed characters and sluggish personalities. That meaner impulse, evident when tribal battles reach a fever pitch, eventually reposes, and more generous sentiments that reside deep in the soul of New York can take over, for most New Yorkers either descend from humble newcomers or are counted among them, and such sympathies have a way of bursting out unexpectedly.

The instinct to progress rather than conserve prevails for a while. Then again, the march is interrupted, as idealist leaders learn to compromise. That is the nature of progressive politics and the delicate alliance that sustains it.

5

Fiscal Collapse, Dreams Deferred

Elected in 1977 as the 105th mayor of New York, Edward I. Koch presided over one of the most significant political and economic transitions in city history. The mood of the country had shifted to the right. A nearly bankrupt New York stood out as the poster child for all that was wrong with American liberalism. The government in Washington was ready to abandon cities and the people who lived in them. It was Ed Koch's job to convince Republican policymakers that the city could live within its means and become worthy of the federal loan guarantees it needed to remain solvent. These demands required him to adopt fiscal priorities that undermined the usual expectations of labor unions, racial minorities, and other components of the city's well-established progressive coalition. The conflicting pressures made him more dependent on business leaders who could be instrumental in restoring the city's fiscal health, and party bosses in the outer boroughs who still thrived on local patronage.

Koch wielded the most formidable mouthpiece of any mayor since La Guardia. He liked to speak his mind bluntly, and sometimes acerbically. To those who admired him, Koch's brash style personified the feistiness of the city he governed. To those on the receiving end of his harsh rhetoric—especially black and Hispanic leaders who challenged his policies—Koch could be seen as insensitive and divisive. He considered himself a "sane liberal," who tried to preserve basic tenets of the progressive creed that defined New York, while at the same time pragmatically negotiating a new set of realities that redefined what was possible. By the end of his third term, Koch faced unprecedented epidemics in crime, homelessness, crack cocaine addiction, an unmerciful outbreak of the AIDS crisis, and a downturn on Wall Street that undermined much of the progress he had made on the economic front.

Ed Koch was born in the Bronx in 1924 to immigrant Jewish parents from Poland.[1] When the family ran into hard times, they were forced to live with his uncle Bernie in Newark. Upon their return to the city, they moved to Ocean Parkway in Brooklyn, a veritable boulevard of Jewish dreams lined with trees, park benches and walking paths stretching from Prospect Park to Brighton Beach.

His father made a decent living as a furrier. Young Edward attended City College, won two battle stars as an infantryman during the war, and received a law degree from New York University. He lived at home until his early thirties. He finally took his own apartment in Greenwich Village to begin his legal and political careers, and stayed in the neighborhood until the end. He retained a modest rent-controlled apartment on Washington Place through his mayoralty with the thought of someday returning there when he had to leave Gracie Mansion. After his defeat in 1989, he took a rented apartment at 2 Fifth Avenue, off Washington Square, where he remained until he died in 2013.

Koch got his first taste of politics campaigning for Adlai Stevenson in 1956. After their candidate's loss, the group of progressives that formed Citizens for Stevenson revamped themselves into the Village Independent Democrats. The change gave them a new purpose: defeating the Tammany Hall organization run by Carmine De Sapio, who still dominated nominations and patronage in the Democratic Party. Koch made a name for himself as the man who deposed the legendary boss by outpolling him in two consecutive primary elections for the district leadership post in 1963 and 1965. The following year, Koch successfully ran for a seat on the City Council, but he had little interest in the work of the local legislature, finding it trivial. In 1968, he decided to make a bid for the congressional seat vacated by John Lindsay, whose Upper East Side district took in Greenwich Village.

As a member of the Council, Koch supported liberal causes such as rent control and school decentralization. He had backed John Lindsay's controversial appeal for a civilian review board in the Police Department, and endorsed Lindsay over Abe Beame for mayor in 1965, antagonizing some Democrats. He was an early supporter of Eugene McCarthy's bid for the White House until Robert Kennedy announced that he would run, when he broke with the Village Independent Democrats and switched sides. Koch was an adamant critic of the Vietnam War, and had traveled to Mississippi to march for civil rights. But Koch also learned to be sympathetic to the needs of more conservative working class people who populated the Italian communities in Greenwich Village, and who continued to vote for him after he defeated Carmine De Sapio. Running on the Democratic and Liberal Party lines, the freshman councilman managed to edge out his Republican opponent Whitney North Seymour Jr. for Lindsay's House seat by only three percentage points. It was a classic New York battle between the son of immigrants and a prominent blueblood from the prestigious legal establishment.

During his eight years in Congress, Koch proved that he could work well with people on both sides of the aisle, including conservatives who did not warm easily to an outspoken Jewish liberal from Greenwich Village.[2] As a member of the Banking and Currency Committee, he had a say on issues that mattered to

Wall Street constituents, and could also influence housing policy, which would remain a personal passion for him. He continued to oppose the Vietnam War and was an unwavering ally of Israel. An advocate for public transportation over automobile travel, Koch was particularly proud of an $89 million federal grant he brought to New York to improve subway service.

Koch also had a long record of supporting gay rights. He publicly chastised Police Commissioner Howard Leary after officers conducted a menacing raid at the Stonewall Inn on Christopher Street in 1969, and repeatedly testified on behalf of anti-discrimination proposals that came before the City Council. While in Congress, he co-sponsored a national anti-discrimination bill, and tried to change the tax code so that single individuals would be taxed similarly to married couples. He opposed a Defense Department policy that labeled homosexuals on their discharge papers, and collaborated with conservative senator Barry Goldwater in 1971 to pass the Privacy Act, which required the government to inform people of records kept on them by federal agencies, and grant them the right to inspect and correct the contained information.

Koch did not hesitate to use his congressional post as a perch from which to intervene in local political issues. One such occasion arose in 1970 when more than a thousand white middle class residents of Forest Hills came out to protest Mayor Lindsay's decision to build scatter-site housing for low-income families.[3] Koch, by then, had ill feelings toward Lindsay. He had gone out on a limb crossing party lines to support the liberal Republican's quest for the mayoralty; Lindsay did not return the favor neither when Koch ran for the City Council nor when he ran for the mayor's former congressional seat. But Koch's appearance at the demonstration was not about getting even—though he was certainly capable of such reckoning. Koch had something important he wanted to say.

Koch wanted to make his voice heard in sympathy with the protesters. He used the episode as a forum to demonstrate what he meant by calling himself a "sane liberal." Sure, he understood the merits of integrated housing. He knew that much of the resistance was racially motivated. He also appreciated why people who had worked hard to buy a home in a stable neighborhood—their most valuable possession—would not want to risk having their property values decline.

Koch sensed that the working class voters who had helped La Guardia (his favorite mayor also) build the New Deal coalition had tangible interests at stake when it came to the racial accommodations championed by Lindsay. He wanted them to know it. More important, he wanted to communicate his position to the clubhouse bosses who relied on these same people for votes and commanded what was left of the rusting political machines in the city's outer boroughs. These same individuals—the likes of Donald Manes in Queens, Meade Esposito in Brooklyn, and Stanley Friedman in the Bronx—would help him attain and retain the mayoralty.

Accountable to a cluster of state agencies established by Governor Hugh Carey as a result of the 1975 fiscal crisis, the city was in virtual receivership during the administration of Mayor Abe Beame. The day-to-day operations of government were handled by First Deputy Mayor John Zuccotti, who had been hand-picked by Albany leaders. Notwithstanding his compromised leadership, Beame thought he could be re-elected. Koch was one of many Democrats who thought otherwise.

The Democratic primary of 1977 attracted a crowded field of candidates. In addition to Koch and Beame, it included Mario Cuomo, liberal congresswoman Bella Abzug, Harlem's Percy Sutton, Puerto Rican icon Herman Badillo, and businessman Joel Harnett. That summer Beame's credibility was further eroded when the city went dark in a power blackout and thousands of rioters took to the streets and broke into local stores, making off with merchandise. *Time* magazine's cover story reported on a "Night of Terror" in which more than 2,000 stores were looted in predominantly black and Puerto Rican neighborhoods such as Harlem, Bedford-Stuyvesant, and the South Bronx, resulting in more than 3,500 arrests.[4] The city had already been panic-stricken by a maniacal serial killer known as *Son of Sam*, who had murdered six people and wounded six others.

Koch had a liberal voting record in Congress, but he took a hard line on crime and supported capital punishment. He made a point of the latter as he campaigned after the blackout, and insisted that if he had been mayor, he would have called out the National Guard to suppress the pillaging.[5] He was the only candidate in a contest among liberals trying to unseat Abe Beame willing to lean so far to the right. The tactic fit well with the strategy his campaign advisor David Garth crafted to appeal to more conservative outer-borough voters. As Garth well understood, it also fit Koch's personality—but it had a downside. Koch's inflammatory words about fighting crime and his railing against "poverty pimps" whom he claimed profiteered from social service programs brought accusations of race baiting from Percy Sutton and other black leaders.

Koch reaped endorsements from the *Daily News* and the *New York Post*. The latter had just been bought by Rupert Murdoch, who was determined to make the once-liberal tabloid into an influential conservative voice. The *New York Times* backed Mario Cuomo, who took a firm stand against the death penalty. Koch came in first (19.8 percent) in the seven-way race, followed closely by Cuomo (18.7 percent) and Beame (18 percent), with Abzug, Sutton, and Badillo not far behind.[6] The primary was followed by a nasty run-off in which somebody within the Cuomo campaign capitalized on rumors that Koch was gay (which he denied), and circulated literature urging people to "Vote for Cuomo, Not the

Homo," hoping to galvanize conservative support. Koch defeated Cuomo by a margin of 54.96 percent to 45.04 percent.[7]

When Cuomo chose to run in the general election on the Liberal Party line, Koch defeated him again: 49.99 percent to 40.97 percent.[8] Cuomo drew most of his support from Catholics, especially Italian voters. Koch drew most of his from Jews, some Irish voters, and a small number of African Americans and Puerto Ricans who did not stay home after the primary was decided.

Upon his swearing in on January 1, 1978, Mayor Koch had twenty days to prepare a four-year financial plan for the U.S. Treasury Department to comply with the terms of a short-term $2.6 billion federal loan the city had received under Mayor Beame. The loan repayment was due on June 30. Under the plan, the city had agreed to balance its budget according to accepted accounting principles, and renegotiate contracts that were about to expire with municipal labor unions. In return, the city asked Congress to provide it with additional long-term loan guarantees for rebuilding its infrastructure.

The new mayor convincingly preached the gospel of sacrifice and austerity from his first day in office. To the chagrin of President Jimmy Carter, he even invited Republican presidential candidate Ronald Reagan for a meeting at Gracie Mansion a month before the 1980 election, knowing he would need GOP members of Congress as the city clawed its way back to fiscal solvency. He developed an amicable relationship with the Republican senator from New York, Alphonse D'Amato. Koch meant what he said when it came to spending, and he got the loan guarantees he sought. He actually balanced the budget by the spring of 1981, a year earlier than required by Congress, prompting Standard & Poor's to restore the city's credit rating, but the cuts enacted went deep. Between 1979 and 1981, the size of the city workforce was shrunk from 192,465 employees to 188,457 through layoffs and attrition. These reductions were in addition to some 34,000 jobs that had been sacrificed since the onset of the fiscal crisis in 1975.[9]

Koch had been critical of how Governor Hugh Carey's Emergency Financial Control Board (EFCB) and Municipal Assistance Corporation (MAC) usurped local policymaking, characterizing the institutions as undemocratic. When he became mayor, he worked well with the two ad hoc agencies. Ironically, they empowered him to make tough fiscal decisions that other chief executives found difficult in the face of pressure from unions and other interest groups. The state institutions could do more than back him up. They could dictate and take the blame for unpopular decisions that politicians typically avoid; as non-elected bodies, their members were less concerned with political repercussions. To borrow a term from political scientist Theodore Lowi, the era of "interest group liberalism," when advocates with political clout could sway decisions in discrete areas of policy, had come to an end.[10] For better or worse.

Koch was not absolved from blame by the unions as he managed the city through a period of austerity, but he took their umbrage in stride. He surmised that the power of organized labor that peaked during the Wagner and Lindsay years was waning. On some level, the public understood that overly generous collective bargaining contracts contributed to the fiscal plight of the city. When the transit workers went out on strike in 1980, Koch defied them. He told city employees that they needed to show up for work, and encouraged others to do the same. He stood at the entrance of the Brooklyn Bridge, greeted workers who were trudging to their offices, and cheered them on. They cheered back with fists raised. The following year, Ronald Reagan abruptly fired 11,000 air traffic controllers when their union, PATCO, called an illegal strike. It was a raw act of union busting on the part of the new president, and it was carried out with minimal public outcry. The writing was on the wall: *the union movement was in decline.*

In order to appease blacks and Puerto Ricans, Koch appointed Basil Paterson and Herman Badillo to his administration as deputy mayors, but neither stayed on very long. Nine months into his second year at City Hall, the mayor was quoted in a *New Yorker* profile by Ken Auletta, accusing blacks of being "anti-Semites."[11] Koch also installed conservative economist Blanche Bernstein as head of the Human Resource Administration. Like the mayor (and President Reagan), she believed welfare perpetuated a state of dependency among the poor.[12] Between 1978 and 1979, she cut the benefits of over 100,000 people. More cantankerous than *Hizzoner* himself, she became so controversial that Koch eventually let her go. Contrary to promises he had made to Harlem politicians during his run-off campaign, Koch closed Sydenham Hospital on West 123rd Street in 1980. It was a decision he later regretted. Although it may have made sense from a budgetary perspective, Sydenham stood out as the first hospital in the country to grant staff privileges to black physicians. Harlem's leadership never forgave him.

Koch had been elected mayor with strong support among Jewish voters. As he looked ahead to a second term, he set out, with the help of county leaders from the outer boroughs, to add to his base those Italian and Irish Catholics who had voted in 1977 for Mario Cuomo. The broad coalition he built included white ethnic middle class voters, joined by financial executives who were impressed with his restoration of the city's fiscal health, and real estate developers sympathetic to his pro-growth agenda.[13] Except for a brief interval with the election of David Dinkins in 1989 for one term, this realignment shaped the contours of mayoral politics in New York right up until Bill de Blasio's election in 2013.

In 1981, the incumbent mayor was so popular that he ran for re-election in both the Democratic and Republican primaries, winning 60 percent of the vote in the former contest and 66 percent in the latter.[14] With his name appearing on both major party lines in the general election, Koch took more than 75 percent of the vote.[15] It was the largest popular landslide in city history. He swept white districts with majorities of ten or twelve to one; he lost black districts by margins of five to one. Speaking at his victory celebration, he cited "racial unity" as a goal of his second term.[16]

Despite his conservative pronouncements, Koch believed that government had an obligation to help people who were truly in need. He urged the state to assume responsibility for Aid to Families with Dependent Children. He was one of the first politicians to advocate the nationalization of health insurance, and resented Presidents Ford and Carter for their refusal to shoulder the costs of Medicaid, to which he attributed half the city's budget gap.[17] After Ronald Reagan declared in his 1981 inaugural address that big government is the problem rather than the solution to our national dilemmas, Koch denounced the president's policies as "a sham and a shame."[18]

Generally supportive of police in their efforts to curb record crime rates, Koch appointed the city's first black Police Commissioner, Benjamin Ward. In 1984, after a white police officer shot and killed Eleanor Bumpurs, a mentally disturbed elderly black woman who was resisting eviction from her apartment in the Bronx, Koch appointed a blue ribbon panel chaired by former deputy mayor John Zuccotti to review the policies and practices of the department. The mayor accepted a set of recommendations from the panel designed to upgrade managerial accountability, increase minority representation, improve training, and experiment with community policing.[19] Koch also prioritized public schools, insisting that the Board of Education, to which he appointed two of seven members, should allow him to choose his own Chancellor, Frank Macchiarola. A university professor with extensive government experience, and an outsider to the entrenched school bureaucracy, Macchiarola raised standards and improved student performance in reading and math.[20]

After the AIDS crisis became public in the early 1980s, the Koch administration came under intense criticism from the gay community for moving too slowly in addressing the disease. In his play *The Normal Heart* that opened in 1985, Larry Kramer portrayed the mayor as a callous, closeted homosexual who did not want to appear closely associated with the gay community. Koch responded with personnel changes in his administration, and he increased funding from $31 to $37 million annually for medical services, hospice care, education, housing, and research.[21] One of Koch's first acts after his election in 1977 (consistent with his congressional record) was to sign a broad executive order prohibiting discrimination against gays in employment, housing, credit, and services. After a state court struck down part of the proclamation as an excessive use of executive power, Koch stood up against opposition from powerful religious leaders to usher a law through a reluctant City Council sustaining the protections.

In the early eighties, New York City experienced its worst homeless crisis since the Great Depression. Unlike La Guardia, who had Franklin Roosevelt to help him through it, Koch had to do it mostly on his own. Before Lower Manhattan began to gentrify, Skid Row on the Bowery had a storied past. Inebriated derelicts begged, coerced, and charmed drivers along Third Avenue for coins to pay for their next bottle of cheap booze and, if they were lucky, a flophouse on cold winter nights. In the late seventies, the state, under pressure from advocates, had decided to release mentally ill patients from state institutions and place them in community-based homes. It sounded like a good idea at the time, for the places that warehoused these poor men and women were just horrible. Unfortunately, the state was never able to provide the community homes, and with the disappearance of single-room occupancy units that once provided shelter for them, many of the indigent population wound up living on the street. Their presence was no longer contained to the Bowery. Others ended up incarcerated.

In 1981, the city, in response to a class action suit, signed a consent decree agreeing to provide shelter and board for each homeless man (eventually expanded in 1983 to include all adults and families with children) who met state standards to qualify for home relief, and who "by reason of physical, mental, or social dysfunction is in need of temporary shelter."[22] The *Callahan* decree was part of a stream of litigation initiated by Robert Hayes, co-founder of the Coalition for the Homeless, that provided homeless people in New York with more legal protection than any other place in the country.[23]

In response to the crisis, the city converted armories into shelters for homeless men. Looking more like wartime hospital wards than homes, the facilities left a lot to be desired, but did offer warmth and sustenance. Desperate for immediate space, the city resorted to the use of "welfare hotels," which could be more seedy than the armories. A report completed by the Community Service Society estimated that the homeless population had grown to 36,000.[24] A survey of a large men's shelter conducted by the city Department of Human Resources in 1982 highlighted the diversification of the homeless population and the factors driving the problem—categorized as psychological (34 percent), economic (19 percent), alcoholic (6 percent), physical disability (6 percent), and drug use (2 percent).[25]

Following the recommendations of a report prepared under the direction of HRA commissioner William Grinker, the Koch administration experimented with jobs and training programs to supplement the provision of basic shelter to the homeless. It also began talks with Governor Mario Cuomo to launch a joint New York/New York program to stem the problem. Final negotiations for the plan would be made by Koch's successor, David Dinkins.

Throughout his incumbency, Koch struggled to fit the deeply ingrained progressive ethos of the city to the harsh realities of a dramatically altered political and economic landscape. Restoring the city's fiscal health involved more than cautious spending. It required the city to replenish the tax base that had been lost in prior decades because of commercial and middle class flight. School improvement was a piece of the strategy to make the city more attractive to businesses and families. Rebranding the image of the city through aggressive public relations was another.[26] In order to incentivize private sector investment in growth, the Koch administration offered tax abatements to businesses and developers. The success of projects such as the Times Square turnaround, which began under Koch, demonstrated that such outreach to the private sector could be effective in anchoring job-producing businesses.[27] This collateral tax relief, however, resulted in the loss of $1 billion in revenue between 1981 and 1990, leading to accusations of corporate welfare.[28]

The federal government was complicit in moving cities toward greater private sector reliance. Although the Nixon administration collapsed a cornucopia of Great Society urban programs into more broadly defined block grants made to state governments, it actually increased social spending by expanding social security benefits and creating a food stamp program. In 1973, however, Nixon called for a moratorium on new housing efforts. In the following year, Congress passed the Housing and Community Development Act that shifted the focus of policy away from building new units to a market-based strategy that subsidized needy families with "Section 8" vouchers that they could use to shop around on their own.

It was during the Carter administration that federal aid to cities actually began to decline, a trend further accelerated by President Reagan. Between 1977 and 1989, the percentage of New York City revenue derived from federal sources declined from 22 percent to 11 percent.[29] New regulations implemented under the Urban Development Action Grant (UDAG) program required that there be a firm commitment of private resources to a project before any federal monies were released. The Koch administration utilized UDAG funding to finance major projects such as the South Street Seaport in Lower Manhattan and the Metrotech Center in downtown Brooklyn. In 1986, Congress amended the tax code to grant credits to businesses that invested in below-market housing. Between 1981 and 1987, the Reagan administration reduced funding for housing by more than 70 percent, from $30 billion to $8 billion.[30]

During the 1970s, 321,000 units of housing had been lost in the city due to arson, landlord neglect, or tax delinquency.[31] Rather than abandon these buildings as other cities did, New York took possession of them (referred to as "in rem" housing) for conversion to public use. The newly formed Housing Preservation and Development Department became the owner and manager of more than 100,000 units in 10,000 buildings. The Koch administration experimented with a variety of approaches to housing, which would be his greatest legacy as mayor. Initially it used small grants, tax abatements, and low-interest loans to cultivate a decentralized network of grass-roots activists and community development corporations, city and state agencies, and private foundations to provide low-income housing in distressed areas.[32] Examples of such efforts include the Nehemiah Houses in East Brooklyn and the Abyssinian Development Corporation in Harlem.

Mayor Koch's full housing plan came together in 1985 when he announced a five-year effort that committed $4.4 billion in city money to build or rehabilitate 100,000 units. In 1989, he expanded the goal, pledging $5.1 billion for 252,000 units. On the public side, Koch's program set out to upgrade all buildings owned by the city, whether they were vacant or occupied. On the private side, it facilitated low-interest loans and property tax reductions for private owners to either renovate existing housing for middle- or low-income tenants, or to build new housing for sale in poor neighborhoods. By 1993, more than 100,000 units of affordable housing were either rehabilitated or constructed as a result of this initiative.[33] During the 1980s, New York spent more of its own money on housing than the next fifty largest cities combined.[34] The effort continued through the administrations of mayors David Dinkins and Rudolph Giuliani.

Koch was reelected to a third term in 1985 with 78 percent of the popular vote.[35] He commanded overwhelming margins among Jewish, Catholic, and, surprisingly, Puerto Rican voters, who at times showed more moderate to conservative leanings. Koch's popularity soon declined, however, and his third term unraveled in a series of disasters that followed one after the other. In early January, a corruption scandal involving patronage, bribery, extortion, and influence peddling was exposed. Although Koch himself was not personally accused of any crime, many of the party bosses with whom he allied were. As a result of aggressive prosecution led by U.S. Attorney Rudolph Giuliani, more than 250 city officials were indicted.[36] An element of high drama highlighted the corruption scandal when Queens Borough President Donald Manes, who was under investigation, committed suicide by plunging a knife into his chest.

Racial strife polarized the city in the winter of 1986 when three black men were brutally beaten by a white mob on Cross Bay Boulevard in Howard Beach, Queens. One of the victims, Michael Griffith, was fatally struck by an oncoming car when he ran into traffic trying to escape the attacks.[37] Soon thereafter, a little known agitator by the name of Al Sharpton led a 100-car motorcade through the neighborhood to protest the violence, where he and other demonstrators were cursed by local residents. Sharpton continued to lead disruptive protests throughout the city, the largest of which was a 5,000-person "Day of Outrage" march up Fifth Avenue scheduled for Martin Luther King Day. Koch had condemned the racial violence; he also ridiculed the marchers for stirring up trouble. Racial tensions were heightened again in his third term, when a white female jogger was allegedly gang raped by a group of black youths in Central Park, and a black man was fatally shot in Ozone Park, Queens, creating a ripe environment for Koch and Sharpton to denounce each others' provocations in the press.[38] Sharpton's Tawana Brawley fiasco involving her false claim of being raped by a gang of white men hit the newspapers at about the same time.

Although Koch was able to restore the jobs he had eliminated from the city payroll, his relationship with organized labor remained sour. Union leaders were particularly riled when Koch granted generous salary increases to his top managers, while negotiating frugal contracts for their members. To the dismay of progressives, the withdrawal of federal funding had the effect of reordering local spending priorities. A budget analysis conducted by the City Comptroller found that between 1978 and 1989, the proportion of dollars spent on redistributive services targeted to vulnerable populations dropped from 40.9 percent to 34.8 percent.[39] Gentrification had been a central feature of Koch's attempt to populate the city with a larger middle class, leading to speculation as to whether the city of the future would be less hospitable to more dependent populations. Koch's broad base of support allowed him to be less responsive to black voters, who chose to sit out his second and third elections. That changed when the Reverend Jesse Jackson became a candidate in the Democratic primary for president in 1988.

Koch had rebuked the charismatic minister from Chicago during his first presidential foray in 1984 because Jackson refused to repudiate anti-Semitic statements made by Black Muslim leader Louis Farrakhan. Jackson himself had referred to New York City as "Hymietown." Even though Jackson had distanced himself from Farrakhan by 1988, Koch said that Jews would have to be "crazy" to vote for him, irritating African Americans who had seen Jackson as their first serious candidate for the White House. While Massachusetts Governor Michael Dukakis won the statewide primary, Jackson came out ahead in the city, also beating Koch's preferred candidate Al Gore. More important, Jackson's candidacy motivated many black people in New York to register to vote. One key person behind that voter registration drive was Bill Lynch.

Lynch, the son of a Long Island potato farmer, had come to New York City to work as a political organizer—first at the community level, then within the labor movement. After serving as political director for Local 1707 of the American Federation of Federal, State, County, and Municipal Employees (AFSCME), he volunteered for the 1980 presidential campaign of Massachusetts senator Edward Kennedy. When he signed up to help Jesse Jackson in 1984, Dinkins was planning a 1985 run for the Manhattan Borough President post and tried to recruit Lynch to manage his campaign. Lynch stayed with the presidential campaign, but lent Dinkins a helping hand. After Dinkins was elected borough president, Lynch oversaw his transition team and became his chief of staff.

David Dinkins married into the Harlem political establishment in 1953 when he wed Joyce Burrows, his college sweetheart from Howard University.[40] Her father was a New York State Assemblyman active in the legendary Carver Democratic Club ruled over by J. Raymond Jones. Many local notables attended their wedding, including the incumbent mayor Vincent Impellitteri. A native of Jersey City, Dinkins served in the U.S. Marine Corps and graduated from Brooklyn Law School before starting his political career. He became a key operative in Jones's Carver Club, where he formed lifelong friendships with Charles Rangel, Basil Patterson, and Percy Sutton. They became famously known as Harlem's Four Horsemen. Dinkins was elected Democratic district leader in 1967 and retained the post for two decades. When Mario Procaccino secured the Democratic nomination to challenge Mayor Lindsay in 1969, Dinkins and his Harlem buddies broke ranks with the party and endorsed the Republican incumbent who also ran on the Liberal Party line.

His support for Lindsay notwithstanding, Dinkins, a product of clubhouse politics, remained a Democratic Party loyalist. As a reward for his service, Abe Beame offered Dinkins a job as Deputy Mayor in 1973. Dinkins was forced to withdraw his name from consideration when it was revealed that he had been negligent in paying his taxes. Two years later, Beame appointed Dinkins City Clerk, a patronage job in the municipal bureaucracy with little responsibility. Dinkins used the position as a base from which to advance his career ambitions. After two unsuccessful tries, he was elected Manhattan Borough President in 1985 when Andrew Stein vacated the position to run for President of the City Council.

David Dinkins was measured in his relationship with Jesse Jackson. Like other Harlem mainstream politicians, he did not want to offend liberal Jews whose votes he depended on. Although Dinkins served in an official capacity as county coordinator during Jackson's 1988 presidential campaign, he was reluctant to make public appearances with the inciteful preacher. But Jackson's growing popularity could not be ignored. In 1984, black voter turnout in the city leaped 83 percent to 293,000, from 160,000 in the 1980 presidential primary.[41]

Jackson was also redefining himself as a representative of organized labor, and he had the muscle to prove it. Two of the largest labor unions in the city had elected an African American and a Puerto Rican as their respective executive directors: Stanley Hill of DC 37 (AFSCME), which represented municipal workers and Dennis Rivera of Local 1199, which represented health workers. These two leaders reflected the changing profile of the city workforce and the increasingly progressive politics that was evolving in some corners. Both threw themselves into the Jackson camp. Rivera actually invited Jackson to use his union offices as a campaign headquarters—a first step on a longer journey taken by Rivera to assemble a progressive coalition in the city.

In 1989, Bill Lynch convinced Dinkins that Jesse Jackson's victory in the New York City primary provided them with a game plan for electing the city's first black mayor. Years later, a similar formula would be applied to bring Bill de Blasio to City Hall. The future mayor had been a young recruit in the volunteer army commanded by Lynch in 1989. De Blasio obviously retained something from the experience. Koch's apparent vulnerability drew other candidates into the primary contest: City Comptroller Harrison Goldin was the choice of the Brooklyn clubhouse; businessman and civic leader Richard Ravitch had the backing of the corporate community. In the end, the primary proved to be a two-way contest, with Dinkins defeating Koch by a wide margin (51 percent to 42 percent).[42] Relying on a strong field operation overseen by Lynch, Dinkins activated a dormant coalition of African Americans, Latinos, white liberals, and organized labor.[43]

In November, Dinkins faced U.S. Attorney Rudolph Giuliani, whose name appeared on both the Republican and Liberal Party lines. In a surprise move, outgoing mayor Edward Koch threw his weight behind the fellow Democrat who had cost him the nomination. A ballot measure to amend the City Charter, the most significant restructuring of the city government since the five boroughs were consolidated into a single municipality, brought a larger-than-usual turnout of voters to the polls. Dinkins also scored endorsements from the *New York Times*, the *Daily News*, and *Newsday*; Giuliani was favored by the *New York Post*. Bolstered by the same progressive coalition that gave him the Democratic Party spot and a share of former Koch supporters, Dinkins edged out Giuliani by less than three percentage points. It was the smallest margin of victory for any mayoral contest since 1905, when George B. McClellan defeated William Randolph Hearst.[44]

David Dinkins was the antithesis of Ed Koch. He was mild-mannered and soft-spoken. He shunned confrontation. He identified closely with organized labor and people who were most dependent on government to get by. Envisioning the city as a "Gorgeous Mosaic," he had hoped to bring people together in greater harmony. His position on racial issues was moderate. Although he took pride in being the city's first black chief executive, he denounced Louis Farrakhan's anti-Semitism and chided Al Sharpton for his antics during the Tawana Brawley imbroglio.[45] His deliberative style of decision making could be a liability in critical times, making him a target for the same news outlets that had endorsed him. One African-American scholar contends that Dinkins was a victim of negative stereotyping by a white-dominated press that routinely questions the competence and intelligence of black politicians.[46]

Dinkins's transition committee included close friends such as Basil Patterson, but it was chaired by Koch's Deputy Mayor Nathan Leventhal. MAC chair Felix

Rohatyn was also a member, signaling the crosswinds the new mayor faced. This dichotomy was also reflected inside the administration. Nobody had more influence on purely political matters than Bill Lynch, who served as Deputy Mayor for Intergovernmental Relations; however, the man with the title of First Deputy Mayor was Norman Steisel, who had worked for Mayors Beame, Lindsay, and Koch. Trained as an engineer, Steisel was a hard-nosed, data-driven manager who supervised the daily operations of the government. Philip Michael, who became budget director, had worked in municipal finance for Merrill Lynch, and was director of the state EFCB before joining the Dinkins team. These differing perspectives created the tensions within the administration that Bill de Blasio later spoke about when he looked back. They were widely reported in the press.

The internal tensions reflected a more fundamental political dilemma the Dinkins administration faced. The stock market crash of 1987 had a damaging effect on the city economy. The national recession that hit in 1990 made things worse. Between 1989 and 1992, New York lost 14 percent of its jobs through layoffs, largely in the financial sector, and the overall unemployment rate climbed to 13 percent.[47] Rents for office space cascaded down as vacancy rates shot up. Personal income tax receipts declined 25 percent, leaving a $1 billion budget gap.[48] In the meantime, the number of people on welfare peaked above one million in a city of less than 8 million. Ed Koch had been able to rely on his electoral base to navigate his way through narrow financial straits; David Dinkins's political base had different expectations. Ed Koch could depend on the backing of state monitors when he had to make tough budget decisions; the same overseers would become Dinkins's chief critics.

The administration's first budget proposal called for $800 million in new taxes and fees. Concerned about record crime rates, the mayor announced the "Safe Streets, Safe City" program that would cost an estimated $1.8 billion over four years partially funded by the state. Dinkins was also committed to improving social services. At the end of 1990, his labor negotiator had granted the teachers union a costly 5.5 percent salary increase, raising expectations for other city workers and anxiety among state watchdogs. Less generous contracts were subsequently negotiated with D.C. 37 and the Teamsters. At around the same time, the mayor announced that he might need to lay off 15,000 workers to balance the budget, throwing the union chiefs who had supported him into a rage, and confusing just about everybody else. Stanley Hill and Dennis Rivera wondered out loud why the mayor did not raise taxes on the rich to pay workers better.

The preliminary budget for the 1992 fiscal year projected a $2.2 billion shortfall, and the loss of 25,000 jobs through layoffs or attrition, with 10,000 slated for the school system. City debt had climbed from $11.5 billion to $17 billion, driving up the costs for debt service. President George H.W. Bush had promised to continue the same policies toward cities enacted by his predecessor, Ronald

Reagan. Dinkins publicly lamented that the partnership between Fiorello La Guardia and Franklin Roosevelt now had become a "sad remembrance" as the Bush administration "turned its back on New York."[49]

To make matters worse, the state faced its own budget gap from the recession, forcing Governor Mario Cuomo to announce he would reduce aid to the city by $400 million to $600 million. At that point, City Hall began talks with the unions asking for a delay in their previously negotiated pay increases. Workers in the Sanitation Department staged a slowdown after 447 men were laid off. Observing the deteriorating fiscal situation, Moody's downgraded the city bond rating, making it more difficult and costly to borrow.

In 1992, the state Financial Control Board intensified its monitoring of city operations to make sure that proposed cuts of $1.6 million, including cuts to social services the mayor had promised to improve, were carried out. Felix Rohatyn warned Dinkins that unless the city imposed a two-year tax freeze and eliminated thirty to thirty-five thousand jobs, MAC would not guarantee the financing of city bonds. If David Dinkins had any thoughts of implementing a redistributive approach to policy, such authoritative commands from above had to dampen them. Dinkins more or less agreed to comply, promising "to make sure our government is not bigger than its checkbook." Striking an agreement with both the City Council and state monitors, his 1993 budget included cuts in capital expenditures and maintenance, larger class sizes in the schools, and workforce reductions of 20,000 over four years.

In order to maintain some of his campaign promises, Dinkins was able to protect spending for health, police, and library services. By the end of his term, he actually cut 15,000 jobs and granted 180,000 other employees an 8.25 percent raise over three years.[50] These raises were premised on the implementation of productivity gains in city agencies, leaving labor representatives grumbling. By the end of 1993, city debt, including MAC obligations, exceeded $26 billion, a 35 percent increase over 1989. These were difficult financial times. Nobody involved could remain very happy for very long, and the mayor was a convenient object of everyone's discontent.

David Dinkins moved forward with Ed Koch's ambitious housing program, and tweaked it to make its "affordable" housing stock more affordable for people at lower income scales. He also kept awarding tax breaks to corporations in order to spur development, to the average tune of $144 million a year between 1990 and 1993—more than his predecessor.[51] He continued to provide homeless people with access to apartments the city acquired through its in rem program and gave them priority in NYCHA public housing projects. In 1993, Dinkins created a stand-alone Department of Homeless Services previously operated by the Human Resources Administration. Dinkins believed that the Koch administration had become too dependent on temporary shelters. Based on a report prepared by his office when he was the Manhattan Borough President, Dinkins argued that the long-term solution to homelessness was permanent housing.[52] As mayor, he discovered that strategy was easier said than done.[53]

Residents of public housing resented the fact that homeless people were given priority when apartments became vacant, and felt unfairly burdened by the problems that many of the new occupants brought with them. It would become an abject legacy, contributing to an image of public housing as an incubator for social dysfunction. Although the administration attempted to involve communities in a participatory process to determine where new housing for the homeless might be located, it learned that most communities did not want it at all. The more the city made new housing available to some homeless families, the more it received applications from others. In 1989, the Dinkins administration, in response to a law adopted by the City Council, released a five-year plan for assisting single homeless adults. It pledged to create 2,500 new beds in model transitional facilities located in twenty-four locations throughout the city.[54] Under the newly adopted City Charter, the facilities and the burdens they might impose were required to be fairly distributed throughout the city. The most innovative feature of the plan was to provide training and rehabilitative services to clients so that they could more easily transition into a normal life.

In August 1990, Mayor Dinkins and Governor Mario Cuomo signed the historic New York/New York agreement pledging to provide 3,314 units of housing for 5,225 mentally ill homeless people by 1992. Negotiations had been underway since the Koch administration, but were delayed during the transition. The final accord dedicated $194.7 million to the project, further investing the city in an area of service that had historically belonged to the state.[55] There was nothing comparable to it in the country.

Mayor Dinkins brought homosexual employees of the city closer to full citizenship when he settled a long-standing suit initiated by teachers to make gay domestic partners eligible for health benefits. He may have reached too far, however, when he entered the culture war undertaken by his schools chancellor Joseph Fernandez. In response to the HIV-AIDS crisis, the chancellor decided to distribute condoms to all high school students. He subsequently attempted to implement the "Children of the Rainbow" curriculum that, in addition to teaching young students about different racial and ethnic cultures, would introduce them to the lifestyle of gay parents and their children. His proposals infuriated parents and religious conservatives, and divided the central school board. Looking back, one might conclude that these proposals were just too far ahead of their time, but the issues at stake were more complicated than that. Opponents raised questions about the age appropriateness of the students involved, and whether parents or school administrators should make such determinations for an individual child. The chancellor's abrupt manner of handling the controversy did not help. To the dismay of Mayor Dinkins, Fernandez was terminated by the Board of Education.

The "Gorgeous Mosaic" of diversity that David Dinkins envisioned for New York crumbled into a pile of controversy that contributed to his undoing. The first incident occurred at Bong Jae Jang's Red Apple grocery store in the Flatbush section of Brooklyn, three weeks after Mayor Dinkins was sworn in. A Haitian woman accused the owner and two of his employees of assaulting her. They contended that she was shoplifting. The confrontation ignited tensions that had long been welling up between Asians and blacks as the newer immigrants began to open businesses in the latter's communities.[56] Sonny Carson, a black nationalist with a long history of militancy dating back to Ocean Hill-Brownsville, demanded that the storeowners be arrested. He organized a boycott of the business that lasted for an entire year. In order to underscore the racial overtones of the conflict and the outsider status of the storeowners, the boycott was also directed at another Korean-owned grocery store across from Red Apple.

Carson taunted Dinkins, calling him a "traitor" for not taking part in the action. The media and public officials, including Ed Koch and Rudy Giuliani, lambasted the mayor for taking no action to end the boycott. The larger Asian community—which was just beginning to realize a more prominent presence in the city—came away feeling that it had no representation at City Hall. In 1992, the U.S. Commission on Civil Rights, citing a rising pattern of bigotry against Asians, issued a report that included criticism of the mayor's handing of the affair.[57] Dinkins's leadership was questioned further that year when six days of rioting, looting, and arson broke out in Washington Heights after a policeman shot and killed an armed twenty-three-year-old Dominican immigrant who had been associated with a drug gang. Police union members picketed City Hall after it was disclosed that the mayor had paid for the dead man's funeral.

All-time record crime rates began to decline in some categories (aggravated assault, burglary, and larceny) during 1989, the last year of the Koch administration, but the murder rate peaked in 1990, with 2,245 New Yorkers losing their lives.[58] In response to growing public alarm, Mayor Dinkins implemented his "Safe Streets, Safe City" initiative that assigned more cops to street patrols, which was moderately successful in reversing the uptick in murders and other major crimes.[59] To his credit, Dinkins was able to keep the city calm in the spring of 1992 as other cities went up in flames after a jury in Los Angeles acquitted four police officers who were filmed beating black motorist Rodney King. After appointing New York's second black Police Commissioner, Lee Brown, Dinkins finally instituted the Civilian Review Board that John Lindsay had attempted to install in 1966.[60] Brown did not support the idea, and it enraged the department rank and file once again, but Dinkins got it done. He also empaneled a commission to investigate police corruption after the department's internal affairs unit failed to uncover a drug-related scam that was accidently discovered by police in Suffolk County.

Dinkins was never able to recover from the great debacle of his mayoralty that took place in Crown Heights, Brooklyn in the summer of 1991. It all started when a Hasidic man's car swerved out of control and struck two black children, leaving seven-year-old Gavin Cato dead. The driver had been in a three-car motorcade transporting the Grand Rebbe Menachem Schneerson of the Lubavitch Hasidic community. As had been the practice for some time, the Grand Rebbe's entourage was led by a police escort, marking his privileged status in the world of New York City politics, and accentuating the second-class citizenship felt by poor African-American minorities living in the same neighborhood.

Witnesses contended that the driver had run a red light and that the Hatzolah community ambulance service protectively whisked him away from the scene, ignoring the more serious medical needs of the children. Three days of unrestrained rioting followed, ending in dozens of injuries, property damage, assaults on the police, and most tragic of all, the fatal stabbing of a rabbinical student named Yankel Rosenbaum. In response to expressions of outrage by the Jewish community, Governor Cuomo asked for an investigation by his director of criminal justice. A report released in July 1993, in the midst of Dinkins' re-election campaign, faulted the mayor for failing to act in a timely manner to protect the lives and property of the people in Crown Heights.[61] Bill Lynch, who personally supervised City Hall's response to the disturbances, humbly took the blame for mishandling the crisis. Lynch's young aide Bill de Blasio got a lesson on the volatility of race relations and the power of organized religion.

The 1993 campaign was a rematch with the man Dinkins had barely defeated in 1989. This time Rudy Giuliani came out on top by an even smaller margin (44,000 as opposed to the 47,000) than that which separated the two men previously.[62] The former prosecutor's take-charge, crime-fighting image resonated in a city that seemed to be coming apart. Most unions continued to support the incumbent, but the membership and some of their leaders had lost enthusiasm. Miffed over heavy layoffs that stung the school system, teachers union president Sandra Feldman decided not to back either candidate. Jesse Jackson campaigned on the mayor's behalf to get black residents to the polls, but fewer blacks voted than in 1989, as was the case with Latinos.[63] In Staten Island, the city's most conservative borough, a ballot issue regarding Staten Island's possible secession from the city brought out many people who cast their votes for Giuliani.[64]

Giuliani recruited David Garth to help manage his campaign, and ran as a fusion candidate on both the Republican and Liberal Party lines. Herman Badillo, a lifelong Democrat who had threatened to challenge Dinkins in the primary, instead declared for the Comptroller's spot, and ran on the fusion ticket with Giuliani. Ed Koch and Robert Wagner Jr., son of the former mayor and grandson of the former New Deal senator, were among the other leading Democrats who openly supported Giuliani. It was a harsh reminder for Dinkins and other progressives that the La Guardia coalition from yesteryear, which had been such a large part of the alliance that kept Ed Koch in office for so long, would continue to move the city to the center right of the political spectrum. Some 64,469 votes the former prosecutor gathered on the Liberal Party line delivered the margin of victory. Raymond Harding, the grand Pooh-Bah of the party, had now abandoned its progressive roots. Hoping to share in the spoils of victory, he became more utilitarian about picking his candidates.

Giuliani's taking of City Hall was more of an about-face from David Dinkins than was Dinkins's replacement of Koch.[65] As a student at Bishop Loughlin High School in Brooklyn and later at Manhattan College, the Long Island-born Giuliani once considered himself a Kennedy Democrat, as had many Catholics of the day. After Giuliani switched parties, President Ronald Reagan appointed him Associate Attorney General in 1981. Upon being elected mayor, the former federal prosecutor promised bipartisan government, and he was able to practice it to a certain extent because the Democratic Party was moving more in his direction. Practically speaking, as Democrats had run City Hall for twenty consecutive years, the pool of experienced talent was dominated by Democrats. Two of Giuliani's four original deputy mayors were Democrats; another identified with the Liberal Party.

The new mayor startled his Republican colleagues when he endorsed incumbent governor Mario Cuomo over Republican challenger George Pataki. He kept a safe distance from GOP firebrands such as Newt Gingrich. He and Council Speaker Peter Vallone shared a commitment to cap rising taxes, motivating labor leaders such as Dennis Rivera of Local 1199 to build a more progressive wing in the local legislature. Giuliani also became a key ally of Bill Clinton when the Democratic president, facing GOP opposition, had difficulty getting his crime bill through Congress. Giuliani's reputation as a tough crime fighter who led the narcotics unit of the U.S. Justice Department lent credibility to the proposal. Its passage brought federal resources to the city that fortified Giuliani's trademark effort to make New York a safer place. This was just the beginning of a mutually advantageous relationship between the Republican mayor and the Democratic president, who had declared, "the era of big government is over," and promised to "end welfare as we know it"—lasting until Giuliani and Hillary Clinton both became hot prospects to fill the U.S. Senate seat vacated by Daniel P. Moynihan.

A month after Giuliani's election in 1993, City Comptroller Elizabeth Holtzman, a Democrat, released a report warning that the city faced an immediate $2 billion deficit that could grow to $3.2 by 1997. [66] The city lagged behind the rest of the country in gains that were bringing the economy out of the recession. With a tax rate nearly twice the national average and more hikes scheduled, New York could lose 265,000 private sector jobs. The new mayor took these warnings to heart. In his first State of the City message in July, he announced plans to cut taxes, reduce the budget by $291 million, consolidate agencies, and eliminate 15,000 jobs, including 2,500 in the city school system. He would also privatize two of eleven public hospitals, put other services such as street paving and park maintenance out for bid, and require the fingerprinting of welfare recipients to eliminate fraud. [67]

This job cut was the first volley fired in many public battles Giuliani fought with the Board of Education. During his tenure he forced two schools chancellors to resign, Ramon Cortines and Rudy Crew—both established career educators. Giuliani's angry threats to "blow up" the system struck a raw nerve with parents and other members of the public school community, causing a backlash that undermined his attempts to achieve reform. That said, the mayor's frustrations with the schools were well-founded. The school headquarters at 110 Livingston Street stood atop an entrenched, bloated, calcified bureaucracy that had demonstrated little capacity for self-improvement. [68] Some parts of the system were downright corrupt. [69]

Although Giuliani was never able to win control of the schools or actualize real change, his unprecedented attacks on the system paved the way for future reforms—some more productive than others. Installing Herman Badillo as Chair of the Board of Trustees at City University did allow Giuliani to raise standards within a system that had lost its way after open admissions was established. [70] New policies moved most remedial instruction from the senior colleges to community colleges, and revised admissions standards created a multi-tiered admissions policy that was better aligned with the diverse needs of students. [71]

Mayor Dinkins's failure to deal effectively with the sight of more homeless people on the city streets contributed to the perception that he was a weak administrator. [72] In 1992, Dinkins had appointed a commission headed by Governor Cuomo's son, Andrew, to study the homeless problem. The report concluded that government cannot be expected to find housing for everyone, and that once a legitimate need is established, service recipients have an obligation to enroll in rehabilitative services to better themselves. [73] The Dinkins team accepted Cuomo's recommendations with ambivalence, and moved slowly to implement them. Giuliani embraced the report, especially the recommendation that assigned responsibility to those who were receiving help. [74] Giuliani dealt with homelessness as a quality-of-life issue that affected all New Yorkers. Squeegee men and street vagrants became symbols of urban disorder he vowed to eradicate.[75] One result of more aggressive enforcement was to "criminalize" homelessness, or at least the minimally disruptive behavior associated with it.

On December 29, 1994, during his last week in office, Governor Cuomo rescinded a state regulation requiring the city to provide a homeless person with immediate emergency housing upon request. The revision gave administrators more time to determine an applicant's needs and to prescribe rehabilitative services when warranted. The Giuliani administration used the change as an opportunity to tighten eligibility requirements and develop protocols under which clients would sign voluntary agreements of cooperation, leading to endless judicial entanglements between the administration and the Coalition for the Homeless. In 1996, Governor Pataki issued new regulations that curtailed the courts' ability to dictate policy.

Following recommendations of the Cuomo (Andrew) Commission, the Giuliani Administration moved with dispatch to convert city-run shelters into private institutions operated by nonprofits. Between 1988 and 1996, the percent of single men's shelters privately operated went from 26.8 percent to 54.3 percent; in 1996, 72 percent of the family shelters were privately run, by 1998 all but a few were.[76] Although private shelters and their stricter expectations for clients proved to be more hospitable than those operated by the city, research continued to show that permanent housing was needed in order to address homelessness effectively.[77] In 1999, Giuliani and Pataki announced a second phase of the "New York/New York" agreement originally signed by Mayor Dinkins and Governor Mario Cuomo, pledging to create 1,500 additional housing units over five years for the mentally ill homeless—a far cry from what was actually needed at the time.[78]

Giuliani's "paternalistic" approach to homeless people was consistent with his larger view of welfare reform.[79] It also coincided with President Clinton's welfare to work policy, which was opposed by progressive groups such as the National Association of Social Workers and ACORN, but widely popular across the country. In his State of the City Speech of 1995, Giuliani declared that it is "just plain wrong" to force more than 1.16 million New Yorkers into a "life of dependency."[80] As an alternative, he purported that his "workfare" program recognizes that "welfare is supposed to be a temporary helping hand." By the end of 1996, the rolls were reduced by 18 percent to 950,000.[81] By 2005, the number of people on welfare would be under 400,000.[82]

As he moved into his second term, Giuliani increased his emphasis on requiring able-bodied welfare recipients to work. Wisconsin had successfully experimented with a "workfare" program that became a model for national reform.[83] Giuliani was so impressed with it that he hired the architect of the program, Jason Turner, to replicate some version of it in New York—just as President Clinton and Senate Republicans were simultaneously putting the final touches on the

Personal Responsibility and Work Opportunity Reconciliation Act of 1996. The city's Work Experience Program (WEP), with 21,000 enrollees by 2000, was the largest welfare to work program in the country.[84] The city Human Resources Administration instituted a "JobStat" information system to monitor the performance of Job Centers, much like the Police Department's Compstat system tracked crime. New York State was also a willing partner to this new approach. Governor Pataki's Welfare Reform Act of 1997 instituted benefit reductions, time limits, and eligibility restrictions.

Taking people off welfare contributed to the growing crisis in affordable housing. A 1996 Housing and Vacancy Survey completed by the city found that nearly one in five households paid more than 50 percent of their income for housing.[85] For twenty years, the federal government had scaled down its commitment to subsidize the construction of affordable housing in favor of privatization and providing direct assistance to tenants. The U.S. Department of Housing and Urban Development (HUD) reduced its budget from $50 billion in 1980 to $20.1 billion in 1995, then to $19.1 billion in 1996, and finally to $16 billion in 1997.[86] The divestment was carried out by Democratic and Republican presidents alike (Carter, Reagan, H.W. Bush, Clinton), and overlapped with Andrew Cuomo's tenure as HUD secretary.

Between 1991 and 1994 the cost of managing property the city had acquired through its in rem program was averaging $294 million annually. Tax arrears on foreclosed walk-up buildings leaped from $28 million to $71 million between 1989 and 1995. The Dinkins administration had been able to dispose of 12,400 units between 1990 and 1993 by transferring ownership to tenants, nonprofit organizations, and for-profit companies, and it began to defer taking title of tax-delinquent properties in 1993 to keep down the inventory.[87] Facing a severe budget, Giuliani pledged to shrink the in rem portfolio with a focus on privatization. In 1995, the city altered its foreclosure policy and sped up the sale of properties. It sold tax liens from commercial and high-end residential properties directly to investors, who would pay tax arrears in exchange for ownership. Marginal residential properties were put through the usual foreclosure process and then deeded to third parties in the for-profit or nonprofit sectors. Between 1995 and 2003, more than 40,000 units were sold or preserved, reducing the city inventory to fewer than 6,000 units.[88]

Privatization was a key feature of Giuliani's thinking on economic development. He came under fire for so-called sweetheart deals he made with high-powered corporations to keep them from relocating, but his actions were hardly unprecedented. Charles Bagli of the *New York Times* had thrashed Mayor Dinkins for giving $75 million in tax breaks to Bear Stearns to build a new headquarters on Madison Avenue, after the global financial giant had extracted $37 million from the city by threatening to move 5,700 employees to New Jersey.[89] Bagli noted that Ed Koch had given Chase Manhattan Bank a $234 million benefits package to move thousands of employees to anchor MetroTech in downtown Brooklyn, and forked over $100 million in benefits to NBC when the network considered abandoning Rockefeller Center. The more progressive Dinkins had also offered financial incentives to Prudential Securities ($106 million), Morgan Stanley ($100 million), and CBS ($49.9 million). Bagli might have also mentioned Solomon Brothers ($79 million), and developers William Zeckendorf, Jr. ($100 million) and Bruce Eichner ($63 million) as riders on the gravy train.[90]

The allure of alternative commercial space grew more tempting as the price of real estate in New York became more prohibitive and leaders in other jurisdictions wooed businesses to relocate with more perks. Bagli, however, faults Giuliani and his predecessors for not creating enough office space outside of Manhattan to compete with their neighbors across the Hudson. Bagli insists that Giuliani brought corporate largesse to a new level, readily granting concessions for the asking, and sacrificing $1 billion in city revenue from some fifty wealthy corporations. A city planning scholar who reviewed the Giuliani deals puts the figure at twice that amount.[91] Giuliani, nonetheless, was following a path that had been paved by his predecessors, and it would soon to be traveled more regularly by his successor, Michael Bloomberg.

Giuliani coasted to a second term in 1997. In the September Democratic primary, Manhattan Borough President Ruth Messinger had to wait for a recount in order to verify the 40 percent plurality she needed to avoid a runoff against the Reverend Al Sharpton, her only opponent. Giuliani walked away with the general election (58 percent to 40 percent).[92] For the first time in many years, things were looking up in the Big Apple. A spurt of immigration from Asia and Latin America once again boosted the size of the population above the 8 million mark. Spurred by a rebound on Wall Street, the city's economy was starting to grow. Despite this, Giuliani continued to negotiate austere contracts with the municipal unions. Although he kept the size of the workforce to its lowest level since the Koch administration for a time, by the end of his second term the mayor took advantage of the good economic times and let the payroll grow again. Giuliani referred to New York as "Comeback City" when he gave his State of the City address in 1998, but not everybody felt that they were sharing in the fruits of the recovery.

The combative chief executive did make good on his promise to install law and order. He not only fought street crime, but also building on his accomplishments as U.S. Attorney, was able to depose mafia kingpins from control of the Fulton Fish Market and rubbish carting industry.[93] His recruitment of William Bratton from Boston was a public relations triumph, and Bratton's prior tenure as chief of the city transit police gave the new commissioner standing with the rank and file. Bratton instituted a computerized management information system in the department (CompStat) to track crime that revolutionized policing and held individual precinct commanders responsible for safety in their jurisdictions.[94]

Heightened accountability, coupled with a "broken windows" approach to patrol that paid more attention to minor infractions, drove arrest rates up.[95] The crime rate dropped 12 percent in Bratton's first year as commissioner compared to 2 percent nationally, and 16 percent in Bratton's second year.[96] Crime statistics would continue to tumble throughout Giuliani's tenure.[97] Once again, however, not everybody was happy with the outcomes, and many felt unfairly treated. The jail population skyrocketed. A disproportionate number of the inmates were African-American and Latino, many of whom were detained for petty offenses. David Dinkins referred to such infractions as "victimless crimes." Giuliani insisted that because poor minorities are disproportionately victimized by crime, they were the major beneficiaries of tough enforcement and new police policies.

New York City, however, was not big enough to accommodate the swelled egos of Rudy Giuliani and William Bratton when the two men were at the top of their games. The mayor was once quoted as saying, "We had a little bit of a Truman-MacArthur problem," recalling tensions between the former president and his commanding general in Korea.[98] The police commissioner was too much of a publicity hound for the mayor's taste. It all came apart in 1996, precipitated by a *Time* magazine story in mid-January featuring a heroic Bill Bratton on the cover. Pointing to a twenty-five-year low in the murder rate, the headline read, "Finally We're Winning the War against Crime."[99] Two months later, feeling pressure from City Hall, Bratton departed to take the top crime-fighting job in Los Angeles. Giuliani chose Fire Commissioner Howard Safir to replace him. Safir, a friend of the mayor with prior experience in law enforcement, was determined to outdo his celebrated predecessor.

More aggressive policing brought officers into greater contact with the public, providing additional opportunities for altercations between citizens and cops. Safir tripled the size of the Street Crime Unit (SCU) (138 to 380), but in a rush to get more personnel on the street, did not provide them with adequate training.[100] In February, 1999, four fresh-faced officers from the Bronx SCU shot and killed an unarmed African immigrant, Amadou Diallo, while looking for a suspect who had committed a string of violent crimes. The unsupervised officers had fired off forty-one shots. Eighteen months earlier, another harrowing episode had played out in Brooklyn, when a police officer used a broomstick handle to sodomize Abner Louima, a Haitian immigrant, while the man was in custody at a precinct house.

Organized demonstrations became commonplace in front of the NYPD Headquarters at One Police Plaza. Celebrities such as Susan Sarandon delighted the media by allowing themselves to be led off in handcuffs in front of news cameras. When leading black politicians such as Congressman Charles Rangel and former Mayor Dinkins were arrested, it only hardened the animosity between the police and minority communities. Al Sharpton and thousands of angry protesters stopped traffic on the Brooklyn Bridge. New York had overcome a crime wave that lasted for more than two decades, but African Americans and Latinos perceived the war waged against crime as a war waged against them.

By now, Sharpton, a devoted adversary of Rudy Giuliani, was moving into the mainstream of city politics. He already had run for mayor and for the U.S. Senate. He and Dennis Rivera had accompanied Jesse Jackson to a Washington rally in support of Bill Clinton when the embattled president was struggling through impeachment hearings. In 2000, Sharpton cohosted and led the questioning in a presidential primary debate between Al Gore and Bill Bradley that was held at the Apollo Theater. From that point forward, Sharpton was a force to behold in local, not to mention national, politics. Office seekers in the Democratic Party were well advised to make a courtesy visit to the headquarters of the minister's National Action Network to demonstrate comity with the black community.

Rudy Giuliani's mayoralty came to a dramatic climax when two jet planes crashed into the World Trade Center towers on September 11, 2001. Nearly 3,000 innocent people perished. He guided the city through its most catastrophic moment ever. The *Time* magazine "Person of the Year" for 2001 was no longer just the mayor of New York; he was now "America's Mayor." Giuliani was so popular for the moment that he considered trying to extend the city's term limits law so that he would be eligible to continue beyond his eight years. He eventually moved on.

* * *

In the previous chapter, we were introduced to the basic precepts of the progressive creed that ordained big, ambitious government with responsibility to enhance the well-being of society's most vulnerable and marginalized. Even in the best of times economically, those political inclinations could not always be followed to the fullest. New Deal Era progressives—nationally and locally—had a disappointing record on race. Fiorello La Guardia, the role model of every modern progressive mayor, and most others for that matter, was forced to execute layoffs and furloughs during his first term. Some of the same labor unions that Robert Wagner empowered to promote economic equality would occasionally situate themselves on the wrong side of the battlefield when they were called upon to advance racial equality.

It is during the worst of times, however, when New York can be counted on to show how deeply the progressive ethos is encoded in its political DNA. La Guardia's creation of public housing during the Depression was a magnificent accomplishment that helped many people. It was no more impressive, though, than the monumental housing program Ed Koch initiated in the shadow of the fiscal crisis without a Franklin Roosevelt in the White House. The political coalition that Koch cobbled together with the sons and daughters of the New Deal generation set the city on a different course, however now affordable housing would have to proceed in the context of a growth agenda, and that required costly concessions to the business sector. A new arrangement was now in place.

At times, the municipality and its chief executives were not as kind to those in need as they should have been. The angry rhetoric around race was especially damaging. And it remained to be seen how long the new centrist realignment that began with Koch would last. There was a brief interlude during the Dinkins years, but it was so short and tenuous that anybody who was paying attention would not have expected the progressive spirit to inhabit New York again, as it would in 2014 with the sudden emergence of Bill de Blasio and the broad coalition he assembled.

Then again, the impulse was there all the while. Even in the throes of a spectacular retreat, New York remained a leader, ahead of other cities and most of the country, in reaching out to its poor, its homeless, its LBGTQ, its black, and its brown people. It never did so to the satisfaction of many residents in need, and perhaps never will, but that lingering restlessness felt by progressive activists is what keeps the spirit alive. Racial tension still existed, and, as the Kerner Commission on Civil Disorder observed fifty years ago, it was most likely to erupt in transactions between minority men and white police officers. Those tensions would carry over into the Bloomberg administration and the city that Mayor Bloomberg eventually handed over to Bill de Blasio.

6

Growing Inequality

If stable leaders are emblematic of the particular time in which they govern, Michael Bloomberg's twelve-year turn as mayor of New York at the dawn of the millennium personified the age of plutocracy—locally and nationally. A self-made entrepreneur who was one of the richest men in New York at the time of his election, Bloomberg was dismissive of ordinary politics, but enjoyed power. He had never worked in government or engaged directly in political activity before becoming mayor, but was confident about what he wanted to accomplish. He twice changed party affiliations—from Democrat to Republican to Independent—to avoid competitive primaries.

The last label—Independent—probably suited him best, especially once he realized how easily the handsome checks he wrote could glide across party lines. He spent more of his own money to get elected than any mayor in history. He was an awkward campaigner, impatient with small talk, and preferred to focus his energy on getting things done. He refused to live in Gracie Mansion, residing instead in his own Upper East Side townhouse. He demolished the exquisite interior of the old Board of Estimate chambers on the second floor of City Hall to make it look more like a corporate headquarters than a seat of government. He celebrated the independence that his personal wealth afforded him, hardly aware that unchecked executive power can undermine the democratic process.

He too idolized Fiorello La Guardia, but the New York that Michael Bloomberg governed bore only a superficial resemblance to the city that belonged to the Little Flower, or even the place once ruled by Robert Wagner, John Lindsay, or Ed Koch. According to census data, the white majority that dominated New York City's population in 1960 (85.33 percent) faded significantly by 1980 (60.72 percent), and became a minority by 2000 (44.66 percent). Blacks, who have historically been the largest racial minority in the city, peaked as a percentage of the population in 1990 (28.71 percent)—just about when David Dinkins was elected, and their numbers have declined since, proportionately and absolutely.[1] By 2010, blacks were 25.55 percent of the population. A perceptible reversal of the Great Migration is taking place, with many African

Americans moving back to the South where the cost of living is more affordable than a rapidly gentrifying New York.[2] The U.S. Census did not count Hispanics as a separate category until 1990. Between 1990 and 2010, the Hispanic population grew 21.1 percent from 1.78 million to 2.1 million, reaching a 27 percent share of the population.[3] Although the majority of Latino immigrants who arrived in New York early came from Puerto Rico, their population has diversified to include Dominicans, Mexicans, and others from Central and South America.

Immigration was a key factor that lifted the total population back above the 8 million mark in 2000. In 1970, only 18.2 percent of the population was foreign born. By 2013, foreign representation rose to 37 percent.[4] A large part of the spike in immigration was generated by the sudden influx of people from Asia. In 1970, Asians and Pacific Islanders made up only 1.20 percent of the population; by 2010, they were 12.76 percent. Although the Asian population is diverse with regard to wealth and income, it is only slightly better-off than other racial minorities in New York.[5]

Between 1980 and 2014, the poverty rate in the city fluctuated between 19 percent and 21 percent. This was a long way from the 14.93 percent rate witnessed in 1970 after President Lyndon Johnson enacted his Great Society initiatives. The situation was actually worse than it appeared. In 2013, Bloomberg's last year in office, the New York City Center for Economic Opportunity (NYC CEO), a city office, published a report indicating that 47 percent of all New Yorkers live at or near the poverty level.[6] The trend in the unemployment rate was also discouraging: according to the U.S. Census, it changed from 5.2 percent in 1960, to 4.9 percent in 1970, to 8.6 percent in 1980, to 9 percent in 1990, to 9.6 percent in 2000, to 10.5 percent in 2010.[7]

Unsurprisingly, poverty is closely aligned with race and citizenship status in New York. According to the NYC CEO, in 2013, the percentage of Non-Hispanic whites (15 percent) that lived below the official poverty line was considerably lower than that of any other group, including Non-Hispanic Blacks (21.5 percent), Non-Hispanic Asians (26.6 percent), and Hispanics (any race) (24 percent). The poverty rate among non-citizens (29.7 percent) greatly exceeded the rate among those who were citizens by birth (18.7 percent) or citizens through naturalization (19.1 percent). It has always been this way in New York: although immigrants build the city's future, they have significant social needs when they first arrive.

The defining economic issue of the last several decades, in New York and elsewhere, concerns income polarization. In sum: the rich got richer, and the poor got poorer. The Fiscal Policy Institute (FPI), which monitors such trends in the city, published a report in 2014 finding that median family income in the city was 5.2 percent lower in 2013 than it was in 2008 at the start of the recession.[8] The erosion of real earnings at the bottom of the income scale is particularly problematic in a city where the cost of living is increasingly prohibitive. In 2010, the City Council completed a study of living costs in the nation's ten most expensive metropolitan areas. Manhattan, Brooklyn, and Queens ranked one, two, and five.[9]

In a paper presented at the American Sociological Association in 2013, FPI's chief economist James Parrott shows that although the share of total income received by the top 5 percent (those earning income above $167,400) grew 28 percentage points between 1990 and 2007, the share of the middle 45 percent (income range from $28,800 to $167,400) dropped by 19.1 percentage points, and the share of the bottom 50 percent (income below $28,800) dropped 7.9 percentage points.[10] For many years, the city has had a regressive tax structure. In 2010, according to Parrott, the top 1 percent (those making $493,579 and above) reaped the highest share of total adjusted income (33.8%), but bore only 25.2% of the local income and property tax burden. Meanwhile, those with incomes between $37,673 and $68,146 accounted for 15.2% of the local income, but paid 17.7% of the local taxes.

In 2012, Parrott observes, 410,000 workers (one in every ten) were paid wages so low that they remained below the poverty level—defined by the federal government as an income of less than $18,284 for a family of three.[11] Anybody who retains a Reagan-era image of welfare recipients sitting double-parked in their Cadillacs while the rest of us head to work in the morning needs to digest that statistic. In human terms, these are the people who fill the ranks of what we call "the working poor." The ever-insightful financial writer Charles Morris has observed that the class-based disparities prevailing in twenty-first century New York City exceed those that existed in France on the eve of the revolution.[12]

This is not to suggest that any mayor, or mayors, can be held responsible for the economic inequality that has afflicted New York more ferociously than just about any other locale in America. There have been significant national forces at play that we will discuss in the next section. However, it is reasonable to ask how a city with such a strong progressive tradition has come to this. How has what began as the New Deal coalition and evolved into the Koch coalition morphed into a political base that has tolerated such profound inequality? How did this city elect a billionaire businessman who epitomized the corporate culture as mayor for three consecutive terms? Recent demographic trends might have prodded the system in another direction. New York, as we have seen, is a city in which racial minorities are the majority, where poverty proliferates, and immigration is on the rise—all basic ingredients of progressive politics. Yet, there are clear explanations for the opposite effect.

It is axiomatic from generations of political science research that racial minorities and poor people don't vote or engage in political activity as regularly and fervently as the more privileged do.[13] Boss Tweed's crooked machine that once turned immigrants into citizens is not around any longer either. Political influence is a function of class and money, which cannot be separated from race. This is the pernicious paradox of progressive politics: those who need help from government the most are the least equipped to demand it. To make matters worse, not many people vote at all. Except for the elections of 1989 (Dinkins) and 2001 (Bloomberg), the number of New Yorkers who have voted for mayor has declined significantly since John Lindsay took office in 1965.[14] A total of 2,652,454 came to the polls that year. Only 1,102,400 people voted in the mayoral election of 2013.

What we see on the rise is campaign spending. In 1989, when the Campaign Finance Board of New York City began keeping track, a total of $24,064,270 was spent on mayoral campaigns.[15] It has become more expensive to be mayor with successive elections. Michael Bloomberg kept breaking his own incredible records for spending, peaking at $108,371,688 in 2009.[16] Bill de Blasio spent $13,583,866 in 2013.[17] Growth in spending also persists in campaigns for the two other citywide offices, and the City Council as well.

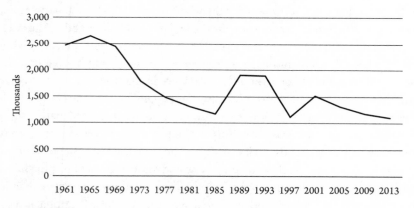

Figure 6.1 Ballot Count. Assembled by Lorraine Minnite, PhD, Rutgers University-Camden.

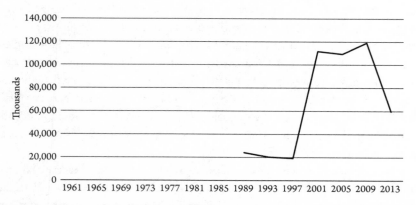

Figure 6.2 Campaign Expenditure. Data retrieved from the New York City Campaign Finance Board.

With voting down and spending up, the democratic process has become severely compromised. It is not hyperbole to allege that public offices are now being bought. When progressive politicians such as Bernie Sanders, Elizabeth Warren, and Bill de Blasio declare there is a need for a populist revolt against plutocracy, they are not just sloganeering. In a majoritarian electoral system, populism can be a friend of progressivism.[18] A process characterized by low popular participation and costly elections is not. What we see in New York City is part of a national pattern. The lopsided economy and lopsided polity feed one another. Who might be at fault for creating this situation is something of a chicken and golden egg riddle.

Perhaps New York should be blamed for the yawning inequality that has overcome the nation. If La Guardia was the tail that wagged a benevolent federal dog to help us get past the Great Depression, Wall Street was the tail of the nasty dog that dragged us into the Great Recession. There is a voluminous scholarly literature on how the economy became so lopsided.[19] Much of the evidence points to federal policy. It wasn't just a random set of developments in world markets, or the effects of Adam Smith's invisible hand. The outcome was largely the result of decisions made by Congress and the White House, and both major political parties were complicit. Bernie Sanders may have popularized the idea of a "rigged system," but research by leading academicians identified the problem long before the Vermont senator took to the podium during the 2016 primary season.[20] The issues are complex, but the influence of Wall Street in Washington is a large part of the explanation.

When the subprime mortgage crisis broke in 2008, millions of families lost their homes to foreclosure, and home values plummeted for many other ordinary folks, eradicating their life savings and leaving them in debt. The federal government responded by bailing out the banks that had caused the crisis through predatory lending and other irresponsible credit practices, setting few conditions that might have incentivized financial institutions to correct their bad behavior.[21] Congress and President Bill Clinton had already given the banks regulatory relief in 1999 by repealing the Glass-Steagall Act of 1933 that separated commercial banks from investment banks and set rules for transparency. Historically, commercial banks took deposits from average folks with modest incomes and invested their money conservatively, whereas investment banks served a wealthy clientele and engaged in more speculative activity with higher risks. A year later (2000), Clinton and Congress passed the Commodity Futures Modernization Act that exempted derivatives and other exotic products from regulations that protect consumers.

To say that Wall Street has exercised inordinate influence over economic policy is an understatement. Nobel Laureate Joseph Stiglitz, himself an appointee of President Clinton as chair of the Council of Economic Advisors, has written that representatives of the financial community have had such a hand in implementing economic policy that at times it has given the appearance of a "conflict of interest."[22] President Clinton's Treasury Secretary Robert Rubin, whose "Rubinomics" called for tightened social spending to reduce the deficit, had previously spent twenty-six years at Goldman Sachs. As a result of his policies, the economy did experience real growth, and Clinton's last three budgets ran surpluses exceeding $300 billion, but not everybody shared in the benefits.[23]

President George W. Bush's Treasury Secretary, Henry Paulson, had served as the CEO of Goldman Sachs. It was on Bush's watch that the tax rate for stock dividends was reduced from 35 percent to 15 percent, and the rate for capital gains went from 20 percent to 5 percent.[24] Timothy Geithner actually had a public service position as President of the New York Federal Reserve Bank when President Barack Obama named him Treasury Secretary. Geithner, however, was roundly criticized for being too close to Citicorp when he engineered the bank bailout during the mortgage crisis.[25] These influential appointments under Clinton and Bush were all just a warm-up for the more complete takeover of Washington by the business class under Donald Trump, who tapped a Goldman Sachs alum (Steven Mnuchin) to become Treasury Secretary, and its president (Gary Cohn) to chair the National Economic Council.

Stiglitz's book is chock-full of examples that illustrate how malignant the political process really is. The purpose of the Securities and Exchange Commission is to protect investors. Yet, it repeatedly allows executives who violate laws and regulations to avoid prosecution and punishment. The Federal Reserve Bank lends money to commercial banks at near-zero interest rates; the banks, in turn, lend the same money to the federal government at a higher rate. The pharmaceutical companies have gotten a law passed that prohibits the federal government from negotiating group discounts on drugs bought through Medicare. As a result Medicare costs are much higher than they ought to be, and some elderly subscribers do not have access to medication that they need to safeguard their health. We could go on.

Wall Street, and the business community in general, are quite adept at using their financial clout to move policy in a direction that is self-serving and economically stratifying to the extent that it undermines societal well-being. The process is best summarized in a seminal article written by Jacob Hacker and Paul Pierson called "Winner-Take-All Politics," based on a book of the same title.[26] The two political scientists begin their essay citing data on income polarization that mirrors the pattern just depicted with reference to New York. Between 1979 and 2005, average incomes of the bottom fifth households rose 6 percent, while the middle quintile rose 21 percent, and that of the richest 1 percent rose 230 percent. The average income of the top 0.01 percent (the 15,000 richest families) leaped from \$4 million to \$24.3 million. Economic inequality in the United States is the highest of any country in the industrialized world.

Hacker and Pierson criticize economists for downplaying the role that government policy plays in producing inequality, and their fellow political scientists for paying insufficient attention to the changing structural dynamics of American politics. They describe the new politics as "organized combat." The real action in policy-making, according to them, is in lobbying. The number of corporations with public affairs offices in Washington increased from 100 in 1968 to more than 500 in 1978. Between 1971 and 1982, the number of firms that employed registered lobbyists rose from 175 to 2,445. The number of corporate PACs increased from fewer than 300 in 1976 to more than 1,200 by the 1980s. The money that corporations spent to influence policy doubled over the first decade of the twenty-first century.

As the role of the big business became more prominent in Washington, the influence of organized labor dwindled. In the aftermath of World War II, more than one-third of wage and salary workers belonged to unions; by 2009, the ratio had dropped to 12.3 percent—a mere 7.2 percent in the private sector. This put more pressure on stable public sector unions such as the ones found in New York to advance the cause of economic equality.

In the early 1970s, most contributions to PACs came from organized labor. By the late 1970s, business was contributing as much. In 1980 unions accounted for less than 25 percent of the total. American unions were never as powerful as their European counterparts where class differences were not so wide, but their recent decline has made matters worse for working people. Like them or not, unions are the only organized interests dedicated to raising the standard of living for those at the lower end of the income scale. In the previous chapter, we saw how President Reagan broke the back of the union representing air-traffic controllers with no effective backlash from organized labor, and how almost every mayor of New York since Ed Koch has been able to cold shoulder union chiefs whose influence daunted their predecessors.

Hacker and Pierson present a picture of politics in the new millennium in which influence is passing from mass-market organizations such as unions to organizations that can better back their demands with dollars. Both parties have responded to the catnip of contributions. The wholesale buying and selling of influence assumed a new air of legitimacy in 2010 when the U.S. Supreme Court handed down the landmark *Citizens United* decision, declaring that contributions to political campaigns are a form of free speech protected by the First Amendment, undermining campaign finance reforms and opening the floodgates for more spending.[27]

Hacker and Pierson mine a rich body of empirical research to demonstrate how policies resulting from the new politics have had tangible effects on the distribution of real income. Citing research by Thomas Piketty and Emmanuel Saez, they show that reductions in tax rates that began during the Reagan years disproportionately benefited the top 10 percent (the richest 150,000 families) and accounted for nearly one-third of their gain in income share between 1970 and 2000.[28] Unregulated corporate governance has allowed executive pay to soar regardless of merit or performance. Between 1970 and 2000, bonuses, stock options, and other obscure benefits drove the average compensation of top executives at the nation's largest firms up from $1 million annually to $6.5 million. From 1930 through 1970, executive pay had remained relatively stable.[29]

Wages and salaries in the financial sector roughly doubled (from 5 percent to 10 percent) as a share of the entire economy between 1975 and 2007.[30] If the new wealth was easily translated into power in the halls of Congress and the White House, one can only imagine its significance in New York, the financial capital of the nation, where the extremes in income skyrocketed through the stratosphere, and the city became more dependent on revenues from Wall Street to remain fiscally solvent. At Goldman Sachs—the pinnacle of New York investment banking excess—average pay for the top five executives averaged $60 million each in 2007; the average pay for all its employees, including clerical workers, was $385,000.[31] Hedge fund and private equity executives did even better, with earnings in the hundreds of millions. All this happened while 20 percent of all New Yorkers lived below the poverty line (under $18,284 for a family of three), and almost half were close to it.

Yes, there is a class war going on in America—and the rich are winning. Since the most decisive battles have been fought and won in Washington, it would be unreasonable to expect a local chief executive to turn the tide. But one might ask what a mayor can do to help blunt the effects of this broad, nationally induced state of inequality. That was not an explicit priority Michael Bloomberg brought to the office.[32] Michael Bloomberg was of, by, and for Wall Street—and proud of it. A native of Boston who had grown up in middle class Medford, Massachusetts, he was determined to apply all the skills he had mastered in the private sector to repair all of what he thought was wrong with New York City government.

After graduating from Johns Hopkins University and Harvard Business School, Bloomberg came to New York in 1966 to work for Salomon Brothers. He had a successful career there, becoming a partner before age thirty, but was let go in a reorganization of the firm in 1981. As dismissals go, it wasn't much of a personal setback. Bloomberg was given a $10 million severance package, which he used to start his own firm. What began as a four-person team and a set of computer terminals has revolutionized the way financial information is distributed, and has grown into a media empire with more than a hundred offices around the world. In 2016, *Forbes* estimated Bloomberg's personal net worth to be at $42.6 billion, making him the eighth richest man in the world.[33]

In 2001, Democrats were lining up like kids at a summer ice cream stand to determine who would succeed Rudy Giuliani as he became the first victim of the city's 1993 term limits law. The primary had been scheduled for September 11th, but was postponed for two weeks so that the city could regain its composure from the tragic events of that fateful day. In a racially charged matchup against three white opponents, the Puerto Rican-born Bronx Borough President Fernando Ferrer came in first with 34 percent of the vote, putting him in a runoff against Public Advocate Mark Green. (City Council Speaker Peter Vallone and City Comptroller Alan Hevesi were the other major contestants). A close association with the Reverend Al Sharpton, which helped Ferrer gain first place in the initial contest, running on a "Tale of Two Cities" platform, proved to be fatal in the run-off. Green won by a margin of 51 percent to 49 percent, the outcome determined along racial lines.[34]

After switching party affiliations to avoid a crowded field in the Democratic Party, Michael Bloomberg faced Herman Badillo (another former Democrat) in the Republican primary. Badillo had no money and no organization to mount a serious campaign, so he was easily defeated by the plodding businessman (65.8 percent to 25.3 percent), who had more money to spend than ever imaginable and was not shy about it. Mark Green, who enjoyed wide name recognition from his city-wide elected post as Public Advocate, and previous service as Consumer Affairs Commissioner, promised to be a more formidable opponent. The *Daily News*, which was owned by Bloomberg's friend Mort Zuckerman, was the only major newspaper to endorse him. The conservative *New York Post*, which endorsed Green during the primary out of fear that Ferrer's election could empower Al Sharpton, stayed neutral in the election.

Throwing its support behind the liberal Mark Green, the *New York Times* editorial board dedicated as much space to denouncing Bloomberg as it did to praising its preferred candidate. Referring to its decision as an "easy call," the editorial noted how the "successful entrepreneur" was "having trouble making a dent on the public consciousness."[35] Recalling that "Voters have historically been suspicious of novice candidates who promise to run government like a company," it deemed Bloomberg "ill matched to the job he covets." Calling Bloomberg's private company a product of his own character, the editorial reminded readers that he had no stockholders or unions to contend with in the business world.

As Bloomberg's candidacy got more exposure, stories emerged in the press about the hostile, degrading environment that confronted women employees at Bloomberg LP: reports of vulgar jokes, unwanted advances, sexual harassment, and outright discrimination—especially against young married females whose productivity in the workplace might be compromised when they became pregnant.[36] As he was the Republican nominee, Bloomberg gleaned endorsements from Governor George Pataki and outgoing mayor Rudolph Giuliani. He also received backing from former mayor Edward Koch who shared a long animosity with his own party's candidate. Still sullen from the primary, Fernando Ferrer offered a grudging endorsement to his Democratic colleague, but did little to mobilize minority voters. Al Sharpton encouraged blacks and Hispanics to stay home.

Bloomberg spent four times more on the election than his opponent ($73.1 million versus $17.4)—astronomical by any measure.[37] He recruited David Garth—the master of electoral politics in New York—to craft a media campaign designed to convince voters that, in the aftermath of 9/11, they needed the steady hand of a non-political businessman to put the city back on its feet. By a small margin, New Yorkers, still in a state of shock, bought the message, and put their faith in a man who was a virtual unknown, who had not engaged in public service since he was a Boy Scout. The margin of victory was 68,040 ballots.[38]

Bloomberg delivered on his promise. Although Ed Koch's former deputy Nathan Leventhal headed up Bloomberg's transition and helped recruit talented public managers for the incoming administration,[39] the new mayor's inner circle was dominated by people from the private sector, starting with Patricia Harris, his closest advisor. Harris began her career as an assistant to then-Congressman Edward Koch, and worked for the former mayor at City Hall. But immediately prior to her appointment in the Bloomberg administration, she had managed the Corporate Communications Department at Bloomberg LP, and was a key advisor to his electoral campaign. Harris was initially named Deputy Mayor for Administration, but eventually became First Deputy Mayor. Kevin Sheekey, who at one time had worked for Senator Daniel P. Moynihan, directed corporate communications at Bloomberg LP before helping with the campaign, and joined the City Hall team as a political advisor and media strategist. He too eventually carried the deputy mayor title.

Daniel Doctoroff, who started out as an investment banker at Lehman Brothers, was heading up a corporate effort to bring the 2012 Olympics— initially slotted for 2008—to New York City when Bloomberg came to office. The plan had significant developmental implications for the city, especially the West Side, making Doctoroff a key player in New York's powerful real estate industry. As Deputy Mayor for Economic Development, Doctoroff oversaw the administration's 127-point *PlaNYC*, the most ambitious development project undertaken in city history. He left the administration in 2008 to become president of Bloomberg LP, where he was tasked with transforming the growing financial information company into an international news organization.

In case one didn't get the message about the corporate culture Bloomberg intended to bring to City Hall, he underscored it graphically when he dismantled the graceful Board of Estimate chambers on the second floor of the landmark building to install a "bullpen" of fifty workstations arranged in cubicles to look like his office setup at Bloomberg LP. The room had been part of New York City history since 1812. Once the seat of the most powerful body in the government, it became a popular venue for ceremonial functions after the Board of Estimate was abolished in 1990. The architect Grosvenor Atterbury renovated it in 1912, installing a cork floor and white wooden benches, recalling the *Ragtime* era courtroom that it once was. The open-air stalls put in by Bloomberg resembled Wall Street trading floors, and were designed to maximize communication and transparency. Bloomberg himself abandoned the mayor's private office on the ground floor of City Hall and set up shop alongside his staff. Fiorello La Guardia's own desk that had been used with reverence by previous chief executives remained downstairs, unoccupied—now a relic of the distant past.

What did the new corporate vision mean for city government? According to one critical scholar, Bloomberg saw himself as the CEO of a private corporation that catered to a customer and client base composed of desirable New York residents and businesses, and the city itself as a product to be branded and marketed.[40] In fact, Bloomberg has referred to New York as a "luxury product."[41] The problem with luxury products is that they are inaccessible to all but a few privileged buyers. Residents are clients of city services, but they are also citizens. In a democratic system, citizens are entitled to a voice in government, and public officials are supposed to be accountable to them.

As Bloomberg was settling in at City Hall, his own office tower designed by Cesar Pelli was rising like a giant candlestick fifty-five stories above Lexington Avenue between East 58th and East 59th Streets. In addition to his own corporate offices and newsrooms, the building houses retail space, restaurants, luxury condominiums, and the studio where the Charlie Rose Show is recorded. A short walk from the Upper East Side townhouse where Bloomberg lives is a six-story Gilded Age building designed by Stanford White that Bloomberg purchased for $45 million to house Bloomberg Philanthropies, which coordinates his varied programs in annual giving.[42] Bloomberg was reported to have made donations exceeding $4.3 billion in his lifetime.[43] Bloomberg Philanthropies identifies five priorities of giving that were very much aligned with his priorities as mayor: the environment, public health, the arts, government innovation, and education.

At the same time that she was serving as First Deputy Mayor, Patricia Harris was appointed CEO of Bloomberg Philanthropies.[44] She served in both functions simultaneously, and retained her position at the foundation after Bloomberg left office. Unlike other individuals who have assumed the title of first deputy, Harris did not carry a large portfolio of agencies for which she had operational responsibility on a daily basis. She functioned more like an alter ego to the mayor who could authoritatively speak on his behalf. How the city's Conflicts of Interest Board (COIB) granted her permission to serve in both positions simultaneously is a true wonder. The arrangement was a prime illustration of how Bloomberg's personal wealth defined his governing style. The COIB's complicity in allowing the arrangement to go forward was a measure of the degree to which Bloomberg dominated the government, with few real checks on his power.

There is nothing wrong or illegal about a billionaire becoming mayor. Nevertheless, when political and financial power are so concentrated in the hands of a single individual, even in a big town such as New York, it raises issues that cannot be ignored. Throw in the mayor's ownership of a news channel that covers local events and the situation becomes more compromised. Fernando Ferrer got a second look at the man when he convinced himself to run again in 2005 and tried to unseat Bloomberg.[45] This time Bloomberg spent $85 million of his own money on the campaign, compared to $10 million that the former Bronx Borough President raised through the city public finance program.[46] Bloomberg won by a margin of 20 percent.

Michael Bloomberg was not supposed to have a third term as mayor. In 1993, the City Charter was amended to limit the tenure of all elected officials to two consecutive terms following a popular referendum that supported the change by a margin of 59-41 percent.[47] The City Council attempted to extend the limits to three terms in 1996, but its proposal was overwhelmingly rejected in a second popular vote by a margin of 54-46 percent. Bloomberg did not fly solo when he approached Christine Quinn and the City Council about allowing him to seek a third term. According to press reports, Bloomberg's envoys contacted individuals and institutions that had benefited from his philanthropy and pressured them to testify before the Council on his behalf.[48] Many complied.

After he got the go-ahead from the City Council to proceed—this time with no referenda asking what the citizens of New York thought—Bloomberg publicly declared that he was prepared to spend $80 million on his re-election campaign, as if to dare anyone to challenge him. Former comptroller William Thompson took up the dare, and came within 79,000 votes of winning.[49] This time Bloomberg spent more than $108 million compared to Thompson's $10 million.[50] It would be naïve to believe that money was not a factor in determining the outcome. In 2010, New Yorkers voted overwhelmingly (74 percent) to amend the City Charter and restore the limit for elected officials back to two terms.[51]

According to biographer Joyce Purnick, a long-time observer of all things New York, Michael Bloomberg is a "control freak" who likes to have his way and is accustomed to getting it.[52] He claims to be politically independent, but sometimes administers private charity the way politicians dole out government pork, which "chills dissent" and keeps the nonprofit sector in line. The former Metro editor of the *New York Times* cuts Bloomberg no slack for his aloof, profane, and occasionally sexist behavior.[53] Purnick, nonetheless, also rates Bloomberg "one of the most effective mayors in city history."[54] That assessment is not unreasonable. He accomplished much of what he set out to do, but fair-minded people can differ about the consequences.

Although Bloomberg was not a progressive mayor, the conservative label does not easily fit him either. During his first year in office, he enacted the highest property tax in city history to overcome a budget deficit, and then implemented cuts that helped middle class homeowners but not wealthy landlords or investors. Early on, he approved generous collective bargaining agreements with teachers and municipal workers; then, by the end of his third term, he refused to negotiate at all, leaving most city employees hanging without contracts.

Bloomberg's curt response to proposals that could have addressed income inequality cemented his reputation as a mayor of the privileged class. He accused legislative leaders of "trying to kill the golden goose" when they proposed a new state tax on hedge fund managers.[55] The City Council needed to override his vetoes in order to pass "living wage" and "prevailing wage" laws that benefited poorly paid workers.[56] He opposed a law enacted by the City Council to provide sick leave to certain businesses, claiming that the costs were prohibitive. At the same time, Bloomberg effectively used his fortune to advance national campaigns for immigration reform, gun control, and same-sex marriage, feeding speculation that he was preparing to run for president.

As discussed in Chapter 1, Bloomberg and his Police Commissioner Raymond Kelly took a tough stand on quality-of-life infractions, continuing the aggressive approach to street enforcement that began under Mayor Giuliani. The results were impressive. The incidence rate in the FBI's seven major felony categories continued to fall between 2000 and 2010, as follows: homicide (33 percent), rape (51 percent), robbery (46 percent), assault (38 percent), burglary (52 percent), auto theft (72 percent), and larceny (23 percent).[57] Criminologists will argue that crime reductions disproportionately benefit poor and minority communities, where crime tends to be higher. However, as noted earlier, some aspects of Commissioner Kelly's signature "stop-and-frisk" tactic were declared unconstitutional because it was disproportionately applied against racial minorities.[58] The practice peaked in 2011 with 685,000 stops, up from 97,000 ten years earlier. Eighty-three percent of those stopped were black or Hispanic. According to a study of 4.3 million stops, presented at the trial, only 12 percent resulted in an arrest or summons, suggesting that 88 percent of those stopped were doing nothing wrong.[59]

One of Bloomberg's first major acts as mayor was to get the state legislature to give him control of the school system. Every mayor since Abe Beame had wanted it. Every mayoral candidate in 2001, except Fernando Ferrer, had vowed to acquire it. The time had finally come.[60] Even the teachers' union, that, in the past, could lean on the five borough presidents (who collectively had five appointees) to exert more influence on the former seven-member Board of Education than the mayor (who had two), finally came around on the issue. Bloomberg's generous contract with the teachers did not hurt in bringing them along. The public was demanding more accountability from the underperforming school system; it wanted somebody to take charge. The mayor, who was the most visible figure in local government, was the most obvious choice. Putting him in charge of the schools would also give the city an incentive to invest more resources in education.[61]

Beyond his personal financial status, Michael Bloomberg was, institutionally, the most powerful chief executive to govern New York in more than a century. The abolition of the Board of Estimate in 1990 eliminated the most formidable check on mayoral power that had existed since consolidation. Contrary to the hopes of those who revised the City Charter, the City Council was never able to fill the vacuum.[62] In fact, it rarely tried. David Dinkins, the first mayor to serve under the new charter, had already been weakened by financial constraints and political crosscurrents that left him treading in troubled waters somewhere between the Koch and Giuliani administrations. Mayor Giuliani and City Council Speaker Peter Vallone shared many of the same priorities. Speaker Christine Quinn would learn to do likewise with Bloomberg. Taking over the schools, which had functioned semi-autonomously—except for reliance on the city for local revenues—was the icing on a very large cake for a new mayor who cherished his executive role.

What Bloomberg did with the schools turned out to be controversial. His choice for Chancellor, Joel Klein, was a former Assistant U.S. Attorney with no relevant experience. It was an extraordinarily high risk for the mayor to put the future of 1.1 million students and the nation's largest school system in the hands of a man who knew nothing about education, and a contemptuous affront to the thousands of professionals who labored in the schools. Klein compounded his own lack of expertise by dismissing many experienced administrators in the central headquarters and replacing them with lawyers, consultants, and private sector types. His agenda was bold, which heightened the risks. To his credit, Bloomberg infused the system with new funding. Local spending on education spiraled from $8.6 billion in 2000 to $14.4 billion in 2013.[63] His chancellor developed the Fair Student Funding method to channel more of those resources into needy schools.[64]

Joel Klein staked his reputation on an agenda that imposed increased accountability, higher standards, and more school choice—all of which were politically divisive propositions. He gave more autonomy to school principals so that they were better able to implement innovations, but the massive data collection system his staff designed could be costly, cumbersome, and impractical.[65] He ended social promotion, but his *Children First* programs did not introduce serious pedagogical interventions that improved teaching and learning. His initial reading curriculum was rejected by the U.S. Department of Education. Under Klein the system was reorganized three times, creating chaos for employees and parents. Teachers and principals complained about the "reform of the day." Organizational analysts might classify such an approach to change as "experimental," but in the hands of a schools chancellor who knew nothing about schools, it seemed more like "hit and miss."[66]

Klein's push for school choice came in three forms. He instituted a program in the high schools that gave entering students more options and discretion in selecting schools, but the effort was undermined by a shortage of desirable schools from which to choose. In a system where most schools are not doing well academically, choice is an empty promise if it does not come with new educational options. Klein also created two hundred small schools to replace large factory-style institutions that were suffering from chronic failure. Assessments of student outcomes suggested that the new small schools were making progress and that the gains were sustained.[67]

More than anything else, Joel Klein opened the door for the growth of charter schools in New York City, with their number increasing from 14 in 2000 to 183 in 2013.[68] Many public school advocates perceive charter schools as a threat to district schools, and the performance record on charters is mixed when viewed on a national scale. Research at the time by reputable scholars, however, was finding that charter schools in New York City outperformed their counterparts in the rest of the country, and that their students did better than their peers attending district schools in New York.[69] These positive trends at charter schools continued after Bloomberg, and quickly became a problem for Bill de Blasio because he instinctively sided with those who opposed them.[70]

Klein also moved swiftly to close schools that were at the lowest end of the performance scale—forty-four in all between 2000 and 2014. Teachers were displaced, parents got angry, and students felt unsettled. When you shut down a faltering institution, it leaves a hole in the community, but when you let students remain in a failing institution for too long, it can leave holes in their lives. The closure strategy is controversial, but the research on it is moderately encouraging. In 2013, Chicago closed forty-seven schools that were underperforming and under-enrolled. An evaluation of the outcomes by researchers at the University of Chicago found that 93 percent of the displaced students transferred to schools with higher performance ratings.[71] An examination of twenty-nine schools being closed in New York revealed that the phaseout did not have a positive or negative effect on students who were already enrolled in the designated schools, but that the students who would have been likely to attend them in the future ended up attending better performing schools.[72]

In 2007, as the law that gave the mayor control of the schools was about to sunset, legislative leaders in Albany asked Betsy Gotbaum, the city's public advocate, to appoint a commission to study the experience with the new governance arrangement and assess its merits. The commission was chaired by Stephen Aiello, a former president of the Board of Education, who had subsequently served in the Carter White House. The commission spent a year meeting with key stakeholders and parent groups, holding public hearings, and soliciting expert reports.[73] It found strong support for mayoral control of the schools, and little interest in returning to the previous system of locally elected school boards. However, it also identified deep concerns about the lack of checks on the power of the mayor and insufficient opportunities for input by parents and other stakeholders into the policymaking process.[74]

Michael Bloomberg's greatest achievement in education was to undo a system that few people had confidence in anymore. What he put in its place was better, but inadequate. The governing structure was too centralized and teachers were micromanaged. The limited expansion of charter schools instituted an alternative service delivery system for instruction that had the potential to elevate academic performance for a diverse population of students. The remainder of the system, the bulk of the schools, however, remained adrift. Scores from tests administered by the National Assessment of Educational Progress (NAEP), commonly called "the Nation's Report Card," indicate that, despite significant increases in spending and several attempts to reorganize the system, there was only a modest improvement in basic academic skills between 2002 and 2011.[75] Bloomberg's faith in private sector credentials reached a point of absurdity when he named publishing executive Cathie Black to succeed Klein. She possessed neither education nor government experience. Her tenure lasted six weeks before she was replaced by Deputy Mayor Dennis Walcott.

The attack on the World Trade Center wreaked havoc on the city economy, which was already suffering from the stock market collapse of 2000 and the national recession that had begun to take hold in March 2001. The devastation itself destroyed or damaged $30 billion worth of office space, displaced 13,000 mostly financial sector workers in the immediate area, and by the fourth quarter of 2001 led to the loss of 75,000 to 100,000 jobs in other industries such as tourism and travel. By July 2002, economic activity had fallen by $17.6 billion. Costs to the municipality resulting from lost revenue and related expenses are estimated at $2.1 billion.[76] After several years of budget surpluses enjoyed at the end of the Giuliani administration, Mayor Bloomberg started off with a budget deficit of $2.4 billion.[77]

The near recovery of Lower Manhattan in just four years was something of a miracle.[78] Governor George Pataki was a driving force. Expecting Mayor Giuliani to be succeeded by a Democrat, he and the outgoing Republican mayor arranged for the state-controlled Empire State Development Corporation (ESDC) to play an outsized role through the creation of the Lower Manhattan Development Corporation, an offshoot of ESDC. Federal aid to the tune of $21 billion was certainly a factor—once again demonstrating both the influence of Wall Street and Washington's role in the fulfillment of big city dreams.[79]

Numerous public, private, and nonprofit institutions such as the Port Authority of New York and New Jersey, the Regional Plan Association, the Real Estate Board of New York, the New York City Partnership and Chamber of Commerce, and the newly formed Lower Manhattan Development Corporation participated in the effort. This may have been the most high profile urban renewal project ever undertaken. The city government was also engaged, but the mayor and his deputy clearly focused their attention elsewhere, and the governor didn't seem to mind.[80]

There was a natural symmetry between Dan Doctoroff's crusade to capture the 2012 Olympics and Mike Bloomberg's determination to redraw the topography of New York. By hosting the international games, New York could show the world that it had recovered magnificently from the destruction of the Twin Towers. Preparations that would enable the city to become a showcase for the world's greatest athletes would stimulate that recovery. Doctoroff, whose mentor at Lehman Brothers had been Koch's deputy mayor for economic development, Peter Solomon, already had aligned many of the city's real estate and economic barons behind the Olympic project before Bloomberg was sworn in. There was giddy anticipation all around with visions of jobs, revenues, and profits that could materialize under the Olympic flag.

An essential element of the bid for the games was a proposal to build a new stadium on the far west side of Manhattan, which was to proceed in tandem with commercial and residential development. The city planning department simultaneously produced the *Hudson Yards Plan* to rezone the area and facilitate building. A metal platform was to be laid over the Long Island Railroad storage yard as a base for new structures. The Jacob Javits Convention Center was slated for expansion. The Farley Post Office would become Penn Station. The Number 7 subway line from Queens would be extended to 11th Avenue. Other game-related amenities were promised for Brooklyn and Queens.

Mayor Giuliani had pushed hard to build a West Side stadium for the Yankees that never came to pass. Doctoroff saw the Olympic stadium as a permanent home for the New York Jets, and an opportunity to return professional football to New York. But the administration underestimated local opposition to the new stadium, and overestimated enthusiasm for the games themselves, weakening its bid to the International Olympic Committee (IOC).[81] Although the IOC's selection of London as the host city for 2012 put an end to Olympic dreams for New York, the decision by no means discouraged the urge for development.

It was a year into his second term, on Earth Day in late April, that Mayor Bloomberg announced the most comprehensive initiative of his administration. Appearing at the American Museum of Natural History after the screening of laudatory video presentations by California governor Arnold Schwarzenegger and British prime minister Tony Blair, Bloomberg presented *PlaNYC: A Greener, Greater New York,* which he described as a blueprint for creating "the first environmentally sustainable 21st-century city."[82] Blind to the home mortgage meltdown and national recession around the corner, the confident entrepreneur mayor declared, "Our economy is humming, our fiscal house is in order, and the near-term horizon looks bright." Looking a quarter century into the future when the size of the population was projected to exceed 9 million, the 127 proposals contained in the plan were all encompassing, bolder than anything Robert Moses could have imagined, certainly more politically palatable than many things the master builder had propagated.

PlaNYC grew out of a study by former City Planning Commissioner Alex Garvin that Deputy Mayor Dan Doctoroff had commissioned.[83] Garvin saw opportunities for growth lying in wait along the city's abandoned industrial waterfront and atop ugly rail yards. He envisioned new public spaces and improved mass transit with recommendations for how growth could be managed with an eye toward sustainability. This was just a kernel of what would be proposed a year after Gavin completed his work.

PlaNYC pledged to build or rehabilitate affordable housing for 1 million New Yorkers, open 290 schoolyards and playgrounds so that every resident was within a ten-minute walk to a recreational facility, clean up 7,600 acres of brownfields, plant 1 million trees, complete major transportation projects such as the Second Avenue Subway, improve efficiency in energy consumption, address climate change, protect waterfront areas from flooding, develop backup systems to the aging water network, upgrade power sources, reduce greenhouse gasses by 30 percent, and reduce water pollution. Borrowing a page from the progressive playbook, the blueprint assumed huge financial commitments from the federal and state governments. It relied on the creation of new state and federal authorities to guarantee financing, implement programs, and enforce new standards for health and safety.

Progressive planners criticized the blueprint for its exclusion of public voices representing the interests of community residents. They portray the process as insular and out of reach, a public relations sham that mimicked real involvement. Tom Angotti, a professor and Director of the Center for Community Planning and Development at Hunter College, described the public forums put on by the administration as such:

> The forums were designed so that civic, environmental and neighbor-hood development groups would be familiar with the plan as it devel-oped, but did not produce a two-way dialogue that could significantly change the plan. Colorful slide presentations showcased the plan, and people who attended were asked to submit their comments, either ver-bally in a limited and highly controlled format, in writing, or on the city's website. All decisions were made outside the public arena. It was essentially a one-way, top-down process, and the discretion about what to put in the plan remained at City Hall.[84]

The most controversial and widely discussed feature of *PlaNYC* was a pro-posal for "congestion pricing" that would charge $8 per day for vehicles entering Manhattan below 86th Street. With sound planning in mind, the initiative was meant to reduce gridlock and air pollution. The $200 million a year in revenue from fees could be invested in mass transit and bike lanes. The plan, however, also reeked of elitism. The $40 per week it cost low and middle-income commut-ers could be prohibitive—as it was meant to be. In the meantime, street passage would be facilitated so that plutocrats could be chauffeured around Manhattan more easily in their oversized limos and SUVs.

Like the plan for an Olympic stadium, congestion pricing went down to astounding defeat. It was never brought to the floor of the State Assembly, where it needed approval. The fate of congestion pricing was another lesson in New York City politics for the entrepreneur mayor. In the public sector there is a difference between deciding and doing. There are many checkpoints in the approval and implementation process for a chief executive. From the perspec-tive of a private sector manager, the process appears cumbersome and hide-bound. From the perspective of democratic governance, the process is a way to give people a voice in policies that affect their lives.

Notwithstanding his setbacks in Albany, Bloomberg boasted a hefty inventory of achievements at the end of his third term that were purportedly brought forth in collaboration with diverse partners from the real estate, business, and not-for-profit communities, as well as the federal and state governments.[85] According to a progress report issued in 2013, the administration had rezoned 36 percent of the total built area in the five boroughs, encompassing over 11,000 city blocks. Affected areas included the 125th Street corridor in Harlem, Coney Island in Brooklyn, Jamaica in Queens, the Lower Concourse in the Bronx, and St. George in Staten Island. It claimed to have created or preserved 92,000 units of housing.

Rezoned areas near targeted transit routes included the East Village/Lower East Side, Bedford-Stuyvesant South in Brooklyn, Williamsbridge/Baychester in the Bronx, and Sunnyside/Woodside in Queens. The city had developed a comprehensive plan setting forth a long-range vision for 520 miles of waterfront property that converted former warehouses and industrial space to residential, commercial, and recreational use. It planted 750,000 trees, and installed 300 miles of bike paths furnished with a new bike share program.

And, of course, Bloomberg was proud to mention, "Times Square is now one of the world's most famous pedestrian plazas." The cleanup effort had dated back to the Koch years, when it was led by Carl Weisbrod, the man who would become Chair of the City Planning Commission for Mayor Bill de Blasio. Tourism had in fact replaced manufacturing as a keystone of the local economy, and the reconfigured shiny new plaza that attracted throngs of visitors was to be an emblem of that change.

The administration was already halfway to its goal of reducing the city's carbon footprint by 30 percent before 2030. Having enacted the "most ambitious green buildings law in the nation," and adopting a green heat program, a green infrastructure plan, and a range of climate resilience initiatives, the mayor asserted that his team had set "the world's standard for municipal sustainability plans." There were tangible measures to support his claim: 95 brownfield cleanup projects under way, 174 city-owned buildings refit to reduce emissions by 24,000 metric tons, 1,900 private buildings converted to clean fuel to reduce heavy oil emissions by 25 percent, a reduction of greenhouse gas emissions by 16 percent, and an increased understanding of climate risk, improving the city's capacity to prepare for storms such as Hurricane Sandy.

Mayor Bloomberg's pledge to leave behind a more sustainable New York was consistent with his personal commitment to public health. Public health was a major priority of his private philanthropy; he had donated hundreds of millions of dollars to the Johns Hopkins University School of Public Health that bears his name. As mayor, he outlawed cigarette smoking in bars, restaurants, and public areas such as parks, beaches, and shopping plazas. He banned the use of trans fats in fast food restaurants, and required eating establishments to post calorie counts. He also tried to prohibit restaurants, food carts, and movie theaters from selling sugary beverages in large containers (16 ounces), but his regulation was tossed out by the courts. When the mayor tried to disqualify the use of food stamps to buy such drinks, President Obama countered that the restriction would be difficult to administer.

Such headstrong interventions to advance public health led to accusations that Bloomberg was running a "nanny state." Tom Farley, his second Commissioner of Health, cites data to suggest that the administration's bold actions reaped positive outcomes: between 2001 and 2010, life expectancy at birth in the city increased 3.0 years to 80.9, as opposed to a gain of 1.8 years nationally to 78.7. The health department traced 50 percent of the change to a decline in heart disease, and another 16 percent to a decline in cancer—two diseases it had targeted.[86]

Whether the recorded improvements in public health can be directly tied to Bloomberg's policies may be debatable, but the value of the administration's campaigns to attack obesity, hypertension, asthma, and smoke contamination is not. The conditions he zeroed in on disproportionately harm poor and minority communities. One has to question why the same mayor opposed a bill in the City Council that required fast food businesses such as McDonalds to provide employees with paid sick days. Is it better to have food handlers show up to work when they are ill? One also has to wonder why a mayor who vowed to redraw the map of the city and create tens of thousands of new housing units allowed the homeless rate to climb to its highest level since the Great Depression.

From the outset, the Bloomberg administration was philosophically committed to pursuing a preventive as well as a responsive approach to homelessness.[87] In 2004, the mayor pledged that he would slash the homeless population of 36,399 by two-thirds within five years by building more housing, investing more in preventive services, and making sure that the shelter system is only being used by people who need it.[88] In 2005, Mayor Bloomberg and Governor Pataki agreed to implement New York/New York III, which was slated to add more than 9,000 units to the affordable housing stock following the template that emerged during the Dinkins and Giuliani years.[89]

The program appeared to be successful for a while, but it was insufficient to address a problem that would accelerate during the recession. A report released by the Independent Budget Office in August 2008 found that although some progress had been made, the administration had failed to meet the goals it had announced in 2004.[90] The number of families living in shelters remained at 8,500, and the number of people living on the street declined by about 25 percent, or 3,300 individuals. The news prompted criticism from Bill de Blasio, who as chair of the City Council's General Welfare Committee had commissioned the report.[91]

In 2007, Mayor Bloomberg, with state support, created the Work Advantage program to give housing subsidies for up to two years to people in shelters on the condition that they work or are enrolled in a job-training program. Architects of the program hoped that it would help participants gain self-sufficiency, but many of those in the program ended up in low-paying or insecure jobs. When the subsidy ran out in two years, they reverted back to homelessness. The Coalition for the Homeless estimated that 25 percent of the enrolled families returned to the shelter system.[92]

At the end of 2009, the New York City Housing Authority (NYCHA) informed 2,600 households that it would need to rescind the rent subsidies they received under the Section 8 Federal Housing Choice Voucher Program. Apparently, NYCHA had miscalculated attrition rates in the program and exceeded its federal cap on the number of vouchers.[93] The Section 8 program had offered its clients a unique opportunity for permanent housing by making up the difference between rent costs and what they could afford. The worst blow to the homeless crisis, however, was yet to come. In 2011 Mayor Bloomberg ended the Advantage program and its subsidies for 9,000 participating families when Governor Andrew Cuomo eliminated its state funding and redirected the funds into other programs, sending more people into the shelter system.[94] The mayor's decision to terminate the Advantage program was temporarily halted by a lawsuit from the Legal Aid Society, but was ultimately sustained by a state appellate court.

By 2014, the size of the homeless population had leaped to more than 50,000. A report prepared by the Coalition for the Homeless found that although median income in the city's poorest neighborhoods decreased 7 percent between 2010 and 2014, rents rose 26 percent; between 2011 and 2014, the city lost 175,000 units renting for less than $1,000 per month.[95] It was clear that the long-term answer to the homeless problem was more affordable housing. With the federal and state government withdrawing from any serious effort to house the poor, this placed the problem back in the lap of the city.

The rules of the game were established well before Michael Bloomberg took office. In order for a serious conversation to take place about housing development, public officials needed to make a pitch to the real estate and finance tycoons who controlled resources. They would want to know what was in it for them. Bloomberg reinforced these rules. When he rolled out his original proposal in December 2002 to build or rehabilitate 65,000 units of affordable housing (raised to 165,000 in 2006), he called it the *New Housing Marketplace Plan* (NHMP).[96] He encouraged leaders in the real estate industry to invest, identify feasible sites, and simply make deals. He encouraged them to be optimistic and aggressive about New York's real estate future. This was not the kind of ambitious public housing program we had seen bear fruit under Fiorello La Guardia, or even Ed Koch. It was an unabashed attempt to stimulate private development to fill in gaps that had been left by the federal government's divestment from affordable housing.

Michael Bloomberg had sworn off corporate welfare when he was elected. In the early days of his administration, he killed a deal made by his predecessor that involved a $1.1 billion subsidy to the New York Stock Exchange. The Exchange was threatening to depart for New Jersey; Bloomberg knew it would not. It did not take long for him to get with the program after that. During Bloomberg's first eighteen months in office, the city executed sixty-three job retention deals. Among those who reaped rewards were Merrill Lynch, American Airlines, Met Life, Forest City Ratner, and the *New York Post*. Between 2002 and 2005, tax expenditures (revenue sacrificed) increased from $2.1 billion to $3.3 billion. Eighty-five percent of these "expenditures" amounting to $2.8 billion was related to property tax abatements. During Bloomberg's first three years in office, the number of applications for assessment reductions submitted to the Tax Commission rose from 2,823 valued at $444 million to 4,672 valued at $2.4 billion. The beneficiaries included the World Financial Center ($108.3 million), Olympia & York ($72.5 million), Citibank ($17 million), and the Millenium Hilton ($32.7 million).[97]

Bloomberg sank a plan hatched by Mayor Giuliani to build a new stadium for the Yankees, but then he signed off on deals to build new ball fields for the Yankees and the Mets, and supported the erection of a basketball arena for the New York Nets as part of the Atlantic Yards project in Downtown Brooklyn. Such stadium deals are complicated, and there is always a question as to whether they benefit the cities involved.[98]

With regard to the Yankees, for example, the team had agreed to assume the cost of putting up a new stadium on land adjacent to the old ballpark.[99] The city, however, assured financing through tax-free bonds (a loss of revenue), and the team's future payments on them were accepted in lieu of taxes (another loss of revenue). The city also assumed costs for the construction of a new transit station, replacement of parks that were destroyed on the location of the new facility, and parking garages. Ticket prices for the new ballpark could run into the hundreds of dollars, but even the cheaper upper-deck seats could be out of reach for local Bronx residents. Might the city have used its scarce resources on something more worthwhile than subsidizing the richest team in major league baseball? How about affordable housing?

As the Bloomberg administration was entering its last year in office, it had arranged financing for 143,305 housing units promised under the NHMP. Unfortunately, much of it was not accessible to poor families living in the very areas where apartments were now available. A report prepared by the Association for Neighborhood and Housing Development found that one-third of the units built have an upper income limit above the median income for New Yorkers. In half the city's community districts, the majority of units built are too costly for households earning the local medium income.[100] Because apartments maintain their "affordable status" only temporarily before they are rented at market rates, the report predicted that by the year 2037, the city could lose as many affordable units as it had gained under NHMP.

In the meantime, the market was abuzz with news of super luxury apartments that were sprouting up in more exclusive neighborhoods. Developers of the tower at 432 Park Avenue, designed by Uruguayan architect Rafael Vinoly and completed in 2015, boasted that it would be the tallest residential building in the Western Hemisphere. Apartments were listed in the $20 million to $80 million price-range. That was a tempting bargain compared to what it would cost you for a comfy abode just a few blocks west at One57, where luxury condominiums already were selling above $90 million.[101] That's where the money is if you are a New York developer.

One person's development project is another's plan for gentrification. Former working class and low-income neighborhoods such as Harlem, Hell's Kitchen, Williamsburg in Brooklyn, and High Bridge in the Bronx might never become Park Avenue, but they have been spruced up with expensive apartments that long-time residents cannot afford.[102] Was the exclusion purposeful or circumstantial? Hadn't we seen this movie before? In the 1960s, the process was derisively referred to as "Negro removal through urban renewal." In the seventies, Housing Commissioner Roger Starr promoted "planned shrinkage." You improved a neighborhood by replacing the poor with a "better" class of people. The shoreline in Williamsburg, Brooklyn, now looks like Battery Park City, and it can cost as much to live there.

The calculations need not be so crude. From a strictly business perspective, it is more profitable to build housing that brings in higher rents. When business people play an outsized role in the decision-making, those criteria hold. Volumes have been written by progressive planners detailing how the public and community residents have been excluded from meaningful participation in the planning process, as was already suggested with regard to *PlaNYC*.[103] We heard similar complaints regarding the public's role in education policy during the Bloomberg administration. It used to be that the building industry in New York was controlled by family dynasties with names such as Zeckendorf, Helmsley, Durst—and yes Trump. In a globalized economy, these family clans now share an embroidered terrain with powerful international conglomerates whose only stake in New York City is their investments.[104]

The erosion of community-based planning was facilitated in 2005 when the U.S. Supreme Court granted local governments broad discretion to condemn and assume possession of privately owned property solely for the purpose of economic development.[105] In New York State, if a state or public authority is assigned responsibility for implementing a development project, the entire community-based procedure for land use review encoded in the City Charter— popularly referred to as ULURP—is legally circumvented. This is what happened when the Empire State Development Corporation took over the Atlantic Yards project in Brooklyn and displaced almost 1,000 residents. This was also the case when the Lower Manhattan Development Corporation engineered the rebuilding of Ground Zero.

If John Lindsay's mayoralty marked the height of decentralized community-based governance for New York, Michael Bloomberg's tenure epitomized a post-fiscal crisis era of corporate governance dominated by the finance, insurance, and real estate industries. The Bronx is no longer burning—but all of New York is on FIRE. At the end of Bloomberg's tenure at City Hall, a *New York Times* poll revealed that a majority of New Yorkers believed his policies favored the rich over the poor and middle class.[106]

* * *

This is the city that Michael Bloomberg handed over to Bill de Blasio. The political culture had the ambience of a comfortable plutocracy. Those who were privileged took it as an entitlement, and they had the power to preserve what they owned. The structure of the government was more centralized than it had been in more than a century. Those who were underprivileged had fewer access points than ever, and lacked the means to control much of their own cheerless destinies. The socioeconomic structure was stratified so that extremes in wealth and poverty were more severe than almost anywhere else in the free world. There may have been a changing of the guard at City Hall underway, but the sultans of Wall Street remained snug in their sinecures of power. Decision-makers in Washington did everything they could to keep the deck stacked against the small guy.

PART III

BEING MAYOR

Let's Take City Hall

It was not the usual kind of event for somebody intending to announce his run for mayor of America's largest city. First, an email went out to friends and supporters in late January 2013 asking, "What are you doing on Sunday?"[1] It was meant to be a family affair—in true de Blasio fashion. As Bill conveyed in his email, "My family is making a very big announcement this weekend." Two hundred people gathered to hear what they had to say in front of 442 11th Street, the modest clapboard house in Park Slope where Bill and Chirlane raised their two children.

Dante, then a sixteen-year-old high school junior, was the first to speak, telling the crowd, "I am here to support my Dad," whom he described as a man who "serves all people," not just "the rich and powerful." Dante then read a statement from his sister Chiara, who was away at college in California. She called her father a "selfless human." Next, Chirlane introduced Bill as "an outer-borough working dad, a public school parent, a lifelong progressive reformer" and "a leader who champions New York as a city of neighborhoods and families."[2] She emphasized their deep roots in the diverse Brooklyn community and how much their modest home meant to them. Bill did the same when he finally spoke, memorializing Little League games in Prospect Park and basketball at the public school gym.

There was something 1950s Americana about the entire scene. With a few demographic adjustments, this is a traditional, intact family dedicated to its home, its community, and each other—a throwback to the past, and yet a projection into the future. They shared the same aspirations as other families, and similar problems. If we did not know better, we might dismiss the scene as a wooden stage set assembled by the campaign staff to mimic Thornton Wilder, instructing us that small town virtue is the bedrock foundation of a dream that was once America's.[3] But this wasn't rural New Hampshire at the turn of the last century; this was Brooklyn at the edge of the twenty-first. This was the man who once left behind a career as a Washington political operative to run for his local school board and city council. This was the college student from Massachusetts who once told his roommate that what he most wanted to do with his life is work for local government in New York. This was the future mayor, who, after his election, baffled reporters when he kept coming back to the neighborhood to work out at the local Y and visit his old haunts.

After de Blasio recounted his personal story and the highlights of his early career, he talked policy. No surprises here: affordable housing, reining in bad landlords, universal childcare and after-school programs for working families, paid sick days, a living wage, and help to small businesses. He focused on "good, clean, safe, strong neighborhoods" and the need to improve police-community relations by mending a "stop-and-frisk" policy that unfairly targeted men of color. He promised to provide early education and after-school programs for all New Yorkers and pay for them by taxing the rich. Then he took aim at the man he was running against. Not at another Democrat he had to beat in the September 10th primary, nor at a Republican he would meet heading into the November general election. His sights were set on Michael Bloomberg, the outgoing three-term mayor, who in de Blasio's mind was largely responsible for distorted priorities that had placed the city on a disastrous course for twelve years.

De Blasio first complimented Bloomberg for his battles against smoking and obesity, and his work on immigration reform, gun control, and climate change. Then he leaned in to denounce the "backroom deal" between the former mayor and the City Council that awarded Bloomberg a third term previously rejected in two popular referenda. In so doing, he also took a swipe at Council Speaker Christine Quinn, who had engineered the deal and was now considered the front-runner in the mayoral contest, with polls predicting that she would take 35 percent of the Democratic Party primary votes to his projected 11 percent.[4] De Blasio also called out his other Democratic Party rivals, who might tip-toe around Bloomberg and pretend that his vision for the city "just needs to be tweaked here and there" and carried into the future. He criticized the past administration for "demonizing teachers" and for choosing a schools chancellor (not referring to Cathie Black by name) "more for her social status than her educational experience."

Invoking the Supreme Court's Citizens United decision that left the American political process open to unprecedented amounts of campaign spending, he reminded the audience that Bloomberg had spent $108 million on his re-election campaign in 2009. He further lamented, "I think maybe we've all gotten a little numb because our democracy has been repeatedly attacked by the power of money. . . ." Noting that one in five New Yorkers lives in poverty, he chided City Hall as a place that "too often has catered to the interests of the elite rather than the needs of everyday New Yorkers." He urged "average New Yorkers" to "refuse to allow their community voices to be stifled." De Blasio, an insider of sorts in New York politics, was running as an outsider—against City Hall.

Taking on Michael Bloomberg in 2013 incurred considerable risk. The former mayor had enormous resources to deploy either to aid or hinder a particular candidate. So far as de Blasio was concerned, it might have been wiser to allow the billionaire powerhouse to ride off into the night and remain neutral. But de Blasio was trying to prove a larger point (to himself and others) about the nature of democratic elections. After three consecutive mayoral contests decided by record amounts of campaign spending, de Blasio saw 2013 as an opportunity to show that a popular vote driven by a more inclusive vision of the public interest could prevail in the voting booth. His emblematic "Tale of Two Cities" mantra was a social, economic, and political reality that could be supported with facts. It was a reality that could no longer be camouflaged behind a naïve notion of the American Dream. The word was out: people were feeling the pain; Michael Bloomberg personified the problem; the popular vote determine the elections.

Manhattan Borough President Scott Stringer had considered entering the race for mayor in 2013, but then he took a safer course by running to succeed City Comptroller John Liu. The first Asian American ever elected to a citywide office, Liu declared his candidacy for mayor, but his campaign was stymied by a federal investigation into his finances. Christine Quinn enjoyed the most name recognition and pulled an early endorsement from Emily's List, the political action committee dedicated to the election of women who are "pro-choice" on the abortion issue. She also got early backing by the United Food & Commercial Workers, and had no difficulty raising the $4.9 million allowed under the city's public financing system.[5]

When Quinn officially announced her candidacy in March, she identified herself as the grandchild of Irish immigrants who was "about keeping New York City a place for the middle class to live and grow and a place that's going to help all those hardworking people get into the middle class."[6] Quinn had grown up in Glen Cove, Long Island. Her father, a devoted campaigner, had been an electrical worker and shop steward for his union. She lost her mother at the age of sixteen, following an agonizing ten-year battle with breast cancer. Her first job in the city was as a tenant organizer before she became head of the New York City Gay and Lesbian Anti-Violence Project.

Quinn referred proudly to her work as Speaker of the City Council, where she passed seven balanced budgets, enacted laws to protect immigrants, expanded preschool programs, saved 4,000 teaching jobs, kept libraries and firehouses open, and (eventually) adopted a living wage law. Sounding like Hillary Clinton running against Bernie Sanders, she insisted, "I'm about getting things done." Hers was another impressive New York story about overcoming modest beginnings and hardship to launch a successful career in public service. Nevertheless, it would be difficult for her to shake her connection to the billionaire businessman-turned-politician with whom she collaborated for three consecutive terms.

To make matters worse for Quinn, she did not receive the kind of support many believed was forthcoming from Bloomberg. In early December, the *New York Times* had run a story, vigorously denied by Deputy Mayor Howard Wolfson, that Bloomberg was shopping around for a more desirable candidate to support, and that he had even approached Hillary Clinton with an offer.[7] There were recurring rumors that Police Commissioner Raymond Kelly might enter the race with the blessing of his admiring boss. Despite Quinn's obvious advantage of having a billionaire incumbent on her side, Bloomberg could have been more helpful in lining up key players from New York's powerful real estate and financial communities behind Quinn.

Quinn had built her own relationships with the business community over time. In the end though, she seemed to reap few of the advantages and many of the disadvantages that could flow from her association with the mega business-man who occupied the other wing of City Hall during her time as Speaker. This was especially problematic in a contest where the dialogue would increasingly be defined in terms of class and income—and where Bill de Blasio was ready to remind voters that Quinn had aligned with Bloomberg to oppose higher corporate taxes, paid sick leave, and a living wage bill (the latter of which she belatedly supported).

Although William (Billy) Thompson was polling at about the same level as de Blasio at the outset of the 2013 race, he had the potential to be a formidable candidate. In 2009, he had come within five percentage points of denying Michael Bloomberg a third term (50 to 46.3), even though Bloomberg had spent a record amount of money to win.[8] Thompson had no serious opponent in the Democratic Party primary that year, and was also granted a ballot line by the Working Families Party. Pundits continue to argue over whether Thompson's votes were really cast for him or against Bloomberg, but he was still starting with a large base of the electorate that already had chosen his name on the ballot line for mayor once before. Thompson's 2009 race also offered a lesson in populist politics that was not lost on Bill de Blasio. It demonstrated that in a city where too many people can't make ends meet, wealth and privilege can be liabilities at the ballot box. De Blasio intended to exploit that disparity more aggressively than the mild-mannered Thompson.

Thompson is the son of a prominent state appellate court judge who was an influential figure in the Brooklyn Democratic party machine, which paved the way for his rise through the ranks of the large and powerful organization. Except for a brief stint on Wall Street, he had spent most of his career amassing an impressive record of public service. As a young man, he served as a congressional aide and Deputy Borough President. In 1994, he was appointed to the

city's Board of Education and became president of the citywide education policy panel two years later, a position he held when Bill de Blasio was making his
pitch for a spot on his neighborhood board. There he worked closely with the
teachers union, which endorsed his candidacy in 2013. Thompson's deep roots
in the party organization also gave him an opportunity to develop strong ties
with the Hasidic Jews of Williamsburg. These and other broad connections he
accumulated across the city had helped him gain two terms as City Comptroller.

Unlike most black politicians in the city, Thompson was not an outspoken critic of the police department's stop-and-frisk tactics, which could have
helped him mobilize a significant portion of his large 2009 minority base. Like
Quinn—and to a lesser extent the weaker candidate Liu—Thompson provided
Democratic primary voters with a moderately liberal alternative to de Blasio in
a city that had just supported five consecutive terms of Republican rule under
Rudy Giuliani and Mike Bloomberg (who later switched his label, without altering his politics).

Identity politics played a historic role in the Democratic Party primary of
2013. Long gone were the days when ticket balancing added up to finding an
Irishman, an Italian, and a Jew to fill Gotham's three top elected offices. This
contest could end with the election of the first woman mayor (a woman with
a wife no less), or the first Asian American, or the second African American to
occupy the coveted position. Bill de Blasio and his family brought their own
unique package of twenty-first century New York-style diversity to the race. He
was a white man married to a black woman, who once identified as a lesbian,
and they had two mixed-race children. Each member of his family was slated to
play an important role in the contest. Charles Barron, the contentious black City
Council member from Brooklyn, had criticized de Blasio back in 2009 for using
his African-American wife and biracial kids as props to attract minority voters.[9]

In their time-honored fashion, New Yorkers took all these recent manifestations of diversity in stride. A Quinnipiac University poll administered that
February indicated that the overwhelming majority of New Yorkers were receptive to candidates who are not straight white males. When asked, 91 percent indicated they were either "enthusiastic" or "comfortable" with a woman candidate,
89 percent with an African American, 89 percent with a Hispanic, and 87 percent
with an Asian. A great majority indicated that they were either "enthusiastic" or
"comfortable" with a candidate who identifies as gay or lesbian (78 percent), or
who is married to a person of the same sex (76 percent). Support dropped to the
lowest level (57 percent) when the respondents were asked the same questions
regarding a business executive.[10]

There was a very dark horse in the primary race who would push the boundaries of New York tolerance further. Anthony Weiner had served in Congress for

thirteen years representing parts of Queens and Brooklyn. He had run in the 2005 Democratic primary for mayor. He was married to Huma Abedin, a close confidante and former deputy chief of staff to Secretary of State Hillary Clinton, and a key member of Clinton's presidential campaign staff. The congressman had attracted national attention in 2010 when he made an impassioned speech on the floor of the House demanding health benefits for 9/11 responders. His new wife was pregnant with their child when he was forced to resign in June 2011, after it was revealed that he had been circulating sexually explicit photos of himself over the Internet. The original incident became public in May when a photo of a man wearing bulging gray underpants intended for a college student in Washington state was accidentally sent to 45,000 people on Weiner's personal Twitter account.[11] At first, the combative representative from the Ninth Congressional district claimed his account had been hacked, purporting that anybody with a name like his was a natural target for such a prank.

An avid hockey player known to explode in anger at his staff, Weiner had cultivated a swaggering macho image of himself. He got into an abrasive confrontation with reporters when they asked why he did not have the "sexting" incident investigated by law enforcement authorities. Then, in a later interview, he said that he could not rule out the possibility that it was his body in the faceless photo, which led MSNBC correspondent Rachel Maddow to confront him on the air with "You must have been doing something creepy here."[12] Weiner finally admitted that he had engaged in intimate "sexting" with six other women, only after several others came forward with more stories and more explicit photos—including a seventeen-year-old high school student with whom he had cultivated an online relationship, a forty-year-old Las Vegas blackjack dealer he had phone sex with from his congressional office, and a porn star.

Weiner had tried to hold on to his position in Washington by promising to get professional counseling. He stepped down in June when national Democrats, including President Barack Obama and House Minority Leader Nancy Pelosi, demanded his resignation. A week before his resignation, during an interview in which Weiner also admitted to the possibility of "more photos out there," CNN's Wolf Blitzer asked the congressman whether, as rumored, he still intended to run for mayor. Weiner responded, "it's the only better job than the one I have."[13] It seemed like a long shot then. As columnist Clyde Haberman of the *New York Times* commented, "lewd behavior may be forgivable for many New Yorkers . . . But rank stupidity is not."[14] Donald Trump, not yet a politician seeking high office, issued a more concise assessment of the outgoing congressman, stating, "He's a psycho."[15]

In July 2012, a year after his dramatic downfall, the *New York Times* published an article indicating that Anthony Weiner still had $4.5 million in the bank that he could use to finance a political campaign, feeding speculation that he might be planning a comeback.[16] In April 2013, as the mayoral campaign was in full swing, he had already begun to make public appearances, and released "Keys to the City," a twenty-one-page policy booklet that outlined proposals for making New York "the capital of the middle class."[17]

An NBC NY/Marist poll taken in April showed that Weiner had a 45 percent favorability rating among Democrats, bunched together with William Thompson (43 percent), Bill de Blasio (42 percent), and John Liu (40 percent). Christine Quinn was in the lead with a 59 percent favorability rating. Weiner also received the highest negative rating (41 percent).[18] He remained a polarizing figure, but could not be discounted. In a Quinnipiac poll taken at about the same time, 41 percent responded yes when asked whether Weiner should run, compared to 44 percent who said no. The same poll indicated that in a five-way primary race, Weiner would come in second (15 percent) behind Quinn (28 percent), trailed by de Blasio (11 percent), Thompson (10 percent), and Liu (9 percent).[19]

Weiner announced his candidacy in May. Earlier that month, two former campaign aides to City Comptroller John Liu were convicted in federal court for engaging in illegal practices to raise money for his campaign. Although Liu was never charged with a crime and he was able to wrest an endorsement from District Council 37, the city's largest public employees union, the scandal, for all practical purposes, put an end to his chances. Citing the convictions, the New York City Campaign Finance Board voted to withhold $3.5 million in public money from Liu's campaign.

Through June, Quinn fell in the polls and it started to look like a flatter distribution of support with de Blasio at the tail end. By the end of the month, Quinnipiac found Democratic voters ranking the candidates as follows: Quinn (19 percent), Weiner (17 percent), Thompson (16 percent), and de Blasio (10 percent).[20] A Marist poll that included undecided Democrats asked to make a "forced choice" put Weiner in the lead: Weiner (25 percent), Quinn (20 percent), Thompson (13 percent), and de Blasio (10 percent).[21]

In early July, it still looked as though Weiner was poised to take the lead, but his candidacy was shattered at the end of the month when a website called *The Dirty* revealed that Weiner had continued to send out obscene messages and photos after his resignation from Congress. In one venue, he took to calling himself "Carlos Danger." As the stories grew more bizarre, every major newspaper in the city demanded that he drop out. He vowed to stay in, but as the campaign moved into its last six weeks, it was clearly becoming a three-way contest. At the end of July, Quinnipiac listed the candidates' popularity among Democratic voters as: Quinn (27 percent), de Blasio (21 percent), and Thompson (20 percent).[22] None of the candidates were near the 40 percent figure they needed to avoid a run-off, but it was clear that de Blasio was on the move. August would belong to him. By the middle of the month, he reached 30 percent in the Quinnipiac poll compared to Quinn (24 percent) and Thompson (22 percent).

Quinn kept sliding. She had union support and endorsements from the *New York Times, Daily News,* and *New York Post,* but she was not popular on the streets of New York. The Speaker drew organized protests for supporting the "stop-and-frisk" policy of Police Commissioner Raymond Kelly. She presented herself as somebody who would carry on with a humbled version of the Bloomberg agenda, which was more appealing to editorial boards than voters. Documentary filmmaker Donny Moss targeted her and distributed "Defeat Chris Quinn" videos through websites, Facebook, and Twitter feeds. Groups with names such as "Outer Boroughs of New York City Against Christine Quinn" and "New York City Is Not For Sale" accused her of being Manhattan-centric. De Blasio, linking Quinn to Bloomberg, called her the "best friend of the real estate industry."[23]

Billy Thompson seemed to start his campaign in second gear and never got out of it as the race approached the finish line. Supporters questioned whether he really had the "fire in the belly" needed to win, and whether he was soft on Bloomberg for fear of alienating his moderate base. Thompson also made a strategic error: he refused to endorse two City Council bills that would have required reforms in the police department. His inaction annoyed many leaders in the black community, and cost him an endorsement from his long-time friend, the Reverend Al Sharpton, which he had taken for granted. The influential black minister instead decided to remain neutral, throwing the Thompson team into a panic. In the meantime, Bill de Blasio cultivated Sharpton by coming forward with a clear position on police issues, recognizing the need for serious change.

For anyone who was wondering, Bill de Blasio shored up his radical credentials in July when he was arrested at a demonstration protesting the closing of Long Island College Hospital in downtown Brooklyn. Other politicians running for high office would not risk such a gesture, but it did not seem to hurt him, and may have contributed to his perceived authenticity. That was only a prelude to de Blasio's sweet August, when he took command of the lead. It is difficult for analysts to pinpoint exactly what puts a candidate ahead of the others. In this case, most observers would point to the "Dante ad" that featured de Blasio's sixteen-year-old son, or more precisely the huge Afro that rose in a halo several inches above his forehead.

Created by John Del Cecato, who also made ads for President Obama, the thirty-second "Dante" spot began to run in early August. In it, the handsome young man rattles off the reasons people should vote for Bill de Blasio, assuring the audience: he's the only candidate willing to break with the Bloomberg years; he will tax the rich to provide preschool and after-school programs; he will build affordable housing; he will end "stop-and-frisk" that targets people of color. There is a short scene with Bill and Chirlane in their kitchen, or at least somebody's kitchen. It ends with a shot of Dante and Bill walking down their tree-lined Brooklyn street together—back in the neighborhood, of course, where all things de Blasio begin and end. You had to love this kid, and he was also delivering a poignant message. The ad caught on like wildfire. It probably handed de Blasio the election.

Bill de Blasio may have just squeaked by the 40 percent (40.3) minimum share of the primary vote to avoid a run-off against one of his two primary opponents (Thompson, 26.2 percent; Quinn, 15.5 percent), but he also managed to sweep nearly every category of voters, whether measured by race, gender, ideology, religion, education, income, or borough.[24] According to *New York Times* exit polls,[25] he performed best among white voters: de Blasio (41 percent), Quinn (22 percent), Thompson (19 percent). He tied Thompson with black voters (42 percent), and won with Hispanics: de Blasio (38 percent), Thompson, (27 percent), and Quinn (14 percent). He beat Quinn among women (39 percent versus 16 percent), but so did Thompson (26 percent). He also beat Quinn among voters who identified as gay, lesbian, or transsexual (47 percent to 34 percent). He took the male vote: de Blasio (40 percent), Thompson (27 percent), and Quinn (14 percent). He won among those who identified as very liberal (50 percent), or somewhat liberal (34 percent), but Thompson did a little better than de Blasio with moderates (35 percent to 32 percent). De Blasio won among Protestants, Catholics, and Jews. He won every education category from those with only a high school diploma to those who attended graduate school. De Blasio took every borough but the Bronx, where Thompson beat him by 3 percent. He excelled in every income category below $170,000; above that, Quinn prevailed.

With regard to issues, the same *New York Times* exit polls indicate de Blasio got his strongest support from those voters concerned with "stop and frisk" (52 percent), and housing (51 percent), but he also won among those who prioritized jobs (39 percent), and education (39 percent). Thompson did better with those concerned about city finances (25 percent to 22 percent). De Blasio excelled among voters dissatisfied with Bloomberg's job performance: de Blasio (36 percent), Quinn (23 percent), and Thompson (20 percent). He surpassed Thompson by a small margin among union families (38 percent to 33 percent).

When the *Times* analyzed the primary results by neighborhood, a slightly different picture emerged, but de Blasio still commanded the lead with most categories of voters.[26] In areas where at least 50 percent of the population was black, he beat Thompson (47 percent to 34 percent), as he did in areas where Hispanics were a majority (35.8 percent to 39.4 percent). He also prevailed in majority white neighborhoods: de Blasio (39.6 percent), Quinn (25.8 percent), and Thompson (21.9 percent). John Liu, whose name remained on the ballot, retained support in majority Asian communities (42.2 percent), with de Blasio coming in a distant second (24.4 percent). Using income as a measure, de Blasio prevailed in neighborhoods at every income average up to $100,990, including: below $35,000 (40.7 percent), with Thompson in second place (25.7 percent); at least $75,446: (39.9 percent) versus Thompson (28.9 percent); and below $100,990 (40.1 percent) versus Thompson (28.4 percent). In the next higher level, where the average income for a neighborhood is below $171,228, de Blasio (38.2 percent) was nearly tied by Quinn (37.9 percent). De Blasio and Quinn actually did tie (38 percent) in neighborhoods where the average income is at $172,302, but Quinn prevailed in neighborhoods where incomes climbed higher.

The Republican primary was less dramatic. Joseph Lhota faced two opponents, neither of whom was much of a threat. John Catsimatidis is the owner of Gristedes, the upscale supermarket chain. George McDonald is the founder of the Doe Fund, a nonprofit organization dedicated to helping the homeless. Neither had a record of government experience. That is the arena in which Lhota excelled—to the point where he picked up an endorsement from the liberal New York Times. It was quite a leap for the Times: lending support to somebody who had served as deputy mayor for Rudy Giuliani, with whom the editorial board was often at odds. Taking into consideration Lhota's role in running the city government and his chairmanship of the Metropolitan Transportation Authority, the editors had to admit, "Few people know better than Mr. Lhota how the city government works."[27] All the other major newspapers made similar endorsements of the seasoned executive.

There were other aspects of his personal story that could make Lhota a contender in a New York election. His father was a cop, his grandfather a fireman. His mother's father was a cab driver. He was Czechoslovakian on his father's side, and his mother was half Italian and half Jewish. He grew up in the Bronx before moving with his family to Long Island. Lhota had been diagnosed with lymphoma in 2005. Friends thought they might lose him, but he faced the malignancy bravely. After seven months of chemotherapy, he emerged "clean," and rightfully proud of the battle he had survived.

Lhota is a self-made man. The first in his family to attend college, he went off to Georgetown, then to Harvard Business School. A stint on Wall Street gave him the financial security to live in a stately Brooklyn Heights brownstone on New York harbor, and to own a summer house on Nantucket Island. Lhota was the only person in the Republican primary with the credentials to run for mayor. New York business leaders admired him. He drew praise from such people as Ken Langone, the cofounder of Home Depot; Peter Kalikow, the real estate developer and former owner of the New York Post; and James Tisch, the chief executive of the Loews Corporation. He won an easy victory with 52.5 percent of the vote, compared to Catsimatidis (40.7 percent) and McDonald (6.8 percent).[28]

The general election was another matter. Now the *Times* switched its endorsement to de Blasio. Joe Lhota got the backing of the Conservative party, but Bill de Blasio got a boost on the Working Families Party line. In an election that would be a refutation of the Bloomberg years, one label was a remnant of the past, the other may be a harbinger of the future. Lhota ran on a platform of safe streets and lower taxes. Ironically, he was a victim of his own and Giuliani's success. Voters were less concerned about crime than they were the last time Lhota worked in the mayor's office; they were more concerned with how the police interacted with their communities. Joe Lhota didn't get it. He promised more of what City Hall delivered under Giuliani and Bloomberg. He praised Police Commissioner Raymond Kelly. He was trounced by de Blasio (73 percent to 24 percent).[29]

Considering race, religion, and a twenty-first century definition of gender and sexuality, Bill de Blasio managed to assemble a large progressive coalition in a city that had elected Michael Bloomberg for three consecutive terms, and Rudolph Giuliani for two before that. Except for those at the very highest brackets, his support also cut across income levels in a contest he was determined to make class-based. For these reasons alone, de Blasio's election was historically significant. It was populist in the sense that it was broad based and mobilized against a plutocracy (real, imagined, or exaggerated) led by a billionaire. Bloomberg himself, one of the few times he spoke out, described de Blasio's rhetoric as "class warfare."[30] It very much was.

De Blasio's triumph—and the part his attractive multi-cultural family played in it—is also a reflection of the city's ever-changing electorate. Between 1990 and 2013, the proportion of the voters who were non-Hispanic white dropped from 54 percent to 42 percent. Blacks have decreased slightly to 24 percent, Hispanics have grown five points to 23 percent, and Asians by four points to 10 percent.[31] His appeal for economic justice and his "Tale of Two Cities" banner allowed him to cut across most of these major groups as he ran against a black candidate with wide name recognition.

De Blasio's pleas were especially well-received among workers in a city where organized labor remains a significant political force, and union membership continues to grow. In 2015, 25.5 percent of the workforce belonged to unions, up for three consecutive years from 21.5 percent in 2012, and more than double the national average (10.9 percent).[32] These high numbers are largely a result of strong public sector unionism in the city, where 70 percent of government employees are members. Union representation among private sector workers (19 percent) in New York City is more than double the national average (7 percent).

De Blasio's victory in the general election could prove to be a historic turn-ing point for another reason. Forging a coalition across racial and class lines has not always been easy, despite the fact that the two demographic variables are so interrelated. John Lindsay was the first New York City mayor to take an aggressive stance on the issue of racial equality. As we have seen, that posture put him at odds with public sector unions in agencies that were old ethnic enclaves controlled by the Irish, Italians, and Jews. According to a census taken of the city workforce in 1971, 67 percent of all employees were white, 25 percent were black, 6 percent were Puerto Rican, and 2 percent were classified as "other." Uniformed services were particularly dominated by whites: Fire (95 percent), Police (87 percent), Sanitation (86 percent), Parks & Recreation (79 percent), and Corrections (53 percent). The Board of Education was 75 percent white.[33]

By 1990, David Dinkins did better with organized labor when minority lead-ers such as Dennis Rivera of Local 1199 and Stanley Hill of DC 37 came onto the scene, reflecting changes in the composition of the city workforce. The pro-file of city employees changed dramatically by the time Bill de Blasio put his name on the ballot. According to a survey completed in 2013, 39 percent of all city employees were white, 32 percent black, 20 percent Hispanic, and 8 per-cent Asian. The Fire Department remains predominantly white (76 percent), and is under court order to address its lack of diversity. The workforce in other large agencies, however, has changed significantly: Police (41 percent white), Sanitation (55 percent), Parks & Recreation (31 percent), Corrections (14 per-cent), and Education (48 percent).[34] The demographic divide between those who live in the city and those employed by it has never been so narrow, enabling politicians such as de Blasio to assemble a broad coalition across race and class lines unlike any that has ever existed.

Whether his 2013 victory could be interpreted to be an ironclad mandate is another matter. The strength of de Blasio's mandate was eroded by the same voter attrition that has affected every New York City election since Mayor Robert Wagner was elected in 1950. According to the Board of Elections, 2.2 million people voted that year—93 percent of those who were eligible. Turnout in the 2013 mayoral election was the lowest on record. Hardly more than 1 million showed up at the polls that day, or 24 percent of those eligible.[35] De Blasio was such a strong favorite in the general election that many voters—whether sup-porters or opponents—may have stayed home because they deemed the out-come a forgone conclusion. That raises another important question regarding the political process.

Supporters of non-partisan elections, who include former Mayor Bloomberg, argue that in a town such as New York where Democrats outnumber Republicans by a margin of 6 to 1, a mayor can be chosen by an even smaller proportion of the public by winning the Democratic primary. [36] That was certainly the pattern for much of New York history—except for being interrupted by the two decades that preceded the de Blasio win. Party primaries attract an even lower turnout than general elections, so a candidate can win with the support of fewer voters. De Blasio won the 2013 primary with approximately 260,000 votes—less than 7 percent of registered voters. Independents do not get to vote in any primary.

There is a theoretical possibility that if Joseph Lhota and his Republican challengers were allowed to enter the original contest that took place among the Democrats, nobody would have gotten 40 percent of the required margin, and a GOP contender could have participated in the runoff against de Blasio or another Democrat. It is improbable, though, and a Democrat probably would have won the final face-off anyway. De Blasio had accumulated more votes in the primary than Lhota did in the general election. Partisan primaries remain popular in Democrat-leaning New York, as they prevail in more than 20 percent of American cities. The arguments will continue, but the process is unlikely to change in the near future.

On January 1, 2014, the more germane question for Bill de Blasio was whether he could turn his electoral coalition into a governing coalition.

The mayor of New York is officially sworn in at midnight on January 1 at a location of his choice, followed the next day with an elaborate inauguration ceremony on the steps of City Hall. Bill de Blasio took the oath of office as the city's 109th mayor in the front yard of 442 11th Street in Brooklyn, right where he announced his candidacy a year earlier. The oath was administered by state Attorney General Eric Schneiderman, followed by an evening of celebration with friends and supporters at Bar Toto, the mayor's favorite neighborhood haunt down the block from his Park Slope home. Where else?

The next morning, Bill, Chirlane, Chiara, and Dante boarded the Number 4 subway to Manhattan for a full day of festivities. When they arrived at the City Hall station beneath the Municipal Building, they ran into Michael Bloomberg, who had commuted downtown from his East Side townhouse. The two men embraced, shook hands, and exchanged brief pleasantries. De Blasio asked, "How does it feel to be a free man?" Bloomberg remarked, "You never forget your first one," having been through three inaugurations of his own. Joined by his lady friend Diana Taylor and an aide, the outgoing mayor climbed the steep stairs to City Hall Plaza and went on his way to take a seat on the stage with other guests. The shouts of a popular nightclub D.J. and the blare of hip hop music composed by Jay Z and Katy Perry loudly proclaimed for all to hear that this was no longer the staid businessman's City Hall.

Bill's brothers Steve and Donald, joined by other members of the Wilhelm clan, were there, including Aunt Jean, who came down from Maine, and cousin John, the labor leader who shared Bill's passion for progressive causes; and so was Chirlane's extended family. Bill's "third brother" Patrick Gaspard, with whom he once shared an office in the Dinkins administration and other formative life experiences for twenty-five years, traveled all the way from his embassy post in South Africa. A magnet for the media, Patrick confidently assured reporters that although Bill was excited about the day, he was more enthusiastic about assuming the responsibilities of governing.[37] Bertha Lewis from ACORN gave Bill a hug. Former mayor David Dinkins sat proudly with the other dignitaries across from the landmarked municipal castle that one day would be named for him.

The first speaker to approach the podium was Harry Belafonte. His was the same soft voice that inspired young audiences during the glory days of the civil rights movement. Weakened by age, it still resonated with a strong message. Denouncing the "Dickensian justice system" and the police tactics of the previous administration, he vowed, "We can become America's DNA for the future."[38] Other speakers sounded a similar militant note. Letitia James, the first woman of color to hold a citywide post, decried, "We live in a gilded age of inequality where decrepit homeless shelters and housing developments stand in the neglected shadows of gleaming multimillion dollar condos." Sanitation department chaplain Fred Lucas Jr. referred to New York City as a "plantation."

It was a difficult morning for Michael Bloomberg, who sat stoically through a ceremony that at times approached incivility toward him and his legacy. This was not the ordinary passage of power that chief executives experience when sitting through the inauguration of a successor. The two-and-a-half hour ceremony was an affirmation of Bill de Blasio's "Tale of Two Cities" refrain. It was a blunt renunciation of Michael Bloomberg and much of what he stood for. Former president Bill Clinton, who at the end of the pageantry came forward to administer the oath of office, was the first person to acknowledge anything positive resulting from the previous twelve years, noting that Bloomberg left the city "stronger and healthier than he found it." Clinton assumed a more temperate posture, condemning "inequalities across the nation and the world" not only as "a moral outrage," but also as an impediment to economic growth. Hillary sat nearby, accompanied by her aide Huma Abedin, Anthony Weiner's wife.

Casting his eyes toward the de Blasios, the ex-president referred to them as a symbol of the future for the city and country, and joked, "With all due respect to the television show. . . . they're our real modern family." Given the governing regime that had been in place for the past twenty years, it was almost hard to believe that somebody of Bill de Blasio's philosophical pedigree was about to take charge. In de Blasio's mind, though, it was all preordained by history. It is he who represents the real New York, and New York needed to reassume its place in pointing the way for the rest of the country. His was a different kind of populism from that which would put Donald Trump in the White House three years later. It remained to be seen whether the Democratic Party could nationalize it to bring alienated voters back to the fold.

After recognizing family, friends, and dignitaries in attendance, de Blasio paid homage to the pantheon of progressive New York leaders who had done just that. Having taken his oath with a Bible that had once belonged to FDR, he paid honor to Franklin and Eleanor. He mentioned Governor Al Smith, who opposed child labor and promoted safe working conditions; Frances Perkins, who brought us the minimum wage and unemployment insurance; and finally, Fiorello La Guardia—"the man I consider the greatest mayor this city has ever had," who battled the excesses of Wall Street, and fought for a progressive income tax. They had all, de Blasio recalled, challenged the status quo. He wanted to do the same.

Pledging to face up to the "inequality crisis" and to convert "two cities" into one, the new mayor presented a vision of New York that was not at all new. He called for a "city that remembers our responsibilities to each other—our common cause—to leave no New Yorker behind." He reviewed a litany of progressive policy proposals that by now were familiar, but gave special attention to his plan to fund universal preschool programs with a tax on the rich, suggesting that this was as much a redistributive fiscal plan as it was an education plan. This centerpiece policy proposal oozed of progressive symbolism. He mapped out details showing that a tax on the rich to provide every New York City child with preschool, and afterschool services for every middle-school student, would cost a person making more than $500,000 annually approximately $973 a year, or less than three bucks a day.[39] It sounded so fair, so compelling. How could any reasonable person disagree?

Before he had even taken the oath to serve as the city's chief executive, Bill de Blasio was exercising his influence as mayor-elect to intervene in an internecine conflict ripening in the City Council. The fifty-one members of the legislative body were scheduled to vote in exactly a week to choose their Speaker. De Blasio's long-time friend and political ally Melissa Mark-Viverito from East Harlem was in contention against Daniel Garodnick, a well-regarded Manhattan Democrat, who had the support of members from the Bronx and Queens delegations, including State Assemblyman Carl Heastie, who would rise to the Speaker's position after Sheldon Silver was forced to resign.

The progressive coalition that de Blasio and the Working Families Party coalesced proved to be a more powerful force. By New Year's Day, Mark-Viverito had lined up thirty votes to Garodnick's nineteen. The leadership question was all but resolved.[40] She is the first Puerto Rican to ever hold the position. It was one of those poignant moments of history: Mark-Viverito had been an activist and protégé of Dennis Rivera, the prescient leader of the SEIU 1199 healthcare workers union, who in 1991 formed the Majority Coalition in an attempt to create a progressive caucus inside the City Council. Then Rivera was ahead of his time; now the time had come, and she would prove it.

When she arrived at the inauguration, one reporter asked Mark-Viverito whether her close relationship with the new mayor would compromise her independence from the executive branch of the government; she immediately denied it. There is always room for conflict when questions are viewed from different institutional perspectives. A speaker needs to collect votes in a diverse body that represents five boroughs and fifty-one communities. Sometimes the task is easier than at other times. The truth is, though, that the Council has not served as an effective check on mayoral power since the new city charter was enacted in 1990. More important, de Blasio and Mark-Viverito are like-minded on most important policy issues. Such amity is a valuable asset to the new mayor as he assumes responsibility for governing the city and attempts to deliver on his campaign promises.

Within six weeks, the City Council overwhelmingly passed an Earned Sick Leave Act. It required employers with five employees or more to provide up to forty hours of paid sick leave to workers who are ill; those with fewer than five employees had to at least provide leave, with or without compensation. The new law revised an ordinance passed over the veto of Mayor Michael Bloomberg in June 2013 that would only have covered employers with twenty (and eventually fifteen) or more employees. Now, for example, food servers at McDonald's would not need to come to work sick, which in the past had aggravated their suffering, prolonged their recovery, and extended the risk of contamination to co-workers and diners.

We may recall that as she got closer to launching her campaign for mayor, Christine Quinn capitulated on a living wage bill that progressives such as Mark-Viverito had been urging for some time. In June 2012, the Council passed a law requiring any employer receiving more than $1 million in contracts or assistance from the city to pay its employees a "living wage." Candidate de Blasio, then the Public Advocate, tweaked his electoral rival as a latecomer to the issue, and deemed the legislation inadequate. In September 2014, Mayor de Blasio, to the applause of progressive Council members, signed an executive order that increased the wage rate and specified additional employees to be covered. By April 2017, the rate would increase to $11.90 for employees with health benefits and $13.65 to employees without benefits. There was a simple principle behind the legislation: people who work for a living deserve a decent life—without relying on food stamps, and without depending on public assistance in any form.

The new wage requirement was still not sufficient for a family trying to eke out a decent living in New York City. Nevertheless, it was a step in that direction. The conversation was apparently changing. New York City had declared war on economic injustice. It was beginning to sound like the city that La Guardia had built.

But there was something missing. La Guardia had a partner in Washington who was willing to provide the resources to lift people out of poverty. Progressivism in New York City had always been reliant on federal largesse, whether it was delivered by Franklin Roosevelt during the New Deal or Lyndon Johnson during the Great Society. Bill de Blasio has no such partner.

President Barack Obama may have been more or less sympathetic, but Congress was not. Washington had become dysfunctional. The institutions of the federal government had ground to a halt because of partisan bickering. When they did move, it could easily be in the wrong direction. The income inequality that de Blasio had written into a local political agenda had been a product of public policy made in Washington. Politically, this meant that Bill de Blasio had taken on a problem he may not have had the power to address—unless he thought he could persuade fellow Democrats at a national level to take up the cause. He certainly tried to do that when he and other progressives made a bid to influence the dialogue around the presidential primary of 2016, but to little avail. It was quite a predicament for the ambitious new chief executive. Then came Donald Trump.

Mayors also need governors to accomplish their goals. According to American law, cities are creatures of the state. Therefore, most significant local actions need state approval in one form or another, particularly when it involves taxation or borrowing. The legal boundaries have been a perennial source of tension between governors and mayors, whether or not they are of the same party. The relationship between Bill de Blasio and Andrew Cuomo is no exception, and would prove to be among the worst in recent memory, surpassing the famous animosity between Nelson Rockefeller and John Lindsay.

New York's late governor Mario Cuomo once eloquently advised rulers, in what ironically became known as the "Two Cities" speech before the Democratic National Convention of 1984, "Campaign in poetry, govern in prose." Mario's son, Andrew, administers his affairs in neither poetry nor prose. If his style has a cadence, it is one of a field officer who issues instructions expecting the troops to fall into line. Bill de Blasio is constantly out of line in the way he plays "state versus city" politics. It is difficult to pinpoint the exact cause of the hostility between de Blasio and Cuomo beyond the institutional strains and excesses of ego that motivate politicians. The two men apparently got along when de Blasio worked for Cuomo at HUD. It probably did not help when Bill resigned from HUD to run the senate campaign of Hillary Clinton, raising his profile in New York while Andrew was left behind in Washington. Now, as de Blasio took up occupancy at City Hall, they were definitely on different paths, and the difference became obvious around the mayor's signature proposal to tax the rich to pay for universal pre-kindergarten (UPK).

Cuomo embraced de Blasio's UPK proposal as a program that should be adopted statewide, and offered to pay the bill. He rejected the idea of raising taxes on the rich. When de Blasio pushed forward in Albany with his "tax the rich" policy, Cuomo claimed that such an approach is unfair to localities that do not have the fiscal capacity to fund such a program. The more the mayor pushed forward with his taxing proposal, the harder the governor pushed back, asking "Why do you need a tax for a service we're going to fully fund?"[41] When he was further questioned by reporters, Cuomo responded more directly, indicating that the discussion had gone beyond education policy and was more driven by economic concerns that the mayor had, stating, "He's [de Blasio] saying part of what he ran on is income inequality, and part of the answer to income inequality is taxing rich people . . . that's a political position . . . If not pre-K, it'll be something else."

Republican legislators in Albany gloated at the sight of public animosity between the two leading Democrats in the state. They liked Cuomo's conservative approach to taxes, and stood to benefit from a pre-K initiative that served their upstate and suburban constituents. De Blasio expressed disappointment, frustration, and fury with the governor at first, but was not about to refuse $300 million the state budget awarded New York City to finance his initiative. The governor's plan did not cover the after-school programs that the mayor had hoped for, but there was nothing preventing de Blasio from funding them on his own. The new state law that came with the funding also included stricter guidelines for teacher certification, curriculum, and family engagement, permitting Cuomo to boast that he had raised the standards for preschool education beyond the usual babysitting activity that such programs typically provide. De Blasio, in return, took credit for demanding the program from the start.

The initial squabble over early childhood education took place just weeks after the mayor was sworn in. It highlighted deep philosophical differences between the two men. It set the tone for their relationship. It demonstrated how far the governor was willing to go to put the mayor in his place, even to the point of tearing down one of de Blasio's major campaign promises. It also exposed a contest of one-upmanship that would characterize their interactions from there on out. People close to the mayor say that he is too absorbed in the personal animosity to appreciate how much he pushes Cuomo to do things he might not be inclined to do. From the perspective of state and local governance, the relationship between the two sometimes makes it seem as though the city tail is wagging the Albany dog; but this big dog enjoys biting his own tail, and he does it whenever it suits him.

De Blasio made a last ditch effort to salvage the relationship when the governor faced re-election in 2014. After leaders in the Working Families Party (WFP) encouraged progressive law professor Zephyr Teachout to oppose Cuomo in the

Democratic Party primary, de Blasio persuaded his WFP friends to stand behind the incumbent governor, even though they were frustrated with Cuomo's fiscal conservatism and his close ties with senate Republicans. In return, Cuomo promised to help his fellow Democrats win a majority of seats in the state senate. The governor did not follow through, and the relationship between him and the mayor further deteriorated.

Inaugurations are telegraphic events. They not only permit a leader to articulate an agenda, they give off a vibe: in music, in the procession of speakers, in their manner of celebration. They exhibit a politician's roots—both deep and newly planted. They tell us who the mayor's friends and supporters are, and who might have influence in the days ahead. More particularly, they tell us who his campaign donors are—or as they say in politics, "who(m) he owes."

Bill de Blasio's inaugural committee was chaired by Gabrielle Fialkoff, a wealthy businesswoman and financier who had served as the finance chair of his campaign, and who was the finance director of Hillary Clinton's 2000 senate campaign. The group included a handful of celebrities such as Dominican writer Junot Diaz, and actors Steve Buscemi, Sarah Jessica Parker, Susan Sarandon, and Rosie Perez. There were four individuals affiliated with the SEIU 1199 healthcare workers union for which Bill and his friend Patrick Gaspard had worked as political advisors. Also listed were Rabbi Heshie Dembitzer of the Bobover Yeshiva B'nai Zion in Borough Park Brooklyn, and two businessmen from the same community who were campaign donors: Jona Rechnitz Jr. and Jeremiah Reichberg.

Transition committees can also showcase celebrity types, such as actress Cynthia Nixon, a friend of the mayor who is an outspoken gay and lesbian rights advocate. But they also have a more practical function. It is their job to help set up the new government. They include experts and old government hands who advise an incoming chief executive in thinking strategically about policy. Most important of all, transition committee members identify talented individuals to occupy key jobs in the government. De Blasio's team included Ken Sunshine, a public relations guru who once supervised young Bill when he worked for David Dinkins, and Harold Ickes, a mentor to him from the beginning, whose father was an architect of the New Deal and helped La Guardia bring federal resources to New York. Others on the team included Peter Madonia of the Rockefeller Foundation, who was once chief of staff for Mayor Michael Bloomberg; and Herbert Sturz, one of the wise men of city government whose involvement goes back to the Lindsay days.[42] John Banks was a Con Edison executive, about to become president of the Real Estate Board of New York, a trade association for the industry. And of course there was Bertha Lewis, the former director of ACORN; and George Gresham, the president of 1199 SEIU.

Bill de Blasio moved slowly in putting together his administration. He had only filled eight of the more than thirty senior level positions in the government by the time he was sworn in—much lower than the norm, giving rise to questions about his managerial prowess. By the first of January, Michael Bloomberg had made thirty such appointments; Rudolph Giuliani had named thirty-two administrators; David Dinkins had chosen twenty.[43] Among de Blasio's early key appointments were three deputy mayors, a budget director, the schools chancellor, and the police commissioner. It was a diverse group of people that shared one basic characteristic: significant experience.

Early on, de Blasio made it clear that he was unlikely to appoint any Republicans to his administration, quipping, "Let's not get crazy about this diversity idea." That remark probably amused de Blasio's more left-leaning supporters; nevertheless, although the mayor's top executives were generally in accord with his agenda, this was not looking like the Red Guard was taking over the reins of government. His key appointees had all been there before; they knew the mechanics of municipal bureaucracy inside and out. They understood the politics of governing. They also appreciated the need to compromise.

Even before naming Bill Bratton Police Commissioner, de Blasio announced his selection of Anthony Shorris as First Deputy Mayor. The first deputy is second in command after the mayor. He is responsible for running the day-to-day operations of the government. Shorris had previously served as Finance Commissioner and Deputy Budget director for Edward Koch and as deputy chancellor of schools during the Bloomberg and Giuliani administrations. He had worked with Governors Andrew Cuomo and Eliot Spitzer as Executive Director of the Port Authority of New York and New Jersey. Shorris had been an architect of Mayor Koch's Ten Year Housing Plan, the largest affordable housing initiative in the nation at the time. He was also a board member of the Regional Plan Association.

De Blasio and Shorris have known each other for many years. Their wives had worked together as speech-writers for Mayor David Dinkins. Shorris's wife, Maria Laurino, was serving as an executive assistant to Governor Andrew Cuomo at the time of his appointment by the mayor. (Dinner conversation must have been interesting at their place.) Most important, de Blasio's top deputy shares his values. As he explained, "I signed up because equality is the core of Bill's agenda, and we both care deeply about it. It is the organizing principle of the administration."[44]

De Blasio turned to the private sector for his next major appointment—to be more precise, Wall Street. If that comes as a surprise, it might be shocking to some that Deputy Mayor for Housing and Economic Development Alicia Glen was recruited from Goldman Sachs, considered by many to be the great villain of Wall Street. At Goldman, she led the Urban Investment Group, where she oversaw $3 billion in real estate properties and companies located in low-income areas across the country. She had previously served as a senior official in the Department of Housing Preservation and Development during the Giuliani administration.

The selection of Glen was greeted with praise from the business sector of the city. Kathryn Wylde, the President of the Partnership for New York City, a corporate alliance founded by David Rockefeller, remarked, "Alicia is widely regarded as an outstanding 'community banker' with particular expertise in affordable housing and community investment. Her appointment is a clear signal that the de Blasio administration will be aggressive in pushing expanded housing and neighborhood development."[45]

Glen would work closely with Carl Weisbrod, who cochaired the mayor's transition team and became Chair of the City Planning Commission.[46] Weisbrod, who started in government as an antipoverty lawyer with the Lindsay administration, has devoted much of his career to revitalizing city neighborhoods. He was the Founding Director of the New York City Economic Development Corporation under Mayor Dinkins. As president of the Times Square Business Improvement District, then as president of the New York State 42nd Street Development Project, he played a key role in the cleanup and development of Times Square. As president of the Lower Manhattan Business Improvement District, he was involved with the recovery after the 9/11 terrorist attack on the World Trade Center. De Blasio had declared affordable housing a major priority. The Glen and Weisbrod appointments affirmed that the newly elected mayor was aware he needed private developers to be successful, and was ready to work with them.

Lilliam Barrios-Paoli served under three mayors before de Blasio recruited her to be Deputy Mayor for Health and Human Services. For Edward Koch, she was an administrator in the Human Resources Administration (HRA) and the Health and Hospitals Corporation before becoming Commissioner of the Department of Employment. For Giuliani, she ran the Personnel Department, the Department of Housing Preservation and Development, and HRA before leaving to become executive director of Lincoln Medical and Mental Health Center in the Bronx. For Bloomberg, she was Commissioner of Aging. Under de Blasio, Barrios-Paoli would assume responsibility for the city's growing homeless problem. When he appointed her, she remarked, "For the first time in my life, I'm going to be working with somebody who really, truly embraces the things I do."[47] Unfortunately, although the mayor and his deputy shared similar values, they had very different working styles. To the dismay of social service advocates, she resigned her deputy mayor post after twenty months, on more or less good terms, and continued as voluntary chair of the Health and Hospitals Corporation for a year.

Mayor Bloomberg had reached an impasse with most of the city labor unions, leaving more than 150 collective bargaining agreements for the new administration to negotiate. For that task, de Blasio recruited Robert Linn, Mayor Koch's chief labor negotiator, who had since developed a career as a labor consultant dealing mostly with public sector clients. He was assisted by Koch's highly regarded former First Deputy Mayor Stanley Brezenoff, who offered his services as an unpaid advisor. The new budget director, Dean Fuleihan, had spent three decades as a senior fiscal advisor to the New York State Assembly.

Like all chief executives, Bill de Blasio also surrounded himself with people with whom he had deeper personal connections. Carmen Fariña, a fifty-year veteran of the school system, was brought out of retirement to become chancellor. She was deputy chancellor to Joel Klein during the Bloomberg years, but her thinking about education was more aligned with the new mayor's, who got to know her when she was an administrator in his Park Slope school district. Emma Wolfe carries the title Director of Intergovernmental Affairs, but she serves in a more expansive role. She had functioned as Political Director of his mayoral campaign, was his Chief of Staff in the Public Advocate Office, and also has a history as a political organizer for the Working Families Party, the 1199 SEIU labor union, and ACORN.

Laura Santucci was the mayor's first Chief of Staff. She had been Executive Director of the de Blasio Transition Committee. Immediately prior to that, she had succeeded Patrick Gaspard as Director of the Democratic National Committee. She and Patrick were colleagues as staffers in the Obama White House and as political operatives at 1199 SEIU. When she left City Hall at the beginning of 2015, she was succeeded by Thomas Snyder. Snyder was the only person in the top echelon with no experience in New York City government, but he came highly recommended. A seasoned labor leader from Boston, he had been an aide to Bill's cousin John Wilhelm, who was head of Unite Here, an influential hotel and restaurant workers union. He also had experience working for Boston mayor Raymond Flynn.

Bill's most trusted advisor was another person he knew back in the Dinkins days. His wife Chirlane McCray had been his partner throughout his political career. At City Hall, she would help screen candidates for jobs in the administration and involve herself in issues pertaining to physical and mental health. The first lady occupies an office at 253 Broadway, where she chairs the Mayor's Fund to Advance New York City, a volunteer position overseeing a $37 million budget supported by private donors to assist needy communities through public-private partnerships.

* * *

The people had spoken. They had cast their votes against plutocracy and inequality. New Yorkers had proved once again that theirs is a tolerant city capable of embracing diversity better than most other places. Their choice had reminded the country that in decent societies people take care of one another; and when they can't do it on their own, government steps in with a helping hand. Bernie Sanders would echo that message in the year ahead. America would hear it, but not as clearly as New York did when spoken by Bill de Blasio in 2013.

As he climbed the ladder of power, Bill de Blasio was studiously determined to stay close to his roots. He marked each step of the journey at his own front door on 11th Street in Brooklyn, surrounded by family and friends. As mayor, he kept returning to the neighborhood to assure supporters, and perhaps himself, that living in the East Side mansion would not put him out of touch with their pleas. If Michael Bloomberg demurred on living in the mayor's official residence for something grander, one of his own private retreats, Bill de Blasio kept his eyes set on something more modest, something that was more real to most New Yorkers.

De Blasio's plurality was broad, but not deep. In assembling a government, he embraced familiar kindred spirits who shared his progressive vision—but he also reached further. He understood that the country had changed since the days when city mayors could rely on sympathetic friends in Washington. He would need to do business with the rich and the powerful, who controlled money and real estate in New York—who, for years, had convinced themselves and previous mayors that they knew what was best for the city. They were now part of the permanent government, and they took their role for granted. At what costs would the compromises come?

8

A New Agenda

Equality is not just an abstract principle that guides the general direction of the de Blasio administration; it is an operational objective. If you join First Deputy Mayor Anthony Shorris in his City Hall office, as I did one Friday afternoon, he will take his cell phone from his pocket and show you a list of metrics that he uses to evaluate the performance of city agencies on a daily basis. Equality measures are near the top of the list. As he explained, "It is not enough to know that we are upgrading parks or playgrounds. I want to know whether we are doing those things in neighborhoods that have been neglected."[1]

As mayor, de Blasio wanted to telegraph these governing values not just to agency heads, but to the entire city. In April 2015, he came forward with *One New York: The Plan for a Strong and Just City (OneNYC).*[2] Taking more than a year to produce, there was nothing subtle about it. It was de Blasio's iteration of Bloomberg's *PlaNYC,* an extension of the "Tale of Two Cities" narrative that defined his electoral campaign. In it the mayor recognized the progress made by his predecessor in promoting a more sustainable, resilient, and greener city, and promised to proceed along a similar path with those goals.

The new blueprint also set down different priorities with "a focus on inequality." It pledged to "implement the nation's most ambitious program for the creation and preservation of affordable housing." It promised to "support a first-class, 21st century commercial sector" that "will foster job growth, and build an inclusive work force by focusing investment in training for high-growth industries as well as programs that provide skills to the hardest-to-employ." The mayor apparently understood the need for a prominent private sector role in the city's future, but his outreach to the business community was infused with his own progressive values.

The words *just* and *equitable* are writ large in the plan's discussion of an inclusive economy. It boldly claims that the city will "lift 800,000 New Yorkers out of poverty or near poverty by 2025." Unlike Mayor Bloomberg, whose first year in office was saddled with a $2.4 billion budget deficit, de Blasio began his with a $2.4 billion surplus.[3] The economy was on sound footing. It was reasonable and fair to ask that the benefits of the city's new prosperity be shared more evenly. Yet, admiring skeptics questioned whether a municipality had the capacity to fight poverty on its own, even with private sector involvement, whose contributions always come at a price.[4] For the de Blasio administration, the answer seemed to be yes, with a caveat.

OneNYC is more than a plan. It is a progressive manifesto on the role that local government can and should play in creating a better life for those who are at risk—with particulars. All the while, de Blasio acknowledges the need for assistance from higher levels of government if progressive dreams are to become realities, and he has acted—or at least tried—to serve as an advocate for distressed people in both Washington and Albany. In so doing, de Blasio is following in the footsteps of other progressive mayors such as Fiorello La Guardia and John Lindsay who became national champions for an urban agenda. *PlaNYC*, in truth, was never intended as a local bootstrap initiative. Mayor Bloomberg had stipulated at the outset that the federal and state governments would have to do their parts. The difference between Bloomberg and de Blasio is in how they respectively defined the local part.

In government, there is no better way to objectively measure the priorities of policymakers than by examining the budget. In New York City, decisions about spending are made collaboratively by the mayor, who proposes the budget, and the City Council, which can amend and must approve the budget. The Council has the authority to reduce or increase the mayor's spending proposals. The mayor must accept the Council's reductions, but can veto its additions; however, the Council can override a veto by a two-thirds supermajority vote.

At no time in recent history has the city had both a mayor and a Council with such a strong progressive orientation aimed at reducing economic and social inequalities. The cooperative relationship between the two branches is facilitated by the political partnership that exists between Mayor de Blasio and City Council Speaker Melissa Mark-Viverito, whose priorities reflect the overall progressive disposition of the fifty-one-person body she leads, and whose assumption of the leadership role he supported.

In order to assess the fiscal consequences of this new partnership, I petitioned the New York City Independent Budget Office (IBO) to provide me with a list of expenditures dedicated to programs that are directed at the needs of vulnerable communities, comparing spending in the last year of the Bloomberg administration (FY 2014) and the current year (FY 2017) of the de Blasio administration.[5] Economists commonly refer to such expenditures as redistributive services, as they rely on tax-generated resources from more wealthy people and corporations to improve the lives of those who are less well off.

Table 8.1 enumerates several new initiatives that were undertaken by the de Blasio administration: rental assistance for the homeless ($112 million), mental

Table 8.1 **Spending on Vulnerable Communities**

Programs	Bloomberg FY2014 (in millions)	de Blasio FY2017 (in millions)	Percentage Change
Child Care	820.6	942.4	+12.92%
Pre-K/UPK	232.5	863.3	+73.07%
Emergency Food	13.3	17.1	+22.22%
Job Training/Placement	82.2	109.5	+24.93%
Workforce1 Centers	22.2	28.1	+21.00%
HIV/AIDS Services	227.1	243.4	+6.70%
Homeless Prevention	6.7	60.7	+88.96%
Rental Assistance (LINC) (homeless)		112	New
Summer Youth Employ	38.2	91	+58.02%
Out of School Time	147.9	336.9	+56.10%
Runaway/Homeless Youth (housing)	12.6	27.9	+54.84%
Community Development Programs	54.3	66.8	+18.71%
Legal Services	17	94.6	+82.03%
Anti-abandonment (housing)	6.3	9.6	+34.38%
THRIVE (mental health)		200.1	New
Young Men/Women Initiative	22.5	36.3	+38.02%
Antipoverty support		2.8	New
H+H subsidy (public hospitals)	90	261.4	+65.57%
Year-Round Youth Employment		11	New

health services ($200.1 million), antipoverty support ($2.8 million), and year-round youth employment ($11 million). The most dramatic increases (above 50 percent) in existing programs are for universal Pre-K (73.07 percent), homeless prevention (88.96 percent), summer youth programs (58.02 percent), out-of-school programs (56.10 percent), runaway/homeless youth services (54.84 percent), legal services (82.03 percent), and public hospitals (65.57 percent). Major increases (between 20 percent and 50 percent) are found in emergency food programs (22.22 percent), job training/placement (24.9 percent), workforce centers (21 percent), housing anti-abandonment (34.38 percent), and the young men/women's initiative (38.02 percent). Other categories with increases include childcare (12.92 percent), HIV-AIDS services (6.70 percent), and community development (18.71 percent). These figures do not include capital expenditures, which will be discussed later on. There is a consistent pattern of increased spending in the items identified by IBO analysts, with no exceptions.

In the fall of 2016, the *New York Times* reported that under Mayor de Blasio, the number of full-time employees on the city payroll was the highest "in modern history," still growing, and projected to reach 287,002, drawing concern from business-oriented watchdogs such as the Citizens Budget Commission for how the hiring might affect spending.[6] Speaking before the Association for a Better New York, another business-oriented civic organization, several days later, de Blasio proudly pled guilty as charged, stating, "We have absolutely increased the amount of public employment," explaining that it is the way the city will improve services in areas such as education and public safety.[7] To the delight of the municipal labor unions, de Blasio's collective bargaining team also moved to negotiate contracts that had been left unsettled by the Bloomberg administration. By the time de Blasio took office, every contract had been allowed to expire. The administration reached agreements with 60 percent of the municipal workforce within six months.[8] By 2016, 98.8 percent of the workforce was under contract.[9] In 2017, a long-delayed contract was signed with the Patrolmen's Benevolent Association.

Although business leaders may have been chagrined by the bulging size of the city workforce, they had reason to be cheered by the general economic picture. The city economy had already experienced four consecutive years of growth prior to de Blasio's taking office, outpacing the national average.[10] That pattern continued. Over 2015 and 2016, the city acquired 250,000 new jobs, bringing the total to 4.3 million, the highest number in history.[11] It had added more jobs in 2014–2015 than forty-six states. Of the 89,500 jobs added by the end of 2016, 84,900 were in the private sector.[12] The unemployment rate ranged between 5.0 percent and 5.9 percent in 2016, somewhat higher than the state rate (4.9 percent) and national rate (4.7 percent), but considerably lower that the city's 7.5 percent average over the last decade.[13]

The economy, at one time more dependent on Wall Street revenues and salaries that began to disappear during the recession, has begun to diversify, making it less vulnerable to swings in the stock market.[14] Nearly half the new jobs are found in the health, education, and technology sectors. There was also significant growth in the food, leisure, and hospitality sectors, no doubt driven by the burgeoning tourist industry. The city had experienced seven consecutive years of visitor growth, reaching a record high of 60.3 million in 2016. That could change if President Trump's attitude towards foreigners discourages international travel.

The administration also released new data produced by the Mayor's Office of Economic Opportunity in May 2017 showing that the city poverty rate had declined from 20.7 percent in 2013 to 19.9 percent in 2015.[15] The percentage of New Yorkers living near poverty had declined from 45.1 percent in 2014 to 44.2 percent in 2015, the largest one-year drop recorded since the city began tracking such data in 2005 and the first statistically significant drop since the Great Recession. This meant that 281,000 people were projected to be lifted from living at or near the poverty line between the end of 2014 and the end of 2017, which is five years ahead of the timeline the mayor had set in his OneNYC report.

It is difficult to estimate how much of the city's economic growth is due to local policy. Since 2009, the nation has experienced renewed prosperity as it emerged from the recession. In 2015, Americans at every rung of the income ladder enjoyed the largest earning gains in a generation.[16] Families at the lowest income levels benefited the most. Poverty and unemployment fell, and as a result of the Affordable Care Act passed by President Obama, more households were covered by health insurance than ever. That said, income inequality in the United States continues to exceed that found in every other major democracy in the world. As explained in an earlier chapter, much of that disparity is driven by federal regulatory and tax policies, leaving local governments to deal with the outcomes. As promised, de Blasio was deliberate in trying to address them.

De Blasio and the council moved quickly to exercise their executive and legislative authority to right some of the wrongs they attributed to the past administration. They revised the Earned Sick Leave Act that the Council had passed over Mayor Bloomberg's veto, so that more private sector employees were covered. Within a year, the mayor signed an executive order to increase benefits under the "living wage" bill Speaker Quinn finally had gotten passed. Then in 2016, de Blasio signed another executive order that guarantees city managers and non-union workers with fifteen years or more on the job at least six weeks of fully paid maternity, paternity, adoption, or foster care leave. Although older managers who are unlikely to take advantage of the new program were not happy to discover that the leave time was paid for by ditching a salary increase scheduled for 2017, 20,000 employees did benefit from it.[17]

And although de Blasio did not convince the legislature in Albany to raise taxes on the rich to pay for his centerpiece pre-kindergarten program, he did get the state to pick up the bill for it (mentioned above). In January 2016, the mayor also announced the implementation of a $15 minimum wage for municipal employees and social service organization workers who provide contracted work for the city. The raise would directly benefit 50,000 families. De Blasio stressed it would also allow the city to lead by example and be a "national leader in the fight to raise the wage."[18] The announcement generated another round of competition between the mayor and the governor. De Blasio had been out in front on the $15 wage issue before Cuomo. The governor initially opposed it. In April, Cuomo signed a $15 minimum wage law that would take effect at around the same time as de Blasio's plan for city workers.[19]

Another early initiative undertaken by Mayor de Blasio and his progressive allies in the City Council involved undocumented immigrants. In January 2015, the mayor and Speaker Melissa Mark-Viverito launched the largest municipal identification program in the country. *IDNYC* issues identification cards to undocumented immigrants, homeless people, and other residents who must navigate their way through the municipal bureaucracy to receive services and other benefits to which they are entitled. The ID can be used to request a library card or open a bank account. It carries a free one-year membership to museums and other cultural institutions. It provides discounts for rentals at Citi Bike and the theater. Simply put, the card validates the identity of people who may still be treated as second-class New Yorkers. According to de Blasio, "the card represents who we are: New Yorkers who value equality, opportunity, and diversity."[20] Immigrants continue to play an important role in the New York economy, making up 45 percent of the city labor force, owning 52 percent of the businesses, and earning 39 percent of household income.[21]

Apparently there is a great deal that a local chief executive, working with a like-minded city council, can do to sensitize government to the needs of people who don't exercise extraordinary influence—especially if he or she wants to, and it coincides with the interests of powerful labor unions. Whether such actions are sufficient is a different but related question that we will discuss in subsequent pages.

In the introductory chapter, we observed the fine line Mayor de Blasio walked between his celebrity police commissioner and civil rights activists who believed that Commissioner Bratton's "broken windows" philosophy was too aggressive. Bratton did drastically cut back on Commissioner Raymond Kelly's controversial "stop-and-frisk" policy—a decision that must have afforded him some not-so-guilty pleasure, as the two New York luminaries are perpetual rivals in the aristocracy of criminal justice circles. And Bratton did not have much of a choice, as a federal court had found aspects of the practice unconstitutional.

Bratton also collaborated with Speaker Melissa Mark-Viverito and City Council leaders to develop legislation that could alleviate tensions between his officers and the minority community. Following a year of negotiations with department officials, the council passed a set of laws in 2016 that reduced penalties for minor offenses, such as having open containers of alcohol, urinating in public, and littering. As a result, police officers are able to issue civil summonses rather than criminal summonses for such offenses. The new practice has the potential to lower arrest and incarceration rates that are disproportionately high in minority communities, and to lower generally the stakes of transactions that take place between civilians and the police.

Mayor de Blasio found himself caught in a nasty public dispute between Bratton and his own Commissioner of Investigation, Mark Peters, when the latter issued a report in 2016 finding that the department's strategy of enforcing "quality of life" crimes does not reduce serious crimes.[22] Analyzing 1.8 million summonses, 600,000 misdemeanor arrests, and 200,000 felony arrests that occurred between 2010 and 2015, the report's conclusions impugn the very logic of "broken windows" policing, which itself is based on substantial social science evidence. Not mincing words, Bratton characterized the report as "fatally flawed" and "useless," suggesting that the inquiry had not looked back far enough in time to determine the impact of the approach when it was originally implemented during the Giuliani administration.[23] Once again, the mayor stood by his police commissioner, and Bratton remarked, "We are joined at the shoulder and the hip."[24]

Speaker Mark-Viverito and Commissioner Bratton also worked closely together on a package of legislation referred to as the "Right to Know Act." In this case the mayor and the police commissioner opposed the law under consideration. According to long-existing practices, a police officer cannot search an individual unless the officer has "reasonable suspicion" that the person is, has been, or will be involved in committing a crime. Such protections are afforded by guarantees against "unreasonable searches" found within the U.S. Constitution. The proposed law would have required police officers who want to conduct a search of a person, car, or home without legal cause specifically to request permission. Once a so-called "consent search" is conducted, an officer would need to provide a business card with his or her identity.

Supportive of the administration's position, Speaker Mark-Viverito delayed voting on the measure until a compromise could be worked out. As a significant concession, she agreed to halt passage of the bill if the changes being considered were added to the Police Department Patrol Guide. Under these terms, the procedures do not have the force of law, and are dependent on the department to enforce them. Although Council members representing minority communities were unhappy with the way the deal came off, it was going to hold.[25] Later on, the Council would pass a stipulation requiring the NYPD to publish its patrol guide.

Another controversy with the NYPD concerns the disclosure of officers' disciplinary records. At issue is New York State Civil Rights Law 50-a, a 1976 statute that prohibits the release of employee disciplinary records without judicial approval. The law protects the privacy of officers in both the police and the correction departments. In 2011, the New York Civil Liberties Union (NYCLU) filed a suit against the NYPD, when the department refused to release a decade's worth of "trial room" decisions in response to a Freedom of Information request. Several news media organizations had joined the suit in support of the NYCLU. The Legal Aid Society also filed a suit to force the NYPD to disclose information on how officers are disciplined. [26]

The disclosure issue recently came to light again during the investigation of Officer Daniel Pantaleo, who had administered a chokehold to Eric Garner on Staten Island in 2014. When a state court ordered the NYPD to release a summary of Officer Pantaleo's previous misconduct findings, the de Blasio administration appealed the ruling. Relying on a narrow interpretation of the law, the city held that the records could not be made available without changing the law itself. Although the mayor has publicly urged the state legislature to amend the law, lawmakers are not likely to tamper with a statute that has such strong backing from the police and corrections officers' unions. In March 2017, a state appellate court handed down separate unanimous decisions upholding the decisions of the de Blasio administration in the two pending cases involving Civil Rights law 50-a.

Despite the mayor's continued support of controversial policies that were important to his police commissioner, it was not enough to keep Bratton on the job. In July 2016, just days after the City Council halted passage of the "Right to Know" Act, Bratton announced that he would be leaving to take a position in the private sector. The news came as a surprise to reporters who had been covering him and fed speculation that the commissioner's departure might throw a wrench into the mayor's re-election campaign, which was now less than a year away. Bratton's appointment had boosted de Blasio's credibility among those who feared that the left-leaning mayor might be soft on crime. That said, the quick transition that linked Bratton's announcement to the immediate selection of a successor was seamless—a political masterstroke on the part of the mayor's office.

A drawn-out selection process would have politicized the crucial appointment and could have fed racial divisions. By choosing Bratton protégé, James O'Neill, as Bratton's replacement, the mayor signaled his intention to stay the course that Bratton had set in suppressing crime. Naming an individual whom Bratton personally groomed as his successor was more likely to keep the outgoing and outspoken commissioner on the reservation in support of the administration's policies. As a career officer who previously served as Chief of the Department— the highest uniformed position on the force—O'Neill had credibility with the rank and file. He had also demonstrated his commitment to a form of community policing that could ease tensions in minority communities. [27] By the time the department was handed over to him, the neighborhood-based program was operative in half the precincts and every public housing district in the city. Most important, O'Neill did not carry around Bratton's supersized ego, which could be a lightning rod for critics, and at times could weaken the hand of the mayor who needed to treat his star appointee almost as if he were a peer.

Bratton's departure may have been a blessing in disguise for the mayor as he faced re-election. Although the "Two Bills" appeared to have a good working relationship, Bratton could also be a liability as the mayor attempted to mobilize his minority base of support, whose votes he had to rely on. There were sharp differences between the two men that underscored the distinct worlds from where they came. De Blasio, who never hesitated to mention his biracial family, identified with the "Black Lives Matter" movement that was very critical of the police, saying that it "hit the right note" and "is a necessary part of the national discussion."[28] The hard-nosed Irish cop from Boston could be provocative in ways that were uncomfortable for the mayor, like the time he referred to rappers as "thugs."[29] Now the marriage had come to an end, and the split seemed to be amicable.

During Bratton's tenure, crime had decreased, even as his department greatly reduced its reliance on the questionable stop-and-frisk policy championed by Police Commissioner Raymond Kelly. During de Blasio's first three years in office, the overall number of crimes declined steadily from 111,335 in 2013 (Bloomberg's last year in office), to 106,722 (2014), to 105,456 (2015), to 101,717 (2016).[30] Although the number of murders in 2015 (352) exceeded the all-time low from 2014 (333), there were only 335 murders in 2016, which equaled the number in the last year of the Bloomberg administration.

The number of stop-and-frisk incidents had peaked at 685,724 in 2011. After a federal judge intervened and questioned the disproportionate effect the policy had on African-American and Latino males, Police Commissioner Kelly de-emphasized the practice, and the number was brought down to 191,558 during Mayor Bloomberg's last year in office (2013).[31] Living up to Mayor de Blasio's campaign pledge, Commissioner Bratton further reduced the number over the next three years by 93 percent. During the same period of time (2013 to 2016), the number of total arrests also dropped consistently from 393,539 to 314,870.[32]

After Bratton's departure, the department agreed to settle the lawsuit brought by the NYCLU in 2012, by amending certain aspects of the stop procedures that the court had found problematic. Under the Trespass Affidavit program, officers would routinely stop individuals who congregated in or around a building after a landlord filed a complaint, whether or not they were involved in suspicious activity. In many cases, individuals who were questioned had actually been residents of the buildings being patrolled. That practice has now ended. Another policy change being implemented as a result of the collective bargaining agreement signed in 2017 would fit all officers on patrol duty with body cameras to record their personal interactions.

Ironically, Bill Bratton, the man who made a reputation reducing crime by taking an aggressive approach to patrolling New York City neighborhoods during the Giuliani administration, inadvertently validated the framework for a new approach to policing that was implemented during his second tour of duty under Mayor de Blasio. He did so by demonstrating that the empirical connection between tough enforcement and the incidence of crime can no longer be assumed—all the while, of course, vowing to abide by his own signature "Broken Windows" policy.

These were different times for sure. Crime had steadily declined throughout the Giuliani and Bloomberg years. The streets had become safer—perhaps because of aggressive policing in the past, or maybe other tactics, such as data-driven policing that took effect under Compstat during Bratton's first tour of duty. Now de Blasio was responding to new demands by minority communities to improve the relationship between NYPD officers and their residents. Apparently, the new approach was reaping dividends. Complaints filed with the Civilian Complaint Review Board plunged from 5,388 in 2013, the last year of the Bloomberg administration, to 4,283 at the end of 2016.[33] Not all was well between the administration and civil rights advocates, however. Civil liberty groups remained unhappy with the defeat of the Right to Know Act, even with the inclusion of many of its provisions in the NYPD Patrol Guide, and disagreements continue over the disclosure of internal investigations of misconduct.

Bill de Blasio also used his powers as mayor to reach beyond the police, making changes in the criminal justice system that could improve conditions for the black and Latino men who are disproportionately caught up in it. Following recommendations made by the Justice Department, the mayor developed a plan to move 200 adolescents out of the Rikers Island Jail complex to the Horizon Juvenile Center in the Bronx, where they are housed if they are serving less than a one-year sentence or are awaiting trial because they could not make bail. He also tripled the number of intensive care units for mentally ill inmates, estimated to be 40 percent of the population.

The latter initiatives were small parts of a much larger campaign to reform the corrections system and root out violence in the infamous Rikers Island multiplex of facilities. In 2015, the city settled a class action suit brought by inmates and the Justice Department by agreeing to appoint a federal monitoring team. In May 2016, the monitors released a report noting that there had been improvements in the jails, but that the use of excessive force by officers remained a problem.

Through the first three years of his administration, Mayor de Blasio resisted pressure from Governor Andrew Cuomo, City Council Speaker Melissa Mark-Viverito, and other political leaders to close the sprawling jail complex on Rikers Island, claiming that it would be impractical. He changed his mind in March

2017, when an independent commission appointed by Mark-Viverito concluded that the notorious institution should be put out of existence.[34] Jonathan Lippman, a retired chief judge of the state court system who chaired the commission, characterized the closing as a "moral imperative."

Standing next to the Speaker at a City Hall news conference, de Blasio announced that he was in basic agreement with the recommendations of the 97-page report and vowed that his reversal on the jail closing was a "very serious, sober, forever decision."[35] The panel's ten-year plan, however, was predicated on lofty aspirations and questionable assumptions that the mayor would have to translate into reality. It projected a reduction of the jail population by half, from 10,000 to 5,000 inmates. This cutback would depend on a continued decline in crime and lower incarcerations rates for minor offenses. It would require substance abusers and mentally ill offenders to be placed in clinics rather than jails. It anticipated the building of new jail facilities throughout the five boroughs; this would not only be costly, but also unwelcome in city neighborhoods. It called for a workforce reduction in the Department of Correction by more than half, from 10,000 employees to 3,700. Labor unions, a key constituency of the progressive mayor, do not take well to job losses of that magnitude. These were all noble objectives, but it remains to be seen whether the mayor's original assessment of feasibility regarding Rikers's demise was right all along.

Getting the administration's universal pre-kindergarten (UPK) program up and running was a notable success. A reported 20,387 seats were filled in the 2014/2015 school year.[36] The program grew to 65,504 in the second year.[37] Although UPK was not specifically targeted at poor or minority children, it could prove especially beneficial to parents who cannot afford private preschool services or do not have the resources to prepare children on their own. Research has shown that early childhood education can have a positive impact on children's cognitive and emotional development.[38] The strategy made good sense, and once again exemplified what local government—in this case with state support—can do to close the opportunity gap. Beyond its educational benefits, the program also provides free childcare for working parents who cannot afford it, allowing them to put in more hours on the job and possibly earning more.

UPK also provided a new reason for de Blasio to do battle with charter schools, and his reliable adversary Eva Moskowitz, the founder of the Success Academy network. Coordinating her efforts with Governor Cuomo's office, Moskowitz had led protests against the mayor when he voiced opposition to the privately run public schools that would compete with regular district schools. On this particular occasion, Moskowitz disputed the oversight authority that the city Department of Education (DOE) exercised over her Pre-K program, claiming that charter schools should be exempt from such regulation. When the State

Education Department (SED) ruled in favor of the DOE, Moskowitz cancelled classes scheduled for about 100 students. SED's decision was upheld by a state court in June 2016.

True to form, the UPK controversy was a convenient vehicle for proponents and opponents of charter schools to renew hostilities in their larger debate over the merits of these privately run public schools. It was another example of adults behaving badly, while the interests of children hang in the balance. Usually, Governor Cuomo and Republican legislative leaders could be expected to line up behind charters, while the mayor and Assembly Democrats would come out less sympathetic. Charter school proponents accuse the other side of being in the pocket of the teachers union and the status quo education establishment; their opponents note how business interests and hedge fund managers invest money in charter schools and the advocacy organizations behind them. There is almost a personal quality to the animosity. Each side selectively cites evidence to support its case, but there isn't a serious discussion about policy.

For the second year in a row (there would be a third), Senate Republicans threatened that they would not renew legislation giving de Blasio control over the public schools. When they finally granted it, they did so for only one additional year. (Mayor Bloomberg was initially afforded seven years of mayoral control to fit what legislators thought would be his full term in office, then it was subsequently renewed through his third term.) De Blasio's renewal was accompanied by new legislation that potentially offered wider latitude for charter schools to operate independently of local control. One law made it easier for charter schools to switch between charter granting institutions. Another specifically authorized the State University of New York (SUNY) Board of Trustees to "promulgate regulations with respect to the governance, structure and operations" of the schools it oversees.[39]

In order to understand the more recent debate over governance, one needs to look back a bit into history to 1998, when Republican Governor George Pataki originally signed the state charter school bill into law. Republicans who controlled the senate had been more amenable to the idea from the outset. Faced with resistance from assembly Democrats who were close to the teachers' union, Pataki agreed to grant the lawmakers a long-debated pay raise they had sought to bring them along. Under the new charter law, three entities were empowered to authorize charter schools: the SUNY Board of Trustees, the State Board of Regents, and the New York City Department of Education. Republicans supportive of charter schools controlled the SUNY board; Democrats who were less supportive controlled the Regents. Democratic governors who succeeded Pataki, especially Cuomo, have remained supportive, as has the SUNY board.

Empowered with newly acquired authority over the school system, Mayor Bloomberg consistently supported the growth of charter schools (from 14 to 183).[40] When de Blasio declared early on that he did not intend to authorize many new charter schools, it made SUNY's governance role all the more important to charter supporters.[41] His suggestion that charters may be required to pay rent in public school buildings further raised anxieties in the charter school community. De Blasio's animosity toward charter schools upon entering office was unfortunate. According to the New York City Charter School Center (NYCCSC), 77 percent of the students who attend charter schools are from disadvantaged backgrounds.[42] There is credible evidence that charter schools in New York have been able to raise the achievement levels of poor and minority children, and in many cases have been more effective than regular public schools. In this way, charter schools can be very much aligned with the egalitarian agenda that Mayor de Blasio has set out to achieve.[43]

Although there are both strong and weak schools within the charter sector, the results of state achievement tests for the 2015/2016 school year for grades 3 through 8 show that charter schools outperform regular public schools in the percentage of students scoring at a proficient level in math (48 percent to 36 percent) and English Language Arts (ELA) (43 percent to 38 percent).[44] The achievement differences are starker among students of color. For black students, the proficiency levels favor charter school enrollees 49 percent to 20 percent in math, and 43 percent to 26 percent in ELA. For Hispanic students, the differences are 47 percent to 24 percent in math, and 46 percent to 27 percent in ELA. No educator or political leader who seeks to improve educational opportunities for low-income populations can ignore such data.

Some have challenged the validity of these comparisons. They argue that parents who apply to charter schools are a highly motivated, self-selected subgroup within minority and poor communities, whose children tend to drive test scores up. That is a valid analytical observation, but a vapid policy argument. Motivated poor and minority parents should have an opportunity to choose a school if they believe it gives their children an opportunity to excel academically the same way that middle class people do. The problem is that there are too few of these sought-after schools. According to the NYCCSC, there are more than 44,000 students on waiting lists for charter schools in the city.

Critics also argue that charter schools have a segregating effect because a disproportionate number of students who seek to enroll in them are from minority communities. If policy advocates want to address the problem of racial segregation, they ought to begin with the regular public schools. New York City has one of the most segregated school systems in the country.[45] A recent report by the Century Foundation found that this segregation begins in preschool, and like the broader pattern of school segregation, it is largely a function of housing segregation.[46] Charter school applicants are disproportionately black and Latino because these groups disproportionately find themselves in failing public schools, and therefore are motivated to seek alternatives. Students who attend charter schools do so as a matter of choice. They are there to take advantage of new educational options. Their situation should not be confused with the years of racial segregation that have prevailed in New York City public schools that are a function either of deliberate policy or of housing patterns.

A more serious charge against charter schools involves the claim that they are inhospitable to low performing students. They have been accused of pressuring students to transfer out, and of discriminating against the disabled. The Legal Aid Society has filed a complaint with the federal Office of Civil Rights against Eva Moskowitz's Success Academy on behalf of the parents of thirteen students or former students, charging that the organization has failed to provide adequate support services to special needs children and tries to push them out.[47] The complaint was joined by Public Advocate Letitia James and City Council Member Daniel Dromm, who chairs the Education Committee. These are serious charges and they should be dealt with appropriately if they are substantiated. They are not a reason to dismiss charter schools as an option for improving the educational opportunities of students who are not getting a quality education elsewhere.

Other than UPK, the most comprehensive education initiative undertaken by the de Blasio administration is the Renewal Program that designated ninety-four low performing institutions as "community schools." The concept behind this approach—sometimes referred to as a full service model—is to develop the whole child by saturating schools with wraparound afterschool, health, social, and other supportive services delivered by local agencies and nonprofit institutions.[48] It fits well with the administration's inclination to treat problems in troubled communities as manifestations of systemic inequality. Renewal schools also receive supplementary staff support and coaching. Community schools can be traced back to the progressive movement of the early twentieth century, when John Dewey conceived of the school as a "social center."[49] School reformer Leonard Covello introduced community schools in East Harlem during the Great Depression, when the neighborhood was still an Italian ghetto, and maintained them as the neighborhood became populated by Puerto Ricans.[50] Now the model is operative in 100 cities across the country.

The Children's Aid Society instituted full service schools in New York during the 1990s. The Wallace Foundation, which has been a major funding source for a broad range of school innovations, has been a loyal supporter of community schools. In 2011, the National Center for Community Schools became a lead partner for developing twenty-one schools in the South Bronx, East Harlem, Washington Heights, and Staten Island. The success of the Harlem Children's Zone has drawn much positive attention to this full-service model of schooling, but it is also very costly. From an organizational perspective, the idea of making schools a focal point for services makes sense because schools are the places where young people are required to congregate on a regular basis.[51]

The overall research on the effectiveness of community schools is somewhat mixed, yet there is sufficient evidence to suggest that if implemented well, they can improve learning and encourage meaningful parent involvement.[52] That said, it is important to point out that community schools were not initially conceived as a model to turn around failing schools. One particular challenge with their application is that the coordination of support services requires adding an extra layer of administrative overhead to institutions that already have difficulty meeting their instructional mandates.

At this point, it is too early to evaluate the program's effectiveness in New York. The logic of providing struggling students with more support is irrefutable. It remains to be seen whether this model can be effectively applied to reverse chronic institutional failure. At the outset, the mayor and his Chancellor Carmen Fariña had rejected the Bloomberg administration's strategy of closing down failing schools. Although their pledge not to give up on any school is commendable in theory, experience with schools that have been unable to meet performance benchmarks has led them to reconsider their approach. At the beginning of 2017, the DOE closed eight Renewal Schools, with plans to close or merge nine more. The administration has also proposed to merge five other pairs of schools that are not part of the Renewal Program in order to reverse patterns of low performance and under-enrollment at chronically weak schools.[53]

In the meantime, overall school performance is improving on de Blasio's watch. State test scores in reading and math were up for the second year in a row in 2016, continuing the upward spiral that began under the Bloomberg administration. Since de Blasio took office, the percentage of students reaching proficiency in math in grades three through eight rose from 34.2 percent to 36.5 percent.[54] In English Language Arts, the improvement was 28.5 percent to 38.0 percent. It is too soon to determine whether the gains are being driven by anything the current administration is doing, or whether the rise might be a residual effect from the work of its predecessor. That said, it is better to be in a position of speculation about improvement than about decline. The mayor has also touted record high school graduation rates (72.6 percent),[55] but because state graduation standards keep changing and about half the graduates are not prepared to assume college level work at the City University of New York, graduation data remain an unreliable measure of progress.

Speaking off the record, one long-time associate of de Blasio put it this way: "We're ok with what he is doing with policy; we understand the limits and the pace of change. It's the silly, sloppy stuff that gets to us. That could really hurt him, and what we hope to get from his being mayor." The person mentioned "annoying" things such as the mayor's lateness when arriving at events, and his harangues with news reporters, then noted all the investigations and allegations brought against de Blasio that, in a worse case scenario, could have brought down.

Bill Bratton's stellar police department was the scene of one set of corruption scandals.[56] In June 2016, federal agents arrested NYPD Sergeant David Villanueva on charges that over a period of five years he had accepted bribes from Alex "Shaya" Lichtenstein to push through applications for 100 to 150 gun permits over a period of five years. Lichtenstein, the leader of the *Shomrim*, a volunteer civilian patrol in the Hasidic Jewish neighborhood of Borough Park, was later convicted of bribery. In a separate case, Deputy Inspector James Grant and Deputy Chief Michael Harrington were arrested and charged with taking gifts from Jona Rechnitz and Jeremiah Reichberg in exchange for special favors from the police department. The two wealthy businessmen were also associated with the Hasidic community in Borough Park, and had been named to Mayor de Blasio's inaugural committee after making generous contributions to his election campaign. Mayor de Blasio has not been directly tied to police scandals, but with friends like these. . ..

Rechnitz is the subject of several other investigations. In one, he pled guilty to arranging for the illegal investment of funds from the corrections officers union, leading to the arrest of its president, Norman Seabrook. In another case, he pled guilty to bribery charges. Rechnitz was turned around to become a cooperating witness in the corrections case against Seabrook, and has cooperated in the investigations involving the mayor's fundraising activities.[57] Altogether, the de Blasio team has been investigated by the U.S. Attorney, the state Attorney General, the Manhattan District Attorney, the State Joint Committee on Public Ethics, the City Comptroller, the City Department of Investigation, and other regulatory bodies.

One major problem involved the Campaign for One New York (CONY), an organization de Blasio founded to advance his policy agenda on issues like universal pre-kindergarten. CONY was incorporated by the state as a social welfare nonprofit under IRS rules, which authorizes it to undertake activities to promote the common good of the entire community. It is not unusual for political leaders to set up such operations. Governors Andrew Cuomo (NY) and Chris Christie (NJ) have set up their own to promote specific causes. After the *Citizens United* decision was handed down by the Supreme Court in 2010, some politicians began using these social welfare nonprofits to hide campaign donations and avoid disclosing their donors.

Several different kinds of questions were raised regarding CONY: whether gifts to the organization were made in exchange for special treatment by the administration, whether the organization itself was a lobbying group, and whether it functioned to supplement the mayor's campaign organization. It reaped more than $4 million in contributions from unions, real estate investors, and firms that conduct business with the city. In addition to donations from Rechnitz and Reichberg, the organization received generous donations from Wendy Neu and Steven Nislick. Both are associated with NYCLASS, an animal rights group that has sought to end the use of horse-drawn carriages in New York, a cause de Blasio has championed. Another donor who raises suspicion is Joseph Dussich, a businessman who has been given a contract from the Parks Department.[58] The list goes on.

A separate area of concern involves contributions to political campaigns. Under state election laws, contributions to individual candidates are limited to $10,300. This limit, however, does not hold regarding donations to county committees, in which the amount can climb to as high as $103,000. The mayor's team was investigated by federal prosecutors to determine whether it circumvented the spending limits by coordinating donations to the Putnam and Ulster Democratic Party county committees and funneling them into two legislative campaigns against Republicans. The outcome of the elections could have determined which party controls the majority in the state senate and ultimately the fate of de Blasio's own legislative proposals in Albany.

Among those subpoenaed in the case is Emma Wolfe, the mayor's Director of Intergovernmental Affairs, who previously served as political director of his campaign and was his chief of staff in the Public Advocate's office.[59] In December 2016, the *New York Times* reported that federal and state grand juries had been empaneled to investigate the fundraising activities, suggesting that the investigation could lead to indictments.[60] De Blasio himself has met with federal prosecutors to discuss the inquiries.

Rivington House was an AIDS hospice located on the Lower East Side. For years, it was protected by a restrictive covenant that did not allow the property to be used for any purpose other than as a not-for-profit residential medicalcare facility. In 2015, the Allure Group that owned the building paid the city $16 million to lift the restriction, and in turn sold the building to a developer for $116 million, making a huge profit. The deal was brokered by James Capalino, one of the most influential lobbyists in town. When questioned by the Investigations Department, city officials claimed that they were not aware of how the former building owner intended to use the property, and the mayor has claimed no knowledge of the deal at all before it was executed.[61]

De Blasio has also come under scrutiny for setting up a "shadow government" of advisors who are paid as consultants and wield influence as "agents of the city," but are not held to the same level of transparency as regular city employees.[62] Some were paid through the Campaign for One New York. Several have public affairs practices and function as media advisors. One, Jonathan Rosen, represents clients from the real estate industry and organized labor that do business with the city, including SL Green, Two Trees Management, Forest City Ratner, the Communications Workers of America, and SEIU. One person listed as an advisor is Patrick Gaspard, the mayor's close friend and associate of many years who had served as ambassador to South Africa in the Obama administration.

In July 2016, the city Campaign Finance Board (CFB) rendered its finding that the CONY did not violate city campaign finance laws, with respect to the mayor's effort to raise private money for his pre-kindergarten initiative before public money was made available by the state. De Blasio had closed down the operation in March. The ruling did not exonerate the mayor from other allegations being investigated at the time. Noting that 95 percent of the funds collected by the foundation would have been prohibited by laws that apply to candidates for office, the CFB concluded that the case "plainly raises serious policy and perception issues."[63] It called on the City Council to institute measures that would tighten the limits on contributions made to nonprofits associated with elected officials. Joining in the conversation, Dick Dadey, executive director of the Citizens Union, called such nonprofits an expansion of the "pay to play" culture.[64]

In March 2017, the U.S Attorney for the Southern District and the Manhattan District Attorney issued coordinated but separate statements indicating that they would not be bringing criminal charges against the mayor or his associates. Marking the conclusion of the investigations, Acting U.S. Attorney Joon H. Kim explained, "Although it is rare that we issue a public statement about the status of an investigation, we believe it appropriate in this case at this time, in order not to unduly influence the upcoming campaign and mayoral election."[65] The Board of Elections maintains separate authority to determine whether election laws were violated, which, if found, could result in civil penalties.

The Manhattan District Attorney, Cyrus Vance, addressed his ten-page letter to the New York State Board of Elections (BOE), which had prompted his investigation by determining that "reasonable cause" existed to believe the mayor's close staff and associates had violated state election laws by channeling funds to county political committees to influence the outcome of state senate races. In his carefully worded letter, Vance stipulated that while "the parties involved cannot be appropriately prosecuted . . . this conclusion is not an endorsement of the conduct at issue." He further elaborated, "the transactions appear contrary to the intent and spirit of the laws that impose candidate contribution limits," citing laws that "are meant to prevent 'corruption and the appearance of corruption' in the campaign financing process."[66]

The district attorney's letter ended with a number of recommendations for consideration by the BOE and the state that were designed to make existing prohibitions more effective in preventing corruption or its appearance—the very kinds of provisions that have been consistently avoided by the governor and the state legislature amidst idle talk of reform. There was a larger lesson to be drawn from the entire episode that cannot be lost in the specifics of these cases. Bill de Blasio's cohorts had followed the law. As have many other political operatives in the state, they had played by the rules that were in place; but the rules themselves were dirty, full of loopholes that undermine serious attempts to control how money corrupts the political process.

* * *

With a progressive City Council in place, the de Blasio administration moved quickly to redirect priorities. These changes were most graphically reflected in the budget—the "put your money where your mouth is" document that explicitly measures what is important to decision-makers. In this case, new resources were invested in services for vulnerable communities. De Blasio's iteration of Bloomberg's *PlaNYC* not only incorporated the language of *equality*, but also it translated equity into a rubric used by the First Deputy Mayor to assess the delivery of services.

The early legislative agenda at the council level revisited old battles and started some anew: expanding the reach of the Earned Sick Leave Act, instituting a $15 minimum wage for city employees and contractors, distributing ID cards to immigrants, the homeless, and marginalized communities to foster a sense of inclusion. The mayor used his executive power to increase benefits guaranteed under the living wage law and to establish paid maternity and paternity leave for city employees.

In the Police Department, the simultaneous drop in crime and stop-and-frisk encounters between officers and citizens resolves a philosophical argument that had been festering since the end of Commissioner Raymond Kelly's tenure, and has the potential to decrease strains in black and Latino communities. The reduction of penalties for minor offenses would lower the stakes of interpersonal encounters at the community level and the number of people arrested or incarcerated. Shrinking the jail population is also an essential prerequisite for plans to close down the Rikers Island facility in ten years.

The "broken windows" approach to quality-of-life issues has remained a source of tension and is still debated. Is quality-of-life policing necessary? Is it just a form of "stop-and-frisk lite"? Will Police Commissioner James O'Neill place less emphasis on it? The reluctance of the City Council to give Right to Know provisions the force of law has left many civil rights activists feeling as though they have been duped by a political sleight of hand. In the meantime, the mayor continues to walk a delicate line between a militant police union he must depend on to protect public safety, and civil rights advocates concerned about the treatment of people in minority neighborhoods. Police Commissioner O'Neill will have an opportunity to put his own signature on policies that are in place, including a renewed focus on community policing. He is being asked to do so in the midst of the mayor's re-election campaign.

Universal Pre-Kindergarten (UPK) has created important developmental opportunities for four-year-olds across the city and free childcare for working parents who could otherwise not afford it. It is encouraging to find that performance continues to improve on state administered tests in reading and math. Nonetheless, with 63.5 percent of all students scoring below proficiency in math and 62 percent below proficiency in reading, there still remains much work to be done. The community school approach holds promise as a strategy for enhancing the capacity of schools, but it has yet to be proven in New York as a method to turn around failing schools. The administration is wise to adopt a more a flexible attitude toward school closings so that children in need of a good education are not allowed to languish in institutions that cannot demonstrate a capacity for improvement.

The administration, however, needs a more comprehensive, "out of the box" strategy to deal with the school system it inherited in which the great majority of students are not learning at a satisfactory level. The mayor and Chancellor Carmen Fariña should have a more open mind on the contribution that charter schools can make in promoting educational and social equality. Although charter schools themselves are not the answer to an educational crisis that disproportionately afflicts low-income students from African-American and Latino communities, there is something that can be learned from those charter schools that are unusually effective at closing the learning gap.

The de Blasio administration has benefited from the strongest local economy in recent history, and it has worked more assertively than any in the past fifty years to assure that the benefits of that economy would be shared more evenly with those New Yorkers who have been deprived of a decent life. But the evidence of the city's lasting inequality has continued to grow, and it keeps presenting itself in raw human dimensions right there on the city streets in the form of epic homelessness.

‖ 9 ‖

No Place Like a Home

Bill de Blasio inherited the largest homeless population in New York's recent history.[1] It has continued to grow on his watch. Their ranks have become increasingly diverse. It used to be a mostly male population that fit certain popular stereotypes. By the 1960s, portraits of down on their luck men panhandling along the Bowery gave way to images of dangerous drug addicts who would steal rather than beg to support their destructive habits. Many mental patients had been turned out on the streets after state institutions were closed in the 1970s adding to the population.[2] In either case, the presence of homeless men was always a conspicuous reminder of human suffering, but their association with personal failure allowed passers-by who stepped around their bodies to reason that maybe these sad old guys, to some extent, were individually at fault for their bleak existence. These stereotypes no longer fit the preponderant population.

A new image emerged in December 2013, when the *New York Times* ran a five-part series on Dasani Coates, a twelve-year-old girl who spent three years at the Auburn Family Residence in Fort Greene, Brooklyn.[3] Dasani shared a small room there with her parents and seven siblings. Both her parents were drug addicts. There were 280 other children at Auburn. The filthy facility was infested with roaches and rodents, layers of mold crept up its peeling walls, the toilets were clogged with human waste, and the showers were trolled by sexual predators. The building itself had thirteen violations, and the fire safety system was broken. According to the investigative report, families make up about 75 percent of the homeless population, and about 40 percent are children. A quarter of the families have at least one adult with a job. The homeless people that New Yorkers see on the street are not representative of those in the shelter system.

The Fort Greene Historic District where Auburn is located is a study in contrasts. It contains two public housing projects populated by poor residents, and some of the finest brownstones in the city. It is the site of the Brooklyn Academy of Music, a destination where chic New Yorkers enjoy classical music, theater, and other cultural offerings. Over a span of three years, nineteen luxury buildings went up in the surrounding area.

Young Dasani became a symbol of much that was wrong with New York as Bill de Blasio came to office: the expansion of the homeless population, the shameful conditions under which they exist, and the bold contrasts between the haves and the have-nots. Dasani sat on stage right behind the new mayor during his inaugural ceremony. She was a special guest of Public Advocate Letitia James. Dasani held the Bible when James took her oath of office, and stood behind her when James spoke of "a gilded age of inequality where decrepit homeless shelters and housing developments stand in the neglected shadow of gleaming, multi-million-dollar condos, where long-term residents are being priced out of their own neighborhoods by rising rents and stagnant incomes."[4]

According to a survey completed by the Coalition for the Homeless in January 2017, there are 62,840 people in the shelter system.[5] This includes 15,899 families with 24,251 children, 10,801 single men, and 4,012 single women. Approximately 58 percent of the population is African-American, 31 percent is Latino, 7 percent is white, and less than 1 percent is Asian. The single adult population tends to suffer from higher incidences of mental illness, addiction disorders, and physical ailments. Most of those who work are women with low paying jobs, such as security guards, sales clerks, home health aides, and office staff. Some are employed by the city. Eviction and overcrowding are among the top five reasons families became homeless, accounting for 42 percent of the shelter residents. Domestic violence is the top reason that families with children entered the shelter system, accounting for 30 percent of the total. Unemployment and the lack of affordable housing also remain critical factors.

Adolescents are an especially vulnerable segment of the homeless population. Many are runaways who have fled abusive family situations and function without adult support.[6] An estimated 30 percent of them have been thrown out or abandoned by their families. Lesbian, gay, bisexual, transgender, and questioning (LGBTQ) youth are overrepresented in crisis shelters, where they comprise at least 20 percent of the population. Many of them have been victims of domestic violence. Former Deputy Mayor Lilliam Barrios-Paoli, who oversaw homeless policy for the first eighteen months of the de Blasio administration, knew these populations well. For several years, she had served as CEO of Safe-Space, a nonprofit organization that provides support services to at-risk children and families who have been victims of poverty, child abuse, and domestic violence.

De Blasio views homelessness as a part of the larger inequality problem, and his approach to health and mental health has been holistic. The fifty-four mental health initiatives he announced with his wife in November 2015 (discussed in Chapter 2) were comprehensive in scope, and designed not just to provide timely treatment, but also to change public attitudes toward people with mental disabilities. The mayor and his wife, Chirlane McCray, drew on their personal family histories to make the point. In education, de Blasio's community schools program was meant to deliver wraparound services to support students who are underperforming. Likewise, his approach to homelessness would focus on supportive housing that provided service as well as shelter.

Three days after being sworn in, de Blasio enacted a "Code Blue" policy that guaranteed shelter to homeless people on the coldest nights of the year. This had been standard policy in the city until Mayor Bloomberg reversed it during his last year in office, and advocates noticed that people were being turned away if they could not prove that they had no place else to go.[7] It was an easy problem to repair for a new mayor wanting to communicate his intent to change direction. With the help of new state funding, the city also doubled its spending on the Homebase program that was started by the Bloomberg administration, and became a casualty of the recession. Homebase sets up offices in communities with high levels of homelessness, and delivers an array of preventive services, such as job training, assistance with benefits, landlord-tenant mediation, and emergency rent payments.

In February, the city began to transfer 400 children and families from the Auburn Family Residence and the Catherine Street Shelter in Lower Manhattan to more suitable places. Over the next year, it adopted an emergency rule under the City Family Exit Plan Supplement Program (CITYFEPS), which provided monthly rent supplements to families with children on public assistance who were at risk of losing their homes through eviction or were already in shelters.[8] The thinking behind the effort was clear and difficult to argue: permanent housing is better than a shelter. Along these lines, the administration reactivated a practice first tried during the Dinkins administration that gave shelter families priority in NYCHA public housing. NYCHA commissioner Shola Olatoye announced she was setting aside 750 units for that purpose.[9] The amount eventually was boosted to 1,500, but homeless advocates, the City Comptroller, and some City Council members insist that twice as many units are needed. Press reports continued to hammer de Blasio for his perceieved slow response to the problem.

To demonstrate further his commitment to the cause, Mayor de Blasio appointed Steven Banks to serve as Commissioner of Human Resources. Banks had been the chief attorney for the Legal Aid Society of New York, where for over three decades he was a leading advocate for the homeless and other vulnerable New Yorkers. He had run against de Blasio for the City Council in 1999. After the 90-day review of its policies and practices the city moved to integrate the Department of Homeless Services and the Human Resources Administration so that both report to Banks, who held the title Commissioner of Social Services. Once he was in place, Banks boosted spending on preventive services.

Desperate for space, the city also resorted to the use of controversial cluster-sites, a program started under the Giuliani administration as an emergency measure to put up homeless families in private apartment buildings. By the middle of 2016, the de Blasio administration placed approximately 11,400 people in cluster units, sometimes paying as much as $3,000 per month to house families.[10] The administration also had to rely on the use of commercial hotels and motels, which also tended to be costly and run down.

Over the course of 2016, the number of rooms the city rented rose from 508 to 2,418, with plans to increase the number by up to 436 additional rooms.[11] These facilities are not received well in city neighborhoods. They draw protests from residents who oppose having an influx of homeless people where they live. One of the ugliest reactions occurred in Maspeth, Queens, where a public meeting with city officials deteriorated into a vulgar screaming match after the city proposed to move homeless families into a 110-room Holiday Inn.[12] In response to inquiries by the *Wall Street Journal*, Steven Banks pled that the city had no choice, and that it would prefer to invest resources to build permanent housing rather than temporary shelters.[13]

De Blasio's most significant early homeless initiative was the Living in Communities (LINC) rental assistance program. LINC was fashioned to replace the Advantage Program that Mayor Bloomberg terminated after Governor Cuomo cut off its state funding. When de Blasio first proposed it in his February 2015 preliminary budget, Cuomo said the city had missed the state deadline for funding and the program would need to wait another year. After that dispute was settled, there was a disagreement over the terms of the plan, with the governor insisting on a higher subsidy amount and lower rent levels. Implementation of the program was further delayed because many landlords refused to accept the lower rents. Finally, de Blasio appropriated city money to assure "Fair Market" rents.[14] Once enacted, the city was able immediately to move 2,300 households out of emergency shelters and into permanent housing.[15] In two years LINC and CityFEPS found placements for 10,242 households comprising 30,129 individuals.[16]

LINC not only replaced Advantage, but also it revamped the previous program in an attempt to overcome some of its shortcomings and improve its benefits to clients. Under Advantage, housing subsidies only lasted for two years. With LINC, they continued for up to five years. Like Advantage, LINC required recipients to participate in a variety of social service programs, but it did not restrict benefits to families with a member who had a job. Its service recipients included the elderly, people who are medically frail, victims of domestic violence, working singles, and families without children.[17]

There was also a futile attempt between Mayor de Blasio and Governor Cuomo to sign a revised New York/New York IV agreement, but the conversations broke down. Homeless service advocates were urging the two leaders to create 30,000 units of housing over ten years, with hopes that the historic effort would be carried forward. Cuomo's father, Mario, had signed the original New York/New York agreement with Mayor Dinkins in 1990. The agreement was renewed by every subsequent mayor and governor. The younger Cuomo first responded to advocates with a plan to create 4,000 units over five years that would impose more financial responsibility on the city. In the past, the state had paid 50 percent of the capital expenses and 80 percent of the operating costs for the units. Cuomo now wanted the city to assume 50 percent of the operating costs.[18] De Blasio blasted the governor for wanting to "take us backward" and alleged that the state reduction would put 500 families on the street.[19]

After a year of failed negotiations with the governor's office, de Blasio decided to go it alone and announced his own plan in November to build 15,000 units of supportive housing over ten years.[20] The program targeted a broad range of clients, including homeless veterans, survivors of domestic violence, people with mental illness, the physically ill, families, single adults, young adults, and older youth. The program would also administer healthcare, social services, and other supportive programs.

The hostilities between the governor and the mayor continued to worsen. In an interview with Errol Louis on NY1 in June 2015, de Blasio accused the governor of taking personal "revenge" and a "vendetta" against him. When asked to elaborate at a later press conference, the mayor referenced an increase in the number of state officials dispatched to inspect city shelters and accused the governor of making unrealistic demands on the city while threatening to cut funding.[21] Shortly afterward, the city Independent Budget Office released a report documenting Albany's divestment from homeless services and its shifting the burden to the federal and city governments. The report showed that over seven years, the federal share of family shelter expenses rose from 32 percent to 58 percent; the city share of sheltering single adults rose from 53 percent to 73 percent.[22]

Cuomo blamed the problems in city shelters on de Blasio's mismanagement. In March 2016, citing incidences of violence and drug abuse at the facilities, he charged, "the system is clearly not well-run and is clearly dangerous."[23] He insisted that the state was responsible for regulating the city, and that there were no personal motivations behind his monitoring.

Not to be outdone by his downstate rival, Cuomo came up with his own new plan for the homeless in January 2016, in which he pledged that the state would build 20,000 units of supportive housing over fifteen years.[24] The outcome of this standoff between the two antagonists is potentially something bigger and better than either had imagined on his own, and more than most advocates had thought possible—a total of 35,000 units of housing for the homeless over fifteen years. Except for the tally of apartments, they were very much in the same place philosophically. De Blasio had once again pushed the governor to take action on an issue more purposefully than he had first intended, but there was another lesson to be learned from this dramatic episode.

The immersion of Cuomo and de Blasio—and one might add Steven Banks—in the same realm of public policy was instructive beyond the usual bickering that characterized the relationship between the mayor and governor. Over the years, there was a clear dichotomy in the language of homeless and welfare policy between the political left and the political right (defined by some Democrats as the political center to dodge the conservative label). The "paternalistic" approach of a younger Andrew Cuomo, Rudy Giuliani, and Bill Clinton demanded an exchange of responsibility for shelter and services.[25] The response of progressives such as David Dinkins, Banks, and de Blasio was voiced in the language of support. It went beyond the usual left/right dispute concerning the proper role of government in a free society.

Both approaches require an active governmental role that involved not only housing provisions, but also an array of social, educational, and employment services. The real differences were attitudinal. One vowed to impose requirements on the needy, the other promised to offer services—even as they both ended up providing more or less the same things. One cast the government in a supervisory position ready to administer a slap on the wrist as needed to get troubled lives on a productive path; the other presented the government as a helping hand. One implied that desperate clients were culpable in determining their own destinies; the other saw them as victims of a larger socioeconomic inequality not necessarily of their own making.

An assessment of de Blasio's polices released by the Coalition for the Homeless (CFH) at the beginning of 2017 was generally positive.[26] At the same time, it recognized that the problem continues to grow without any signs of abating. The city had managed to move more than 10,000 families into stable housing situations in a period of two-and-a-half years—more than any time since 2004, and seven times the number accommodated during the last four years of the Bloomberg administration. Nevertheless, 950 more families entered the shelters during the 2016 fiscal year than moved out. Some of the growth in the shelter population was attributed to more lenient policies implemented by de Blasio toward applicants who previously would have been turned away.

Referring to the "lost decade" from FY 2005 to 2014, the CFH report placed considerable blame for the growing homeless population on the "failed policies" of the Bloomberg administration, which created a backlog of families in need of assistance. It specifically cited Bloomberg policies that cut off NYCHA public housing and Section 8 vouchers for 32,000 homeless families, and the use of temporary subsidies that returned half of their users back into the shelter system—all policies that had been reversed by the de Blasio administration. The CFH complimented the de Blasio administration for newly funded rent subsidies and anti-eviction initiatives it had adopted (discussed below). But none of these changes altered the fact that the size of the homeless population had exceeded all previous records, leading CFH to insist that the city and state do more to stem the tide. Underscoring a point that had been apparent since the beginning of the crisis, the report concluded, "The serious lack of affordable housing in New York City continues to be the primary driver of homelessness among families."

Shortly thereafter, in February 2017, the de Blasio administration issued its own brief on homelessness.[27] It promised to continue efforts to protect and develop affordable housing, but signaled a change in strategy with regard to the shelter system. The long-term plan now is to remove residents from 360 cluster site apartments and hotels, and place them in 90 newly built shelters or additional space provided by the expansion of 30 existing shelters. The new spaces promised to be less costly and more habitable.

De Blasio wants to locate the new shelters in areas with the largest homeless populations so that placements will be less disruptive to clients. From a policy perspective, his plan makes sense. Homeless people are more likely to get back on their feet if they have access to friends, churches, and other supportive institutions to help them through hard times. Children are less likely to be absent from school if they are not moved around and do not need to commute long distances to get to class. According to a report completed by the Independent Budget Office, one out of thirteen students in the entire public school population are homeless.[28]

But de Blasio's approach could be a tough sell to communities resistant to having more shelters in their neighborhoods. Simultaneous with the release of the mayor's plan, the City Council put out its own report. The report cited "fair share" provisions in the city charter that require the municipal government to distribute burdens and benefits evenly throughout the city. Concerned that the new shelters would be concentrated in poorer areas of the city, the council put the mayor on notice that his shelter plan would not proceed without challenge.[29] It is unusual for a chief executive to announce such an unpopular program as he is about to launch his own re-election campaign. More than that: it was bold. Facing opposition, de Blasio vowed to move ahead, and there was a logic to his thinking. We place more police officers in communities with high crime rates, more fire companies in neighborhoods with high alarm rates, more pre-schools in neighborhoods with younger children. Why not put more homeless shelters in neighborhoods with more homeless people?

According to the mayor's February 2017 report, the process of conversion from cluster sites and hotels to shelters will be gradual, with twenty new facilities added in 2017 and an additional twenty in 2018.[30] Probably the most telling

statistic in the entire report referred to the projected size of the homeless population into the future, which had stabilized at about 60,000. According to the
report, the administration was anticipating a reduction of 2,500 within the next
five years. For all practical purposes, the mayor had accepted the fact that he
would preside over the largest homeless population in history through his second term in office. Candidly responding to reporters in the course of his press
conference, de Blasio conceded, "It is a deep rooted problem . . . I today cannot
see an end. I can see improvement and constant progress if we all do things right.
But again, I am not going to lie to the people of New York City and say I have a
defined end in sight."[31]

As it had done in other quarters, the de Blasio administration first went for the
low-hanging fruit when it came to housing policy. Within three months, the
mayor appointed five new members to the Rent Guidelines Board, which sets
the rates for about 1 million privately owned apartments. He eventually replaced
all nine members. In June, the board voted 5 to 4 to allow landlords a 1 percent raise for one-year leases and 2.75 percent for two-year leases. It was the
lowest increase in the forty-five years since the rent stabilization program was
launched. In the next two years, the board voted unanimously to approve 0 percent increases for one-year leases. De Blasio later appealed to the state legislature
to strengthen rent regulations so that fewer apartments would lose regulatory
protections and become subject to market rates, but his proposal was squelched
by the Republican-controlled state senate.

De Blasio also threw himself into a conversation about tenant evictions and
the lack of representation for poor people who find themselves in housing court
with predatory landlords. Too many of the latter have been known to buy buildings intent on harassing occupants of rent-regulated units to get them out and
have the apartments deregulated. Under American law, individuals have a constitutional right to representation in criminal cases, but not civil proceedings.
Given the epidemic of evictions that victimize people who cannot afford to hire
lawyers, civil rights advocates have been arguing for guaranteed legal representation to protect people's homes.[32] In 2013, the number of evictions in New York
City had reached 28,849.[33] Over two years, de Blasio increased spending for tenant legal services from $6.4 million to $62 million, bringing evictions down 18
percent.[34] The City Council subsequently passed legislation guaranteeing legal
representation for tenants with incomes below $50,000, and legal assistance for
tenants earning more.

The new mayor also picked up the ball on real estate projects he inherited
from the Bloomberg administration that were still under negotiation. Within
three months, he made a deal with Jed Walentas, whose Two Trees Management
was the developer of the Domino Sugar Factory in Williamsburg, Brooklyn, to

increase the number of affordable units in the high profile 2,300 apartment complex from 660 to 700. After eleven years of lawsuits and delays, he got Forest City Ratner, the developer of the massive Pacific Park Project (formerly Atlantic Yards) that includes the Barclays Center near downtown Brooklyn, to accelerate the construction of 2,250 affordable apartments by 2025—ten years ahead of schedule.

De Blasio's most consequential intervention involved Stuyvesant Town and Peter Cooper Village. They were the complexes, with a combined 11,200 units situated north of the East Village, built by Metropolitan Life during the La Guardia administration to house middle-income families. For years they provided homes for civil servants, schoolteachers, and office workers with modest incomes. In 2006, Tishman-Speyer and the Blackrock Realty bought it for $5.4 billion with plans to push out many of the tenants and convert their rentals to market rate. The investors wound up defaulting on their loans, but not before more than half the units were rented at market rates. In some cases, they had been deregulated illegally, and were returned to regulated status. After the Blackstone group acquired the complexes in 2015, the de Blasio administration negotiated an agreement to preserve 5,000 middle-income apartments for twenty years. In return, the city provided Blackstone with a $77 million tax break and a $144 million interest-free loan for twenty years.[35]

The big challenge with housing—as it had been for generations—remained the need to increase the overall number of affordable apartments, especially low-rent ones. According to the *Housing New York* plan that Mayor de Blasio released in May 2014, the median monthly rent across the city rose by 11 percent between 2005 and 2012, while real income practically stagnated at about $40,000 to $41,000.[36] In 2012, almost 55 percent of all renter households were "rent burdened," meaning that they paid more than 30 percent of their income on rent. This was an 11 percent rise from 2000.

To make matters worse, between 1994 and 2012 the city experienced a net loss of 150,000 rent-regulated units due to decontrol provisions that allow rents to rise to market levels. Shortages are especially harsh for households in the "Extremely Low Income" and "Very Low Income" categories—calculated respectively as earning below $25,150 and below $41,950 for a family of four. In 2014, a total of 979,142 New York households fell within these Area Median Income (AMI) categories. Unfortunately, there were only 424,949 units available that these households could reasonably afford.

When Mayor de Blasio announced his plan in 2014 to build or preserve 200,000 affordable apartments over ten years, he called it "a central pillar in the battle against inequality."[37] Touting it to be the "largest and most ambitious affordable housing initiative by any city. . . in the history of the United States," he invoked the memory of his hero Fiorello La Guardia, who so triumphantly dealt with his own housing crisis during the Great Depression.[38] But de Blasio should have known better than to draw the analogy. It was Harold L. Ickes, the father of one of his own mentors, Harold M. Ickes, who helped La Guardia persuade Franklin Roosevelt to create the federal public housing program, which financed the bulk of the low-income housing built by the New York City Housing Authority. Roosevelt and the Congress he prodded were long gone. Under de Blasio's $41.1 billion plan, the combined federal and state contribution is $2.9 billion. An additional $8.2 billion is to be absorbed by the city. The big money—$30 billion— would have to come from the private sector.[39]

Federal support had already evaporated when Mayor Ed Koch launched his $5.1 billion housing plan in 1986, but Koch had acquired a large stock of repossessed in rem housing units to offer developers that strengthened his bargaining hand. Some of that housing stock remained for Mayors Dinkins and Giuliani to use, and much less for Mayor Bloomberg. Bloomberg's commitment to build or preserve 165,000 units was somewhat encumbered by the economic crisis of 2008–2009, and a further acceleration of federal divestment that carried over into the de Blasio administration. Between 2011 and 2012, Congress reduced funding for the New York City HOME grant by 52 percent, and Community Development Block Grants (CDBG) by 23 percent. HOME funds are an essential resource for developing supportive housing and low-income housing; CDBG gives critical support for enforcement and service programs.

In the past, it was assumed that federal voucher programs and other subsidies directed at the poor could meet the needs of those at the lowest end of the income ladder. That no longer being the case, in 2015 the city launched the Our Space initiative to set aside 15 percent to 30 percent of the units in some new construction projects for formerly homeless households. Rents under the Our Space program range from $215 per month for a studio to $512 for a three-bedroom apartment. Developers contend that the real problem with the current arrangement remains the lack of an operating subsidy to support extremely low-income units, which can be attributed largely to the federal government's retreat from Section 8 vouchers, as well as the state's termination of the short-lived Advantage Program for homeless people. As mentioned earlier, the de Blasio administration has tried to compensate for the latter loss by establishing the LINC program.

Section 8 vouchers give assistance to tenants in the "Very Low" and "Extremely Low" AMI categories who rent affordable or market rate apartments in the private and nonprofit sectors. Under this program, tenants pay approximately 30 percent of their income, and the housing voucher covers the difference. In 2013, Congress sequestered $37 million (10 percent) from the program's allocation to the NYC Department of Housing Preservation and Development

(HPD) and $81 million from its allocation to NYCHA. In the meantime, 123,000 economically disadvantaged households in New York City were relying on the program to meet their monthly rental expenses. Although Section 8 funding was restored by 2015, it furnished only half the amount needed to recoup 67,000 vouchers previously lost—and still tens of thousands of vouchers short of meeting the needs of all families who qualify for them.[40]

In addition to the loss of Section 8 funding, NYCHA was facing its worst financial crisis in its eighty year lifetime. By 2015, it was projecting a $2.5 billion deficit in its operating budget over ten years, and a $17 billion shortfall for unmet capital needs. De Blasio took immediate steps to ease the fiscal stress by waiving the $70 million annual payment the authority made to the city for police services, and relieving $30 million in annual Payments in Lieu of Taxes (PILOT). This established a foundation for launching NYCHA's "Next Generation" plan for significant investments to address the long-delayed maintenance and repair needs of the agency's 178,000 apartments and the 400,000 people they house.[41]

The more one understands the situation that de Blasio walked into, the easier it is to appreciate why he recruited a housing team familiar with the business community led by Deputy Mayor Alicia Glen and City Planning Chair Carl Weisbrod. With three of every four dollars invested in the mayor's plan coming from the private sector, he was highly dependent on the leaders of New York's powerful real estate industry to execute it successfully. Having a minimal in rem housing stock to fall back on and little capital from other government sources, he was in a relatively weak position to strike a productive bargain. The real estate and finance barons not only held the high cards, but also they had most of the chips stacked in front of them as he came to the table. That said, de Blasio was in a relatively strong position compared to previous mayors since the 1975 fiscal crisis, because the city real estate market was now booming, and the financial condition of the municipal government was in better shape. As a result, de Blasio made a lot more capital dollars available for housing, and he pushed for terms that would make subsidy dollars go further.

Although the de Blasio administration increased the city's capital budget for affordable housing, the city's capacity to subsidize directly the development and preservation of affordable housing remains limited. As such, the administration fell back on the city's zoning authority to support the mayor's affordable housing goals by allowing developers to build taller structures in exchange for a requirement to provide affordable housing.[42] This, however, does not always sit well with neighborhood residents who care about the character of their communities or worry about gentrification that can drive poor people and small businesses out. A progressive City Council, which must approve zoning changes made by the planning commission, can be sensitive to such concerns.

De Blasio's housing plan was a departure from Mayor Bloomberg's in several respects. Generally speaking, Bloomberg's approach was more market driven; de Blasio's favored a more interventionist governmental role. De Blasio's was also more ambitious. His predecessor had invested $5.3 billion in city money and leveraged more than three times that amount from other sources to build or preserve 165,000 units over twelve years. De Blasio has promised to put up $8 billion in city funding, leveraging more than three times that amount from other sources to reach his goal of 200,000 units in ten years.

According to *Housing New York*, the administration intended to meet that goal by preserving subsidies for 120,000 affordable apartments and subsidizing the construction of an additional 80,000. To a greater extent than Bloomberg's plan, it promised to address the needs of people from the middle to extremely low income categories. De Blasio's plan also was projected to create 194,000 construction jobs and 7,100 permanent positions that would continue after building was completed. It raised the prospect of reducing construction costs and delays by streamlining the regulatory and approval processes.

In response to criticisms of the Bloomberg plan, de Blasio also made a commitment to shift the emphasis toward housing for "very low" and "extremely low" income households, and away from "moderate" and "middle income" ones. In some cases, the latter tenants could help to subsidize the former. Using HUD determined categories as a guide (as outlined in Table 9.1), his initial plan set the following targets: 11 percent middle income, 11 percent moderate income, 58 percent low income, 12 percent very low income, and 8 percent extremely low income.

Both Bloomberg and de Blasio relied on zoning—more specifically up-zoning particular neighborhoods, which the City Planning Commission has the power to do once certain charter-required land use procedures are followed that allow communities to have a say in any changes that are proposed. Rezoning not only involves altering height restrictions on buildings, it can also allow land to be

Table 9.1 **What Is Affordable Housing?**

Income Band	Percentage of AMI	Monthly Rent Required to Prevent Rent-Burden	Annual Income (for a four-person household)
Extremely Low Income	0–30%	Up to $629	<$25,150
Very Low Income	31–50%	$630–$1,049	$25,151–$41,950
Low Income	51–80%	$1,050–$1,678	$41,951–$67,120
Moderate Income	81–120%	$1,679–$2,517	$67,121–$100,680
Middle Income	121–165%	$2,518–$3,461	$100,681–$138,435

put to different uses, for example changing an area from manufacturing to residential use, as Mayor Bloomberg did with much of the waterfront in Brooklyn and Queens. Each mayor used benefits granted by the city, such as a specific tax break or subsidy, to encourage developers to build. The most significant difference between the approaches of the Bloomberg and de Blasio administrations is the expectations they set for private developers. One of de Blasio's signature initiatives was to amend the City Zoning Resolution through two separate proposals to facilitate the creation of more affordable housing.

Announced in 2016, the Zoning for Quality and Affordability (ZQA) amendment was meant to modernize zoning laws that inhibited the development of affordable housing with regard to such factors as height limits and parking requirements. ZQA's counterpart, Mandatory Inclusionary Housing (MIH), requires all future rezoning or up-zoning to include affordable housing. Under Bloomberg, a developer could decide whether or not to build a larger structure in exchange for affordable housing in a rezoned area. Under de Blasio, it became mandatory for developers building in rezoned areas or seeking zoning changes for their projects to include affordable housing. Unlike most inclusionary zoning laws elsewhere, and the previous Bloomberg program, a distinct element of the de Blasio plan is that it specifies the percentage of a building space rather than the percentage of apartments to be affordable. This is done to discourage developers from building an excessive number of large market rate units and fewer small below market ones, which do not serve low-income families well.

There was initially strong opposition to the MIH plan proposed by the de Blasio administration. One fundamental concern many housing groups have arises from the fact that the federally (HUD) established AMI categories that determine access to federal subsidies are based on regional averages that encompass not just the city, but parts of Rockland, Westchester, and Putnam counties, where incomes are higher. The assumption is that tenants in most places operate within a regional housing market rather than one defined by city limits. The Association for Neighborhood and Housing Development (ANHD) has pointed out that while the median household income (AMI) in the metropolitan region was $83,900 in 2014, the AMI for the five boroughs was just above $50,000 for a family of four.[43] That clearly skews calculations of affordability.

Many housing advocates claimed that the plan does not target the majority of people who are at the lowest income levels. The original Mandatory Inclusionary Housing (MIH) proposal developed by the de Blasio administration offered three options for the required AMI levels and percentage of space dedicated to affordable units in developments built under MIH. The most affordable option required that 25 percent of the building units be set aside at an average of 60 percent AMI, meaning that they could provide deeper affordability in some units in exchange for higher AMIs in others. The ANHD has calculated that although the plan devoted 58 percent of units to "low income" housing at 51–81 percent AMI, a third of New Yorkers fall below 40 percent AMI.[44]

Fifty of fifty-nine community boards, and four of the five borough boards voted de Blasio's zoning plan down in March 2016, expressing concerns that it would not help the poorest residents but instead displace them by introducing more expensive housing. Deputy Mayor Alicia Glen was heckled when she first appeared before the Council to defend the plan. Not deterred, she warned the legislators, "We are in a true housing crisis." She conceded, "Is it enough? Of course not," but explained that it was the best the city can do under the political and economic circumstances. Glen later told reporters, "This is the strongest, most rigorous program in the U.S."[45] HPD Commissioner Vicki Been admonished the Council, "Don't make the perfect the enemy of the good," elaborating on how difficult it is to build housing for the poor without federal and state subsidies.

The plan garnered strong backing from groups such as the American Association for Retired Persons (AARP) and powerful progressive unions that included 1199 SEIU, Local 32BJ SEIU, the United Federation of Teachers, and DC 37 of AFSCME. Business advocate Kathryn Wylde of the Partnership for New York City, a long-time champion of privately built affordable housing, supported the plan, but criticized its "social engineering that requires affordable units in luxury buildings."[46] Real Affordability for All, a coalition of housing advocates, reversed its original opposition to support the plan after City Hall promised to study deeper affordability and job standards. Explaining the change, Maritza Silva-Farrell, the coalition's campaign director, declared, "This plan is a big step forward for the city. . .. We know Mayor de Blasio shares our core progressive values, and has listened to our concerns."[47]

Later in March, Mayor de Blasio's Mandatory Inclusionary Housing (MIH) and Zoning for Quality and Affordability (ZQA) plans were approved by forty and forty-two members of the fifty-one member City Council respectively, enacting the changes to the city's Zoning Resolution. In response to demands from critics, the final version of MIH was amended to provide developers with a "Deep Affordability" option. This fourth option required developers benefiting from zoning changes to guarantee 20 percent of floor area to households making an average of 40 percent of AMI, or about $31,000 annually for a household of three.[48] The City Council made some changes to the original three options to make them more affordable as well. They made modifications to ZQA centered on "ensuring robust public review, narrowing and focusing the proposal to maximize affordable and senior housing development, meeting the parking needs of communities with limited transit access, and protecting the character of our neighborhoods."[49] The requirements outlined in MIH will apply to all future rezoning, including seven areas the de Blasio administration has specifically designated for rezoning: East New York in Brooklyn, Bay Street on Staten Island, Flushing and Long Island City in Queens, Jerome Avenue in the Bronx, and East Harlem and Inwood in Manhattan.

Having been the target of criticism by advocacy groups, in January 2016, Governor Cuomo released his own $20 billion blueprint for housing and home-less services throughout the state. It pledged to build or preserve 100,000 units of affordable housing, including 6,000 permanent units of supportive housing for homeless people, and 1,000 emergency shelter beds over five years, earmark-ing $2 billion in the state's FY 2017 budget.[50] Cuomo's blueprint offered few details on where the housing would go or when it would be finished.

There was one conspicuous detail of uncertainty in the respective plans the mayor, the Council, and the governor had generated that could prove to be the noxious fly in the ointment. All of them were premised on the assumption that the city would be able to offer developers a controversial tax break referred to as 421-a. Enacted by the state in 1971 during harder times, when the real estate industry was reluctant to invest in new construction in New York City, 421-a grants property tax exemptions to developers as an incentive to build.

As the city housing market improved, revisions to the law required develop-ers with projects in high-demand neighborhoods—such as the area between 14th and 96th Streets in Manhattan—to reserve, for an initial period, 20 per-cent of the units for low and moderate-income tenants. That provision, however, only covered 16.5 percent of the area in the entire city, so developers could build elsewhere and still receive abatements without providing affordable housing. In some cases, 421-a served as a giveaway program for developers who built luxury housing and shunned the lower end of the market. One article in the *New York Times*, for example, drew attention to a property with a $100 million penthouse that received a 95 percent tax break.[51] De Blasio pledged to undo these abuses by limiting the program to rental buildings, thus excluding condos and co-ops where tax abatements transferred to homeowners.

Another provision of 421-a that has been a source of controversy is that it does not require the builder receiving the exemption to use union labor. When 421-a was due to expire in June 2015, the construction unions and some contractors went to Albany to demand prevailing wages. Despite his ties to organized labor, de Blasio did not support the trade unions' push for higher compensation, tak-ing a position that favored increased production of affordable housing at lower costs. His proposal would double the number of affordable apartments built under the program, reduce the subsidy to developers by one-third, and target families with lower incomes. He also recommended a mansion tax that would affect 10 percent of the residential real estate transactions in town: a 1 percent flat tax on residential sales over $1.75 million, and a 1.5 percent marginal tax on apartments over $5 million. The new revenues were to be invested in affordable housing.[52]

The mansion tax sounded a lot like de Blasio's early appeal to fund Pre-K education by taxing the rich. It had the same populist ring, and it evoked a similar response from the governor and senate Republicans. Ironically, the idea of a mansion tax dates back to 1989, when Governor Mario Cuomo introduced a state tax on real estate sales over $1 million.[53] That was not about to sway the incumbent Governor Cuomo. Now the proposal was "dead on arrival" when it got to Albany.

Cuomo had denounced 421-a for being a "giveaway to developers" but supported labor demands for prevailing wages—aligning himself more closely with the building trades than the proudly progressive mayor. This was around the same time that the mayor had his fateful "revenge" and "vendetta" interview with Errol Louis on *Inside City Hall*.[54] In it, he did not fail to mention the mansion tax he had proposed. He derided the governor's motives, claiming, "He (Cuomo) did not act in the interest of people who need affordable housing." He also accused the governor of working closely with senate Republicans to undermine attempts by Assembly Democrats and himself to refashion 421-a, thereby positioning Cuomo as antagonistic to a progressive agenda.

Cuomo recommended that lawmakers should extend 421-a until a resolution of the labor issues could be found, handing the problem back to the builders and the trade unions. The legislature did just that. It extended the subsidy program for six months while requiring that wage requirements be negotiated between the unions and the real estate industry. The unions and the industry did arrive at a broad outline, but failed to reach a specific agreement by Christmas 2015, so the program lapsed. In the meantime, the Independent Budget Office published a report finding that union-level wage requirements would increase costs of the mayor's housing plan by $4.2 billion.[55]

Cuomo finally reached an agreement with the Real Estate Board of New York and the Buildings and Trade Council in January 2017, when he triumphantly announced that 421-a would be replaced by a new program called "Affordable New York."[56] Not everyone was persuaded of its merits. A fiscal brief released by the New York City Independent Budget Office in February 2017 found the 421-a program to be an inefficient investment in tax dollars.[57] In the past, the report found, 421-a remained the city largest tax expenditure, totaling $1.4 billion in 2016; however, because condominium owners accrue benefits intended to incentivize development, it does not spur the building of more affordable housing. If enacted, the governor's plan could cost the city $8.4 billion over ten years. A report disseminated by the Association for Neighborhood and Housing Development (ANHD) at about the same time found that of 152,400 residential units subsidized by the program in 2014, only 12,700 were affordable, while the remainder were either luxury or market rate.[58]

Under the final deal appoved by the legislature in April 2017, 100 percent tax abatements for developers would be extended from twenty years to thirty-five years. In exchange, developers agreed to set aside twenty-five to thirty percent of the units for low and moderate income renters, and to extend the life of affordable units from thirty-five to forty years. A pay schedule for workers was set at $60 per hour in Manhattan below 96th Street, and $45 per hour for projects in "Enhanced Affordability Areas" in Brooklyn and Queens. Building projects in other parts of the city that involved 300 units or more could also qualify. The final legislative package released more than $2 billion in state funds earmarked earlier for building 100,000 units of affordable housing and 6,000 units of supportive housing throughout the state.

At the urging of Mayor de Blasio, Governor Cuomo and Assembly Democrats managed to defeat an attempt by Senate Republicans to make luxury condominiums eligible for tax reductions. Although the new plan could cost the city $82 million more in lost revenue than the mayor's original 2015 proposal would have, he conceded that the new program was "certainly something I can live with."[59] With the announcement of the new legislation, ANHD issued a statement saying, "Taxpayers and Tenants Should Be Disgusted."[60]

Since East New York was the first location slated for Mandatory Inclusionary Housing (MIH), it attracted much attention. One of the poorest areas of the city that was the scene of violent racial confrontations during the Lindsay years, it was chosen for development because of its extensive transit amenities that were accessible by subway, bus, and the Long Island Rail Road. City planners envisioned new schools, a medical center, refurbished parks, repaved streets, and bustling commercial activity. In response to a draft of the plan, City Comptroller Scott Stringer issued a report indicating that more than half the residents of East New York would not be able to afford the "affordable" apartments that would come on line.[61]

The final rezoning plan for East New York, approved by a 45-1 vote of the City Council in April 2016, called for an expedited 1,300 units of affordable housing. As a result of changes made in the MIH plan, builders were able to offer the "Deep Affordability" option for families of three with incomes below $39,943 in exchange for subsidies. Developers could also apply for the Extremely Low and Low Income Affordability Program (ELLA) that "funds the new construction of low income multi-family rental projects affordable to households earning a range of incomes from 30% to 60% of the AMI."[62] In all, 6,000 new apartments would be available by 2030. Half of these will be priced below market, including a quarter that will be offered for families with incomes at $31,000 or less.[63] The East New York Neighborhood Rezoning Plan developed by local representatives had recommended that 5,000 new apartments be made available to local residents.[64]

Reporting on the demographics of the two community boards located in East New York, ANHD has claimed that more than half the households in CB 5 make less than $34,000 annually, and about half those in CB 16 earn less than $27,800, suggesting that relatively few local residents would benefit from the program.[65] Similar questions were being raised about affordability in East Harlem, Inwood, the South Bronx, and other neighborhoods slated for rezoning. A revised blueprint developed by the City Planning Department for East Harlem—Speaker Mark-Viverito's district—was more aligned with the community's own plan.[66]

Other criticism of the mayor's housing plan has been harsher, and has come from unexpected corners. Bertha Lewis, the former leader of ACORN, and a long-time ally of de Blasio, accused him of adopting the talking points of real estate developers, and neglecting the needs of the most vulnerable New Yorkers. She told the City Council that his plan would replace people of color with more wealthy people and "accelerate the whitening of New York City."[67] Echoing Lewis's racially tinged objections, Harlem historian Michael Henry Adams penned an op-ed for the *New York Times* under the title, "The End of Black Harlem," just about suggesting that de Blasio had betrayed the black people who voted for him. Comparing de Blasio to his own progressive heroes, Adams wrote:

> The man we saw as "our mayor" may talk about housing affordability, but his vision is far from the rent control and public housing that President Franklin D. Roosevelt and Mayor Fiorello H. LaGuardia once supported, and that made New York affordable for generations. Instead he has pushed for private development. . . . He and the City Council have effectively swept aside contextual zoning limits, which curb development that might change the very essence of a neighborhood.[68]

De Blasio was not deterred. In January 2017, the mayor issued a progress report indicating that his administration was ahead of schedule with regard to the Housing New York plan announced in the spring of 2014.[69] During his first three years in office, the administration doubled capital spending in the HPD budget. It added 62,506 apartments to the affordable housing stock, including 20,854 new units and 41,652 preserved. More than a quarter of the units financed under the mayor's plan serve residents earning $31,100 a year, or $40,800 for a family of three. The inventory included 5,160 units for the homeless and 4,043 for seniors. There had been more affordable housing created in 2016 than any time since 1989, when the Koch administration launched its ambitious initiative. The report also mentioned that one in four tenants brought into housing court in 2016 had the benefit of legal representation, compared to one in one hundred in 2014. Evictions were down 24 percent. De Blasio also crowed that his administration had allowed a 0 percent increase in rent-regulated apartments for two years running.

The statement put out by City Hall carried words of praise from many local politicians and union leaders, including the Brooklyn Borough President, several state legislators, Council members, and the heads of District Council 37 and 32BJ of SEIU. To the contrary, Benjamin Dulchin of ANHD declared that although it was "truly impressive" to see the administration surpass its goals, more apartments need to be set aside for the poorest New Yorkers.[70] Katie Goldstein, of Real Affordability for All, was more stinging in her criticism, claiming, "At a time of record homelessness in the city, Mayor de Blasio's self-congratulatory victory lap on affordable housing is offensive and wrong."[71]

In his February 2017 State of the City Address, Mayor de Blasio announced that the city would invest $1.9 million to add 10,000 more affordable units to his *Housing New York* plan to accommodate households earning less than $40,000 annually. Half would be dedicated to seniors, and 500 to veterans. He also announced a new Elder Rent Assistance Program to help 25,000 seniors with monthly subsidies up to $1,300 that he proposed to support with a 2.5 percent mansion tax on real estate transactions valued above $2 million. The latter, however, was a legislative nonstarter in the state capitol, where approval is needed.

Housing had become a key component of Bill de Blasio's policy agenda. His plan has been as controversial as it is bold. He has made it a lynchpin of his attempt to address the growing economic and racial inequality that he had campaigned against in 2013. Its actual implementation on the ground in distinct neighborhoods overwhelmed with the cost of living could please many of its beneficiaries as a promise delivered on, but also erode some secure elements of his electoral coalition who were not persuaded he had done enough.

* * *

Homelessness is beginning to seem like an intractable problem. Despite a record commitment of new resources by well-intended people, the homeless population has stabilized at the highest level ever and is not about to subside. The mayor himself has accepted that discouraging reality. His announced decision to build more shelters in city neighborhoods that don't want them on the eve of his own re-election campaign appears counterintuitive by most political calculations; but putting shelters in communities with large homeless populations makes sense. The decision itself demonstrates that the mayor views the homeless population as a legitimate public service clientele rather than a public nuisance. It is consistent with his promise to serve all New Yorkers.

The administration's dedication of more funding to mental health and supportive services is also a major step in the right direction; but as the mayor himself has argued, homelessness is a function of a larger inequality that has been abetted by the political process. Many of these issues and their fundamental causes are not altogether solvable at the local level of government; but local government has no choice but to deal with the fallout of misguided polices enacted elsewhere. As scores of advocates for the needy have insisted, the ultimate answer to a homeless crisis that has affected individuals, families, and children is the provison of more affordable housing.

Here again, there are short-term methods that can come into play for a local chief executive, and the mayor has utilized those tools. He was prudent to move quickly on containing monthly charges for rent-regulated apartments, offering attorneys to tenants who might be wrongfully evicted, alleviating financial stress in the Housing Authority so that facilities can be better maintained, and closing deals that were already in negotiation during the Bloomberg administration. That said, it is imperative to expand the affordable housing stock through preservation and construction to keep up with rising demand. Doing so is not as easy as saying so. There are genuine concerns about the rising cost of construction and maintenance that are greatly exacerbated by the loss of federal funding. Working with real estate developers in the city allows the mayor to apply private resources to a public problem, but his dependence on them puts him in a compromised position to negotiate deals that are most beneficial to the city. To his credit, de Blasio has exercised more pressure in this regard than any of his predecessors. To his advantage, he has more local resources to apply.

Beyond affordability, there are larger questions about the goals of a housing program in a city such as New York that seems primed for growth. This is no longer the New York of the 1980s when businesses and families were fleeing to other places. New York is now popular. It is a destination for young people who want to build careers and families that want to settle. This demand accelerates the housing market and drives up rental costs to the detriment of low-income families. It propels gentrification. Gentrification displaces the very people who stood so strongly behind de Blasio when he declared for mayor, and some have threatened to abandon him as he runs for re-election.

Taking Stock, Looking Ahead

As Steven Banks, the city's director of homeless services, explained to me in conversation one afternoon, "Homelessness is a reflection of larger systemic failures built up over many years in terms of income, rents, mental health and criminal justice, and the hacking away of social safety nets that were once in place."[1] It is symptomatic of other problems gone unattended over time. And the abandonment of policies and programs he speaks of, especially at the federal level, was deliberate. After spending more money on the problem than any mayor in history, Bill de Blasio has called homelessness his "number one frustration."[2]

We used to be more mindful about keeping our indigent out of sight. The state institutions were shameful, but at least they gave shelter, often provided permanent housing, and always administered some kind of care. Now the mentally ill are out there staring us in the face. Some were once healthy young men and women who served their country on battlefields in Vietnam and the Middle East. Today they are considered a public nuisance. We try to collect them on the coldest nights and enter them into the temporary shelter system, but many are too scared to go inside. Shelters also serve as transition posts where former convicts from places as far away as Pennsylvania re-enter society, and their journey is seldom easy—for them, or for those they meet along the way.

More and more, our temporary shelters are used to house families with children. Most of the adults are unable to find jobs, and those who work are paid so little that they are unable to make ends meet. Some have been accused of gaming the system. Experts use the term "perverse incentives" to describe how the system works. It is said that these mothers and fathers bring their children to the shelters to get themselves on expedited lists for affordable housing. It sounds like an act of desperation to me. What parent wouldn't want to give her child a real home? Why would parents bring their children to a shelter if they had more desirable alternatives?

The waiting lists for affordable apartments are endless—too long to accommodate the demand. The government used to do a better job furnishing a stock of livable units for those of modest means, but at some point turned the job over to the private sector. That was asking a lot. Real estate developers, after all, are set up for profit. Since New York has grown so popular with the filthy rich, it is more lucrative to build luxury and high-rent housing. Although ostentatious generosity can burnish a company's image, free enterprise is not about charity. It is propelled by self-interest. As Adam Smith taught, the market is a stern master. It fosters competition: dog-eat-dog, survival of the fittest, and all that. Inevitably, people fail and companies vanish. If you follow the laissez-faire creed, decline and extinction are part of a natural order that, in the end, is supposed to better us all.

But, the market can leave one with a cold perspective on life. Fortunately, outside of Darwin's jungle, not everyone abides by its admonitions. Good-natured social theorists have advanced a notion of *enlightened self-interest* that could move us in a more flattering direction. It serves to elevate our aspirations. It establishes different expectations for humanity by reminding us of our shared destiny. You have heard its appeals before: we are all brothers and sisters; the chain of human relationships is only as strong as its weakest link; we all have a stake in taking care of our most vulnerable neighbors. . ... If we don't, they will be out there to remind us of their miserable existence and disrupt our lovely lives.

Perhaps there is an even higher motivation. If we dug further, we could come to terms with a more basic understanding that *it is simply wrong to leave people on the street when we could afford to do better.* It is that kind of sentiment that gives us our common humanity; it is access to that basic truth about the nature and requirements of our existence that makes us equal. As a child, I first heard these wise words of kindness from a semi-literate, immigrant man who repaired shoes for a living. That same instinct, over the years, has given New York its soul.

New York Exceptionalism?

No place has ever taken in more people seeking a better life. The city doesn't treat them very well at first, but eventually it gives them a break and in odd ways makes life better for them—if not entirely satisfactory. Boss Tweed's corrupt machine gave the Irish their American citizenship and the right to vote: power, in other words—more efficiently than our present immigration offices do, if you knew the right guy. Now there is no right guy. Tammany was not so receptive to the next wave of immigrants from Southern Europe, who couldn't speak English and had odd customs and contrary religious practices.

When conditions became really bad during the Great Depression, La Guardia, after casting his lot against Tammany, convinced the White House that it needed to build infrastructure and housing. That was certainly a boost for most, but the attitude toward black New Yorkers then was a harbinger of things to come.

They were kept segregated, and the spoils of patronage—or what was left of it—were awarded to them sparingly. They always came up short. Robert Wagner empowered unions to advance what there was of a class war, but the new power arrangement that eventually replaced Tammany was at first another impediment to black people and the Puerto Ricans who arrived at about the same time.

It took John Lindsay, a Republican patrician from the Upper East Side, to take up the racial cause wholeheartedly. His congressional record suggested that his sympathies were genuine. Lindsay understood that he had to take on Wagner's powerful unions to advance racial justice, but he got too absorbed in the battles to appreciate that what the white working class had in common with the black and Puerto Rican underclass could build a political foundation for real progress. Yet, his inquisitive intellect and sense of justice also drove him to push the boundaries of gender beyond what most mid-twentieth century elected officials were prepared to do. He spoke up for women before other politicians did, then woke us from the binary gender wars that had been waged for generations to alert us to the ascendant issue of sexual orientation and the rights of gays and lesbians. Throw in his prescient appreciation of environmental threats, his imaginative use of public space, and his harnessing of the arts as a magnetic urban force, and you begin to understand Lindsay's claim for progressive leadership.

La Guardia, Wagner, and Lindsay each played a distinct part in imbuing New York with a progressive spirit. The true test of that spirit, however, came later, after the country adopted different priorities and the funding dried up. Ed Koch's post-fiscal crisis housing plan, built on the remains of the city's crumbling residential inventory, was remarkable in itself. It stands out more when seen in the context of what was happening to public housing in other cities at the same time.

President Roosevelt had never been enamored with the idea of having the government build public housing. Senator Wagner of New York, its chief legislative sponsor, presented it to him as a public works project that would produce jobs and invigorate the economy. In a futile attempt to appease a real estate industry that opposed public housing development as a form of socialism, the senator also felt obliged to explain during congressional hearings that the government's commitment to build housing for low-income people would not compete with the private housing market. He reasoned, "To reach those who are really entitled to public assistance, and to get into the field where private enterprise cannot operate, is the object of this bill."[3] There is an interesting policy assumption in the latter statement that we will return to later. For now, let it be noted that before the president, senator, and mayor from New York City breathed life into the construction of public housing by the federal government, Governor Al Smith, at the urging of Tammany, was already doing it in the Empire State.

During the New Deal, public housing projects were more directed toward working class families than the very poor. That changed after the war, when poor Southern blacks began to replace upwardly mobile white families who moved from the cities to the suburbs. And so did the national commitment to public housing by both the federal government and cities themselves. Public housing projects became an extension of the welfare state. They were increasingly identified with a growing black "underclass." Over a six-year period in the 1980s, President Reagan reduced allocations for subsidized housing by 80 percent, while New York went on a building binge.[4] As funds for repairs and maintenance disappeared, "the projects" became a national disgrace, an emblem of urban decay, and another nail in the coffin for liberal social policy. With the tacit approval of the federal government, many cities began to tear them down—but not New York.[5]

The process of dismemberment was gradual.[6] The Housing Act of 1937 forbade local Public Housing Authorities (PHA) from phasing out housing projects without prior permission. Approval was to turn on the determination that a facility was no longer meeting its goal of providing decent housing for the poor; but, of course, lack of adequate funding made it impossible for many to do that. In the 1960s, operating costs and payments in lieu of taxes started to exceed revenues, so some cities resorted to rent increases, making apartments unaffordable for the poorest residents. In response, Congress passed the Brooke amendment, capping rents at 25 percent of a tenant's income, which, although well-intentioned, imposed additional financial burdens on struggling PHAs.

The first stage of abandonment came in the form of purposeful neglect. Decision-makers in Newark and Kansas City, for example, figured that if they let conditions in the projects get bad enough, they could justify tearing them down. In 1969, Congress amended the Housing Act to allow the demolition of public housing so long as local authorities replaced one-in-four lost units with new facilities. That is quite an exchange. In 1983, the Reagan administration abandoned the one-in-four rule. It adopted a new housing policy that de-emphasized the building of new units from scratch, and focused on providing subsidies in the form of vouchers that could be used in either public or private housing, a strategy first endorsed by President Nixon. Cities such as San Diego, for example, sold off the housing projects to private developers. Others, including Los Angeles, eventually privatized the management of the projects.

In 1992, President Clinton's HUD secretary Henry Cisneros actively encouraged PHAs to tear down the projects, and provided more tenants with vouchers that could be used to promote mixed-income, privately built developments. The idea was to "de-concentrate poverty." Calls for ending poverty no longer filled the air. That was the distant chant of LBJ's Great Society. The Hope VI program enacted by Congress in 1992 provided resources for cities to demolish public housing units that were deemed to be pockets of failure. Residents of Houston and Baltimore celebrated at the sight of huge projects coming down. The most dramatic exhibit of mass destruction took place in 2003, when, after a decade of litigation by housing advocates, Chicago cleared the sixty-acre Cabrini-Green complex. That mass of property is now the site of condominiums that sell for more than $600,000.[7]

According to one urban scholar, HUD reported that there were 285,000 units of public housing slated for demolition throughout the country in 2012.[8] That total did not include 250,000 that had been already taken down. The sacrifice of public housing either through demolition or privatization has transpired unevenly, reflecting the priorities of local governments. Between 1990 and 2007, Hartford, Memphis, St. Petersburg, and Detroit lost more than half their units; Atlanta, Tucson, Hampton (Va.), Tampa, Little Rock, and Columbus lost in excess of 40 percent.[9] During that same period, New York removed less than 1 percent. NYCHA, one of the lasting monuments of New Deal New York, has been safeguarded through the post-fiscal crisis administrations of mayors Koch, Dinkins, Giuliani, and Bloomberg—most of whom are not consistently identified with progressive causes. New York City does have a progressive soul.

New York City has not done as well when it comes to issues of race. In fact, it has never done well with racial issues. Fiorello was blindsided by the Harlem riots, and saw fit to bury his own report on the angry rebellion. Mayor Wagner was immobilized by demands for black power. John Lindsay was an ardent champion for racial justice and he quickened the political incorporation of blacks and Puerto Ricans like no other mayor, but his awkward relationships with working class whites could spark reactions that were self-defeating. Beame and Dinkins were too absorbed by fiscal constraints to do much, although the latter's election gave African Americans and Latinos a reason to believe in the ballot box. Koch was capable of undermining whatever good he had done with his own inflammatory rhetoric.

Giuliani's determination to make the city safer through aggressive police action was bound to raise tensions in minority communities, although he would argue that African Americans and Latinos were the major beneficiaries of the crime reductions he brought about. Michael Bloomberg, who has distinguished himself as a national leader on progressive issues such as immigration, the environment, public health, and gun control, never seemed to grasp the damaging effects of income polarization and the disproportionate burden it imposed on people of color. His police policies also inflamed racial tensions.

Racial injustice is the original sin of American history. At times, New York has asserted itself to take a leading role in the cause of racial equality. However, even after the election of an African-American president, the nation is still divided over race, and there are usually police involved when the most violent eruptions occur. New York is no exception. La Guardia consistently heard complaints about police brutality in black communities, and such stories date back a century before him. Since then, the NYPD has grown more professional, and it is one of the most respected police agencies in the entire world. On too many occasions, that apparently isn't enough, and the tensions continue, often through life-threatening encounters between officers and civilians. We expect our police to negotiate boundaries of social change before the rest of us do, and the challenge seems endless.

Perhaps it was fortuitous that the historic Stonewall uprising occurred on John Lindsay's watch, handing him an opportunity to jump-start the discussion on gender equality that was not taking place elsewhere. Although some have displayed more enthusiasm than others, for the past fifty years, New York City mayors have consistently supported the rights of gays and lesbians. New York was one of the first states to enact a marriage equality law. We are now entering a new phase of the gender wars as the needs of transgender and gender-nonconforming people enter the public consciousness. New York appears well positioned to take a lead on this issue, as other parts of the nation lag behind.

Ever since John Lindsay forced a bartender to serve a drink to a woman in a male-only establishment, women have played increasingly important roles in city government. They have twice occupied the positions of Public Advocate and Speaker of the City Council, but a woman has yet to be elected mayor, the top electoral prize. Even in areas where the city exceeds the achievements of other localities, progressive New Yorkers are not satisfied with the progress that has been made with regard to gender, broadly defined, and they ought not to be. It is this spirit of discontent in the face of progress that makes New York exceptional.

De Blasio's Leadership?

John Lindsay was able to make his fabled walk to calm the streets of Harlem on the evening that Martin Luther King was killed because he had been there before. He had taken controversial stands on hot-button racial issues, and he made it a regular practice to visit communities that were tinderboxes. He had credibility among people who had been ignored by other white politicians. Bill de Blasio started out with a deep reservoir of credibility among marginalized communities before he stepped out the front door of his own home. His diverse family grants him that. When he speaks about the anxieties black parents feel about their sons' encounters with the police, he speaks from personal experience. He has had "the talk."[10] When he and his wife, Chirlane McCray, describe how mental illness can wreak havoc on families, they have their own wounds to show for it. She in particular can discuss with authentic conviction the barriers people endure on account of their race, gender, or sexual orientation, because she has been there.

So de Blasio started out with a stockpile of political capital that most white progressive politicians don't have, and he has built on it through his own actions. He has deep roots in progressive causes, and his closest associates share those same values. Few politicians have made economic inequality so central a feature of their agendas. Working with a sympathetic City Council, he moved rapidly to fix what they could at their own discretion. The presence of a local legislature with such inclinations for the first time ever, after many false starts in earlier times, may be a sign that New York is about to enter a new era of politics; but it is too soon to tell. What's clear so far is that de Blasio has built a coalition that cuts across race, class, and gender boundaries better than any mayor in New York City history. The changing demographics of the city and workforce make it easier for him than it was for Lindsay or Wagner, but he has taken advantage of the situation and run with it. His being the only mayoral candidate in the 2013 election to adopt income inequality as a defining issue got the attention of voters as no others had.

Like Lindsay, de Blasio sees himself as playing by different rules from most politicians. He explained this in his now famous *Inside City Hall* interview from 2015 with Errol Louis on NY1, where he derided the governor and attacked his leadership.[11] It is understandable that the mayor's accusations against the state's highest-ranking official and fellow Democrat caught the headlines. A closer look at the exchange reveals how de Blasio defines his own leadership style. He criticizes a "transactional model" of leadership that functions "within the status quo" where elected officials simply trade with other players to get done whatever the political circumstances at the time allow. Instead, he advocates a "transcendent" model of leadership that operates from a "bigger vision," in which leaders "talk about where we need to go and what changes we need to make." In this sense, his pragmatism is guided by underlying principles that lie outside the ordinary realm of political decision making. What other politician do we know who promises to bring jails and homeless shelters to communities on the eve of his re-election campaign?

Here again in the interview with Louis we hear de Blasio speak of the need for clarity, saying, "What the public would like to see is forceful leadership with clear values." Not surprisingly, he mentions "income inequality" as the uppermost concern on people's minds. He was energized by his own election, and reads it as a mandate. That's a fair assertion on his part, given the consistency and clarity of his campaign message, and the response it got from New York City voters. His confidence may have been overstated in light of the close primary results and low turnout in the general election of 2013.

As a populist, de Blasio regards the public as a powerful resource for forceful leaders, declaring, "the best hand to play is to mobilize the people." He may have overplayed his hand thinking he could move Hillary Clinton and the mainstream of the Democratic Party further to the left during the 2016 presidential campaign, but that's history. Closer to home, the mayor cites his fight for universal pre-kindergarten as an example of how a leader's mobilization of public sentiment can work. De Blasio recalls how he was "told a thousand times it was not viable," when he first took his pleas for UPK to Albany, but notes that public support for the initiative created its own unstoppable momentum. His claim is probably valid, and there is a larger pattern here in the relationship between the mayor and governor that needs to be considered.

The press may have become too preoccupied with the personal bombast between the two headstrong Democrats to fully appreciate how their petulant dynamic translated into public policy. Alienating the governor is not good strategy for a mayor who needs his support. Beyond their personal animosity, however, the truth is that the two men have serious philosophical differences—or at least have through the first three years of de Blasio's mayoralty. This is not a rerun of the Rockefeller-Lindsay wars, in which the antagonists were both liberal Republicans. Cuomo and de Blasio have actually disagreed on important policy matters. Cuomo was more aligned with centrist to right-leaning Senate Republicans on some key issues than he was with progressives in his own party. That across-the-aisle comity between the governor and GOP lawmakers killed serious talk of a "mansion tax" on high-end real estate transactions, but it also forced the governor and the legislature to pick up the cost of UPK to hold off higher income taxes on the wealthy to pay for it.

Following the tenets of leadership he laid out for Errol Louis, de Blasio did marshal public opinion to get the governor and legislature to do things they were unlikely to do. This is not only so with regard to UPK, but also with other salient issues such as housing, homelessness, and the minimum wage. The ultimate outcome of the back and forth between City Hall and Albany was that the state invested more resources than it would have without de Blasio's prodding, and the consequences were felt statewide.

De Blasio, of course, had to make his own bargains. And they are the basis upon which he will be judged as he seeks re-election. The stakes are high. As I mused at the outset of this exploration, he could lose his head, or worse, his soul. The closest he came to the latter may have been his support of *metzitzah b'peh*. De Blasio can be admired for not having the same insensitivity toward deeply religious communities that other left-leaning political actors do—a tendency to which I have taken exception in another venue.[12] Supporting a religious ritual that puts the health of infants at risk without closer monitoring, however, crosses the line of what is acceptable. His support of Hillary Clinton over philosophical compatriot Bernie Sanders, even belatedly—whether out of loyalty, pragmatism, or conviction—also had to be soul-wrenching.

Then there is what one political ally of de Blasio called "the dumb stuff." De Blasio has been associated with some unsavory characters, and his fundraising has raised suspicion in too many places. He has been exonerated of criminality by federal and local prosecutors; but no doubt he has flirted with disaster. Given the role that money plays in politics, such risks may be an occupational hazard in what ought to be a noble profession. It has become increasingly difficult for decent people to dip their toes into politics without feeling as though they have taken a swim in the Gowanus. Rules against unethical practices have been written so that they can be easily circumvented.

Let's face it: if you want to launch a serious career in American politics, you can't do it without the constant feed of political contributions. If you decide to be above it all and don't have enough money of your own, you will be at a distinct disadvantage, and will probably lose. The shrewd operators know how to navigate their way through the sludge, so unseemly behavior does not cross over into breaking the law. That's not to say, however, that the legal is a reliable measure of the good. Lobbyists have figured out ways to bend laws and regulations having to do with matters such as campaign finance, economic regulation, and tax policy that legalize questionable practices. George Washington Plunkitt, the turn-of-the-century rascal of Tammany, called such knavery "honest graft."[13]

In our own time, the New York City Campaign Finance Board found no problem with the fact that Mayor Bloomberg's top deputy was simultaneously serving as the CEO of his private foundation. Many of the grant recipients were organizations and individuals that had influence over policies that were important to the mayor. There are some situations, I'm afraid, when it just is not any better to give than to receive. Critics of the Clinton Foundation may differ with that assertion, I suppose. In all, most modern day practitioners of American politics do not believe that what they do undermines the public interest, but neither did George Washington Plunkitt. And now the Trump administration in Washington makes conflicts of interest at the highest levels of government appear to be business as usual.[14]

It is not the purpose of this project to examine the conscience of Bill de Blasio, or any contemporary political figure for that matter. It is fair to present the facts as known, and let others decide on their own. It is certainly within the bounds of this project to highlight flaws in the political system, especially with regard to the role money plays in it, and how the current rules reinforce political and economic inequality. As true reform of the political process is in the hands of those who benefit from the status quo, we cannot be hopeful that serious change is on the horizon. It is a legislative matter, nationally and locally. Here in New York, the state legislature has functioned as an anteroom for the federal penitentiary. Over the past ten years, more than two dozen members of the legislature have been convicted, sanctioned, or accused of wrongdoing, including the top leaders of both houses, who have been sentenced to jail.

Nevertheless, change always starts with a conversation that somebody is willing to have despite all opposing odds that it will alter objectionable behavior. John Lindsay did it with regard to race and gender. Bill de Blasio is one of the few who has done it with regard to economic inequality and the Supreme Court's *Citizens United* decision that legitimizes practices warping our political process. Campaign finance laws in New York City are among the best nationally, but provisions that allow wealthy candidates to spend as much of their own money as they please to win office distort the norms of democracy.

What about Policy?

So far as Bill de Blasio is concerned, all policy roads in his first administration have led to affordable housing. It is the cornerstone of his agenda. Housing policy is also an instructive arena for exploring both the extent and the limits of what local government can do to improve the lives of the disadvantaged. By necessity, de Blasio, like every mayor since Ed Koch, is highly dependent on the private sector to build or maintain affordable housing.[15] His overall approach has been to promote mixed-income development. The obvious financial advantage of this method is that high-rent apartments can cross-subsidize lower-income units. His efforts have led to quarrels with housing advocates over two interrelated issues that go to the heart of the progressive agenda in all its complexity: gentrification and access for the very poor.

Gentrification has been with us for a while. Older New Yorkers saw Greenwich Village and Tribeca transformed from edgy bohemian enclaves where artists and vagabonds once thrived to urban shopping malls with glass towers occupied by well-heeled corporate executives. For the soulful New Yorker of today, these places are more attractive for what they once were rather than what they have become. Younger folks are more familiar with the rapid development of Williamsburg, Brooklyn, a neighborhood of modest homes that once housed dockworkers, rail yard mechanics, and utility men, where the waterfront now resembles Lower Manhattan. As income polarization became a fact of life and real earnings evaporated at the bottom of the scale, the stakes of gentrification have become fiercer for the very poor.

Bill de Blasio finds gentrification to be inevitable, and describes it as a "double edged sword."[16] Research on gentrification demonstrates that concerns about displacement are well-founded, but the overall effects are more complex and end up pitting one set of progressive goals against another. A report produced by New York University's Furman Center in 2015 identifies fifteen of fifty-five neighborhoods in New York as "gentrifying."[17] These are described as areas populated by relatively low-income families (bottom 40 percent) in 1990 that experienced higher than average rent growth over the next twenty years. Other neighborhoods in the study are classified as either low-income but "non-gentrifying" or "high-income."

Gentrification is not universal in the city, and neighborhoods that experience it have distinguishing characteristics beyond rent increases. Several demographic shifts observed citywide are more pronounced in gentrifying neighborhoods. These include trends toward younger, more educated, and single person households, and households with unrelated adults. The report also shows an increase in white populations in gentrifying areas despite their relative decrease in the city as a whole, and a larger decrease in black populations than the city as a whole.

Between 1990 and 2014, the average household income in gentrifying neighborhoods rose by 14 percent, while the average for non-gentrifying areas dropped by 8 percent. Many poor people still live in gentrifying neighborhoods, but their numbers are falling off. Citywide, roughly half the households in all types of neighborhoods are "rent burdened," but low and moderate income neighborhoods had the greatest increases in the number of people who are. Rental units that recently came on the market were less affordable to low-income households in all neighborhoods, but especially so in gentrifying neighborhoods. In 2000, 77.2 percent of the recently available units in gentrifying neighborhoods were affordable to those earning 80 percent of the AMI; by 2014, the share of affordable units at the same income level dropped to less than half. The evidence produced in this report is quite clear: in short, gentrification displaced poorer minority residents.

A second study completed by the Furman Center in 2016 focused on how neighborhood changes affected people living in three NYCHA housing projects that are surrounded by increasingly or persistently high-income communities: Long Island City, in Queens; Chelsea, in Manhattan; and Morris Heights, in the Bronx.[18] According to the report, two-thirds of all NYCHA residents live in developments that are surrounded by more privileged communities. As a result, these developments exist, for all practical purposes, as communities within communities, and residents see the public housing projects as their primary reference points. To state it another way, these communities are somewhat integrated on the basis of race and class, and the outcomes for residents are multifaceted.

On the positive side, these NYCHA residents experience lower violent crime rates than those who live in housing projects surrounded by persistently low-income communities. Their children are also zoned for public elementary schools with higher standardized test scores, and they score higher on standardized tests in math and reading at both the elementary and middle school levels. Neighborhood change, however, can also have an isolating effect. As high-end businesses that cater to new residents replace bodegas and laundromats, NYCHA residents find fewer places that sell groceries and other staples they can afford.

This form of "side-by-side" integration (my term) may not be what civil rights advocates of the 1950s and 1960s had in mind when they envisioned integration of the races, where people of different backgrounds shared their lives more fully—living next to each other, attending the same schools, playing in the same parks, shopping in the same stores, becoming more familiar on a personal level, developing friendships.[19] It does, however, move us in that direction and advances some of the secondary societal goals integrationists strove for with regard to community safety and education. Straightaway, it is axiomatic among criminologists that neighborhoods with high concentrations of poor and minority residents have higher crime rates.

School integration, on the other hand, has a special place in the history of the civil rights movement. The story has not always been an uplifting one, and we need to explore it more carefully before closing this discussion about housing. School segregation is largely a function of housing segregation. Boston is probably the classic case study of how attempts at forced school integration through busing in the 1970s and 1980s sparked an ugly and divisive reaction by opponents that only led to further racial antagonism.[20] Just last year, all hell broke out on the liberal Upper West Side when the New York City Department of Education rezoned schools to achieve more racial balance. A decision handed down by the U.S. Supreme Court in 2007 that reviewed integration plans in Seattle and Louisville placed significant restrictions on the use of race as a criterion for school assignments.[21] Racial integration of our schools has never been easy, and now there are additional legal impediments in the way.

More recent experiments in school integration by class and race rely on voluntary participation and cooperation. They show that integration has a positive effect on the academic achievement of students from low-income and minority backgrounds without having detrimental effects on more advantaged students.[22] Beyond the development of cognitive skills, allowing students to study, work, and play with others from different backgrounds and cultures can be an enriching experience that promotes genuine social integration among young people and future adults.

The Century Foundation in New York has been tracking experiments in school integration for twenty years. There are some one hundred districts and charter schools throughout the country implementing such programs. A recent study of nine of these urban districts found that participating students excel academically and leave school better prepared to live in a diverse society.[23] Housing policy is no substitute for a standards-based program of school reform to bridge the learning gap defined by race and class. Mixed income and housing of the sort being fostered under the de Blasio plan brings us a step closer to breaking patterns of school segregation and forming integrated communities that can potentially help overcome boundaries of race and class.

There is a justifiable apprehension in minority communities about displacement, though, which needs to be addressed. We can't deny that it is happening. Beyond these misgivings, however, even if the effects of gentrification can be controlled so that a racial balance is achieved through housing policy, expressions of alarm by minority advocates about the "whitening" of Harlem, or all of New York for that matter, should not be dismissed as alarmist either. Here again, history can serve as an able instructor. Experiences with "urban renewal" and "planned shrinkage" have demonstrated what is possible, and it usually was not favorable to low-income people of color.

Looking back to the 1960s, the admonitions of black power activists who parted ways with integrationists such as the Reverend Martin Luther King Jr. and a young John Lewis are worthy of consideration also. When Stokely Carmichael and his fellow activists concluded that desegregation was a hopeless cause, they urged the black community to turn inward and take charge of its own destiny.[24] They sought to convert the demographic concentration of racial isolation into an asset that could contribute to community power. They spoke of racial pride and independence. Mainstream politicians wrote them off for their provocative rhetoric. Not long afterward, voting rights advocates and the Supreme Court recognized that the geographic concentration of black people in voting districts could be translated into political power that sent representatives such as John Lewis to Congress.[25] It became a matter of public policy sanctioned by law.

Once again, de Blasio's housing policies must be put to the reasonableness test. There are conflicting values at stake here, each of which has merit in the progressive lexicon of priorities. In the end, the judgment must turn somewhat on an assessment of a political actor's intentions, and whether they are aligned with some version of the progressive cause to advance equality. Given de Blasio's progressive political pedigree, the tone of his campaigns, and the choices he made on issues over which he had control, his approach to mixed-income housing is a reasonable one—which does not necessarily mean that all progressives need to agree with him. One might add, though, that it is also consistent with federal law. Although the U.S. Supreme Court has discouraged the use of racial criteria to make school assignments, the Fair Housing Act of 1968 requires localities to break historic patterns of racial and income segregation.

The question remains, however, whether Mayor de Blasio's housing policy will meet the needs of those New Yorkers who are at the lowest end of the income scale. For years, NYCHA provided a safety net for many of them in a way that few other cities did. Federal cutbacks since the 1980s continued to rip a hole in those cushions so that many households that would have been rescued fell to the ground. As part of the *Next Generation* initiative, the mayor had offered budget relief to NYCHA by absorbing all the authority's costs of police protection and payments in lieu of taxes. That gesture had a symbolic significance of its own. According to NYCHA chair Shola Olatoye, "Mayor de Blasio's assumption of costs for police protection and in lieu of taxes was more than budget relief. It represented his recognition that the people who live in public housing are an integral part of New York City entitled to all its benefits."[26] With that, the waiting lists for NYCHA housing continue to grow.

To increase the supply of housing, Mayor Bloomberg elicited private and not-for-profit developers to build 6,500 new units on land belonging to NYCHA. As part of NYCHA's *Next Generation* plan initiated in 2016, the de Blasio administration launched its own experiment of public-private partnership by issuing a request for proposals (RFP) for building 800 units of new housing on two NYCHA sites in Manhattan and Brooklyn.[27] Residents of the two public housing complexes were involved in the development of the plans. According to the RFP, a developer or nonprofit entity would design, finance, and construct the buildings. Reflecting the mixed income strategy of the administration, half the units would be dedicated to affordable housing, and the remainder would be available at market rates. NYCHA would retain ownership of the land and the developer would manage the properties.

Some critics of the NYCHA initiative have seen it as a first step in the privatization of the public authority, but 800 units out of a total of 177,657 is hardly a critical mass. And there is not much of a choice if the objective is to build more public housing units for the city. A law signed by President Clinton in 1998 prohibits local PHAs from using federal capital or operating funds to increase the net number of housing units under their jurisdictions.[28]

Considering the de Blasio administration's *Housing New York* plan on the whole, it remains to be seen how far public/private partnerships can go to meet the needs of New Yorkers at the very lowest income levels. Historically, the only time political leaders in New York City came close to that goal was when the federal government did it for them. Even that New Deal project was originally directed at working class New Yorkers who were not at the very bottom of the income scale, and the housing built was intentionally segregated by race. Federal policymakers did have the good sense then to fill the void, once they saw that private developers were not prepared to build housing for the poor. In Senator Wagner's words, they deemed it an area where "private enterprise cannot operate." That is not likely to happen now with Donald Trump in the White House and Republicans controlling both houses of Congress.

Progressive Cities?

Progressivism could be the suicide pill of American politics in the twenty-first century. The chasm that stretches between the declared aspirations of local progressive leaders and the resources they possess to realize them is vast. Bill de Blasio has sought to build housing that is integrated by race and class, while serving the needs of extremely low income New Yorkers and many homeless families who need additional support services. The federal retreat from subsidized housing has proceeded without much interruption through the Democratic administrations of Presidents Bill Clinton and Barack Obama, and it's not about to get better.

President Donald Trump has vowed to rebuild the eroding infrastructure of American cities. It remains to be seen what he means by that, and how it will unfold. A lot is on the line. There is only so much that fiscally healthy cities such as New York, Boston, Denver, and Seattle can do on their own. There is very little that financially strapped cities such as Detroit, Cleveland, Milwaukee, Baltimore, and Memphis can achieve without serious assistance from Washington. The country is facing an urban infrastructure crisis. The problem received little attention in a presidential campaign that was short on the discussion of real and pressing policy issues.

Under the current circumstances, progressive big city mayors have little choice but to work within the structure of the Democratic Party to move it off the center, where it has been stuck for more than three decades. Only then will the country be offered real alternatives to policies that have created disparities in income and wealth exceeding every other major democracy in the world. Until then, cities will be left to deal with the symptoms of that larger inequality in the form of homelessness, ineffective schools, and other societal dysfunctions without the resources they need to do so effectively.

In the tradition of La Guardia and Lindsay, Bill de Blasio has taken his responsibility to speak out against injustice on a national stage very seriously. Perhaps, as a new mayor, he tried to do too much, too soon. The mainstream leaders of the Democratic Party were not yet ready to hear what de Blasio, Bernie Sanders, Elizabeth Warren, and others had to say in the course of the 2016 presidential campaign. De Blasio took a huge political risk by delaying his endorsement of the powerful home-state standard-bearer of his party. Hillary Clinton and her campaign team ignored his plea for a progressive forum during the Iowa caucus. WikiLeaks of emails reveal that campaign chair John Podesta actually asked his staff, "Should we care about this?"[29] Other exchanges among the staff indicate that they were not about to support de Blasio's call for a $15 minimum wage.[30]

Once de Blasio endorsed her, Clinton was cool to his offers to campaign for her. Her top aides dealt with him warily, underscoring concerns that dated back for years. At the national party convention, Clinton gave former mayor Michael Bloomberg, the independent billionaire who was de Blasio's main philosophical adversary in New York, a more prominent speaking role. It was an unusual snub for a sitting Democratic mayor of the nation's largest city. Aside from the personal

tensions arising from the endorsement issue, one cannot ignore real philosophical differences between Clinton and de Blasio. Bloomberg was probably more in
accord with the Clinton agenda. De Blasio has since said that Sanders's message
would have prevailed over Trump.[31]

Although Bernie Sanders did not win the Democratic nomination in 2016,
he unleashed a populist progressive movement within the party that has more
potential after the defeat of Hillary Clinton. The election of Donald Trump
starkly demonstrates that populist sentiment needs to be taken seriously in
American politics, and it is not easily checked by sophisticated campaign operations with unlimited resources. Trump's election also shows that populism can
have destructive tendencies, when it is not properly guided by strong leadership.
Bill de Blasio's ability to build a progressive alliance in New York that cuts across
the boundaries of race, class, and gender can help show the way. It is a case study
of what progressive mayors can do (and can't) without much support from other
levels of government, and it is about to face its biggest test imagined.

To the extent that Trump's victory can be read as an endorsement of racist,
misogynist, homophobic, nativist bigotry, it is tragic. To the extent that his election is a rejection of American politics "as we know it" and an economy that
has hurt too many people, it is an opportunity for the progressive wing of the
Democratic Party to broaden its base. Republicans will need to go beyond their
usual litany of lower taxes and smaller government to retain support from those
Americans facing economic hardship to convince them that the GOP represents
Main Street—and Back Street—as well as Wall Street. The GOP does not appear
poised to do that, despite the uptick of support among working class whites. The
Trump administration has recruited more Cabinet and high level officials from
the privileged class than any in recent memory.[32]

Back in New York City, the man from nowhere who scored an upset victory
for the mayoralty in 2013 is running for re-election. As a new mayor, he assumed
such easy credibility among progressives that he might have raised expectations
beyond his own reach. It is ironic that, after four years of intense activity to reset
the priorities of the city, he draws some of his most intense criticism from former
allies within that same progressive coalition. That discontent may betray a bit of
vulnerability as he seeks a second term. But incumbent mayors don't make easy
targets at the ballot box. And the large roster of labor leaders that has lined up
with the Working Families Party to pledge him their support in 2017 does not
make the contest inviting to potential challengers.[33] De Blasio enjoys an impressive wall of defense as he advances to the goal line.

It was not so long ago that Michael Bloomberg declared his intention to seek
a third term and spend as much of his own money as needed to win. It was a
potent dare in itself, backed by a different firewall of defense. A lot has changed.
New York may be rediscovering its soul. The country needs it more than ever

now, with the election of a president who has stoked the flames of division and promises to set the clock back on social spending. The country needs to hear the sound of a different voice that speaks to the values of opportunity, fairness, and tolerance for all people. Throughout history, that sound has resonated from New York with poignant clarity.

What about the Future?

Few New York progressives ever believed the future would involve Donald Trump residing in the White House. Many still can't. Could this man who wants to build a wall at the Mexican border actually have come from Queens, one of the most immigrant-rich, demographically diverse counties in all America? Did a billionaire real estate tycoon really manage to carry off so many white working class voters that were once part of the Democratic Party base? How will leaders in the Democratic Party respond?

One scenario, mentioned earlier, holds that in the hope of returning many former loyalists to its fold, the results of the 2016 election will create opportunities for progressives within the national party to have more sway. A more discouraging scenario—not at all unreasonable—suggests that with Republicans in Washington attempting to move the national agenda so far to the right, Democrats will be preoccupied with holding ground on battles fought and won generations ago.

At least since the Clinton administration, and in some respects going back to President Jimmy Carter, when federal spending on cities began to subside, moderate Democrats contented themselves with focusing on a rights-based agenda built around issues of race and gender without taking much serious action to stem the tide of economic inequality that began to rise in the 1980s. To the contrary, mainstream Democrats, responding to the same corporate and financial interests that influenced their Republican colleagues, were complicit in the passage of regulatory and tax legislation that propelled income polarization. Most recently, President Barack Obama did manage to pass Dodd-Frank legislation in 2008 to provide protection for investors from unscrupulous practices in the financial sector, but those protections are a prime target of the Trump administration.

Having an administration in Washington plump with plutocrats, and a lineup of Cabinet officials who do not support the core missions of the socially attuned agencies they run—think, for example, justice, housing, the environment, and education—mainstream Democrats will be all too absorbed in protecting the status quo ante to take on new challenges urged on by economic progressives such as Bernie Sanders and Elizabeth Warren. That was always their instinct to begin with, and they could do so without offending the lobbyists that have kept them in office all along. The years ahead could usher in a new era of civil rights battles on behalf of racial and ethnic minorities, women, gays, and immigrants. It could suit Democratic moderates just fine. Republicans who control Washington are not about to take on issues of economic justice in any case.

The political landscape of New York is different. Within days of the 2016 election, both Governor Cuomo and Mayor de Blasio declared (separately, of course) that New York would remain a safe haven for all minorities who had fallen victim to discrimination, including immigrants. Before President Trump was sworn in, Governor Cuomo, looking toward his own re-election in 2018, and a possible run for the presidency in 2020, unleashed a bevy of policy proposals that positioned him to claim the mantle of progressive leadership that was once his father's. With Bernie Sanders at his side, he proposed free tuition at the state and city universities of New York for families with incomes below $125,000. He vowed to cut taxes on the middle class, but urged the legislature to extend higher taxes on people who earn more than $300,000 annually. He proposed more spending on housing, infrastructure, clean water, and education— all within the bounds of responsible budgeting (less than 2 percent increase) he had set down for himself earlier.[34]

The governor's discovery of his progressive self better aligns him with the priorities of his fellow Democrats in the state legislature and discomfits some of his former Republican allies. It is not likely to ease his personal tensions with Mayor de Blasio; however, it would be difficult for Cuomo to implement his plan without benefiting the city in ways that supported the mayor's agenda, even though Cuomo's pitch to middle class voters—epitomized in his free college tution plan—is not entirely coherent with City Hall's determination to reach people at the lower end of the economic ladder.

Both the governor and the mayor could see their dreams go up in smoke, of course, if the federal government makes steep cuts in areas such as housing, health, and education, and that seems probable. De Blasio insists, however, that he will not be deterred by political prognostics of impending doom. In a wideranging conversation at Gracie Mansion, he remained upbeat, bordering on defiant when asked about progressive prospects for the future.[35]

Queried about the possibility of change in the mainstream Democratic Party, he responded, "I think it will take a lot of work, and a lot of people will have to see the need for change. They will need to recognize from the 2016 election how the Democratic Party must be identifiably progressive and economically populist." Then, he reached back to his experience in the 1990s with the Majority Coalition that Dennis Rivera of Local 1199 had organized to install a progressive presence in the Democratically controlled New York City Council, declaring, "I never followed a party line. I did not want to go along to get along. I had deep roots in progressive politics long before I ran for office myself, and appreciated what coalition politics tied to labor could do to promote change. I still do."

When confronted with the realities of a changing political climate in Washington, de Blasio was his pragmatic self, claiming: "I never expected much from Washington when I was elected mayor. Even during the Obama years, Congress would not cooperate. I could not expend my energy thinking about what I did not have; I needed to work with what I had. Washington cannot take away what you don't have."

But, Washington could take away what we do have, as relatively little as it may be. Unlike La Guardia and Lindsay who had sympathetic presidents such as FDR and LBJ to support their progressive goals, I retorted, he (de Blasio) is out there on his own. At this point, de Blasio became philosophical, and his New York spirit of idealism began to show through. He looked back further into history and, with an air of self-assurance, remarked that he had inherited "a city that was in a lot better shape than the one that either La Guardia or Lindsay governed." The mayor further explained that he did not have a Depression to deal with, and the city was no longer in decline as it was by the end of the Lindsay years. He noted how, beginning with Ed Koch through the Bloomberg years, his predecessors were able to recuperate from the damaging fiscal crisis of 1975. He recalled how the crime rate began to come down under Mayor Dinkins, with the decline accelerating under Giuliani and continuing under Bloomberg.

He assured me, "New York City is stronger than ever, and we will continue our work to promote an inclusive, fair, and more equal society, no matter what happens in Washington."

We shall see.

NOTES

Preface

1. Joseph P. Viteritti, ed., *Summer in the City: John Lindsay, New York, and the American Dream* (Johns Hopkins University Press, 2014).
2. Joseph P. Viteritti, Interview: "What Bill de Blasio Can Learn from John Lindsay," talkingnote. blogs.nytimes.com.2015/05/18/what-bill-de-blasio/can/learn/from/john/lindsay.

Chapter 1

1. Joseph P. Viteritti, "Epilogue: The New Charter: Will It Make a Difference?", in Jewel Bellush and Dick Netzer, eds., *City Politics, New York Style* (M.E. Sharpe, 1990), pp. 413–428.
2. Robert W. Bailey, *Gay Politics, Urban Politics: Identity and Economics in the Urban Setting* (Columbia University Press, 1999), pp. 215–248.
3. Catie Edmondson, "Suing the Hand That Feeds You," *Gotham Gazette*, August 19, 2015.
4. Betsy Gotbaum, interview with the author, January 18, 2016.
5. Vivian Toy, "Term Limits Stay 8 Years as Extension Is Rejected," *New York Times*, November 6, 1996.
6. Quinnipiac Poll, taken January 16, 2013, three weeks after de Blasio declared his candidacy. The same poll gave Christine Quinn 35 percent of the vote. A Marist/NY1 Poll taken as late as April 24th also gave de Blasio 11 percent.
7. Jill Calvin, "Joe Lhota on Bill de Blasio's Strategy: Right Out of the Marxist Playbook," *New York Observer*, September 24, 2013.
8. https://www.youtube.com/watch?v+mGVDSr0-PFY.
9. http://www.nytimes.com/projects/elections/2013/general/nyc-mayor/map.html.
10. J. David Goodman, "Bratton to Lead New York Police for a Second Time," *New York Times*, December 5, 2013. This claim is supported in Joe Domanick, *Blue: The LAPD and the Battle to Redeem American Policing* (Simon & Shuster, 2015).
11. The concept was first described and popularized in James Q. Wilson and George L. Kelling, "Broken Windows: The Police and Neighborhood Safety," *Atlantic Monthly*, Vol. 249 (March 1982). For Bratton's own account of his first tour in New York, see William Bratton, *Turnaround: How America's Top Cop Reversed the Crime Epidemic* (Random House, 1998). For other assessments of Bratton's tenure in New York, see Eli Silverman, *NYPD Battles Crime: Innovative Strategies in Policing* (Northeastern University Press, 1999), which also accounts for developments preceding Bratton's tenure; and Frank E. Zimmering, *The City That Became Safe: New York's Lessons for Urban Crime and Its Control* (Oxford University Press, 2013), which also accounts for developments subsequent to Bratton's tenure.
12. Ken Auletta, "Fixing Broken Windows," *The New Yorker*, September 7, 2015.
13. Lilliam Barrios Paoli, interview with the author, December 8, 2015.

14. Pervaiz Shallwani, "Mayor and Police Commissioner Pressured on NYPD," *Wall Street Journal,* July 31, 2014.

15. Al Sharpton, "'Homos,' 'Chinamen,' the 'N' Word," https://www.youtube/watch?v=4ltjow C37AM.

16. Transcript: Mayor de Blasio Holds Media Availability with Police Commissioner Bratton on the Death of Eric Garner, July 18, 2014.

17. Transcript: Mayor de Blasio Holds Media Availability with Police Commissioner Bratton on the Death of Eric Garner, July 16, 2014.

18. Ross Barkan, "At Round Table, Sharpton Claims Dante de Blasio Could Have Been a Chokehold Target," *The Observer,* July 31, 2014.

19. Transcript: Mayor de Blasio, "This Week," ABC News, December 7, 2014.

20. Transcript: Erin Durkin, "Bill de Blasio Details Talks with Son about Interacting with Police," December 8, 2015.

21. Durkin, "Bill de Blasio Details Talks with Son about Interacting with Police."

22. Durkin, "Bill de Blasio Details Talks with Son about Interacting with Police."

23. Durkin, "Bill de Blasio Details Talks with Son about Interacting with Police."

24. http://www.nycpba.org/miscellaneous/council-funeral.pdf.

25. Matt Pearce, "New York's Embattled Mayor Meets with Police Union Leaders," *Los Angeles Times,* December 19, 2014.

26. John Marzulli and Corky Siamaszko, "NYPD Captain's Leader: Don't Turn Your Backs on de Blasio during Wenjian Liu's Funeral," *Daily News,* December 30, 2014.

27. For the story of consolidation, see Edward G. Burrows and Mike Wallace, *Gotham: A History of New York to 1898* (Oxford University Press, 1999), pp. 1219–1236.

28. James Traub, *The Devil's Playground: A Century of Pleasure and Profit* (Random House, 2004), p. 19.

29. See Sam Roberts, *Grand Central: How a Train Station Transformed America* (Grand Central Publications, 2013).

30. Lynne Sagalyn, *Times Square Roulette: Remaking a City Icon* (MIT Press, 2003).

31. http://www.nyc.gov/html/dot/downloads/pdf/broadway_report_final2010_web.pdf

32. "Mayor Bloomberg, Transportation Commissioner Sadik-Khan, and Design and Construction Commissioner Barney Cut Ribbon on the First Phase of Times Square Reconstruction (23 December 2013)," http://www1.nyc.gov/office-of-the-mayor/news/432-13/mayor-bloomberg-transportation-commissioner-sadik-khan-design-construction-commissioner/#/0

33. http://www:timessquarenyc.org/do-business-here/market-facts/pedestrian-counts/index.aspx#.

34. Michael M. Grynbaum, "Mayor de Blasio Raises Prospect of Removing Times Square Pedestrian Plaza," *New York Times,* August 20, 2015.

35. P. Mc Gleehan, "Times Square Topless Women Should Be Regulated, Mayor Says," *New York Times,* August 18, 2015.

36. Gleehan, "Times Square Topless Women Should Be Regulated."

37. 1010 WINS, Interview: "Bratton Suggests Tearing Up Times Square Pedestrian Plaza," http://newyork.cbslocal.com/2015/08/20/bill-bratton-times-square/

38. Grynbaum, "Mayor de Blasio Raises Prospect of Removing Times Square Pedestrian Plaza."

39. Transcript: "City Task Force on Times Square Announces Recommendations," October 1, 2015, http://www1.nyc.gov/office-of-the-mayor/news/668-15/ciyu-task-force-times-square-recommendations

40. In 2016, the City Council enacted a law setting up "designated activity zones" for costumed (and uncostumed) characters who offer services for tips.

41. Sharon Otterman, "Board Votes to Regulate Circumcision, Citing Risks," *New York Times,* October 13, 2012.

42. Press Release: "Health Department Issues Statement Strongly Advising That Direct Oral Suction Not Be Performed during Jewish Ritual Circumcision," #017-12, June 6, 2012.

43. "Neonatal Herpes Simplex Virus Infection following Jewish Ritual Circumcision That Included Direct Orogenital Suction—NYC," *Morbidity and Mortality Weekly Report,* Vol. 61 (22), pp. 405–409, July 8, 2012. Washington, D.C.: Centers for Disease Control and Prevention.

44. NYC Rules, Sec. 181.21: Consent for Direct Oral Suction as Part of Circumcision (2012).

45. http://www.nytimes.com/video/multimedia/100000002254335/candidates-on-circumcision-ritual.html.

46. Sharon Otterman, "Mayor de Blasio and Rabbis Near Accord on Circumcision Rule," *New York Times,* January 14, 2015.

47. Will Brederman, "De Blasio Cuts Deal on Controversial Circumcision Ritual," *New York Observer,* February 24, 2015.

48. Edward Burns, et al., "NYC *Metzitzah* Policy Is Insufficient," *The Jewish Week,* June 22, 2015.

49. Sharon Otterman, "De Blasio's Prekindergarten Expansion Collides with Church-State Divide," *New York Times,* August 4, 2014.

50. Nikita Stewart, "Mayor de Blasio and Cardinal Dolan Highlight Plan to Add Beds for Homeless," *New York Times,* September 2015.

51. Glen Thrush, "The New Icon of the Left: An Interview with New York Mayor Bill de Blasio," *Politico,* September/October 2014.

52. Molly Ball, "The Equalizer: Bill de Blasio vs. Inequality," *The Atlantic,* December, 2015.

53. http://dailycaller.com/2015/09/29/bill-de-blasio-hillary-clinton-need-to-clarify-her-vision-further-video/.

54. Meet the Press, Transcript: April 12, 2015.

55. https://twitter.com/hillary/status/587280737088491520#.

56. Vivian Yee, "WikiLeaks Emails Show Mayor de Blasio Venting at and Appealing to Clinton Campaign," *New York Times,* October 12, 2016.

57. Josh Robib, "In NY1 Interview Mayor Suggests Biden Should Sit Out 2016 Democratic Presidential Primary," *NY1,* September 11, 2015.

58. Michael M. Grynbaum, "Bill de Blasio Endorses Hillary Clinton, to Little Fanfare from Campaign," *New York Times,* October 30, 2015.

59. Grynbaum, "Bill de Blasio Endorses Hillary Clinton."

60. Jill Jorgensen, "Bill de Blasio Finally Endorses Hillary Clinton for President," *New York Observer,* October 30, 2015.

61. Ball, "The Equalizer."

Chapter 2

1. Donald Wilhelm, *Theodore Roosevelt as an Undergraduate* (John Luce and Company, 1910).

2. Shah Mohammed Reza, *Mission for My Country* (Hutchison of London, 1974), p. 26.

3. Jean Wilhelm, correspondence with the author, January 29, 2017.

4. Jean Wilhelm, correspondence with the author, January 29, 2017.

5. Maria de Blasio Wilhelm, *The Other Italy: The Italian Resistance in World War II* (Norton, 1988). Herbert Mitgang, "Review/Book; How the Italians Resisted the Occupying Germans," *New York Times,* September 8, 1988.

6. On Chambers, see Sam Tanenhaus, *Whittaker Chambers: A Biography* (Modern Library, 1998).

7. Federal Bureau of Investigation, interview with J. David Whittaker Chambers, December 29, 1951, obtained under Freedom of Information Act from the U.S. Information Agency, request No. 1319259-001 for Warren Wilhelm and 1319246-001 for Maria de Blasio.

8. Javier Hernandez, "From His Father's Decline, de Blasio 'Learned What Not to Do,'" *New York Times,* October 13, 2013.

9. Steven Wilhelm, interview with the author, January 31, 2017.

10. Hernandez, "From His Father's Decline, de Blasio 'Learned What Not to Do.'"

11. Bill de Blasio, interview with the author, January 28, 2017.

12. Chris Smith, "The 99% Mayor," *New York Magazine,* October 27, 2013.

13. Greg Smith, "Mayoral Hopeful Bill de Blasio Has Had Three Different Legal Names, Court Records Show," *New York Daily News,* September 9, 2011.

14. Bill de Blasio, interview with the author, January 28, 2017.

15. Mark Binelli, "Mayor Bill de Blasio's Crusade," *Rolling Stone,* May 6, 2015.

16. Binelli, "Mayor Bill de Blasio's Crusade."

17. Peter Dicpinigaitis, interview with the author, February 25, 2016.

18. Allan Frei, interview with author, November 17, 2015.

19. Smith, "Mayoral Hopeful Bill de Blasio Has Had Three Different Legal Names."

20. Javier Hernandez, "A Mayoral Hopeful Now, de Blasio Was Once a Young Leftist," *New York Times,* September 22, 2013.
21. http://www.icj-cij.org/docket/?sum=367&p1=3&p2=3&case=70&p3=5
22. Chris Hedges, "Sandinista's U.S. Friends: Case of Dashed Ideals," *New York Times,* July 21, 1990.
23. Dana Rubinstein, "The Right Thing to Do: De Blasio Explains His Nicaragua Work," *Capital New York,* September 25, 2015.
24. Chirlane McCray, interview with the author, January 28, 2017.
25. Andrew Marantz, "Significant Other," *The New Yorker,* August 5, 2013.
26. Lisa Miller, "Chirlane McCray's City," *New York Magazine,* May 18, 2014.
27. Heidi Evans, "Bill de Blasio Dishes on His Romance with Chirlane McCray," *Daily News,* October 28, 2013.
28. Boris Kachka, "Hillary, Michelle, Chirlane: Chirlane McCray Is a New Kind of First Lady," *Elle,* December 9, 2013.
29. Nikita Stewart, "Mayoral First Couple Talk about Love and Hard Times," *New York Times,* April 21, 2014.
30. Chirlane McCray, "I Am a Lesbian," *Essence,* September 1979.
31. Miller, "Chirlane McCray's City."
32. Kachka, "Hillary, Michelle, Chirlane."
33. Miller, "Chirlane McCray's City."
34. Chirlane McCray, personal communication with the author, January 29, 2017.
35. Teresa Mastin, "Why Chiara de Blasio Matters," *Ebony,* January 20, 2014.
36. Chiara de Blasio, "I'm Chiara de Blasio and I'm a Young Woman in Recovery," *xojane.com,* May 6, 2014.
37. Kate Taylor, "In a Speech and Essay, Chiara de Blasio Details Her Depression and Addiction," *New York Times,* May 7, 2014.
38. Emily Tess Katz, "Chirlane McCray Opens Up about Daughter Chiara's Struggle with Depression," *Huffington Post,* May 12, 2015.
39. Transcript: "Mayor de Blasio, First Lady McCray Release Thrive NYC: A Mental Health Roadmap for All," November 22, 2015.

Chapter 3

1. For a brief introduction, see Lisa Duggan, *The Twilight of Equality: Neoliberalism, Cultural Politics, and the Attack on Democracy* (Beacon, 2004); David Harvey, *A Brief History of Neoliberalism* (Oxford University Press, 2007).
2. Jillian Jorgenson, "Bill de Blasio to Rename Municipal Building for David Dinkins," *New York Observer,* October 2, 2015.
3. Chris Smith, "The 99% Mayor," *New York Magazine,* October 27, 2013.
4. Chris McNickle, *The Power of the Mayor: David Dinkins: 1990–1993* (Transaction, 2012).
5. Juan Gonzalez, "Mayor de Blasio, Ambassador Friend Are Dinkins Success Stories," *Daily News,* January 2, 2014.
6. Adam Dickter, "The Political Education of Bill de Blasio," *The Jewish Week,* July 16, 2013.
7. http://www.seiu1199.org/about-our-union/union-history/.
8. Steven Greenhouse and Noam Scheiber, "Two Big Labor Unions Share Efforts to Gain Power and Scale," *New York Times,* May 5, 2016.
9. Sam Roberts, "Primary Day: Council's New Era Takes Shape in New York Vote," *New York Times,* September 13, 1991.
10. Bob Liff, "Vallone Set to Retain His Power," *Newsday,* October 13, 1991.
11. Dennis Rivera, interview with the author, March 11, 2016.
12. For a brief history of the New Party, see Micah L. Sifry, *Spoiling for a Fight: Third Party Politics in America* (Routledge, 2003), pp. 226–257.
13. www.acorn.org.
14. Sifry, *Spoiling for a Fight,* p. 230.
15. Dennis Rivera, interview with the author, March 11, 2016.
16. Bob Liff, "Hillary Could Use Millions on Mall," *Newsday,* May 18, 1993.

17. Maurice Carroll, "Why Roy Innis Is Money Man," *Newsday*, June 11, 1993.
18. Robert Shogan, "Liberals Fear Further Loss of Political Clout," *Los Angeles Times*, July 6, 1993.
19. *Timmons v. Twin Cities Area New Party*, 520 U.S. 351 (1997).
20. See Sifry, *Spoiling for a Fight*, pp. 258–276.
21. Raymond Hernandez, "Rangel Easily Defeats Five Primary Rivals," *New York Times*, September 14, 2010.
22. David Firestone, "Effort to Preserve Political Dynasty in East Harlem Falls by a Wide Margin," *New York Times*, March 15, 1993.
23. Firestone, "Effort to Preserve Political Dynasty in East Harlem Falls by a Wide Margin."
24. Kenneth R. Bazinet and William Goldschlag, "Prez Says He's Proud Wife's in Senate Race," *Daily News*, November 25, 1999.
25. Michael Tomasky, "The Sure Thing," *New York Times Magazine*, March 11, 1996.
26. Kevin McCabe, interview with the author, August 18, 2016.
27. James Dao, "Second Prominent Democrat Foregoes Race against Pataki," *New York Times*, August 8, 1997.
28. http://www.cnn.com/ALLPOLITICS/stories/1998/09/16/primary.results/new.york.html.
29. http://www.elections.ny.gov/NYSBOE/news/gvot98.pdf.
30. Jill Colvin, "The Tall Man Cometh: Bill de Blasio Will Bring His Own Brand of Leadership to City Hall," *New York Observer*, October 29, 2013.
31. Michael Shnayerson, *The Contender: Andrew Cuomo, A Biography* (Twelve, 2015), pp. 218–219.
32. Joel Siegel, "Hill Picks Veteran to Run Her Run," December 4, 1999.
33. Sifry, *Spoiling for a Fight*, p. 271.
34. Randall C. Archibald and Elissa Gootman, "Behind Four Pardons, a Sect Eager for Political Friends," *New York Times*, February 5, 2001; Larry Cohler-Esses and Joel Siegel, "The Wooing of Hillary Clinton: Pardons on Mind of New Square Rabbi," *New York Daily News*, February 12, 2001; Richard Kreitner, "The Shady Ties between de Blasio and the Clintons," *Counterpunch*, October 25, 2013.
35. Randal Archibald, "Man Pleads Guilty to Fraud and Conspiracy in Hasidic Enclave," *New York Times*, January 24, 2002; Josh Gerstein, "Clinton Pardon Records Offer Fuel for Hillary Foes," January 28, 2016, www.politico.com/story/2016/01/hillary-clinton-pardon-record-218331.
36. G.A. Casebeer, "Comey Has a Long History of Letting the Clintons Off the Hook," July 8, 2016, thebernreport.com/comey-long-history-letting-clintons-off-hook/.
37. http://www.fec.gov/pubrec/fe2000/2000senate.htm#NY
38. David Chen, "In 2000, a War Room Didn't Fit de Blasio Style," *New York Times*, August 25, 2013; Smith, "The 99% Mayor."
39. Bill de Blasio, interview with the author, January 28, 2017.
40. Josh Benson, "Clinton West Winger Bill de Blasio Runs Midlife-Crisis Council Race," *New York Observer*, April 16, 2001.
41. Joel Siegel, "A Powerbroker Goes Broke for a Council Race," *Daily News*, December 31, 2000.
42. Benson, "Clinton West Winger Bill de Blasio Runs Midlife-Crisis Council Race."
43. Elizabeth Mitchell, "Cuomo vs de Blasio: How a Friendly, Airtight Relationship between the Democratic Heavyweights Turned Ugly. Is It Beyond Repair?," *New York Daily News*, October 29, 2016.
44. Bill Egbert, "Biggest Bills for BEEP Race," *Daily News*, September 11, 2001.
45. Kreitner, "The Shady Ties between de Blasio and the Clintons."
46. http://www.elections.ny.gov?NYBOE/news/gvot98.pdf.
47. http://vote.nyc.ny.us/downloads/pdf/results/2003/general/g2003recaps.pdf
48. Jillian Jonas, "Edwards Has Helped the Democrats," *United Press International*, March 3, 2004.
49. As a young man, de Blasio also worked on the presidential campaigns of Morris Udall (1976), Edward Kennedy (1980), and Jesse Jackson (1984). Bill de Blasio, interview with the author, December 28, 2016.
50. http://query.nytimes.com/get/fullpage.html?res=9900E7DF123EF933A25752C1A9639C8B63
51. http://vote.nyc.ny.us/downloads/pdf/results/2009/General/2.11CitywidePublicAdvocateRecap.pdf

52. Sam Roberts, "City of 8 Million Was Ghost Town at the Polls," *New York Times,* October 6, 2009.
53. Board of Elections of the City of New York, "Statement and Return Report for Certification: General Election 2009," November 3, 2009.
54. These estimates are from Mark Green, "Green to Bloomberg: Don't Cut the Public Advocate," *Huffington Post,* May 5, 2011.
55. Dana Rubinstein, "Bill de Blasio Thinks Occupy Wall Street Could Be a Good Thing, with Some Refining," *Capitol New York,* October 6, 2011.
56. Chris Bragg, "Appelbaum Lashes Out at Stupefying de Blasio," *Crain's New York,* March 26, 2013.
57. Ross Barkan, "De Blasio Wishes Quinn Would Wield Her Wrath for Paid Sick Leave Days," *New York Observer,* March 26, 2013.
58. CNN Wire Staff, "Preliminary Report Clears ACORN on Funds," CNN, June 14, 2010, http://www.cnn.com/2010/POLITICS/06/14/congress.acorn/
59. Dan Cantor, interview with the author, August 3, 2016.
60. "Working Families Party Announces Endorsement for Bernie Sanders for President," Working Families Party, December, 2015.
61. https://web.archive.org/web/19961112083542/; http://www.newparty.org/1996.html

Chapter 4

1. The authoritative historical text on New York through the nineteenth century is Edwin G. Burrows and Mike Wallace, *Gotham: A History of New York City to 1898* (Oxford University Press, 1999). For a lovely short history, see also Joanne Reitano, *The Restless City: A Short History of New York from Colonial Times to the Present,* 2nd ed. (Routledge, 2006). For a comprehensive history of immigration, see Tyler Anbinder, *City of Dreams: The 400-Year Epic Story of Immigrant New York* (Houghton Mifflin, 2016).
2. Joelle Attinger, "The Rotting of the Big Apple," *Time,* October 17, 1990. The cover read, "The Decline of New York."
3. Steven Erie, *Rainbow's End: Irish Americans and the Dilemmas of Machine Politics, 1840–1985* (University of California Press, 1988), p. 18.
4. The fights between Irish immigrants and Protestant nativists, and Tweed's clever embrace of the former, are vividly portrayed in Martin Scorsese's *Gangs of New York,* which was released by Mirimax Films in 2003, and is loosely based on Herbert Asbury, *The Gangs of New York* (Knopf, 1927).
5. Erie, *Rainbow's End,* pp. 5, 27, 51.
6. Erie, *Rainbow's End,* p. 89.
7. There is a voluminous and colorful literature on Tammany. Among the standard histories are: Jerome Mushkat, *Tammany: The Evolution of a Political Machine, 1789–1865* (Syracuse University Press, 1971); Alexander Callow, *The Tweed Ring* (Oxford University Press, 1965); Seymour J. Mandelbaum, *Boss Tweed's New York* (Ivan Dee, 1965). For a biography of Tweed, see Kenneth D. Ackerman, *Boss Tweed: The Rise and Fall of the Corrupt Pol Who Conceived the Soul of Modern New York* (Carroll & Graff, 2005). On Tammany as a democratizing institution, see Terry Golway, *Machine Made: Tammany Hall and the Creation of Modern American Politics* (Liveright, 2014). For a positive reading of the contribution made by political machines in urban America, including New York, see Jon Teaford, *The Unheralded Triumph: City Government in America, 1870–1900* (Johns Hopkins University Press, 1984).
8. Rosemary C. Salomone, *True American: Language, Identity, and the Education of Immigrant Children* (Harvard University Press, 2010), pp. 15–45.
9. Samuel P. Hayes, "The Politics of Reform in Municipal Government in the Progressive Era," *Pacific Northwest Quarterly* (1964), pp. 157–169.
10. James Bryce, *American Commonwealth* (Macmillan, 1888), Vol. II, p. 281.
11. La Guardia was first elected to Congress in 1916 to represent Lower Manhattan, but resigned after volunteering for military service.
12. See generally, Arthur Mann, *La Guardia: A Fighter Against His Times, 1882–1933* (J. B. Lippincott, 1948); Howard Zinn, *La Guardia in Congress* (Cornell University Press, 1959).

13. Thomas Kessner, *Fiorello H. La Guardia and the Making of Modern New York* (McGraw-Hill, 1989), p. 182.
14. Mason B. Williams, *City of Ambition: FDR, La Guardia, and the Making of Modern New York* (W.W. Norton, 2013), p. 83.
15. See Louis Gribitz and Joseph Kaye, *Jimmie Walker: The Story of a Personality* (Dial Press, 1932).
16. Arthur Mann, *La Guardia Comes to Power: 1933* (J. B. Lippincott, 1965), pp. 123–159.
17. Bryan Burrough, "Bill de Blasio's Battle to Save New York—and Himself," *Vanity Fair*, October, 2015.
18. Williams, *City of Ambition*, p. 97.
19. Williams, *City of Ambition*, p. 110.
20. Kessner, *Fiorello La Guardia*, p. 175.
21. Moses played an important role in La Guardia's capital projects. See Robert Caro, *The Power Broker: Robert Moses and the Fall of New York* (Knopf, 1974), pp. 347–402.
22. For an excellent history of NYCHA, see Nicholas Dagen Bloom, *Public Housing That Worked: New York in the Twentieth Century* (University of Pennsylvania Press, 2008).
23. Kessner, *Fiorello La Guardia*, pp. 323–325.
24. Williams, *City of Ambition*, p. 183.
25. Williams, *City of Ambition*, p. 155.
26. See Ira Katznelson, *Fear Itself: The New Deal and the Origins of Our Time* (Liveright, 2014).
27. *The Complete Report of Mayor La Guardia's Commission on the Harlem Riot of March 19, 1935* (Arno Press, 1969).
28. See Dominic J. Capeci Jr., *The Harlem Riot of 1943* (Temple University Press, 1977).
29. City of New York, Office of the Mayor, "Interim Order in the Conduct of Relations between the City of New York and Its Employees," July 21, 1954.
30. Chris McNickle, *To Be Mayor of New York: Ethnic Politics in the City* (Columbia University Press, 1993), pp. 144–145.
31. Richard Flanagan, *Robert Wagner and the Rise of New York City's Plebiscitary Mayoralty* (Palgrave Macmillan, 2015), p. 69.
32. See Joshua B. Freeman, *Working Class New York: Life and Labor since World War II* (The New Press, 2000); Mark H. Maier, *City Unions: Managing Discontent in New York City* (Rutgers University Press, 1987).
33. Raymond Horton, *Municipal Labor Relations: Lessons from the Lindsay-Wagner Years* (Praeger, 1973), pp. 23–27.
34. See Joseph P. Viteritti, "The Tradition of Municipal Reform: Charter Revision in Historical Context," in Frank J. Mauro and Gerald Benjamin, eds., *Restructuring the New York City Government: The Reemergence of Municipal Reform* (Academy of Political Science, 1989), pp. 16–30.
35. Flanagan, *Robert Wagner and the Rise of New York City's Plebiscitary Mayoralty*, pp. 35–36.
36. Jerilyn Perine and Michael H. Schill, "Reflecting on New York City's Housing Policy: 1987 to 2004," in Harris Beider, ed., *Neighborhood Renewal & Housing Markets: Community Engagement in the US and UK* (Blackwell, 2007), p. 98.
37. Diane Ravitch, *The Great School Wars: A History of the New York City Schools* (Basic Books, 1974), pp. 251–286.
38. Barry Gottehrer, ed., *New York City in Crisis: A Study in Depth of Urban Sickness* (Pocket Books, 1965).
39. The most comprehensive analysis of the Lindsay administration is Vincent Cannato, *The Ungovernable City: John Lindsay and His Struggle to Save New York* (Basic Books, 2001). For a more sympathetic, though hardly uncritical assessment, see the collection of essays in Joseph P. Viteritti, ed., *Summer in the City: John Lindsay, New York, and the American Dream* (Johns Hopkins University Press, 2014). See also the collection co-sponsored by the Museum of the City of New York, Sam Roberts, ed., *America's Mayor: John V. Lindsay and the Reinvention of New York* (Columbia University Press, 2010).
40. "Text of Lindsay's Address to New York Lawyers," *New York Times*, May 21, 1965.
41. See Geoffrey Kabaservice, "On Principle," in Viteritti, *Summer in the City*, pp. 27–58.
42. See Richard Norton Smith, *On His Own Terms: A Life of Nelson Rockefeller* (Random House, 2014), pp. 471–479, 507–510, 559–561.

43. Kabaservice, "On Principle," p. 40.

44. Joshua B. Freeman, "Lindsay and Labor," in Roberts, *America's Mayor*, pp. 118–131.

45. See Joseph P. Viteritti, *Police, Politics, and Pluralism in New York City: A Comparative Case Study* (Sage Publications, 1973).

46. There is a rich literature on this seminal episode. See Ravitch, *The Great School Wars*, pp. 251–404; Cannato, *The Ungovernable City*, pp. 301–351; Richard Kahlenberg, *Tough Liberal: Albert Shanker and the Battles over Schools, Unions, Race, and Democracy* (Columbia University Press, 2007), pp. 93–111; Jerald E. Podair, *The Strike That Changed New York: Blacks, Whites, and the Ocean Hill-Brownsville Crisis* (Yale University Press, 2004); Clarence Taylor, *Knocking at Our Own Door: Milton Galamison and the Struggle to Integrate New York City Schools* (Columbia University Press, 1997), pp. 176–207.

47. Joseph P. Viteritti, *Bureaucracy and Social Justice: The Allocation of Jobs and Services to Minority Groups* (Kennikat Press, 1979), pp. 66–71, 89–110.

48. Clarence Taylor, "Race, Rights, Empowerment," in Viteritti, *Summer in the City*, pp. 61–80.

49. Kabaservice, "On Principle," in Viteritti, *Summer in the City*, p. 49.

50. *Report of the National Advisory Commission on Civil Disorders* (Bantam Books, 1968), pp. 5–6.

51. There is an abundant literature on Johnson's legislative record. For an early journalistic account, see Robert Evans and Robert Novak, *Lyndon Johnson: The Exercise of Power* (New American Library, 1966), pp. 406–434. For insider accounts, see Joseph A. Califano, *The Triumph and Tragedy of Lyndon Johnson: The White House Years* (Texas A&M University Press, 2000), pp. 106–164; Eric Goldman, *The Tragedy of Lyndon Johnson* (Knopf, 1968), pp. 305–399. For fuller biographies, see Robert Caro, *The Passage of Power: The Years of Lyndon Johnson* (Knopf, 2012), pp. 558–570; Robert Dallek, *Flawed Giant: Lyndon Johnson and His Times* (Oxford University Press, 1998), pp. 185–287; Randall B. Woods, *LBJ: Architect of Ambition* (Harvard University Press, 2006), pp. 440–482, 557, 592, 649–692.

52. For a recent assessment of Johnson's long-term legacy, see Randall B. Woods, *Prisoners of Hope: Lyndon B. Johnson and the Limits of Liberalism* (Basic Books, 2016).

53. See generally Sar Levitan, *The Great Society's Poor Law: A New Approach to Poverty* (Johns Hopkins University Press, 1969); Daniel P. Moynihan, *Maximum Feasible Misunderstanding* (Vintage, 1971).

54. See Viteritti, *Bureaucracy and Social Justice*, pp. 76–82.

55. Statutes of the State of New York, Chapter 634, May 26, 1972.

56. See Viteritti, "The Tradition of Municipal Reform."

57. David Rogers, "Management versus Bureaucracy," in Viteritti, *Summer in the City*, pp. 107–136.

58. Charles R. Morris, "Of Budgets, Taxes, and the Rise of a New Plutocracy," in Viteritti, *Summer in the City*, p. 84.

59. Lizabeth Cohen and Brian Goldstein, "Governing at the Tipping Point: Shaping the City's Role in Economic Development," in Viteritti, *Summer in the City*, p. 167.

60. Paul Goldberger, "A Design Conscious Mayor: The Physical City," in Viteritti, *Summer in the City*, pp. 139–260; Hillary Ballon, "The Physical City," in Roberts, *America's Mayor*, pp. 132–146.

61. See Mariana Mogilevich, "Arts as Public Policy: Cultural Spaces for Democracy and Growth," in Viteritti, *Summer in the City*, pp. 195–222.

62. On the causes and effects of the fiscal crisis, see generally Charles R. Morris, *The Cost of Good Intentions: New York City and the Liberal Experiment* (Norton, 1980); Martin Shefter, *Political Crisis/Fiscal Crisis: The Collapse and Revival of New York City* (Basic Books, 1985); William K. Tabb, *The Long Default: New York City and the Urban Fiscal Crisis* (Monthly Review Press, 1982).

63. Data in the following two paragraphs are taken from Morris, "Of Budgets, Taxes, and the Rise of Plutocracy", pp. 87–96.

64. For a detailed telling of Carey's role, see Richard Ravitch, *So Much to Do: A Full Life of Business, Politics, and Confronting Fiscal Crises* (Public Affairs, 2014), pp. 71–99; Seymour P. Lachman and Robert Polner, *The Man Who Saved New York: Hugh Carey and the Great Fiscal Crisis of 1975* (State University of New York Press, 2010), pp. 75–166.

65. For an institutional roadmap, see Robert W. Bailey, *The Crisis Regime: The MAC, the EFCB, and the Political Impact of the New York City Financial Crisis* (State University of New York Press, 1984).

66. Bailey, *The Crisis Regime*, pp. 179–190.

67. Cannato, *The Ungovernable City*, p. ix. See also Fred Siegel, *The Future Once Happened Here: New York, D.C., L.A., and the Fate of America's Big Cities* (Encounter Books, 1997).

Chapter 5

1. The most comprehensive scholarly work on Koch is Jonathan Soffer, *Ed Koch and the Rebuilding of New York* (Columbia University Press, 2010), but see also *Koch* (2012), the documentary film by Neil Barsky that was released in 2013 days after Koch's death. For an unrestrained personalized *critique* (perhaps *attack* is a more accurate designation) by three respected journalists, see Arthur Browne, Dan Collins, and Michael Goodwin, *I Koch: A Decidedly Unauthorized Biography of the Mayor of New York City, Edward I. Koch* (Dodd Mead, 1985).

2. Soffer, *Ed Koch*, pp. 89–93.

3. Scatter-site housing is an approach to racial and economic integration that "scatters" publicly subsidized low-income housing though middle-income neighborhoods. Clarence Taylor, "Race, Rights, Empowerment," in Joseph P. Viteritti, ed., *Summer in the City: John Lindsay, New York, and the American Dream* (Johns Hopkins University Press, 2014), pp. 61–80; Mario Cuomo, *Forest Hills Diary: The Crisis of Low Income Housing* (Random House, 1974).

4. "The Blackout: A Night of Terror," *Time*, July 25, 1977. For a snapshot of that year that intertwines politics, baseball, and popular culture, see Jonathan Mahler, *Ladies and Gentlemen, the Bronx Is Burning: 1977, Politics, and the Battle for the Soul of the City* (Picador, 2006).

5. See Dennis Hamill, "Hi, I'm for Capital Punishment. Are You?," *Village Voice*, September 5, 1977, p. 35.

6. See Soffer, *Ed Koch*, pp. 129–142; Chris McNickle, *To Be Mayor of New York: Ethnic Politics in the City* (Columbia University Press, 1993), pp. 262–270.

7. http://www.ourcampaigns.com/RaceDetail.html?RaceID=78427

8. http://www.ourcampaigns.com/RaceDetail.html?RaceID=79303

9. See James R. Brigham and Alair Townsend, "The Fiscal Crisis," in Michael Goodwin, ed., *New York Comes Back: The Mayoralty of Edward I. Koch* (Powerhouse Books/Museum for the City of New York, 2005), pp. 29–33. The authors of this essay had, at different times, served as budget directors in the Koch administration.

10. Theodore J. Lowi, *The End of Liberalism: The Second Republic of the United States* (W.W. Norton, 1969). See also Lowi, *At the Pleasure of the Mayor: Patronage and Power in New York City, 1898–1958* (Free Press, 1964).

11. Ken Auletta, "Profiles: E.I. Koch," *The New Yorker*, September 10, 1979.

12. Blanche Bernstein, *The Politics of Welfare: The New York Experience* (Abt Books, 1982).

13. John Hull Mollenkopf, *A Phoenix in the Ashes: The Rise and Fall of the Koch Coalition in New York City Politics* (Princeton University Press, 1992), pp. 100–128.

14. http://www.ourcampaigns.com/RaceDetail.html?RaceID=87220; http://www.ourcampaigns.com/RaceDetail.html?RaceID=84398

15. http://www.ourcampaigns.com/RaceDetail.html?RaceID=79306

16. McNickle, *To Be Mayor of New York*, p. 278.

17. Soffer, *Ed Koch*, p. 151.

18. Ward Moorehouse III, "New York Mayor Koch Joins in Criticism of Reagan," *Christian Science Monitor*, December 30, 1981.

19. A three-volume final report and recommendations were released on February 24, 1987. See Joseph P. Viteritti, "Police Professionalism in New York City: The Zuccotti Committee in Historical Perspective," Center for Research in Crime and Justice, New York University School of Law, 1987. In the spirit of full disclosure, I should mention that I served as Executive Director of the Commission.

20. See Joseph P. Viteritti, *Across the River: Politics and Education in the City* (Holmes & Meier, 1983). Again, in the spirit of full disclosure, I served as special assistant to Chancellor Macchiarola from 1978 to 1983.

21. Soffer, *Ed Koch*, p. 311, and see more generally pp. 305–316.

22. *Callahan v. Carey*, Index No. 42582/79 Sup. Ct. NY County, final judgment by consent.

23. For a review of that legal history, see Thomas J. Main, *Homelessness in New York City: Policy Making from Koch to de Blasio* (New York University Press, 2016), pp. 13–69.

24. Kim Hopper and L. Stuart Cox, "Litigation in Advocacy for the Homeless: The Case of New York City" (Community Service Society, 1982).

25. Stephen Crystal et al., "Chronic and Situational Dependency: Long Term Residents in a Shelter for Men" (Human Resources Administration, 1983).

26. See generally Miriam Greenberg, *Rebranding New York: How a City in Crisis Was Sold to the World* (Routledge, 2008).

27. Lynn B. Sagalyn, *Times Square Roulette: Remaking the City Icon* (MIT Press, 2001), pp. 104–133.

28. Soffer, *Ed Koch*, p. 289.

29. Bruce F. Berg, *New York City Politics: Governing Gotham* (Rutgers University Press, 2007), p. 66.

30. Soffer, *Ed Koch*, p. 300.

31. Jerilyn Perine and Michael H. Schill, "Reflecting on New York City's Housing Policy: 1987 to 2004," in Harris Beider, ed. *Neighborhood Renewal & Housing Markets: Community Engagement in the US and UK* (Blackwell, 2007), p. 97.

32. Nicholas Dagen Bloom and Matthew Gordon Lasner, eds., *Affordable Housing in New York* (Princeton University Press, 2016), pp. 245–289.

33. Jonathan Soffer, "The Koch Plan," in Bloom and Lasner, *Affordable Housing in New York*, pp. 273–276.

34. Eileen B. Berenyi, "Locally Funded Housing Programs in the United States; A Survey of the Fifty-One Most Populated Cities" (New School for Social Research, 1989).

35. http://www.ourcampaigns.com/RaceDetail.html?RaceID=79307

36. Jack Newfield and Wayne Barrett, *City for Sale: Ed Koch and the Betrayal of New York City* (Harper Collins, 1988).

37. See Charles J. Hynes and Bob Drury, *Incident at Howard Beach: The Case for Murder* (Putnam, 1990).

38. It was later determined that five teenagers had been wrongfully convicted, and that the victim had been attacked by a single assailant.

39. Mollenkopf, *A Phoenix in the Ashes*, p. 132.

40. To date, there are three scholarly books on Dinkins: Chris McNickle, *The Power of the Mayor: David Dinkins, 1990–1993* (Transaction Publishers, 2013); Wilber C. Rich, *David Dinkins and New York City Politics: Race, Images, and the Media* (State University of New York Press, 2007); and J. Philip Thompson III, *Double Trouble: Black Mayors, Black Communities, and the Call for Deep Democracy* (Oxford University Press, 2006).

41. Thompson, *Double Trouble*, p. 183. For a general account of the Jackson campaigns, see Thompson, *Double Trouble*, pp. 182–188.

42. "The New York Primary: Dinkins Sweeps Past Koch for Nomination: Giuliani Easily Wins Republican Primary: Mayor Offers Help," *New York Times*, September 13, 1989.

43. McNickle, *The Power of the Mayor*, pp. 35–46.

44. Sam Roberts, "The 1989 Elections: The New York Vote; Almost Lost at the Wire," *New York Times*, November 9, 1989.

45. The Associated Press, "Dinkins Faults the Tactics," *New York Times*, June 28, 1988, p. B5.

46. Rich, *David Dinkins and New York City Politics*.

47. McNickle, *The Power of the Mayor*, p. 62.

48. Rich, *David Dinkins and New York City Politics*, p. 51.

49. Transcript: Mayor David Dinkins "The Reform and Renaissance of New York City Government—Making the Future Work for Us," July 30, 1991.

50. The material in the previous three paragraphs is drawn from McNickle, *The Power of the Mayor*, pp. 71–114, 124–137.

51. Kim Moody, *From Welfare State to Real Estate: Regime Change in New York City, 1974 to the Present* (The New Press, 2007), p. 123.

52. "A Shelter Is Not a Home," Manhattan Borough President's Taskforce on Housing for Homeless Families, March 1987.

53. For an overview of Dinkins's approach to homelessness, see Main, *Homelessness in New York City*, pp. 69–104.

54. Main, *Homelessness in New York City*, p. 91.

55. Main, *Homelessness in New York City*, p. 64.
56. See Claire Jean Kim, *Bitter Fruit: The Politics of Black-Korean Conflict in New York City* (Yale University Press, 2003).
57. "Racial and Ethnic Tensions in American Communities: Poverty, Inequality, and Discrimination—A National Perspective," United States Commission on Civil Rights, May 21, 1992.
58. George James, "New York Killings Set a Record, While Other Crimes Fell in 1990," *New York Times*, August 23, 1991.
59. City crime had decreased 15 percent from 1990, subway crime by 31 percent, with the addition of 6,000 officers. Office of the Mayor, "Safe City, Safe Streets II: A Futureprint for Success," September, 1993, p. 2.
60. On the history of the review board, see Joseph P. Viteritti, "Civilian Review Board," in Kenneth T. Jackson, ed., *Encyclopedia of New York City*, 2nd ed. (Yale University Press, 2010), pp. 262–263.
61. Richard H. Girgenti, "A Report to the Governor on the Disturbances in Crown Heights: Vol. 1," December, 1993.
62. Todd S. Purdam, "The 1993 Elections: Mayor Giuliani Ousts Dinkins by a Thin Margin," *New York Times*, November 3, 1993.
63. Mollenkopf, *A Phoenix in the Ashes*, pp. 210–211.
64. For an analysis of the secession question, see Joseph P. Viteritti, "Municipal Home Rule and the Conditions for Justifiable Secession," *Fordham Urban Law Journal*, Vol. 23 (1995), pp. 3–68. Full disclosure: I served as Executive Director of the state commission appointed by Governor Mario Cuomo to study the feasibility and possible impact of Staten Island secession. It was a tribute to the leadership and statesmanship of both Mayor David Dinkins and state Senator John Marchi, who chaired the commission, that the debate over Staten Island's possible separation from the city did not deteriorate into the highly charged racial controversy it might have been.
65. The three most comprehensive books on Giuliani's mayoralty are: Fred Siegel, *The Prince of the City: Giuliani, New York, and the Genius of American Life* (Encounter Books, 2005) (a sympathetic insider); Andrew Kirtzman, *Rudy Giuliani, Emperor of the City* (William Morrow, 2000) (more critical); Jack Newfield, *The Full Rudy: The Man, the Myth, the Mania* (Nation Books, 2002) (most negative). For more acidic brief assessments by journalists, see Wayne Barrett, *Rudy! An Investigative Biography of Rudolph Giuliani* (Basic Books, 2000); Robert Polner, ed., *America's Mayor: The Hidden History of Giuliani's New York* (Soft Skull Press, 2005). See also James Traub, "Giuliani Internalized," *New York Times Magazine*, February 2, 200 (admiring).
66. "The State of the City Economy," Comptroller's Report to the City Council, December 1993.
67. Siegel, *Prince of the City*, pp. 112–113.
68. See Diane Ravitch and Joseph P. Viteritti, "New York: The Obsolete System," in D. Ravitch and J. P. Viteritti, eds., *New Schools for a New Century: The Redesign of Urban Education* (Yale University Press, 2007), pp. 17–36.
69. See Lydia Segal, *Fighting Corruption in America's Public Schools* (Harvard University Press, 2005).
70. See Benno Schmidt, "The City University of New York: An Institution Adrift," Report of the Mayor's Advisory Task Force on the City University of New York, June 7, 1999; James Traub, *City on a Hill: Testing the American Dream at City College* (Perseus, 1995).
71. For a critical assessment of early changes, see David E. Lavin and David Hyllegard, *Changing the Odds: Open Admissions and the Life Chances of the Disadvantaged* (Yale University Press, 1996).
72. See J. Philip Thompson, "The Failure of Liberal Homeless Policy," *Political Science Quarterly*, Vol. 11 (1996–1997), pp. 639–660.
73. "The Way Home: A New Direction in Social Policy," New York City Commission on the Homeless, February, 1992.
74. See generally, Main, *Homelessness in New York City*, pp. 102–139.
75. Alex Vitale, *City of Disorder: How the Quality of Life Campaign Transformed New York Politics* (New York University Press, 2008), pp. 115–143.

76. Main, *Homelessness in New York City*, p. 110.
77. Sam Tsemberis and Ronda E. Eisenberg, "Pathways to Housing: Supported Housing for Street-Dwelling Individuals with Psychiatric Disabilities," *Psychiatric Services*, Vol. 51 (April 2000), pp. 487–493.
78. See Ted Haughton, "A Description and History of the New York/New York Agreement to House Homeless Mentally Ill Individuals" (Corporation for Supportive Housing, May 2001).
79. See Lawrence M. Mead, *The New Paternalism: Supervisory Approaches to Poverty* (Brookings Institution Press, 1997), describing the approach.
80. State of the City Address: Archives of Rudolph W. Giuliani, http://www.nyc/htlm/records/rwg/html96/city95.html.
81. Siegel, *Prince of the City*, p. 162.
82. Moody, *From Welfare State to Real Estate*, p. 285.
83. Lawrence M. Mead, *Government Matters: Welfare Reform in Wisconsin* (Princeton University Press, 2005).
84. "Welfare Reform: Work-Site Based Activities Can Play an Important Role in TANF Programs," Federal Accounting Office, 2000.
85. Michael H. Schill and Benjamin P. Scafidi, "Housing Conditions and Problems in New York City," in Michael H. Schill, ed., *Housing and Community Development in New York City: Facing the Future* (State University of New York Press, 1998), p. 30.
86. Alex F. Schwartz and Avis C. Vidal, "Between a Rock and a Hard Place: The Impact of Federal and State Policy Changes on Housing in New York City," in Schill, *Housing and Community Development*, pp. 235–236.
87. Frank P. Braconi, "In Re *In Rem*: Innovation and Expediency in New York's Housing Policy," in Schill, *Housing and Community Development*, pp. 102–109.
88. Perine and Schill, "Reflecting on New York City's Housing Policy: 1987 to 2004," in Beider, *Neighborhood Renewal*, p. 102.
89. Charles Bagli, "Largesse," in Polner, *America's Mayor*, pp. 49–61.
90. Moody, *From Welfare State to Real Estate*, p. 123.
91. Susan S. Fainstein, *The City Builders: Property Development in New York and London, 1980–2000* (University Press of Kansas, 2001), p. 59.
92. http://www.ourcampaigns.com/RaceDetail.html?RaceID=55046.
93. James Jacobs, *Gotham Unbound: How New York Was Liberated from the Grip of Organized Crime* (New York University Press, 1999).
94. Eli Silverman, *NYPD Battles Crime: Innovative Strategies in Policing* (Northeastern University Press, 1999), pp. 97–204.
95. See James Q. Wilson and George L. Kelling, "Broken Windows: The Police and Neighborhood Safety," *Atlantic Monthly*, Vol. 249 (March 1982). See also the discussion in Chapter 1.
96. Silverman, *NYPD Battles Crime*, p. 6
97. FBI data indicates a drop in all seven index offenses from 1990 to 2000: homicide (73 percent), rape (52 percent), robbery (70 percent), assault (46 percent), burglary (72 percent), auto theft (73 percent), and larceny (53 percent). Franklin E. Zimring, *The City That Became Safe: New York's Lessons for Urban Crime and Its Control* (Oxford University Press, 2012), p. 6.
98. Al Baker, "Bratton, Who Shaped an Era in Policing, Tries to Navigate a Racial Divide," *New York Times*, July 25, 2016.
99. Eric Pooley, "One Good Apple," *Time*, January 15, 1996.
100. Siegel, *Prince of the City*, p. 232.

Chapter 6

1. American Community Survey, U.S. Census.
2. See Isabel Wilkerson, *The Warmth of Other Suns: The Epic Story of the Great Migration* (Random House, 2010).
3. "Decennial Census–Census 2000," NYC Planning, http://www1.nyc.gov/site/planning/data-maps/nyc-population/census-summary-2000.page

4. U.S. Census Bureau, 2006–2010, American Community Survey.
5. There is a misperception about Asians being a "model minority." There are, however, serious class cleavages among them and incidents of economic exploitation. See Peter Kwong and Dusanka Miscevic, *Chinese America: The Untold Story of America's Oldest New Community* (New Press, 2007).
6. "The CEO Poverty Measure, 2005–2011," Annual Report by the New York City Center for Economic Opportunity, April 2013.
7. Unemployment data are drawn from U.S. Census published rates. See also Patrick McGeehan, "Jobless Rate in June Rose to 10% in City, Despite Hiring," *New York Times,* June 20, 2012.
8. "NYC Median Family Income up for the First Time since Great Recession," Fiscal Policy Institute, October 15, 2014.
9. "The Middle Income Squeeze: A Report on the City's Middle Class," The City Council of New York, February 2010.
10. James Parrott, "Patterns of Income Polarization in New York City," paper presented at the American Sociological Association, New York City, August 13, 2013.
11. "While Some Improvement Crept in during 2012, NYC's Family Incomes and Poverty Status Are Still Much Worse than before the Recession," Fiscal Policy Institute, September 20, 2014.
12. Charles R. Morris, "Of Budgets, Taxes, and the Rise of a New Plutocracy," in Joseph P. Viteritti, ed., *Summer in the City: John Lindsay, New York, and the American Dream* (Johns Hopkins University Press, 2014), p. 100.
13. See, for example, Kay Lehman Schlozman, Sidney Verba, and Henry E. Brady, *The Unheavenly Chorus: Unequal Political Voice and the Broken Promise of American Democracy* (Princeton University Press, 2012).
14. The 1989 balloting also included an important referendum on the City Charter that restructured the government. Bloomberg spent unprecedented amounts of money on his 2001 campaign.
15. New York City Campaign Finance Board, *Campaign Finance Summary 1989 Citywide Elections,* June 9, 2016.
16. He had spent $73,109,266 and $84,587,319 in 2001 and 2005 respectively, according to the New York City Campaign Finance Board.
17. New York City Campaign Finance Board, Bill de Blasio (2013 Mayor Financial Summary).
18. Of course, as Donald Trump's election as president in 2016 has demonstrated, populism can also move politics to the right, in many directions simultaneously, or to a total state of confusion for that matter.
19. Among the most influential economists, see Emmanuel Saez and Gabriel Zucan, "Wealth Inequality in the United States since 1913: Evidence from Capitalized Income Data," *Quarterly Journal of Economics,* Vol. 13 (2016), pp. 519–578; Thomas Piketty, *Capital in the Twenty-First Century* (Belknap Press, 2014) (a historical international analysis); Joseph E. Stiglitz, *The Price of Inequality* (W.W. Norton, 2012); Paul Krugman, *The Conscience of a Liberal* (W.W. Norton, 2009). Among the most commonly cited works in political science are Jacob S. Hacker and Paul Pierson, *Winner-Take-All Politics: How Washington Made the Rich Richer—and Turned Its Back on the Middle Class* (Simon & Schuster, 2010); Larry M. Bartels, *Unequal Democracy: The Political Economy of the New Gilded Age* (Princeton University Press, 2010); Jeffrey A. Winters and Benjamin Page, "Oligarchy in the United States," *Perspectives on Politics,* Vol. 7 (2009), pp. 731–751.
20. This should not be confused with Donald Trump's reference to a "rigged election" in 2016.
21. Stiglitz, *The Price of Inequality,* pp. 187–202.
22. Stiglitz, *The Price of Inequality,* p. 253.
23. Charles R. Morris, *The Two Trillion Dollar Meltdown: Easy Money, High Rollers, and the Great Credit Crash* (Public Affairs, 2008).
24. Stiglitz, *The Price of Inequality,* p. 110.
25. Sheila Bair, *Bull by the Horns: Fighting to Save Main Street from Wall Street and Wall Street from Itself* (Simon & Shuster, 2013), pp. 165–174. See also Neil Barofsky, *Bailout: An Inside Account of How Washington Abandoned Main Street while Rescuing Wall Street* (Free Press, 2012).
26. Jacob S. Hacker and Paul Pierson, "Winner-Take-All Politics: Public Policy, Political Organization, and the Precipitous Rise of Top Incomes in the United States," *Politics and Society,* Vol. 38 (2010), pp. 152–204.

27. *Citizens United v. Federal Election Commission*, 558 U.S. 10 (2010).
28. Thomas Piketty and Emmanuel Saez, "How Progressive Is the U.S. Federal Tax System? A Historical and International Perspective," *Journal of Economic Perspectives*, Vol. 21 (2007), pp. 3–24.
29. Carola Frydman and Raven Saks, "Historical Trends in Executive Compensation, 1936–2003," working paper, Massachusetts Institute of Technology, Cambridge, MA, 2005.
30. Hacker and Pierson, "Winner-Take-All Politics," pp. 192–193.
31. Morris, "Of Budgets, Taxes, and the Rise of a New Plutocracy," p. 101.
32. There are two books on Bloomberg's mayoralty thus far: Joyce Purnick, *Mike Bloomberg: Money, Power, Politics* (Public Affairs, 2009); Julien Brash, *Bloomberg's New York: Class and Governance in the Luxury City* (University of Georgia Press, 2011). As I write, Eleanor Randolph is at work on a new book, which will probably have appeared at about the same time as the one you are reading.
33. http://www.forbes.com/profile/michael-bloomberg/
34. http://vote.nyc.ny.us/downloads/pdf/results/2001/primaryelection/2001runoff.pdf
35. "Mark Green for Mayor," *New York Times*, October 29, 2001.
36. Geoffrey Gray, "Baby Bust at Bloomberg?," *New York Magazine*, October 2, 2006; Ed Vulliamy, "Is Michael Bloomberg the New Citizen Kane?," *The Guardian*, May 20, 2001; Dean Murphy, "Campaigning for City Hall: Controversies, Questions Raised over a Gag Gift to Bloomberg from 1990," *New York Times*, September 8, 2001.
37. The exact amounts were $73,109,266 versus $17,359,109. New York City Campaign Finance Board, Mark Green (2001 Mayor Financial Summary).
38. http://vote.nyc.ny.us/downloads/pdf/results/2001/generalelection/general2001.pdf
39. Bloomberg did hire experienced, highly regarded public sector managers: Peter Madonia, a veteran of the Koch administration, was his Chief of Staff; Deputy Mayor for Operations Marc Shaw, who had previously served as CEO for the Metropolitan Transportation Authority, eventually became First Deputy, but stayed for only one term; Budget Director Mark Page remained throughout; and Dennis Walcott, after serving as deputy mayor became schools chancellor when Joel Klein left; but none of the aforementioned wielded the same influence as Harris, Doctoroff, or Sheekey.
40. Brash, *Bloomberg's New York*, p. 17.
41. Diane Cardwell, "Mayor Says New York Is Worth the Cost," *New York Times*, January 8, 2003.
42. Diane Cardwell, "Mayor to Put His Charity in Upper East Side Building," *New York Times*, July 2, 2006.
43. Paul Sullivan, "Giving Like Michael Bloomberg: 'Find One Small Thing,'" *New York Times*, May 20, 2016.
44. Michael Barbaro and David Chen, "Top Bloomberg Aide Will Lead His Charity Board," *New York Times*, March 31, 1010.
45. Ferrer had beaten Public Advocate Gifford Miller and Congressman Anthony Weiner in the Democratic primary to win the nomination.
46. Michael Bloomberg (2005) Mayor, Financial Summary from New York City Campaign Finance Board; Fernando Ferrer (2005) Mayor, Financial Summary from New York City Campaign Finance Board.
47. Steven Lee Myers, "The 1993 Elections: New York City Roundup: Vallone Says Term Limits Issue Is 'Not Dead,'" *New York Times*, November 4, 1993.
48. David Chen, "Dust-Up of the Debate Occasionally Obscures Some Facts," *New York Times*, October 14, 2009.
49. "Statement and Return Report for Certification: General Election 2009," Board of Elections of the City of New York, November 3, 2009.
50. "Campaign Finance Summary: 2009 Citywide Elections," New York City Campaign Finance Board, January 15, 2010.
51. Javier C. Hernandez, "Once Again, City Voters Approve Term Limits," *New York Times*, November 3, 2010. Full disclosure: I served as Research Director of the Charter Commission chaired by Matthew Goldstein that placed the term limit question on the ballot. I do not support term limits philosophically, and actually testified against it at the request of Speaker Peter Vallone when the City Council was considering overturning it in 1996. I agreed, however,

with the chair and a majority of members of the 2010 Charter Commission who believed that the voters were entitled to another opportunity to voice their preferences and make a final determination on the issue.

52. Purnick, *Mike Bloomberg*, p. 49.
53. Purnick, *Mike Bloomberg*, p. 197, quoting David Jones of the Community Service Society.
54. Purnick, *Mike Bloomberg*, p. 3.
55. David Seifman, Kaya Witehouse, and Jennifer Gould Kiel, "Bloomie Blitz Aims to Halt Hedge Clippers," *New York Post*, January 23, 2010.
56. Michael Grynbaum, "Bloomberg Sues City Council to Overturn Two Laws Raising Wages," *New York Times*, July 28, 2012.
57. Franklin E. Zimring, *The City That Became Safe: New York's Lessons for Urban Crime and Its Control* (Oxford, 2012), p. 6.
58. *Floyd et al. v. City of New York*, U.S. Court of Appeals, Second Circuit, decided October 31, 2014.
59. "Policing the Police on Stop-and-Frisk," *New York Times*, June 23, 2016.
60. See Joseph P. Viteritti, "Abolish the Board of Education," *New York Times*, January 6, 2002.
61. See generally, Joseph P. Viteritti, ed., *When Mayors Take Charge: School Governance in the City* (Brookings Institution Press, 2009).
62. See Joseph P. Viteritti, "The New Charter: Will It Make a Difference?," in Jewel Bellush and Dick Netzer, eds., *Urban Politics, New York Style* (M.E. Sharpe, 1990), pp. 413–428.
63. New York City Independent Budget Office, Focus on Schools, http://www.ibo.nyc.ny.us/ publicationsEducation.html
64. Leanna Stiefel and Amy Schwartz, "Financing K-12 Education in the Bloomberg Years, 2002–2008," in Jennifer A. O'Day, Catherine S. Bitter, and Louis M. Gomez, eds., *Education Reform in the Nation's Most Complex School System* (Harvard Education Press, 2011), pp. 55–84.
65. Stacy Childress, Monica Higgins, Ann Ishimaru, and Sola Takahashi, "Managing for Results at the New York City Department of Education," in O'Day, Bitter, and Gomez, *Education Reform in the Nation's Most Complex School System*, pp 87–108; Joan Talbert, "Collaborative Inquiry to Expand Student Success in New York City Schools," in O'Day, Bitter, and Gomez, pp. 155–177.
66. Jennifer O'Day and Catherine Bitter, "Reflections on Children First," in O'Day, Bitter, and Gomez, *Education Reform in the Nation's Most Complex School System*, pp 293–335. See also Joseph P. Viteritti, "Stumbling Through: How Joel Klein Reinvented the New York City Schools," *Journal of School Choice*, Vol. 6, pp. 411–422.
67. Harold S. Bloom, Saskia Levy Thompson, and Rebecca Unterman, *Transforming the High School Experience: How New York City Small Schools Are Boosting Student Achievement and Graduation Rates* (MDRC, 2010); Harold S. Bloom and Rebecca Unterman, Sustained Progress: New Findings about the Effectiveness and Operation of Small Public High Schools of Choice in New York City (MRCC, 2013).
68. "School Indicators for New York City Charter Schools, 2013–2014 School Year." New York City Independent Budget Office, July 2015.
69. C. M. Hoxby, S. Murarka, and J. Katz, *New York Charter School Education Project: How New York City's Charter Schools Affect Achievement* (August 2009 Report, Second in a Series). Center for Research on Educational Outcomes (CREDO), *Charter School Performance in New York City*, Palo Alto, CA, 2010.
70. Center for Research on Education Outcomes (CREDO), *Urban Charter School Study, Report on 41 Regions* (Palo Alto, CA, 2015).
71. "Closings in Chicago: Understanding Families' Choices and Constraints for New School Enrollments," University of Chicago Consortium on Chicago School Research, January 2015.
72. James Kemple, "School Closures in New York City," *Education Next*, Vol. 16 (Fall 2016).
73. *Final Report of the Commission on School Governance*, prepared for Betsy Gotbaum, Public Advocate for New York City, September 4, 2008. Full disclosure: I served as Executive Director of the Commission and oversaw its research.
74. See Viteritti, *When Mayors Take Charge*, especially the chapters by Diane Ravitch, Clara Hemphill, and Joseph Viteritti.

75. Between 2002 and 2013, average fourth grade reading scores increased from 206 to 216; from 2003 to 2013, eighth grade reading scores increased from 252 to 256; from 2003 to 2013, fourth grade math scores increased from 226 to 236; from 2003 to 2013, eighth grade math scores increased from 266 to 274. National Assessment for Education Progress. Results on state performance tests showed more improvement, but because the tests and their standards were altered midway through Bloomberg's term, they were an unreliable measure of progress.

76. See Howard Chernick, ed., *Resilient City: The Economic Impact of 9/11* (Russell Sage Foundation, 2005), pp. 1–3, 295–296.

77. The Citizens Budget Commission estimated a deficit of $2.3 to $2.5.billion. Citizens Budget Commission, "A Review of the January 2001 Financial Plan for New York City for Fiscal Years 2002 to 2005," March 29, 2001, http://www.cbcny.org/sites/default/files/report_nycfy0205_03292001.pdf. In his FY 2003 budget, Bloomberg was projecting a shortfall of $4.8 billion.

78. For a detailed overview of the project, see Lynne B. Sagalyn, *Power at Ground Zero: Politics, Money, and the Remaking of Lower Manhattan* (Oxford University Press, 2016).

79. See Lynn B. Sagalyn, "The Politics of Planning the World's Most Visible Urban Development Project," in John Mollenkopf, ed., *Contentious City: The Politics of Recovery in New York City* (Russell Sage, 2005), pp. 23–72.

80. Mitchell I. Moss, "The Redevelopment of Lower Manhattan: The Role of the City," in Mollenkopf, *Contentious City,* pp. 95–111.

81. Brash, *Bloomberg's New York,* pp. 144–253.

82. Thomas J. Lueck, "Bloomberg Draws a Blueprint for a Greener City," *New York Times,* April 23, 2007. *PlaNYC 2011* expanded on these initiatives to strengthen the focus on environmental stability and livable neighborhoods. *PlaNYC: A Stronger, More Resilient New York* was published in 2013 to document lessons learned from Hurricane Sandy.

83. Alex Gavin and Associates, "Visions for New York City: Housing and the Public Realm," prepared for the New York City Economic Development Corporation, 2006.

84. Tom Angotti, "Is New York's Sustainability Plan Sustainable?," paper presented at the Joint Conference of the Association of Collegiate Schools of Planning and the Association of European Schools of Planning, ACSP/AESOP, July 2008.

85. "PlaNYC: Progress Report 2013," June 7, 2013.

86. Tom Farley, *Saving Gotham: A Billionaire Mayor, Activist Doctors, and the Fight for Eight Million Lives* (W.W. Norton, 2015), p. 258.

87. Thomas Main, *Homelessness in New York City: Policymaking from Koch to de Blasio* (New York University Press, 2016), pp. 140–184.

88. "Uniting for Solutions beyond Shelter: The Action Plan for New York City," September 22, 2004.

89. Thomas Main, *Homelessness in New York City,* pp. 158–159.

90. "The Rising Number of Homeless Families in NYC, 2002–2012: A Look at Why Families Were Granted Shelter, the Housing They Had Lived In, and Where They Came From," November, 2014.

91. Fernanda Santos, "Mayor's Effort to Reduce Homelessness Is Off Pace, Study Says," *New York Times,* August 7, 2008.

92. Patrick Markee and Giselle Routhier, "The Revolving Door Spins Faster: New Evidence That the Flawed 'Advantage' Program Forces Many Formerly-Homeless Families Back into Homelessness," Coalition for the Homeless, February 16, 2011.

93. "Broken Promises: Examining the Cost of New York City Housing Authority Reneging on Its Commitment to Vulnerable New Yorkers," Office of the Public Advocate, June 19, 2010.

94. Michael Howard Saul, "End of Rent Subsidies Has Critics Pouncing," *Wall Street Journal,* February 4, 2012; Elisabeth Brown, "As Rental Subsidies for Families End, Time in Shelter Grows," Independent Budget Office, February 23, 2012.

95. Giselle Routhier, "State of Homelessness in 2016: Beyond the Rhetoric: What Will Turn the Tide?" Coalition for the Homeless, April, 2016.

96. "The New Housing Marketplace Plan 2003–2014," New York City Department of Housing and Preservation Development.

97. The data in this paragraph are cited in Kim Moody, *From Welfare State to Real Estate: Regime Change in New York City, 1974 to the Present* (The New Press, 2007), pp. 170–172, drawing on reports from the New York City Finance department.

98. Mark S. Rosentraub, *Major League Losers: The Real Cost of Sports and Who's Paying for It* (Basic Books, 1997); Mark S. Rosentraub, *Reversing Urban Decline: Why and How Sports, Entertainment and Culture Turn Cities into Major League Winners* (CCRC Press, 2014).

99. Susan S. Fainstein, *The Just City* (Cornell University Press, 2010), pp. 106–131.

100. "Real Affordability: An Evaluation of Bloomberg's Housing Program and Recommendations to Strengthen Affordable Housing Policy," Association for Neighborhood and Housing Development, February, 2013.

101. Gina Bellafante, "When Affordable Is Just a Word," *New York Times*, April 12, 2013.

102. See *My Brooklyn*, a touching personal story by documentary filmmaker Kelly Anderson about the remaking of the Fulton Mall in Downtown Brooklyn.

103. See Tom Angotti, *New York for Sale: Community Planning Confronts Global Real Estate* (MIT Press, 2008); Susan Fainstein, *The City Builders: Property Development in New York and London, 1980–2000* (University Press of Kansas, 2001); Michael Sorkin and Sharon Zukin, eds., *After the World Trade Center: Rethinking New York City* (Routledge, 2012); Brash, *Bloomberg's New York*.

104. Saskia Sassen, *The Global City: New York, London, and Tokyo* (Princeton University Press, 2001); Hank V. Savitch and Paul Kantor, *Cities in the International Marketplace: The Political Economy of Urban Development in North America and Europe* (Princeton University Press, 2004).

105. *Kelo v. New London*, 545 U.S. 469 (2005).

106. Michael Barbaro and Megan Thee-Brenan, "Poll Shows New Yorkers Are Deeply Conflicted over Bloomberg's Legacy," *New York Times*, August 16, 1013.

Chapter 7

1. Bill de Blasio, personal communication, January 2013.

2. De Blasio mayoral candidacy announcement (Full Speech), January 27, 2013.

3. I am referring, of course, to Thornton Wilder's *Our Town* (1938), the Pulitzer Prize-winning masterpiece.

4. Jonathan Van Meter, "Madam Would-Be Mayor," *New York Magazine*, January 27, 2013.

5. Quinn raised about $7.9 million in total: http://www.nyccfb.info/VSApps/CandidateSummary. aspx?as_cand_id=204&as_election_cycle=2013&cand_name=Quinn,%20Christine%20 C&office=Mayor&report=summ

6. Christine Quinn, *Christine Quinn Launches Her NYC Mayoral Campaign*, March 10, 2013.

7. Van Meter, "Madam Would-Be Mayor."

8. He spent $102 million of his own fortune, or about $174 per vote. Michael Barbaro, "Bloomberg Spent $102 Million to Win Third Term," *New York Times*, November 27, 2009.

9. Sheila McClear, "Bill de Blasio Is Running for Mayor, but His Son's Afro Is Winning Popularity," *New York Daily News*, January 28, 2013.

10. Quinnipiac University Poll, "Quinn Close to 40% in New York City Dem Primary, Quinnipiac University Poll Finds; Voters More Comfortable with Gay than Biz Exec Mayor," February 27, 2013.

11. "Lewd Photo Sent Over Rep. Weiner's Hacked Twitter Account," NBC New York, May 29, 2011.

12. The Rachel Maddow Show, June 1, 2011, http://www.msnbc.com/transcripts/rachel-maddow-show/2011-06-01

13. CNN, The Situation Room with Wolf Blitzer, June 1, 2011, CNN, http://cnnpressroom. blogs.cnn.com/2011/06/01/rep-weiner-i-dont-know-what-photographs-are-out-there-in-the-world-of-me.

14. Clyde Haberman, "Yet Again, A Politician's Instinct Is to Lie," *New York Times*, June 7, 2011.

15. Donald Trump, "From the Desk of Donald Trump 6/7/11," June 7, 2011, https://www. youtube.com/watch?v=QNRXpDIX0uQ.

16. Kate Taylor, "Anthony Weiner Longs for a Second Chance in Politics, Friends Say," *New York Times*, July 15, 2012.

17. https://web.archive.org/web/20130929133401/http://keystothecity.uberflip.com/i/121474

18. NBC New York-Marist Poll, "New York City Mayoralty: Weiner Candidacy Could Scramble Democratic Primary Contest," Marist College Institute for Public Opinion, April 16, 2013.

19. Quinnipiac University Poll, "With Big Negatives, Weiner at 15% among NYC Democrats, Quinnipiac University Poll Finds; All Voters Divided on Whether He Should Run," April 19, 2013.

20. Quinnipiac University Poll, "Quinn, Thompson, Weiner Tied in New York City Primary, Quinnipiac University Poll Finds; Kelly Loses to Dem, Tops Lhota in 4-Way Race," June 26, 2013.

21. NBC New York-Marist Poll, "Weiner Surpasses Quinn among NYC Dems . . . Lhota Tops GOP Field in Quest for NYC Mayoralty," Marist College Institute for Public Opinion, June 26, 2013.

22. Quinnipiac University Poll, "Weiner Should Drop Out, NYC Likely Dem Voters Tell Quinnipiac University Poll; Quinn Leads, With de Blasio, Thompson Tied for Second," July 29, 2013.

23. Kate Taylor, "With Democratic Mayoral Field in Flux, de Blasio Assails Quinn," *New York Times*, April 30, 2013.

24. http://vote.nyc.ny.us/downloads/pdf/results/2013/2013SeptemberPrimaryElection/01011000000Citywide%20Democratic%20Mayor%20Citywide%20Recap.pdf

25. Exit Polls, *New York Times*, September 10, 2013.

26. "The Mayoral Primaries," *New York Times*, September 16, 2013, http://www.nytimes.com/projects/elections/2013/nyc-primary/mayor/map.html

27. The Editorial Board, *New York Times*, August 24, 2013.

28. "The Mayoral Primaries," *New York Times*, September 16, 2013.

29. http://www.nytimes.com/projects/elections/2013/general/nyc-mayor/map.html

30. Chris Smith, "In Conversation: Michael Bloomberg," *New York Magazine*, September 7, 2013.

31. Andrew Beveridge, "New York's Changing Electorate: What It Means for the Mayoral Candidates," *Gotham Gazette*, June 16, 2013.

32. Ruth Milkman and Stephanie Luce, "The State of the Unions, 2016: A Profile of Organized Labor in New York City, New York State, and the United States," Murphy Institute for Worker Education and Labor Studies, September, 2016.

33. Joseph P. Viteritti, *Bureaucracy and Social Justice: The Allocation of Jobs and Services to Minority Groups* (Kennikat, 1979), pp. 94–107.

34. Workforce Profile Report, NYC Government, The Mayor's Office of Operations and the Department of Administrative Services, http://www.nyc.gov?html/dcas/downloads/pdf/misc/workforce-_profile_report_12_30_2013.pdf

35. Sam Roberts, "New York Voter Turnout Appears to Be Record Low," *New York Times*, November 6, 2013.

36. Phil Keisling, "The Wrong Way to Elect America's Mayors," *Governing*, November, 2013.

37. Javier Hernandez, "Patrick Gaspard, a Trusted Advisor," *New York Times*, January 1, 2014.

38. "Highlights from the Inauguration," *New York Times*, January 1, 2014.

39. "The Inaugural Address of Bill de Blasio," Associated Press, January 1, 2014.

40. Kate Taylor, "In the Seats, Politicking in the Speaker's Race," *New York Times*, January 1, 2014.

41. Thomas Kaplan, "Cuomo Sweetens Pre-K Deal: Whatever' Mayor Needs," *New York Times*, January 23, 2014.

42. See Sam Roberts: *A Kind of Genius: Herb Sturz and Society's Toughest Problems* (Public Affairs, 2009).

43. Michael Grynbaum, "For de Blasio, So Many Jobs to Fill," *New York Times*, December 31, 2013.

44. Anthony Shorris, interview with the author, July 29, 2016.

45. Jill Colvin, "De Blasio Appoints Goldman's Alicia Glenn as Deputy Mayor," *New York Observer*, December 23, 2013.

46. Weisbrod served as Chair of the City Planning Commission and director of the City Planning Department until the end of 2016. He has been replaced by Marisa Lago, an assistant secretary for international markets and development in the U.S. Treasury Department, who had previously worked with Weisbrod in the administration of Mayor David Dinkins.

47. Miyera Navarro, "Deputy Mayor for Social Services Now Has a Boss Who Shares Her Agenda," *New York Times,* January 26, 2014.

Chapter 8

1. Anthony Shorris, interview with the author, July 29, 2016.

2. *One New York: The Plan for a Strong Just City,* April, 2014.

3. New York City Independent Budget Office, "For the New Mayor and City Council: A Big Budget Surplus and Even Bigger Challenges Ahead," December, 2013.

4. Steven Cohen, "From PlaNYC to OneNYC: New York's Evolving Sustainability Policy," *Huffington Post,* July 27, 2015.

5. IBO was created as part of the 1989 City Charter reforms to provide non-partisan information about the city budget. In order to protect its independence, it was guaranteed an annual budget equivalent to 10 percent of the mayor's Office of Management and Budget (increased to 12.5 percent in 2009). The figures in this table were derived from the NYC Office of Management and Budget's Function Analysis, from the Adopted Budget Financial Plans of Mayors Michael Bloomberg and Bill de Blasio.

6. J. David Goodman, "Now Hiring: Under de Blasio New York's Government Grows to Record Level," *New York Times,* October 11, 2016.

7. Editorial, "De Blasio's Budget Busting Hiring Spree," *Daily News,* October 15, 2016.

8. http://www1.nyc.gov/office-of-the-mayor/labor-contracts.page

9. http://www1.nyc.gov/site/olr/labor/labor-updates.page

10. Office of the New York City Comptroller, "The State of New York City's Economy and Finances," December 11, 2015.

11. Transcript: Mayor de Blasio Delivers Remarks at Crian's 2016 New York City Summit, November 1, 2016.

12. January 2017 Financial Plan Detail: Fiscal Years 2017–2021 (Released January 24, 2017).

13. Office of the New York City Comptroller, "The State of New York City's Economy and Finances," December 11, 2015.

14. January 2017 Financial Plan Detail: Fiscal Years 2017–2021 (Released January 24, 2017).

15. "Mayor de Blasio Announces Release of Poverty Measure Report: First Statistically Significant Decline in Near Poverty Since the Great Recession," May 16, 2017.

16. Binyamin Appelbaum, "Incomes in the U.S. Are Up Sharply: Poor Gain Most," *New York Times,* September 14, 2016.

17. "Mayor de Blasio Signs Paid Paternal Personnel Order for NYC Workers," January 7, 2016, http://www1.nyc.gov/office-of-the-mayor/news/025-16/mayor-de-blasio-signs-paid-parental-leave-personnel-order-nyc-workers#/0

18. "Mayor de Blasio Announces Guaranteed $15 Minimum Wage for All City Government Employees—Benefiting 50,000 Additional New Yorkers," January 6, 2016, http://www1.nyc.gov/office-of-the-mayor/news/019-16/mayor-de-blasio-guaranteed-15-minimum-wage-all-city-government-employees--#/0

19. "Governor Cuomo Signs $15 Minimum Wage Plan and 12 Week Paid Family Leave Policy into Law," April 4, 2016, https://www.governor.ny.gov/news/governor-cuomo-signs-15-minimum-wage-plan-and-12-week-paid-family-leave-policy-law

20. "Mayor's Office, Mayor de Blasio, and Speaker Melissa Mark-Viverito Launch IDNYC, The Country's Most Ambitious Municipal Identification Program," January 12, 2015.

21. Office of Management and Budget: The City of New York Preliminary Budget Fiscal Year 2018: Financial Plan Summary.

22. The City of New York, Department of Investigation, Office of the Inspector General for the NYPD, *An Analysis of Quality-of-Life Summonses, Quality-of-Life Misdemeanor Arrests, and Felony Crime in New York City, 2010–2015,* June 22, 2016.

23. Josh Dawsey and Zolan Kanno-Young, "Mayor, Police Commissioner Bash 'Windows' Report," *Wall Street Journal*, June 23, 2016.

24. Transcript: Mayor de Blasio, Police Commissioner Bratton Discuss NYC Pride March and Public Safety, June 23, 2016, http://www1.nyc.gov/office-of-the-mayor/news/556-16/transcript-mayor-de-blasio-police-commissioner-bratton-nyc-pride-march-public-safety.

25. J. David Goodman, "New York Council Won't Vote on Police Reform Bills, but Agency Agrees to Changes," *New York Times*, July 13, 2016.

26. Press Release: "The Legal Aid Society and Cleary Gottlieb File a Petition for Disclosure of NYPD Administrative Summaries of Police Officer Discipline," *The Legal Aid Society*, December 6, 2016.

27. Rocco Parascandola and Graham Rayman, "Bratton's Possible Successor, James O'Neill, Has Sought to Boost Police-Community Relations in an Era of Heightened Tension," *Daily News*, July 25, 2016.

28. William Neuman, "Mayor de Blasio, Informed by His Family, Steps Into Debate on Race," *New York Times*, July 12, 2016.

29. Ross Barkan, "The Unnatural (and Possibly Doomed) Symbiosis between Bill de Blasio and Bratton," *Village Voice*, June 28, 2016.

30. The data in this section was provided by Assistant Commissioner J. Peter Donald of the NYPD on January 30, 2017.

31. New York Police Department, CVS zip archive 2011–2016.

32. The consecutive drop in arrests went from 394,539 in 2013, to 388,368 in 2014, to 339,524 in 2015, to 314,870 in 2016. Arrest data was provided by Assistant Commissioner J. Peter Donald of the NYPD on January 30, 2017.

33. The decline in complaints was as follows: 5,388 (2013), 4,777 (2014), 4,462 (2015), 4,283 (2016). Data obtained from Edison Alban of the Civilian Complaint Review Board on January 30, 2017.

34. "Towards a More Just NYC," Report of the Independent Commission on New York Criminal Justice and Incarceration Reform, March 31, 2017.

35. J. David Goodman, "De Blasio Vows to Close Rikers, Ending an Era," *The New York Times*, April 1, 2017.

36. Press Release: In First Wave of UPK Implementation Mayor de Blasio Announces More than 4,200 New Full-Day Pre-K Seats Added to Public Schools, April 2, 2014.

37. Press Release: Pre-K for All: Mayor de Blasio and Chancellor Fariña Kick Off First Day of School with Full-Day Pre-K for Every Four-Year-Old, September 9, 2015.

38. See, for example, William T. Gormley Jr., Ted Gayer, Deborah Phillips, and Brittany Dawson, "The Effects of Universal Pre-K on Cognitive Development," *Developmental Psychology*, Vol. 41 (2005), pp. 872–884; Vivian Wong, Thomas D. Cook, W. Steven Barnett, and Kwanghee Jung, "An Effectiveness Based Evaluation of Five State Pre-Kindergarten Programs," *Journal of Policy Analysis and Management*, Vol. 27, pp. 122–154.

39. Kate Taylor, "Late Deal in Albany Could Allow Charter Schools to Hire More Uncertified Teachers," *New York Times*, June 22, 2016.

40. School Indicators for New York City Charter Schools 2013–2014 School Year, July, 2015.

41. Victoria Bekiempis, "With a Mayor de Blasio, Fate of Charter Schools in Limbo," *Newsweek*, November 15, 2013.

42. Source: New York City Charter School Center, Fact Sheets.

43. There is a long-running debate among pro-choice scholars between market adherents on the Right who define choice in terms of competition, and egalitarians on the Left who define it in terms of opportunity. See Joseph P. Viteritti, *Choosing Equality: School Choice, the Constitution, and Civil Society* (Brookings Institution Press, 1999).

44. Source: New York City Charter School Center, Fact Sheets.

45. John Kucsera, with Gary Orfield, "New York State's Extreme Segregation: Inequality, Inaction, and a Damaged Future," March 2014, https://civilrightsproject.ucla.edu/research/k-12-education/integration-and-diversity/ny-norflet-report-placeholder/Kucsera-New-York-Extreme-Segregation-2014.pdf.

46. Halley Potter, "Diversity in New York City's Pre-K Classrooms," Century Foundation, September 20, 2016. Housing patterns can reinforce racial segregation more in lower grades because parents are reluctant to send their children far from home to attend school.

47. http://www.legal-aid.org/media/201034/012016_complaint_success_academy.pdf
48. According to IBO, the administration committed $149 million to the effort over three years beginning in 2015. "Alternative to School Closure: Significant Resources Directed towards 94 Renewal Schools," NYC Independent Budget Office, 2015.
49. John Dewey, "The School as Social Center," *Middle Works,* Vol. 2 (1902), p. 80. For a general history of community schools, see John S. Rogers, *Community Schools: Lessons from the Past and Present* (UCLA IDEA, 1998).
50. Leonard Covello, "The School as a Center of Community Life in an Immigrant Area," in Samuel Everett, ed., *The Community School* (Appleton-Century, 1938).
51. Joseph P. Viteritti, "Urban Governance and the Idea of a Service Community," in Frank J. Macchiarola and Alan Gartner, eds., *Caring for America's Children* (Academy of Political Science, 1989), pp. 110–121.
52. Mark R. Warren, "Communities and School: A New Vision for Urban Education Reform," *Harvard Educational Review,* Vol. 75 (Summer, 2005), pp. 133–173; John H.W. Houser, "Community and School Sponsored Program Participation and Academic Achievement in a Full Service Community School," *Education and Urban Society,* Vol. 48 (May, 2016), pp. 324–345; Ming E. Chin, Jeffrey Alvin Anderson, and Lara Watkins, "Parent Perceptions of Connectedness in a Full Service Community School Project," *Journal of Child and Family Studies,* Vol. 25 (July, 2016), pp. 2268–2278.
53. Kate Taylor, "City to Close or Merge 9 Schools That Are in Program Offering Extra Help," *New York Times,* January 7, 2017.
54. New York State Common Core Tests.
55. "This Is Your City," Mayor Bill de Blasio's 2017 State of the City Address, delivered at the Apollo Theater in Harlem, February, 13, 2017.
56. William K. Rashbaum, "NYPD Commanders Are Arrested on Corruption Charges," *New York Times,* June 20, 2016.
57. William K. Rashbaum, "De Blasio Donor Emerges as a Key Witness in Corruption Case: What Else Does He Know?," *New York Times,* June 6, 2016.
58. Josh Dawsey and Rebecca Davis O'Brien, "Investigations into Mayor de Blasio's Fundraising Focuses on Specific Donors," *Wall Street Journal,* June 16, 2016.
59. Josh Dawsey, "Mayor de Blasio's Political Allies Subpoenaed in Fundraising Probes," *Wall Street Journal,* April 27, 2016.
60. William K. Rashbaum, "De Blasio Inquiries Said to Go to Grand Jury," *New York Times,* December 16, 2016.
61. Josh Dawsey, "Bill de Blasio Failed to Protect Public Interest on Rivington Deal, Report Finds," *Wall Street Journal,* July 14, 2016.
62. J. David Goodman and William Newman, "De Blasio Pressed to Clarify New Advisor Role: 'Agent of the City'," *New York Times,* May 19, 2016; Laura Nahmias and Dana Rubinstein, "De Blasio Lists Advisors He Considers Exempt from Transparency Law," *Politico,* May 19, 2016.
63. "CFB Statement of Determination Regarding the Campaign for One New York," New York City Campaign Finance Board, July 6, 2016.
64. Vivian Yee, "Agency Clears Mayor de Blasio and Nonprofit of Campaign Finance Violations," *New York Times,* July 6, 2016.
65. "Acting U.S. Attorney Joon H. Kim Statement on the Investigation of City Hall Fundraising," United States Attorney's Office, Southern District of New York, March 16, 2017.
66. Letter from Cyrus Vance to Risa S. Sugarman, regarding the January 2016 Referral Pursuant to Election Law Sec. 3-104(5)(b), March 16, 2017.

Chapter 9

1. "State of the Homeless 2014," Coalition for the Homeless, March 12, 2014.
2. Between 1965 and 1979, the number of resident patients in state psychiatric hospitals declined from 85,000 to 27,000. Coalition for the Homeless, "Why Are So Many People Homeless?," http://www.coalitionforthehomeless.org/the-catastrophe-of-homelessness/why-are-so-many-people-homeless/.

3. The five-part series began with Andrea Elliot, "Invisible Child," *New York Times,* December 9, 2013.

4. Jill Colvin, "Tish James Declares Dasani Coates Is Her 'New BFF,'" *The Observer,* January 1, 2014.

5. Giselle Routhier, "Family Homelessness in New York City: City and State Must Meet Unprecedented Scale of Crisis with Proven Solutions," Coalition for the Homeless, January, 2017.

6. Anna L. Oliveira and Jeanne B. Bullgrav, "All Our Children: Strategies to Prevent Homelessness, Strengthen Services, and Build Support for LGBTQ Youth," New York City Commission on Lesbian, Gay, Bisexual, Transgender, and Questioning Runaway and Homeless Youth, June, 2010.

7. Tina Moore, "The City's 'Code Blue' Policy That Provides Shelter for People When Temperatures Drop below Freezing Is Leaving Families out in the Cold," *New York Daily News,* February 17, 2013.

8. Sara Stefanski, "Further Increases to Homeless Rental Assistance, but Additional Funds for Shelter Still Necessary," New York City Independent Budget Office, May 20, 2015.

9. Kim Velsey, "NYCHA to Allocate Approximately 750 Units a Year to Homeless Families," *New York Observer,* June 3, 2014.

10. Nathan Tempey, "NYC Will Phase Out Infamous Apartment Building Homeless Shelters," *Gothamist,* January 4, 2016.

11. William Newman, "City Expands Costly Use of Hotels as It Confronts Surging Homelessness," *New York Times,* December 8, 2016.

12. Andy Mai and Erin Durkin, "New York City Won't Convert Queens Holiday Inn into Shelter After Fierce Public Opposition," *Daily News,* October 10, 2016.

13. Josh Dawsey and Mark Morales, "New York City Relies on Motels to House Homeless," *Wall Street Journal,* August 28, 2016.

14. Patrick Markee, "State of the Homeless 2015," Coalition for the Homeless, March 19, 2015.

15. Mary Brosnahan and Giselle Routhier, "The Current State of Homelessness and Crucial Next Steps," Coalition for the Homeless, October 27, 2015.

16. Jennifer Fermino, "Over 30,000 Poor New Yorkers Granted Permanent Housing in Just Two years through City's Rental Assistance Programs," *Daily News,* March 8, 2016.

17. Thomas J. Main, *Homelessness in New York City: Policy Making from Koch to de Blasio* (New York University Press, 2016), pp. 188–189.

18. Nikita Stewart, "De Blasio Unveils Plan to Create 15,000 Units of Housing," *New York Times,* November 18, 2015.

19. Will Breddman, "Bill de Blasio Slams Andrew Cuomo's Homeless Proposals," *The Observer,* February 25, 2015.

20. Office of the Mayor, "De Blasio Administration Announces Plan to Create 15,000 Units of Supportive Housing," November 18, 2015.

21. Office of the Mayor, Transcript: Mayor de Blasio Holds Press Gaggle, June 20, 2015.

22. "Albany Shifts the Burden: As Cost for Sheltering the Homeless Rises, Federal and City Funds Are Increasingly Tapped," New York City Independent Budget Office, October, 2015.

23. Laura Nachmias, "Cuomo Blames Homeless Issues on de Blasio's Mismanagement," March 17, 2016.

24. Governor Cuomo Outlines 2016 Agenda: Signature Proposals That New York Is—And Will Continue to Be—Built to Lead, January 13, 2006, http://www.governor.ny.gov/news/governor-cuomo-outlines-2016-agenda-signature-proposals-ensuring-new-york-and-will-continue-be

25. For an explanation of this approach, see Larry M. Mead, *The New Paternalism: Supervisory Approaches to Paternalism* (Brookings Institution Press, 1997).

26. Routhier, "Family Homelessness in New York City."

27. "Turning the Tide on Homelessness in New York City," City of New York, February, 2017.

28. "Not Reaching the Door: Homeless Students Face Many Hurdles on their Way to School," New York City Independent Budget Office, October, 2016.

29. "Doing Our Fair Share, Getting Our Fair Share: Reforming NYC's System for Achieving Fairness in Siting Municipal Facilities," New York City Council, February, 2017.

30. "Turning the Tide on Homelessness in New York City."

31. Office of the Mayor, "Transcript: Mayor de Blasio Delivers Speech on Vision and Plan to Combat Homelessness," February 28, 2017.

32. For heartbreaking stories about how eviction has affected the lives of eight families in the poorest section of Milwaukee, see Matthew Desmond, *Evicted: Poverty and Profit in the American City* (Crown, 2016).

33. Mireya Navarro, "Push to Provide Lawyers in New York City Housing Court Gains Momentum," *New York Times*, December 16, 2014.

34. Jessica Silver-Greenberg, "For Tenants Facing Eviction, New York May Guarantee a Lawyer," *New York Times*, September 26, 2016.

35. Kevin Sweeting, "How Stuy Town Gets a Tourniquet while Blackstone Gets Billions," *Gothamist*, March 31, 2016.

36. *Housing New York: A Five Borough, Ten Year Plan,* City of New York, May, 2014.

37. Mireya Navarro and Michael Grynbaum, "De Blasio Sets 10-Year Plan for Housing, Putting the Focus on Affordability," *New York Times*, May 5, 2014.

38. Transcript: Mayor de-Blasio Unveils Housing New York: A Five Borough, 10 Year Housing Plan to Protect and Expand Affordability May 5, 2014.

39. *Housing New York.*

40. https://www.ncsha.org/resource/2015-housing-choice-voucher-voucher-program-qa

41. Press Release: "De Blasio Unveils NextGeneration NYCHA: A Comprehensive Plan to Secure the Future of Public Housing," April, 2015.

42. Other tools available to the city include tax exempt bonds and Low Income Housing Tax Credits. Up-zoning is only effective in neighborhoods where the market value is high enough to cross-subsidize affordable units. Otherwise, some subsidy still may be required.

43. http://www.anhd.org/wp-content/uploads/2011/07/ANHD-Complete-Analysis-of-Mayors-Housing-Plan-5-2014.pdf (Part 3).

44. Barika Williams, "City's Mandatory Inclusionary Zoning Misses Out, Association for Neighborhood and Housing Development," November 16, 2015.

45. Steven Wishnia, "What Does Affordable Housing Really Mean in de Blasio's New York? We're About to Find Out," *Gothamist*, February 10, 2016.

46. Steven Wishnia, "De Blasio's Controversial Zoning Plan Stretches Definition of 'Affordable,'" *Gothamist*, December 18, 2015.

47. Sally Goldenberg, "With Promise of Future Study, Opponents Back de Blasio's Housing Plan," *Politico*, March 13, 2016.

48. http://labs.council.nyc/land/land-use/plans/mih-zqa/mih/

49. http://labs.council.nyc/land/land-use/wp-content/uploads/sites/53/2016/05/ZQA-Summary-Council-modifications.pdf

50. https://www.governor.ny.gov/news/governor-cuomo-directs-new-york-state-division-budget-sign-2-billion-homelessness-and-housing

51. Charles V. Bagli, "In Program to Spur Affordable Housing, $100 Million Penthouse Gets 95% Tax Cut," *New York Times*, February 1, 2015.

52. Office of the Mayor, "Mayor de Blasio Calls for Sweeping Overhaul of Tax Benefits to Spur More Affordable Housing," May 7, 2015, http://www1.nyc.gov/office-of-the-mayor/news/295-15/mayor-de-blasio-calls-sweeping-overhaul-tax-benefits-spur-more-affordable-housing. After this proposal was rejected in Albany, de Blasio proposed in 2017 a 2.5% tax on sales above $2 billion.

53. Matt A.V. Chaban, "This Apartment Is Not $1 Million. It's Only $999,000," *New York Times*, October 12, 2015.

54. Bill de Blasio, interview with Errol Louis, *Inside City Hall*, NY1, June 30, 2015.

55. "Requiring a Prevailing Wage Would Increase Housing Plan Costs by an Estimated $4.2 Billion," New York City Independent Budget Office, January, 2016.

56. Office of the Governor, "Governor Cuomo Advancing New Legislation to Create 'Affordable New York' Housing Program after Agreement between REBNY and the Building Trades," January 15, 2007.

57. "An Efficient Use of Tax Dollars? A Closer Look at Market Effects of the 421-a Tax Break for Condos," New York City Independent Budget Office, Fiscal Brief, January, 2017.

58. "What Happened to Housing Development When 421-a Was Suspended?," ANHD White Paper, February, 2017.

59. Charles Bagli, "Overhauled Affordable Housing Program Requires a 'Fair Wage' for Builders," *The New York Times*, April 11, 2017.
60. "Albany Agrees to Resurrect the 421-a Tax Exemption, Association for Neighborhood and Housing Development," April 8, 2017.
61. Scott Stringer, "Mandatory Inclusionary Housing and the East New York Rezoning," Office of the New York City Comptroller, December 2, 2015.
62. http://www1.nyc.gov/site/hpd/developers/development-programs/extremely-low-low-income-affordability-program.page
63. For more detail, see Abigail Savitch Lew, "Affordable Housing: How Low Can de Blasio Go?," *City Limits*, May 2, 2016.
64. Emma Whitford, "East New York Rezoning Plan Flies Through City Council," *Gothamist*, April 20, 2016.
65. Amy Zimmer, Danielle Tcholakian, Carolina Pichardo, and Maya Rajamani, "The Mayor's Rezoning Plan Is Six Months Old. Here's How It's Going So Far," *DNAInfo*, September 20, 2016.
66. Abigail Savitch-Lew, "City's East Harlem Plan Tracks Community Blueprint," *City Limits*, October 19, 2016.
67. Bertha Lewis, "The Whitening of New York City," *City and State*, March 10, 2006.
68. Michael Henry Adams, "The End of Black Harlem," *New York Times*, May 27, 2016.
69. Office of the Mayor, "'Still Your City': Mayor de Blasio Announces Major Progress Helping New Yorkers Afford Their Homes and Neighborhoods," January 12, 2017.
70. Charles Bagli, "City Gains More Affordable Housing, but Critics Say It's Not Enough," *New York Times*, January 12, 2017.
71. Jeff Mays, "More Affordable Housing Created in 2016 than Any Year since 1989: De Blasio," *DNAInfo*, January 13, 2017.

Chapter 10

1. Steven Banks, interview with the author, November 3, 2016.
2. J. David Goodman and Nikita Stewart, "Mayor de Blasio Scrambles to Curb Homelessness after Years of Not Keeping Pace," *New York Times*, January 13, 2017.
3. J. Paul Mitchell, *Federal Housing Policy and Programs: Past and Present* (Rutgers University Center for Urban Policy Research, 1985), p. 247.
4. Edward G. Goetz, *New Deal Ruins: Race, Economic Justice, and Public Housing Policy* (Cornell University Press, 2013), p. 9.
5. For the history of NYCHA, see Nicholas Dagen Bloom, *Public Housing That Worked: New York in the Twentieth Century* (University of Pennsylvania Press, 2009). For more general histories of housing policy in New York, see Nicholas Dagen Bloom and Michael Gordon Lasner, eds., *Affordable Housing in New York: The People, Places, and Politics That Transformed New York* (Yale University Press, 2015); Richard Plunz, *A History of Housing in New York* (Columbia University Press, 1990).
6. See generally Goetz, *New Deal Ruins*.
7. Goetz, *New Deal Ruins*, p. 15.
8. Goetz, *New Deal Ruins*, p. 4.
9. Goetz, *New Deal Ruins*, p. 71.
10. For an illuminating film on the subject, see the PBS documentary, "The Talk: Race in America," 2017.
11. Bill de Blasio, interview with Errol Louis, *Inside City Hall*, NY1, June 30, 2015.
12. Joseph P. Viteritti, *The Last Freedom: Religion from the Public School to the Public Square* (Princeton University Press, 2007).
13. William Riordan, *Plunkitt of Tammany Hall: A Series of Very Plain Talks on Very Practical Politics* (Signet, 2015), p. 8.

14. Eric Lipton, Ben Protess, and Andrew W. Lehren, "Raft of Potential Conflicts in President's Appointees: 'No Transparency' and Revised Rules for Ex-Lobbyists Raise Ethics Concerns," *The New York Times*, April 16, 2017.

15. Earlier this year, conceding reliance on the private sector for money to build affordable housing, de Blasio explained, "So we try to, as intelligently as possible, use the private market dynamics to our favor—channel them with regulation to get the most out of the private market, and create a financially viable building that's going to be long term." Transcript: Mayor de Blasio Announces Major Progress Helping New Yorkers Afford Their Homes and Neighborhoods, January 12, 2017.

16. Transcript: Mayor de Blasio Announces Major Progress Helping New Yorkers Afford Their Homes and Neighborhoods.

17. "State of New York City's Housing and Neighborhoods in 2015," NYU Furman Center, 2015.

18. "The Effects of Neighborhood Change on NYCHA Residents," NYU Furman Center, 2016.

19. For a more positive analysis of gentrification in six Brooklyn neighborhoods, see Kay S. Hymowitz, *The New Brooklyn: What It Takes to Bring a City Back* (Rowman and Littlefield, 2017).

20. Ronald P. Formisano, *Boston against Busing: Race, Class, and Ethnicity in the 1960s and 1970s* (University of North Carolina Press, 2004).

21. *Parents Involved in Community Schools v. Seattle District 1*, 551 U.S. 701 (2007).

22. See Raz Chetty, Nathaniel Hendron, and Lawrence F. Katz, "The Effects of Exposure to Better Neighborhoods on Children: New Evidence on the Moving to Opportunity Experiment," NBER Working Paper No. 21156, May, 2015; Gerald Grant, *Hope and Despair: Why There Are No Bad Schools in Raleigh* (Harvard University Press, 2009); Heather Schwartz, "Housing Policy Is School Policy: Economically Integrative Housing Promotes Academic Success in Montgomery County, Maryland," Century Foundation, 2010; see also Amy Stuart Wells, Lauren Fox, and Diana Cordova-Cobo, "How Racially Diverse Schools and Classrooms Can Benefit All Students," February 9, 2016.

23. Richard Kahlenberg, "School Integration in Practice: Lessons from Nine Districts," Century Foundation, October 14, 2016.

24. Stokely Carmichael and Charles V. Hamilton, *Black Power: The Politics of Liberation* (Vintage, 1967). See also the illustrative historical essays in Sylviane A. Diouf and Komozi Woodard, eds., *Black Power 50* (The New Process, 2016).

25. For a history of these districting battles and their resolution by the federal courts, see Joseph P. Viteritti, "Unapportioned Justice: Local Elections, Social Science, and the Evolution of the Voting Rights Act," *Cornell Journal of Law and Public Policy*, Vol. 4 (1994), pp. 199–271.

26. Shola Olatoye, interview with author, November 3, 2016.

27. Press Release: "NYCHA and HPD Release Request for Proposals for NEXTGEN Neighborhood Development Sites," June 30, 2016.

28. U.S. Code, Title 42, Chap. 8, Sub. 1, Sec. 1437 (1998).

29. Marc Santora, "Hillary Clinton Aides Kept de Blasio at Arm's Length, WikiLeak Emails Reveal," *New York Times*, October 10, 2016.

30. Laura Nahmias and Conor Skelding, "Leaked Emails Show Clinton Camp Eyeing de Blasio Warily," *New York Times*, October 10, 2016.

31. Laura Nahmias, "De Blasio: Sanders' Message 'Would Have Won the Election,'" *Politico*, December 12, 2016.

32. Editorial, "Mr. Trump's Big Money Establishment," *New York Times*, January 24, 2017.

33. At this writing, several individuals have announced their intention to challenge de Blasio in the Democratic Party primary and general election, but none have gathered any momentum of support.

34. Office of the Governor, "Governor Cuomo Outlines FY 2018 Executive Budget to Maintain Fiscal Responsibility, Reduce Taxes, and Invest in New York's Middle Class," January 18, 2016.

35. Bill de Blasio, interview with the author, December 28, 2016.

INDEX

Note: Tables and figures are indicated by italic page numbers. Note content is indicated by an italic "*n*" and note number.